# BUILDING BLOCKS OF RABBINIC TRADITION

## *The Documentary Approach to the Study of Formative Judaism*

Jacob Neusner

Studies in Judaism

University Press of America,® Inc.
Lanham · Boulder · New York · Toronto · Plymouth, UK

**University Press of America,® Inc.**
4501 Forbes Boulevard
Suite 200
Lanham, Maryland 20706
UPA Acquisitions Department (301) 459-3366

Estover Road
Plymouth PL6 7PY
United Kingdom


Printed in the United States of America
British Library Cataloging in Publication Information Available

Library of Congress Control Number: 2007933357
ISBN-13: 978-0-7618-3868-5 (paperback : alk. paper)
ISBN-10: 0-7618-3868-6 (paperback : alk. paper)

™ The paper used in this publication meets the minimum requirements of American National Standard for Information Sciences—Permanence of Paper for Printed Library Materials, ANSI Z39.48—1984

# Studies in Judaism

## CONTENTS

# Preface

This book responds to a question that came to me from Professor Maren Niehoff of the Hebrew University of Jerusalem: Have you written a simple introduction to your documentary theory and method, which can serve as a starting point for my students? I assumed that I had written such a book — I certainly had meant to — but a survey of my bibliography turned up nothing that served. I had written a number of scattered theoretical articles but had not composed them into a coherent introduction. In this book I have gathered eight of the more fundamental items of documentary theory and practice — three in theory, five in practice — for Professor Niehoff's students and anyone else who takes an interest in the formative history of Judaism.

The documentary thesis of Rabbinic literature holds that the document — the Mishnah, Sifra, Lamentations Rabbah, the Bavli, for example — forms the basic building block of the Rabbinic tradition. Excluded by that definition are sayings attributed to, and stories told about, named sages. These cannot serve in the reconstruction of the Rabbinic tradition, its literature, history, religion, and theology.

What led me to the recognition that documents, not named authorities, form the starting point of all inquiry, literary and religions-historical? It was a journey of some four years, from when in 1970 I rejected as gullible for accepting at face value the historicity of attributions and narratives ten years of work. That wrong approach marked my *Life of Yohanan ben Zakkai* and *History of the Jews in Babylonia.*1 In three projects I then experimented with other approaches to historical study. The journey came to an end in 1974 when I determined to start all over again, this time with *A History of the Mishnaic Law,* a systematic form-analytical study of the Mishnah and the Tosefta, that is, studying a document rather than a historical figure or large-scale topic. In between 1970 and 1974 came *Development of a Legend, Rabbinic Traditions about the Pharisees before 70,* and *Eliezer ben Hyrcanus, the Tradition and the Man.* These critical historical works marked the end of the old and the beginning of the new.

The work of the next years, 1974-1980, reached fruition in my *History of the Mishnaic Law* (in forty-three volumes) and in the recapitulative work, *Judaism: The Evidence of the Mishnah* (1981). That book struck me as a collection of truisms but turned out to be intensely controversial. It appeared in Hebrew and in Italian and was the subject of several major reviews. The next decade, 1981-1991, produced the first set of works in the documentary method in the reading of the Rabbinic canon after Mishnah-Tosefta, on the one side, and in the documentary or canonical history of ideas, on the other. This culminated in my *Transformation of Judaism: From Philosophy to Religion* (1991). The next stage, from 1991, also involves a drastic critique of the former one and an inquiry into problems of phenomenology as a route toward the penultimate and antepenultimate structures that the documents contain. In simple language, I went in search of the continuities among documents, tracing the logic of theology that pervaded them.

My path thus began with *Development of a Legend: Studies on the Traditions Concerning Yohanan ben Zakkai.* There I began to try to find out how historically to deal with diverse versions of a story, and this required the analysis of the blatantly formalized character of much of the Rabbinic literature. The choice of Yohanan ben Zakkai for the first break with the established way of doing things was dictated by the simple fact that, eight years earlier, I had written a biography in the accepted manner, organizing all the stories about, and sayings attributed to, the man, in the order and categories indicated by their content. In my narrative I had further assembled pretty much everything everyone else had said about the same stories and sayings in the same believing spirit, thinking of course that that was scholarship. Then the great scholar of biblical theology, Brevard Childs, a profound, formative influence on me for nearly fifty years now,2 asked me, "Is it possible that you are doing history too soon, and might you be asking the wrong questions?" Since I didn't know the answer, I determined to find it out. Both he and I supposed that form-criticism provided the key to the historical lock, and neither one of us imagined that a completely different approach from the one centered on free-standing compositions — the bits and pieces of evidence, identified by the name of a given authority — would be required.

I thought it best to begin again from my own beginning. Since I had written Yohanan's life without analyzing the sources but, essentially, by merely alluding to, or just citing, them as facts, I realized that the new beginning had to start with the specification, translation,3 and analysis of all relevant materials. Laying all the cards on the table seemed the right way. That explains *Development of a Legend.* Uncomprehending colleagues asked, why not just paraphrase or summarize "the sources"? But that is the very point. The source— the saying or the story is what is meant here — is not the answer but the question, not the solution but the problem. So the paramount trait of my scholarship, beginning with *Development* and onward to the present, was going to be a massive labor of new translation, and, of more importance, totally fresh exegesis. I soon realized that the translation would have to expose the document's traits of composition, the main lines and secondary interpolations and the like; an analytical translation would be necessary — and every single canonical writing would have to be retranslated (or translated for the first time) with the problem of form-analysis translated into clearly-signaled solutions.

*Development* forced my attention on the boundaries of documents, which I had never realized marked out anything that made a difference. But I could not ignore that a given saying made its way hither and yon. When confronting the same story running through Mishnah, Tosefta, the Talmuds, and the Tannaite and other Midrashic compilations, I decided to see whether there were fixed relationships as the story moved from one document to another, and, if so, how I might account for them. In other words, does the document define a variable? What made matters difficult is that there is some doubt about the dating and even the relative priority of the various documents. What I found, to sidestep that difficulty, was that relationships tend to be fixed, no matter the priority or posteriority of the documents. The general result is that the simplest version would be the Mishnah's, then, details omitted would be given by Tosefta, usually further enriched by the Palestinian Talmud, and, at the end, by the Babylonian one. Since I was able to show that details added in a given version dealt with questions left open, or even generated, by another version, I showed that what we have are not several incidents, each of which happened on yet another and gaining or losing weight in its peregrinations. So we have to bid adieu to Rabbinical equivalent of the Sermon on the Mount and the Sermon on the Plain.

A second point struck me then. It was possible to make sense of the sorts of materials occurring in one document and not in some other. That leads me to the whole issue of forms. I specifically wanted to know whether there really were fixed literary forms and rhetorical devices in the Rabbinic literature. What I found was that while there clearly are highly formalized traits attached to sayings and stories of Yohanan ben Zakkai, they form no coherent unit associated distinctively with his name. They conformed to the formal preferences of the *documents* in which they occur, and that suggests that documents form the basic and definitive literary category, and not the name of a given authority that is tied to a story or saying. So documents, not historical personages or events, formed the first line of inquiry, the building block of the title of this book. I had reached the end of the historical road, and the beginning of a different path altogether.

At this point I had already reached what I would come to understand as the pivot of all further work, but I did not see it as such. I had stumbled across the simple fact that all analytical and critical work in Rabbinical literature must begin in the study of specific documents, their formal traits, redactional preferences, and substantive interests. That is the documentary theory. Now before I expand on that simple and obvious proposition, I have to say it did not even impress or occur to me for two more, sizable projects, *The Rabbinic Traditions about the Pharisees before 70* and *Eliezer ben Hyrcanus. The Tradition and the Man.* Both of these lengthy projects — on the Pharisees and the transition from the Pharisees before 70 to Yavneh and its Rabbis after 70 — continued to ask essentially historical questions. That is to say, they continued to treat topics which carried me through the far reaches of diverse collections. I dealt in enormous detail with the character of what Rabbinic literature had to say about the Pharisees; in volume III of *The Rabbinic Traditions about the Pharisees before 70* I made some tentative remarks about who and what the historical Pharisees might have been, and, in a companion text-book, *From Politics to Piety*, I summarized these results and speculations for a broader readership.

What I wanted to know in *Rabbinic Traditions* — as the title of the work said in so many words — was what the later Rabbis had to tell us about the Pharisees, how they tell it to us, and whether it is so. What I found out — as distinct from what I wanted to know — was a great deal about the use of form-criticism as a rather sharp tool for literary analysis, about the mnemonic traits of important strata of the Rabbinic literature, about the overall shape of the Rabbinic traditions about the Pharisees, and about the difficulty of interpreting materials assigned to a given name or set of names when approached totally outside of the documents — that is to say, the systems — in which they occur.4

What I wanted to know about Eliezer ben Hyrcanus was what in fact we can say about the man. What I found out was a great deal about the history of a tradition associated with a given name. Not all of that history called into question the possibility of speaking of the man, as distinct from the tradition about him. But most did, and from that point onward, I regarded as a waste of time sustained work on Rabbinic biography. In the interim, my students of that period and I had accomplished the examination of the sayings and stories assigned to or told about all the major figures of the Yavneh period, down to Aqiba.5 The results proved marginally interesting in the study of the history of traditions, since, over all, the kind of materials in a given document about various names proved uniform, different from the kind of materials in other documents about those same various names. That result, achieved with much hard work (we were still imagining at some point biography might be possible), underlined the centrality of the document, the peripherality of attributions, in the formation and presentation of the Rabbinic literature.

Quite what that meant about documents or "books" — the large components of the canon, whatever we call them — and how they were to be studied and interpreted, was slowly becoming clear. What was emerging was a new episteme: the systematic analysis of documents and their traits, the systems they set forth one by one, on a long path toward the analysis of the writings aimed at a synthesis, properly set forth, of the same writings. That accounted for the title toward which I then aimed, and ultimately achieved: *Judaism: The Evidence of the Mishnah.* That meant, what Judaic system is set forth by this document. It did not mean, what was Judaism. But all critics of the book thought that is precisely what it meant.

The move from biography to documentary analysis came about for three other reasons as well.

[1] First, I found that in my historical work I covered a wide range of topics, but each one superficially. By that I mean I perceived only the law in the episodic setting of this item and that item tied to a particular name. Accordingly, I concluded I never really grasped the law in its own terms as a coherent whole. But,

clearly, given the character of the canon, to present the law in its own terms meant, in the terms in which the principal documents were formulated. The counterpart for scholarship on early Christianity would be to read Augustine for everything but his theology, or Aphrahat for everything but his polemic. The inner logic of a given ruling and its place in the unfolding frame of the chapter of law in which it found its place never fully revealed themselves. Consequently for reasons quite divorced from the epistemological problems that I recognized but left unsolved, I could not find entire satisfaction in my results.

[2] Second, and quite separate from the foregoing, I could not even in theory explain how to deal with sayings lacking attributions. So the state of a law at a given point in time could not be ascertained. The oft-repeated mantra coming out of the received scholarship held, "If it's unattributed, it's old." But that left me wondering about two matters. First of all, how old? Second, why old at all? To the contrary, in the Mishnah, studded as it is with disputes, we have unattributed sayings alongside contrary sayings assigned to named masters. In the context of the Mishnah — everyone who knows the literature recognizes — the purpose of leaving a saying without attribution is to signal that it represents the consensus of sages. That is said in so many words in the Talmuds. So the absence of an attribution signals the status of a saying, not a judgment on its origins, earlier or later.

A further consideration intruded, and that is the unanimous judgment that we deal with a profoundly traditional, conservative culture. But that premise, which the canon itself reinforces in every line, challenges the premise about the antiquity of what is unassigned. Specifically, in the context of the dispute, if the named saying is young and the anonymous saying old, then how is it possible that Meir or Judah should take a position contrary to an old, received legal tradition? The same good folk who repeat the mantra also describe "Judaism" as a tradition, so we are asked to believe that the authorities of the tradition are not traditional.

Finally, in the context of a dispute, the unassigned saying and the assigned one always, everywhere, without exception, match in every respect: form, wording, topic and problematic, and the literary evidence invariably tells us that the sentences, unattributed and attributed, belong to the same authorship, the same period, and so on. How the dogma of the "antiquity" of the unassigned saying got going need not detain us; why people take at face value a claim so utterly at variance with the literary evidence they purport to interpret "historically" leads us out of scholarship and into murky corners of personal preference and private, idiosyncratic belief.

[3] Third, I recognized that, when all was said and done, I relied for my periodization of materials on attributions of sayings to specific figures and on that alone. What I saw in *Eliezer* was that while I did not take for granted everything in the name of Eliezer really was said by him, I did tend to assume that everything said about Eliezer in the name of some later authority really was said by that later authority. So it was a case of postponing the act of gullibility, not abandoning it. Thus, a growing, unsolved dilemma no longer could be avoided. I found myself on

that same slippery turf which I had many times thought to have abandoned, because the only grounds I had for assigning a saying to a given man or period was that the sources said he had said so. I had not moved far from the world in which the traditionalists would say that our sages would not lie, and the modernists — without even the merit of piety — would say that they would not have assigned a saying to a given man if they did not have a reason (which is precisely what the old timers were telling us in their quaint way). When I was at work on the history of the Jews in Babylonia, as I said just now, Brevard Childs had told me that I might be asking the historical question too soon. He certainly was right. But I now realized, not only was it a premature historical question. It also was a question meant to precipitate the writing of the wrong kind of history to begin with.

The documentary thesis in the literature and history of Rabbinic Judaism came about, then, in response to a negative fact. The "Neusner revolution" to which I see reference made here and there is understood in that negative framework. It may be simply stated. I could not either validate or falsify the attributions of sayings to named authorities, upon which my, and all other, historical work rested. I reached the conclusion that the foundations, in irrefutable fact, of the utilization of all evidence were irreparably flawed, and that nothing I had done, or anyone else for that matter, met the simple test: how do you know that what you say, on the basis of the sources in hand and the way you read them, is so? What we cannot show, we do not know. Then, I asked myself, what are the facts we really do have in hand? The simplest is, the facticity of the documents, one by one. While the wordings may vary from one textual witness to the next, while the repertoire of materials may shift from one manuscript to another, the various documents viewed one by one do exhibit distinctive and differentiating traits; these awaited discovery and elucidation, and that is what, I determined, I had to do. That decision explains how and why this Introduction forms the culmination of so many years of work.

For on the basis of the simple fact that the document forms an irreducible fact, but the facticity of the attribution of sayings in a given document or in all of them together to a single named authority, was subject to serious doubt, I concluded the work resting on attributions — which is to say, historical work of one kind. Now began historical work of another kind, for I required a different starting point for all future work, besides the one provided by the attribution of a saying to a named authority, on the one side, or the telling of a story about him, on the other. Since everything I had done, and the entire scholarly literature and tradition within which I worked, presupposed the facticity of what in fact lay beyond all rigorous testing, I went off in search of some other way of studying the Rabbinic literature, besides the uncritical one that I knew and followed.

As is clear, by way of working hypothesis I determined that the irrefutable fact, the uncontingent, independent variable, was the document. I could think of no candidates besides the attribution, on the one side, or the documentary locus, on the other. It is the simple fact that everything we have received from Rabbinic

Judaism in late antiquity comes to us in the documents of Rabbinic literature. So all future study depended upon the systematic characterization of those documents.

In the early 1970s I started with the first of these, which is the Mishnah, and, two decades later, concluded with the last, which is the Talmud of Babylonia. The documentary description of the Rabbinic canon yielded my *Introduction to Rabbinic Literature* and *Rabbinic Judaism. The Documentary History of the Formative Age*. I have since gone on to a series of theological problems. I provided a form-analytical translation of the canon, for, in the interim of two decades I translated for the first time approximately a third of the volume of that literature — the Tosefta, the Talmud of the Land of Israel, Sifra, and some other documents — and retranslated, but for the first time providing a form-analytical presentation, all of the other documents, the Mishnah, the Talmud of Babylonia, and the Midrash-compilations in their entirety. That explains why I have now translated and introduced every document that with confidence is assigned to late antiquity's Rabbis (as distinct from other than Rabbinic sources, on the one side, or writings that came to closure after the Muslim conquest marked the end of antiquity and the beginning of the Middle Ages, on the other). Each, furthermore, has now been systematically translated and fully analyzed as to rhetoric, logic of coherent discourse, and topical and propositional program, by me.6 That is the considerable *oeuvre* that is summarized here in a systematic and succinct way in the pages of this book.

Because I have collected free-standing essays, some overlap among the chapters is unavoidable. I have tried to keep it to a minimum.

Jacob Neusner
Distinguished Service Professor of the History and Theology of Judaism
Bard College
Annandale-on-Hudson, New York 12504 USA
Jneusner@frontiernet.net

ENDNOTES

[1]The appendix contains the bibliographical information on the titles to which I made reference here.

[2]When he came to the Jewish Theological Seminary summer program to study Rabbinic texts, in 1958 and 1959, we were roommates; he was then an Assistant Professor at Yale Divinity School and I was a student at Jewish Theological Seminary of America and Columbia University. From that time to the present, I have looked up to him.

[3]I formulated a theory of translation spelled out in *Translating the Classics of Judaism. In Theory and in Practice*. Atlanta, 1989: Scholars Press for Brown Judaic Studies. This involved supplying a reference system to the entire canon and framing a theory of translation, which

clearly displayed the forms of the Hebrew. My form-analytical translations were completed by the early 1990s.

[4]The matter of mnemonics is summarized in *Oral Tradition in Judaism: The Case of the Mishnah.* N.Y., 1987: Garland Publishing Co. *Albert Bates Lord Monograph Series* of the journal, *Oral Tradition.* I find quite startling the insistence upon the oral character of the entirety of the Rabbinic canon, absent clear evidence that sustains that view. I spent a great deal of effort to discern the mnemonic system of the Mishnah. But then, it struck me, where I do not find a mnemonic system, then the same considerations that lead me to think on the basis of internal evidence that the Mishnah is orally formulated and orally transmitted make me wonder why I should suppose any other document, lacking those traits or their counterparts, should have been orally formulated and orally transmitted.

[5]The work of Rabbinic biography, a principal staple for a century and a half of Wissenschaft des Judenthums, now came to an end. So far as I know, apart from some silly articles in Tarbiz (in Hebrew), not a single systematic biography of a Talmudic Rabbi has been attempted. Compare Alon Goshen-Gottstein. *The Sinner and the Amnesiac. The Rabbinic Invention of Elisha ben Abuya and Eleazar ben Arach.* Stanford, CA., 2000: Stanford University Press. In the series, CONTRAVERSIONS. JEWS AND OTHER DIFFERENCES, ed. By Daniel Boyarin, Chana Kronfeld, and Naomi Seidman. 416 pp.,

[6]I collected and printed as a single volume all of the important negative reviews, down to 1990, of various volumes of this *oeuvre* in *The Origins of Judaism. Religion, History, and Literature in Late Antiquity* (New York, 1991: Garland Press.) XX. *The Literature of Formative Judaism: Controversies on the Literature of Formative Judaism.* I collected some of my reviews of the results of others, past and present, in my *Ancient Judaism. Debates and Disputes.* Chico, 1984: Scholars Press for Brown Judaic Studies; *Ancient Judaism. Debates and Disputes. Second Series.* Atlanta, 1990: Scholars Press for South Florida Studies in the History of Judaism; and *Ancient Judaism. Debates and Disputes. Third Series. Essays on the Formation of Judaism, Dating Sayings, Method in the History of Judaism, the Historical Jesus, Publishing Too Much, and Other Current Issues.* Atlanta, 1993: Scholars Press for South Florida Studies in the History of Judaism; and also *Judaic Law from Jesus to the Mishnah. A Systematic Reply to Professor E. P. Sanders.* Atlanta, 1993: Scholars Press for South Florida Studies in the History of Judaism.

# THE DOCUMENTARY APPROACH IN THEORY

# 1

# INTRODUCTION

## I. Defining Rabbinic Literature

Rabbinic literature is the corpus of writing produced in the first seven centuries C.E. by sages who claimed to stand in the chain of tradition from Sinai. They maintained that they uniquely possess the oral part of the Torah, revealed by God to Moses at Sinai for oral formulation and oral transmission, in addition to the written part of the Torah possessed by all Israel. Among the many, diverse documents produced by Jews in late antiquity, the first seven centuries of the Common Era (C.E. = A. D.), only a small group cohere and form a distinctive corpus, called "Rabbinic literature." Three traits together suffice to distinguish Rabbinic literature from all other Jewish (ethnic) and Judaic (religious) writing of that age.

[1] These writings of law and exegesis, revered as holy books, copiously cite the Hebrew Scriptures of ancient Israel ("written Torah").

[2] They acknowledge the authority, and even the existence, of *no* other Judaic (or gentile) books but the ancient Israelite Scriptures.

[3] These writings promiscuously and ubiquitously cite sayings attributed to named authorities, unique to those books themselves, most of them bearing the honorific title "Rabbi."

Other writings of Jews, e.g., Josephus, to begin with do not claim to set forth religious systems or to form holy books. Other Judaic writings ordinarily qualify under the first plank of the definition, and the same is to be said for Christian counterparts. The second element in the definition excludes all Christian documents. The third dismisses all writings of all Judaisms other than the one of the dual Torah. Other Judaisms' writings cite Scriptural heroes or refer to a particular authority; none except those of this Judaism sets forth, as does every Rabbinic document,[1] extensive accounts of what a large number of diverse authorities say, let alone disputes among them. "Rabbinic" is therefore an appropriate qualifier for this Judaism, since what distinguishes it from all other is the character of its authorities (the matter of title being a mere detail) and the myth that accounts for its distinctive character.

Any book out of Judaic antiquity that exhibits these three traits — focus upon law and exegesis of the Hebrew Scriptures, exclusion of all prior tradition except for Scripture, and appealing to named sages called Rabbis, — falls into the category of Rabbinic literature. All other Jewish writings in varying proportions exhibit the first trait, and some the second as well, but none all three. It goes without saying that no named authority in any Rabbinic writing, except for scriptural ones, occurs in any other Judaic document in antiquity (excluding Gamaliel in Acts), or in another Jewish one either (excluding Simeon b. Gamaliel in Josephus's histories).

Rabbinic literature is divided into two large parts, each part formed as a commentary to a received part of the Torah, the one oral, the other written. The written part requires no attention here: it is simply Scripture (Hebrew: "the written Torah," TaNaKH, Torah, Nebi'im, Ketubim, a.k.a. "the Old Testament" part of the Bible). The oral part begins with the Mishnah, a philosophical law code that reached closure at the end of the second century, the written part of course comprises the Pentateuch and other books of ancient Israelite Scripture. Promulgated under the sponsorship of the Roman-appointed Jewish authority of the Land of Israel ("Palestine"), Judah the Patriarch, the Mishnah formed beyond Scripture the first document of Rabbinic literature and therefore of the Judaic system, "Rabbinic Judaism," or "the Judaism of the dual Torah," that took shape in this period. The attributed statements of its authorities, named sages or Rabbis called Tannaites ("repeaters," "memorizers," for the form in which the sayings were formulated and transmitted), enjoyed the standing of traditions beginning at Sinai. Numerous anonymous sayings, alongside the attributed ones and bearing upon the same controverted questions, appear as well.

THE MISHNAH AND THE EXEGETICAL TRADITION OF THE ORAL TORAH: Comprising six divisions, dealing with agriculture, holy seasons, women and family affairs, civil law and politics, everyday offerings, and cultic purity, the Mishnah served as the written code of the Patriarch's administration in the Land of Israel, and of that of his counterpart, the Exilarch, in Iranian-ruled Babylonia as well. Alongside the Mishnah's compilation of sages' sayings into well-crafted divisions, tractates, and chapters, other sayings of the same authorities circulated, some of them finding their way, marked as deriving from Tannaite authority, into the Tosefta and the two Talmuds.

Three exegetical documents formed around parts of the Mishnah. These were, specifically,

[1] the Tosefta, a compilation of supplementary sayings organized around nearly the whole of the Mishnah as citation and gloss, secondary paraphrase, and freestanding complement thereto, of no determinate date but probably concluded

about a century after the closure of the Mishnah, hence ca. 300; and two Talmuds, or sustained and systematic commentaries to the Mishnah,

[2] the Talmud of the Land of Israel, which reached closure in ca. 400, a commentary to most of the tractates of the Mishnah's first four divisions,

[3] the Talmud of Babylonia, concluded in ca. 600, providing a sustained exegesis to most of the tractates of the Mishnah's second through fifth divisions.

The Tosefta's materials occasionally form the basis for exegetical compositions in the two Talmuds, but the second Talmud's framers know nothing about the compositions, let alone compositions, of the prior Talmud, even though they frequently do cite sayings attributed to authorities of the Land of Israel as much as of Babylonia. So the line of the exegesis and extension of the Mishnah extends in an inverted Y, through the Tosefta, to the two, autonomous Talmuds.

Mishnah

Tosefta

Talmud of Land of Israel (Yerushalmi)   Talmud of Babylonia (Bavli)

SCRIPTURE AND THE EXEGETICAL TRADITION OF THE WRITTEN TORAH: Parts of the written Torah attracted sustained commentary as well, and, altogether, these commentaries, called Midrash-compilations, form the counterpart to the writings of Mishnah-exegesis. It should be noted that both Talmuds, in addition, contain large composites of Midrash-exegesis, but they are not organized around books or large selections of Scripture. The part of Rabbinic literature that takes Scripture, rather than the Mishnah, as its organizing structure covers the Pentateuchal books of Exodus, Leviticus, Numbers, and Deuteronomy, and some of the writings important in synagogue liturgy, particularly Ruth, Esther, Lamentations, and Song of Songs, all read on special occasions in the sacred calendar. Numbering for late antiquity twelve compilations in all, the earliest compilations of exegesis, called midrash, were produced in the third century, the latest in the sixth or seventh.

SAGES AND THE EXEMPLARY TORAH: There is a third, small type of writing in Rabbinic literature, which concerns teachings of sages on theological and moral questions. This comprises a very small, freestanding corpus, tractate Abot ("the fathers," or founders) and Abot deRabbi Nathan ("the fathers according to Rabbi Nathan"). The former collects sayings of sages, and the later contributes in addition stories about them. But the bulk of Rabbinic literature consists of works of exegesis of the Mishnah and Scripture, which is to say, the principal documents of the Torah, oral and written respectively. But throughout the documents of the oral Torah also are collected compositions and large compilations that are devoted to the sayings and exemplary deeds of named sages. No documents took shape to be made up out of that kind of writing, which, nonetheless, was abundant.

MISHNAH AND MIDRASH, *HALAKHAH* AND *AGGADAH* : Viewed as a whole, therefore, we see that the stream of exegesis of the Mishnah and exploration of its themes of law and philosophy flowed side by side with exegesis of Scripture. Since the Mishnah concerns itself with normative rules of behavior, it and the documents of exegesis flowing from it ordinarily are comprised of discussion of matters of law, or, in Hebrew, *halakhah.* Much of the exegesis of Scripture in the Midrash-compilations concerns itself with norms of belief, right attitude, virtue and proper motivation. Encased in narrative form, these teachings of an ethical and moral character are called *aggadah*, or lore.

Midrash-exegesis of Israelite Scripture in no way was particular to the Rabbinic literature. To the contrary, the exegesis of the Hebrew Scriptures had defined a convention of all systems of Judaism from before the conclusion of Scripture itself; no one, including the sages who stand behind Rabbinic literature, began anywhere but in the encounter with the Written Torah. But collecting and organizing documents of exegeses of Scripture in a systematic way developed in a quite distinct circumstance.

For Rabbinic literature, the circumstance was defined by the requirement of Mishnah-exegesis. The Mishnah's character itself defined a principal task of Scripture-exegesis. Standing by itself, providing few proof texts to Scripture to back up its rules, the Mishnah bore no explanation of why Israel should obey its rules. Brought into relationship to Scriptures, by contrast, the Mishnah gained access to the source of authority by definition operative in Israel, the Jewish people. Accordingly, the work of relating the Mishnah's rules to those of Scripture got under way alongside the formation of the Mishnah's rules themselves. It follows that explanations of the sense of the document, including its authority and sources, would draw attention to the written part of the Torah.

We may classify the Midrash-compilations in three successive groups: exegetical, propositional, and exegetical-propositional (theological).

[1] Exegetical Discourse and the Pentateuch: One important dimension, therefore, of the earliest documents of Scripture-exegesis, the Midrash-compilations that deal with Leviticus, Numbers, and Deuteronomy, measures the distance between the Mishnah and Scripture and aims to close it. The question is persistently addressed in analyzing Scripture: precisely how does a rule of the Mishnah relate to, or rest upon, a rule of Scripture? That question demanded an answer, so that the status of the Mishnah's rules, and, right alongside, of the Mishnah itself, could find a clear definition. Collecting and arranging exegeses of Scripture as these related to passages of the Mishnah first reached literary form in Sifra, to Leviticus, and in two books, both called Sifré, one to Numbers, the other Deuteronomy. All three compositions accomplished much else. For, even at that early stage, exegeses of passages of Scripture in their own context and not only for the sake of Mishnah-exegesis attracted attention. But a principal motif in all three books concerned the issue of Mishnah-Scripture relationships.

A second, still more fruitful path in formulating Midrash-clarifications of Scripture also emerged from the labor of Mishnah-exegesis. As the work of Mishnah-exegesis got under way, in the third century, exegetes of the Mishnah and others alongside undertook a parallel labor. They took an interest in reading Scripture in the way in which they were reading the Mishnah itself. That is to say, they began to work through verses of Scripture in exactly the same way — word for word, phrase for phrase, line for line — in which, to begin with, the exegetes of the Mishnah pursued the interpretation and explanation of the Mishnah. Precisely the types of exegesis that dictated the way in which sages read the Mishnah now guided their reading of Scripture as well. And, as people began to collect and organize comments in accord with the order of sentences and paragraphs of the Mishnah, they found the stimulation to collect and organize comments on clauses and verses of Scripture. This kind of verse-by-verse exegetical work got under way in the Sifra and the two Sifrés, but reached fulfillment in Genesis Rabbah presents a line-for-line reading of the book of Genesis. Characteristic of the narrowly-exegetical phase of Midrash-compilation is the absence of a single, governing proposition, running through the details. It is not possible, for example, to state the main point, expressed through countless cases, in Sifra or Sifré to Deuteronomy.[2]

[2] From Exegesis to Proposition: A further group of Midrash-compilations altogether transcends the limits of formal exegesis. Beyond these two modes of exegesis — search for the sources of the Mishnah in Scripture, line-by-line reading of Scripture as of the Mishnah — lies yet a third, an approach we may call "writing with Scripture," meaning, using verses of Scripture in a context established by a propositional program independent of Scripture itself. To understand it, we have to know how the first of the two Talmuds read the Mishnah. The Yerushalmi's authors not only explained phrases or sentences of the Mishnah in the manner of Mishnah- and Scripture-exegetes. They also investigated the principles and large-scale conceptual problems of the document and of the law given only in cases in the Mishnah itself. That is to say, they dealt not alone with a given topic, a subject and its rule, the cases that yield the rule, but with an encompassing problem, a principle and its implications for a number of topics and rules.

This far more discursive and philosophical mode of thought produced for Mishnah-exegesis sustained essays on principles cutting across specific rules. Predictably, this same intellectual work extended from the Mishnah to Scripture. Exegesis of Scripture beyond that focused on words, phrases, and sentences produced discursive essays on great principles or problems of theology and morality. Discursive exegesis is represented, to begin with, in Leviticus Rabbah, a document that reached closure, people generally suppose, sometime after Genesis Rabbah, thus ca. 450 C.E. and that marked the shift from verse-by-verse to syllogistic reading of verses of Scripture. It was continued in Pesiqta deRab Kahana, organized around themes pertinent to various holy days through the liturgical year, and Pesiqta Rabbati, a derivative and imitative work.

Typical of discursive exegesis of Scripture, Leviticus Rabbah presents not phrase-by-phrase systematic exegeses of verses in the book of Leviticus, but a set of thirty-seven topical essays. These essays, syllogistic in purpose, take the form of citations and comments on verses of Scripture to be sure. But the compositions range widely over the far reaches of the Hebrew Scriptures while focusing narrowly upon a given theme. They moreover make quite distinctive points about that theme. Their essays constitute compositions, not merely composites. Whether devoted to God's favor to the poor and humble or to the dangers of drunkenness, the essays, exegetical in form, discursive in character, correspond to the equivalent, legal essays, amply represented in the Yerushalmi. The framers of Pesiqta deRab Kahana carried forward a still more abstract and discursive mode of discourse, one in which verses of Scripture play a subordinated role to the framing of an implicit syllogism, which predominates throughout, both formally and in argument.

[3] SAYING ONE THING THROUGH MANY THINGS: Writing with Scripture reached its climax in the theological Midrash-compilations formed at the end of the development of Rabbinic literature. A fusion of the two approaches to Midrash-exegesis, the verse-by-verse amplification of successive chapters of Scripture and the syllogistic presentation of propositions, arguments, and proofs deriving from the facts of Scripture, was accomplished in the third body of Midrash-compilations: Ruth Rabbah, Esther Rabbah Part I, Lamentations Rabbah, and Song of Songs Rabbah. Here we find the verse-by-verse reading of scriptural books. But at the same time, a highly propositional program governs the exegesis, each of the compilations meaning to prove a single, fundamental theological point through the accumulation of detailed comments.

HALAKHAH AND AGGADAH, MISHNAH AND MIDRASH IN A SINGLE DEFINITIVE DOCUMENT: The Talmud of Babylonia, or Bavli, which was the final document of Rabbinic literature also formed the climax and conclusion of the entire canon and defined this Judaism from its time to the present. The Talmud of Babylonia forms the conclusion and the summary of Rabbinic literature, the most important document of the entire collection. One of its principal traits is the fusion of Mishnah- and Scripture-exegesis in a single compilation. The authors of units of discourse collected in the Talmud of Babylonia or Bavli drew together the two, up-to-then distinct, modes of organizing thought, either around the Mishnah or around Scripture. They treated both Torahs, oral and written, as equally available in the work of organizing large-scale exercises of sustained inquiry. So we find in the Bavli a systematic treatment of some tractates of the Mishnah. And within the same aggregates of discourse, we also find (in somewhat smaller proportion to be sure, roughly 60% to roughly 40% in a sample made of three tractates) a second principle of organizing and redaction. That principle dictates that ideas be laid out in line with verses of Scripture, themselves dealt with in cogent sequence, one by one, just as the Mishnah's sentences and paragraphs come under analysis, in cogent order and one by one.

DATING RABBINIC DOCUMENTS: While we have no exact dates for the closure of any of the documents of Rabbinic literature, — all the dates we have are mere guesses — we have solid grounds on setting them forth in the sequence [1] Mishnah,

Tosefta, [2] Yerushalmi, [3] Bavli for the exegetical writings on the Mishnah, and the three corresponding, and successive groups — [1] Sifra and the two Sifrés, [2] Leviticus Rabbah, Pesiqta deRab Kahana, Pesiqta Rabbati, then [3] Ruth Rabbah, Esther Rabbah Part One, Lamentations Rabbah, and Song of Songs Rabbah — for the exegetical writings on Scripture. The basis in the case of the sequence from the Mishnah is citation by one compilation of another, in which case, the cited document is to be dated prior to the document that does the citing. The basis in the case of the sequence from Scripture is less certain; we assign a post-Mishnah date to Sifra and the two Sifrés because of the large-scale citation of the former in the latter. The rest of the sequence given here rests upon presently-accepted and conventional dates and therefore cannot be regarded as final.

THE DOCUMENTARY THESIS: Study of the history of Rabbinic Judaism through the literature just now set forth must proceed document by document, in the sequence presently established for their respective dates of closure. In such a study of documentary sequences, e.g., how a given topic or theme is set forth in one writing after another, we learn the order in which ideas came to expression in the canon. We therefore commence at the Mishnah, the starting point of the originally-oral part of the canon. We proceed systematically to work our way through tractate Abot, the Mishnah's first apologetic, then the Tosefta, the Yerushalmi, and the Bavli at the end. Along the same lines, the sequence of Midrash-compilations is to be examined and the results, if possible, correlated with those of the Mishnah and its companions. In tracing the order in which ideas make their appearance, we ask about the components in sequence so far as we can trace the sequence. The traits of documents govern, and the boundaries that separate one from another also distinguish sayings from one another. The upshot is the study of the documents one by one, with emphasis on their distinguishing traits. When properly analyzed data are in hand, the work of forming of the facts a coherent, historical account of the whole may get underway. A further, theological task, within Judaism, is to form of the facts a cogent system and structure.

## II. ATTRIBUTIONS OF SAYINGS TO SAGES AND THEIR PLACE IN RABBINIC LITERATURE

The documentary examination of the Rabbinic literature is not the only way taken to describe the writings. Another approach to the examination of Rabbinic literature takes as the units of study not the successive documents and their definitive qualities, but rather, the sayings attributed to named authorities. This approach to the examination of Rabbinic literature treats as inconsequential the task of describing the documents in their own terms, one by one. It deals with the themes of the literature read as a single corpus, rather than the traits of documents inclusive of their topical programs. The topical-biographical reading of Rabbinic literature rests on the (definitive) fact that nearly every composition in Rabbinic literature will contain an attributed statement, as well as anonymous ones. Some therefore suppose that instead of reading Rabbinic literature document by document, we should collect all the sayings assigned to a given authority without regard to the document in which they appear and provide an account of the literature solely in terms of its contents. These sayings found in diverse documents then are to be classified as to time and place by the names associated with given compositions, rather than classified as to sequence by the presently-assumed order of closure of the writings themselves. The result is that a principal mode of describing Rabbinic literature alternative to the one followed here is biographical.[3]

It would follow that the traits of documents might take subordinate position, attributions of sayings defining the correct modes of categorization and ordering of the literature. Without regard to the documentary origin of those assigned sayings, such an approach to the study of Rabbinic literature then would work out the intellectual-biographical sequences, e.g., all the sayings given to a given authority, or topical ones, assuming the validity of the attribution of a saying to a sage who lived at a given time and therefore assigning that opinion to the age in which that sage lived. This approach ignores the lines of structure and order set forth by the documents themselves and takes for granted that the compilers of documents played no role in the shaping of the compositions that they collected. Documents then are taken to represent random points of compilation, not purposive and deliberate statements.

Examining attributions of sayings to named authorities, by contrast, and ignoring the documentary traits of individual writings present problems. The decisive one is that we cannot demonstrate, and therefore cannot take as fact, that what is attributed to a given sage really was said by him. The facticity of the documents is beyond question; the reliability of attributions is not. The reason is simple. No tests of validation or falsification of attributions have yet been devised to indicate which attributions are reliable, which not. The kind of internal evidence that would suffice — authenticated writings of said authority in his own style and on his own account — such as we have for earliest figures in Christianity, such as Paul or Justin, Origen or Augustine — does not exist. The Rabbinic documents rarely assign to named authorities sayings that exhibit traits of an individual character; most sayings exhibit the stylistic traits that predominate in the document that contains them. That means traits of individual style and form are obliterated, and that fact raises the question of how reliable what is attributed to that name is going to be.

Tests of falsification of the entire body of attributions, by contrast, yield positive results. When we seek evidence that attributions served a purpose other than factually assigning a given saying to a given name, we find ample indication that that was the case. What is attributed to a given name is not consistently assigned to that name; or we may find attributed to a given name both a statement and its very opposite. A saying assigned to a given authority in one document is assigned to someone else in another; a saying that is assigned to a given authority in one document occurs in different form altogether in his name in some other; and it is routine in the two Talmuds to revise attributions, reversing the sponsorship of a given position, for instance, so that Rabbi X, originally thought to have said A, is given opinion B, and Rabbi Y, who is supposed to have said B, is given opinion A. It follows that whatever the semiotic meaning of attributing sayings to named authorities, considerations of historical accuracy in the contemporary sense figured only in a limited way. While the writings before us are characterized by the attribution of numerous sayings to named authorities, those attributions do not provide secure evidence that the named authority really said what was attributed to him.

Sayings of individual sages come down to us in collective compositions, so we cannot demonstrate that Rabbi X wrote a book in which his views are given, preserved by his immediate disciples for instance. We do not know that a given Rabbi really said what is imputed to him at all, since there are no external witnesses to any attribution. All we have in hand is that the framers of document A have assigned diverse sayings to various names. Some facts make us wonder whether those assignments rest on the facts of a given figure's actual statements. First, the same saying may occur in more than a single name. What document A gives to Rabbi X, document B gives to Rabbi Y. Second, the actual wording of sayings assigned to individuals rarely bears distinctive traits and most commonly conforms to an overall pattern, imposed, in a given document, upon all sayings. These specific negative factors join a general one. In the picture we have of the formation of the documents and of the sayings in them, we cannot point to evidence of processes of individual writing, e.g., Rabbi X wrote book Y, or even to a program of preserving the very words of Rabbi X on the part of his disciples. The collective character of the writings before us testifies to a different purpose altogether from one which would preserve the particular views of a given individual. In Rabbinic literature we have in hand something other than minutes of meetings, actual words spoken by particular authorities, that is, the results, for conditions pertaining in antiquity, of the counterpart of careful observations by trained reporters, with tape recorders or TV cameras.

Not only so, but the documents formalize in their own distinctive patterns whatever they use and impose their own documentary-rhetorical preferences on nearly everything in hand. Some maintain that while we do not have in hand the actual words, we do have the gist of what someone said. They suppose that, while we do not know exactly what he said, he do know what he was thinking. But that carries us onto still more dubious ground. For attributions even of the gist of what is said by themselves cannot be shown to be reliable. We have no way of demonstrating that a given authority really maintained the views assigned to him – even if not in the actual words attributed to him. There are no sources in which we can check what is attributed, e.g., a given authority's own writings, preserved by his disciples; diaries, notes, personal reflections of any kind. We have only the judgment and record provided by the collectivity of sages represented by a given authorship: that is, the document and that alone. What we cannot show we do not know.

Since the various compositions of the canon of formative Judaism derive not from named, individual authors but from collective decisions of schools or academies, we cannot take for granted that attributions of sayings to individuals provide facts. We cannot show that if a given Rabbi is alleged to have made a statement, he really did say what is assigned to him. We do not have a book or a letter he wrote such as we have, for example, for Paul or Augustine or other important Christian counterparts to the great Rabbis of late antiquity. We also do not know that if a story was told, things really happened in the way the storyteller says, in some other way, or not at all.

Accordingly, we cannot identify as historical in a narrow and exact sense sayings or stories that come down to us in the canon of Judaism. Attributions of sayings, narratives of stories — these tell us only what those who assigned the sayings approved, on the one side, or what they believed ought to have happened, on the other. Sayings and stories therefore attest to the viewpoint of the framers of the documents who collected the sayings and stories and gave them a position of authority in the compilations they produced. What is absolutely firm and factual, therefore, is that these books represent views held by the authorship behind them. At the point at which a document reached conclusion and redaction, views of a given group of people reached the form at that moment of closure in which we now have them (taking account of variations of wording). That is why we do not know with any certainty what people were thinking prior to the point at which, it is generally assumed, a given document was redacted. Accordingly, if we wish to know the sequence in which views reached their current expression, we have recourse to the conventional order and rough dating assigned by modern scholarship to the several documents, from the Mishnah through the Bavli. All of the Rabbinic compilations are collective, official writings of their institutional sponsors, and none of them speaks for an individual authority. We examine Rabbinic literature document by document because the documents alone form solid facts, starting points for further study of history, religion, and the literature of Judaism itself.

### III. The Relationships among the Documents of Rabbinic Literature

If, however, we read documents one by one, as autonomous of one another, we have also to know how they interrelate. Describing the documents one by one therefore marks only the first step in the analysis of Rabbinic literature. Only when we know to what degree a document speaks for its authorship and to what degree it carries forward a received position can we come to an estimate of the character of that document's testimony to the unfolding of the system of Rabbinic Judaism as a whole:

[1] essentially its own and representative of the authorship of its stage in the unfolding of the canon, — or

[2] essentially continuous with what has gone before — or

[3] somewhere in the middle.

Seen one by one, moreover, documents stand in three relationships to one another and to the system of which they form part, that is, to Judaism, as a whole. Three stages, therefore, mark the analysis of documents, corresponding to the three possible relationships that can characterize the canonical writings as a whole.

[1] Each document is to be seen all by itself, that is, as autonomous of all others (though all documents may well concur on some basic, commonly inert facts, e.g., the unity of God).

[2] Each document is to be examined for its connections or relationships with other documents universally regarded as falling into the same classification, as Torah.

[3] And, finally, in the theology of Judaism each document is to be allowed to take its place as part of the undifferentiated aggregation of documents that, all together, constitute the canon of, in the case of Judaism, the "one whole Torah revealed by God to Moses at Mount Sinai."

These several relationships that situate the documents of Rabbinic literature may now be described in the terms of [1] autonomy, the stage of description; [2] connection, the stage of analysis, comparison and contrast; and [3] continuity, the stage of interpretation (whether historical or theological). That is to say, each of the writings is to be read as an autonomous statement in its own terms, with close attention to its distinctive, definitive traits of rhetoric, logic, and topic. Each further has to be brought into relationship with other writings of its species, e.g., exposition of the Mishnah or of Scripture, and sayings found in more than a single document are to be compared and contrasted as well. Finally, all writings are to be seen as part of a single coherent literature, a canon, meant to make a statement, elements of which derive from all of the documents equally. The first stage is descriptive, defining each writing; the second is analytical, comparing one writing with another; the third is synthetic, joining all the documents into a whole statement. The three stages of documentary study may be characterized as follows:

[1] AUTONOMY: if a document comes down to us within its own framework, exhibiting its own distinctive traits of rhetoric, topic, and logic, as a complete book with a beginning, middle, and end, in preserving that book, the canon presents us with a document on its own and not solely as part of a larger composition or construct. So we too see the document as it reaches us, that is, as autonomous.

[2] CONNECTION: if, second, a document contains materials shared verbatim or in substantial content with other documents of its classification, or if one document refers to the contents of other documents, then the several documents that clearly wish to engage in conversation with one another have to address one another. That is to say, we have to seek for the marks of connectedness, asking for the meaning of those connections.

[3] CONTINUITY: finally, since the community of the faithful of Judaism, in all of the contemporary expressions of Judaism, concur that documents held to be

authoritative constitute one whole, seamless "Torah," that is, a complete and exhaustive statement of God's will for Israel and humanity, we take as a further appropriate task, if one not to be done here, the description of the whole out of the undifferentiated testimony of all of its parts. These components in the theological context are viewed, as is clear, as equally authoritative for the composition of the whole: one, continuous system. In taking up such a question, we address a problem not of theology alone, though it is a correct theological conviction, but one of description, analysis, and interpretation of an entirely historical order.

The several documents that make up Rabbinic literature relate to one another in yet three other important ways.

[1] All of them refer to the same basic writing, the Hebrew Scriptures. Many of them draw upon the Mishnah and quote it. So the components of the canon join at their foundations.

[2] As the documents reached closure in sequence, the later authorship can be shown to have drawn upon earlier, completed documents. So the writings of the Rabbis of the talmudic corpus accumulate and build from layer to layer.

[3] Among two or more documents some completed units of discourse, and many brief, discrete sayings, circulated, for instance, sentences or episodic homilies or fixed sayings (e.g., moral maxims) of various kinds.

So in some (indeterminate) measure the several documents draw not only upon one another, as we can show, but also upon a common corpus of materials that might serve diverse editorial and redactional purposes. The extent of this common corpus of floating sayings can never be fully known. We know only what we have, not what we do not have. So we cannot say what has been omitted, or whether sayings that occur in only one document derive from materials available to the editors or compilers of some or all other documents. That is something we never can know.

## IV. Intertextuality or Intratextuality: Rabbinic Literature as a Community of Texts

Since the several Rabbinic documents stand distinct from one another, each with its own rhetorical, logical, and topical program, they relate not "intertextually" but "intratextually." That is to say, when the framers of a composition wish to allude to another document, e.g., Scripture, they say so in so many words. They ordinarily give a clear signal that that document is cited, ordinarily using such citation-language as "as it is said," or "as it is written." The accepted definitions of intertextuality, which emphasize the implicit bonds that form an invisible web holding together all writings, therefore do not apply. Rabbinic literature forms a library, in which a common collection unites discrete items, rather than an undifferentiated body of writing.

To clarify this perspective, consider the analogy of a library. Books brought together form a library. Each title addresses its own program and makes its own points. But books produced by a cogent community constitute not merely a library but a canon: a set of compositions each of which contributes to a statement that transcends its own pages. The books exhibit intrinsic traits that make of them all *a community of texts*. We should know on the basis of those characteristics that the texts form a community even if we knew nothing more than the texts themselves. In the Judaic writings, moreover, the documents at hand are held by Judaism to form a canon.

Seeing the whole as continuous, which is quite natural, later theology maintains that all of the documents of Rabbinic literature find a place in "the Torah." But that is an imputed, and theological, not an inductive and intrinsic fact. It is something we know only on the basis of information — theological convictions about the one whole Torah God gave to Moses in two media — deriving from sources other than the texts at hand, which, on their own, do not link each to all and all to every line of each. Extrinsic traits, that is imputed ones, make of the discrete writings a single and continuous, uniform statement: one whole Torah in the mythic language of Judaism. The community of Judaism imputes those traits, sees commonalities, uniformities, deep harmonies: one Torah of one God. In secular language, that community expresses its system — its world view, its way of life, its sense of itself as a society — by these choices, and finds its definition in them. Hence, in the nature of things, the community of Judaism forms a *textual community*. That cogent community that forms a canon out of a selection of books therefore participates in the process of authorship, just as the books exist in at least two dimensions.

Let us turn to the problem of the community of texts, utilizing the dimensions just now defined in our description of the canon. We take the measure of two of the three dimensions just now introduced, *autonomy*, on the one side, and *connection*, on the second. (Continuity among all documents introduces theological, not literary problems for analysis.) That is to say, a book enjoys its own autonomous standing, but it also situates itself in relationship to other books of the same classification. Each book bears its own statement and purpose, and each relates to others of the same classification. The community of texts therefore encompasses individuals who (singly or collectively) comprise (for the authorships: compose) books. But there is a set of facts that indicates how a book does not stand in isolation. These facts fall into several categories. Books may go over the same ground or make use in some measure of the same materials. The linkages between and among them therefore connect them. Traits of rhetoric, logic, and topic may place into a single classification a number of diverse writings. Then there is the larger consensus of members who see relationships between one book and another and so join them together on a list of authoritative writings. So, as is clear, a book exists in the dimensions formed of its own contents and covers, but it also takes its place in the second and third dimensions of relationship to other books.

Then the relationships in which a given document stands may be expressed in the prepositions *between* and *among*. That is to say, in its intellectual traits a document bears relationship, to begin with, to some other, hence we describe relationships between two documents. These constitute formal and intrinsic matters: traits of grammar, arrangements of words and resonances as to their local meaning, structures of syntax of expression and thought. But in its social setting a document finds bonds among three or more documents, with all of which it is joined in the imagination and mind of a community. These range widely and freely, bound by limits not of form and language, but of public policy in behavior and belief. Documents because of their traits of rhetoric, logic, and topic form a community of texts. Documents because of their audience and authority express the intellect of a textual community.

The principal issue worked out in establishing a community of texts is hermeneutical, the chief outcome of defining a textual community, social and cultural. The former teaches us how to read the texts on their own. The latter tells us how to interpret texts in context. When we define and classify the relationships between texts, we learn how to read the components — words, cogent thoughts formed of phrases, sentences, paragraphs — of those texts in the broader context defined by shared conventions of intellect: rhetoric, logic, topic. More concretely, hermeneutical principles tell how, in light of like documents we have seen many times, to approach a document we have never before seen. Hermeneutics teaches the grammar and syntax of thought. Memorizing a passage of a complex text will teach the rhythms of expression and thought that make of the sounds of some other document an intelligible music. Not only so, but documents joined into a common classification may share specific contents, not only definitive traits of expression — meaning and not solely method.

## v. Compositions and Composites: The Prehistory of Rabbinic Documents

Any introduction to Rabbinic literature must answer the question, what about the materials upon which the various documents draw? The question concerns sources or traditions utilized by framers of Rabbinic documents but not made up by those compilers. The documents give ample evidence that before the work of compilation got underway, a process of composition had gone forward and in some passages had reached conclusion That is not by reason of the citations, of indeterminate reliability, of sayings to named figures, even though these have to be addressed, if not treated as irreducible historical facts. It is because the literary traits of the documents themselves ordinarily permit us to identify compositions that are quite distinct in indicative traits from the larger composite of which they now form a component.

For example, a given document defines for us its definitive structure — the paramount literary forms, the rhetorical preferences of the editors, the modes of logical coherence, even the topical program. Then materials clearly not put together in conformity with the document's protocol present themselves as candidates for inclusion in a list of compositions utilized, but not made up, by the document's own framers. Most of the Rabbinic writings exhibit the character of compilations, and only few of them appear to conform to a single convention of thought and expression, beginning to end. The Mishnah and Sifra typify the latter kind of document, Tosefta, the two Talmuds, and most of the Midrash-compilations, the former. In the composite-documents, as we shall see at some length, one principle of coherent discourse, that of propositional logic, serves in compositions, while another, that of fixed association to a set of statements (e.g., verses of Scripture or clauses of the Mishnah), molds compositions into composites. It follows that Rabbinic documents on the very surface implicitly attest to the availability of statements — whether writings or oral traditions — made up prior to inclusion in the documents in which they now occur.

Internal evidence within the documents themselves guides us toward an answer to the question of the prehistory of Rabbinic documents. Specifically, we may categorize the completed units of thought that comprise each of the documents by appeal to external, redactional traits. Some of those completed units of thought, which we may call compositions, clearly serve the purposes of the framers of the document in which they occur; others accomplish the goals of compilers of a kind of document we do have, but not the document in which we now find them. And still others present the anomaly of writings composed for a kind of compilation that we simply do not have at all.

It is a fact that the Rabbinic writings make occasional use of freestanding individual sayings that circulated in ways we cannot now define. But, to a much more considerable extent, they all utilize for the formation of their composites sizable numbers of previously completed compositions and even composites of such compositions, and any account of the Rabbinic literature requires attention to the materials that contribute to the formation of those books. We know that that is a fact, because, while each of the documents that make up the canon of Judaism exhibits distinctive traits in logic, rhetoric, and topic, so that we may identify the purposes and traits of form and intellect of the authorship of that document, they also use compositions and even composites that do not exhibit those distinctive traits at all.

Most Rabbinic documents in various proportion contain some completed units of thought — propositional arguments, sayings, and stories for instance. A few of these may travel from one document to another. It follows that the several documents intersect through shared materials. Furthermore, these completed compositions compiled in two or more documents by definition do not carry out the rhetorical, logical, and topical program of a particular document. So while documents are autonomous but also connected through such shared materials, therefore, we must account for the history of not only the documents in hand but also the completed pieces of writing that move from here to there.

Three stages mark the formation of Rabbinic documents, viewed individually. We work from the finished writing backward to the freestanding compositions that framers or compilers or authors of those documents utilized.

[1] Moving from the latest to the earliest, one stage is marked by the definition of a document, *its* topical program, *its* rhetorical medium, *its* logical message. These are definitive traits we have now explained, and some of the compositions compiled in a document exhibit the traits of the document as a whole. The document as we know it in its basic structure and main lines therefore comes at the end of the process. It follows that writings that clearly serve the program of that document and carry out the purposes of its authorship were made up in connection with the formation of *that* document.

[2] Another, prior stage is marked by the preparation of writings that do not serve the needs of a particular document now in our hands, but can have carried out the purposes of an authorship working on a document of a *type* we now have. The existing documents then form a model for defining other kinds of writings worked out to meet the program of a documentary authorship.

[3] But — and now we come to the heart of the matter — there are other types of writings that in no way serve the needs or plans of any document we now have, and that, furthermore, also cannot find a place in any document of a type that we now have. These writings, as a matter of fact, very commonly prove peripatetic, traveling from one writing to another, equally at home in, or alien to, the program of the documents in which they end up. These writings therefore were carried out without regard to a documentary program of any kind exemplified by the canonical books of the Judaism of the dual Torah. They form the earliest in the three stages of the writing of the units of completed thought that in the aggregate form the canonical literature of the Judaism of the dual Torah of late antiquity.

As a matter of fact, therefore, a given canonical document of the Judaism of the dual Torah draws upon three classes of materials, and these were framed in temporal order. Last comes the final class, the one that the redactors themselves defined and wrote; prior is the penultimate class that can have served other redactors but did not serve these in particular; and earliest of all in the order of composition (at least, from the perspective of the ultimate redaction of the documents we now have) is the writing that circulated autonomously and served no redactional purpose we can now identify within the canonical documents. Let us consider a concrete example of the distinction between writings that conform to the purposes of a document we now have and those that do not, with the Mishnah and the Talmud of Babylonia as our illustrative cases.

[1] The Mishnah: A document that is written down essentially in its penultimate and ultimate stages, taking shape within the redactional process and principally there, is the Mishnah. In that writing, the patterns of language, e.g., syntactic structures, of the apodosis and protasis of the Mishnah's smallest whole units of discourse are framed in formal, mnemonic patterns. They follow a few simple rules. These rules, once known, apply nearly everywhere and form stunning evidence for the document's cogency. They permit anyone to reconstruct, out of a

few key phrases, an entire cognitive unit, and even complete intermediate units of discourse. Working downward from the surface, therefore, anyone can penetrate into the deeper layers of meaning of the Mishnah. Then and at the same time, while discovering the principle behind the cases, one can easily memorize the whole by mastering the recurrent rhetorical pattern dictating the expression of the cogent set of cases. For it is easy to note the shift from one rhetorical pattern to another and to follow the repeated cases, articulated in the new pattern downward to its logical substrate. So syllogistic propositions, in the Mishnah's authors' hands, come to full expression not only in *what* people wish to state but also in *how* they choose to say it. The limits of rhetoric define the arena of topical articulation.

The Mishnah's formal traits of rhetoric indicate that the bulk of the document has been formulated all at once, and not in an incremental, linear process extending into a remote past. These traits, common to a series of distinct cognitive units, are redactional, because they are imposed at that point at which someone intended to join together discrete (finished) units on a given theme. The varieties of traits particular to the discrete units and the diversity of authorities cited therein, including masters of two or three or even four strata from the turn of the first century to the end of the second, make it highly improbable that the several units were formulated in a common pattern and then preserved, until, later on, still further units, on the same theme and in the same pattern, were worked out and added. The entire indifference, moreover, to historical order of authorities and concentration on the logical unfolding of a given theme or problem without reference to the sequence of authorities, confirm the supposition that the work of formulation and that of redaction go forward together.

The principal framework of formulation and formalization in the Mishnah is the intermediate division rather than the cognitive unit. The least-formalized formulary pattern, the simple declarative sentence, turns out to yield many examples of acute formalization, in which a single distinctive pattern is imposed upon two or more (very commonly, groups of three or groups of five) cognitive units. While an intermediate division of a tractate may be composed of several such conglomerates of cognitive units, it is rare indeed for cognitive units formally to stand wholly by themselves. Normally, cognitive units share formal or formulary traits with others to which they are juxtaposed and the theme of which they share. It follows that the principal unit of formulary formalization is the intermediate division and not the cognitive unit. And what that means for our inquiry, is simple: we can tell when it is that the ultimate or penultimate redactors of a document do the writing.

Now let us see that vast collection of writings that exhibits precisely the opposite trait: a literature in which, while doing some writing of their own, the redactors collected and arranged available materials.

[2] THE TALMUD OF BABYLONIA: In the pages of this document we find a kind of writing that in no way defines a document now in our hands or even a type

of document we can now imagine, that is, one that in its particulars we do not have but that conforms in its definitive traits to those that we do have may also be identified. The final organizers of the Talmud of Babylonia had in hand a tripartite corpus of inherited materials awaiting composition into a final, closed document.

First, in the initial type of material, in various states and stages of completion, sages addressed the Mishnah or took up the principles of laws that the Mishnah had originally brought to articulation. These compositions the framers of the Bavli organized in accord with the order of those Mishnah-tractates that they selected for sustained attention.

Second, they had in hand received materials, again in various conditions, pertinent to Scripture, both as Scripture related to the Mishnah and also as Scripture laid forth its own narratives. These they set forth as Scripture-commentary. In this way, the penultimate and ultimate redactors of the Bavli laid out a systematic presentation of the two Torahs, the oral, represented by the Mishnah, and the written, represented by Scripture.

And, third, the framers of the Bavli also had in hand materials focused on sages. These in the received form, attested in the Bavli's pages, were framed around twin biographical principles, either as strings of stories about great sages of the past or as collections of sayings and comments drawn together solely because the same name stands behind all the collected sayings. These can easily have been composed into biographies. This is writing that is utterly outside of the documentary framework in which it is now preserved; nearly all narratives in the Rabbinic literature, not only the biographical ones, indeed prove remote from any documentary program exhibited by the canonical documents in which they now occur.

The Bavli as a whole lays itself out as a commentary to the Mishnah. So the framers wished us to think that whatever they wanted to tell us would take the form of Mishnah commentary. But a second glance indicates that the Bavli is made up of enormous composites, themselves closed prior to inclusion in the Bavli. Some of these composites — around 40% of Bavli's whole — were selected and arranged along lines dictated by a logic other than that deriving from the requirements of Mishnah commentary. The components of the canon of the Judaism of the dual Torah prior to the Bavli had encompassed amplifications of the Mishnah, in the Tosefta and in the Yerushalmi, as well as the same for Scripture. As we have already noted, these are found in such documents as Sifra to Leviticus, Sifré to Numbers, another Sifré, to Deuteronomy, Genesis Rabbah, Leviticus Rabbah, and the like. But there was no entire document, now-extant, organized around the life and teachings of a particular sage. Even The Fathers According to Rabbi Nathan, which contains a good sample of stories about sages, is not so organized as to yield a life of a sage, or even a systematic biography of any kind. Where events in the lives of sages do occur, they are thematic and not biographical in organization, e.g., stories about the origins, as to Torah-study, of diverse sages; death-scenes of various sages. The sage as such, whether Aqiba or Yohanan ben Zakkai or Eliezer b. Hyrcanus, never in that document defines the appropriate organizing principle for sequences of stories or sayings. And there is no other in which the sage forms an organizing category for any material purpose.

Accordingly, the decision that the framers of the Bavli reached was to adopt the two redactional principles inherited from the antecedent century or so and to reject the one already rejected by their predecessors, even while honoring it.

[1] They organized the Bavli around the Mishnah.

[2] They adapted and included vast tracts of antecedent materials organized as scriptural commentary. These they inserted whole and complete, not at all in response to the Mishnah's program.

[3] While making provision for small-scale compositions built upon biographical principles, preserving both strings of sayings from a given master (and often a given tradent — a disciple responsible to memorize sayings of a given master) as well as tales about authorities of the preceding half millennium, they never created redactional compositions, of a sizable order, that focused upon given authorities. But sufficient materials certainly lay at hand to allow doing so.

While we cannot date these freestanding writings, we may come to a theory on their place in the unfolding of the Rabbinic literature. We ask in particular about the compositions and even large scale composites that stand autonomous of any redactional program we have in an existing compilation or of any we can even imagine on the foundations of said writings. Compositions of this kind, as a matter of hypothesis, are to be assigned to a stage in the formation of classics prior to the framing of the now-available documents. For, as a matter of fact, all of our now extant writings adhere to a single program of conglomeration and agglutination, and all are served by composites of one sort, rather than some other. Hence we may suppose that at some point prior to the decision to make writings in the model that we now have but in some other model people also made up completed units of thought to serve these other kinds of writings. These persist, now, in documents that they do not serve at all well. And we can fairly easily identify the kinds of documents that they can and should have served quite nicely indeed. These then are the three stages of literary formation in the making of the classics of Judaism.

Of the relative temporal or ordinal position of writings that stand autonomous of any redactional program we have in an existing compilation or of any we can even imagine on the foundations of said writings we can say nothing. These writings prove episodic; they are commonly singletons. They serve equally well everywhere, because they demand no traits of form and redaction in order to endow them with sense and meaning. We can understand these compositions entirely within the information their authors have given us; no context in some larger document or even composite is required to make sense of what is before us. So these kinds of compositions are essentially freestanding and episodic, not referential and allusive. They are stories that contain their own point and do not invoke, in the making of that point, a given verse of Scripture. They are sayings that are utterly ad hoc. A variety of materials fall into this — from a redactional perspective — unassigned, and unassignable, type of writing. They do not belong in books at all. Whoever made up these pieces of writing did not imagine that what he was forming required a setting beyond the limits of his own piece of writing; the story is not only complete in itself but could stand entirely on its own; the saying spoke for itself and required no nurturing context; the proposition and its associated proofs in no way were meant to draw nourishment from roots-penetrating nutriments outside of its own literary limits.

Where we have utterly hermetic writing, able to define its own limits and sustain its point without regard to anything outside itself, we know that here we are in the presence of authorships that had no larger redactional plan in mind, no intent on the making of books out of their little pieces of writing. We may note that, among the "unimaginable" compilations is not a collection of parables, since parables rarely stand free and never are inserted for their own sake. Whenever in the Rabbinic canon we find a parable, it is meant to serve the purpose of an authorship engaged in making its own point; and the point of a parable is rarely, if ever, left unarticulated. Normally it is put into words, but occasionally the point is made simply by redactional setting. It must follow that, in this canon, the parable cannot have constituted the generative or agglutinative principle of a large-scale compilation.

The three stages in the formation of materials ultimately compiled in the Rabbinic documents in our hand correspond, as a matter of fact, to a taxic structure, that is, three types of writing.

[1] The first type — and last in assumed temporal order — is writing carried out in the context of the making, or compilation, of a classic. That writing responds to the redactional program and plan of the authorship of a classic.

[2] The second type — penultimate in order — is writing that can appear in a given document but better serves a document other than the one in which it (singularly) occurs. This kind of writing does not likely fall within the same period of redaction as the first. For while it is a type of writing under the identical conditions, it also is writing that presupposes redactional programs in no way in play in the ultimate, and definitive, period of the formation of the canon: when people did things this way, and not in some other. That is why it is a kind of writing that was done prior to the period in which people limited their redactional work and associated labor of composition to the program that yielded the books we now have.

[3] The third kind of writing originates in an indeterminate period, probably prior to the other two — before the documentary norms had reached definition. It is carried on in a manner independent of all redactional considerations such as are known to us. Then it should derive from a time when redactional considerations played no paramount role in the making of compositions. A brief essay, rather than a sustained composition, was then the dominant mode of writing. People can have written both long and short compositions — compositions and composites — at one and the same time. But writing that does not presuppose a secondary labor of

redaction, e.g., in a composite, probably originated when authors or authorships did not anticipate any fate for their writing beyond their labor of composition itself.

Along these same lines of argument, this writing may or may not travel from one document to another. What that means is that the author or authorship does not imagine a future for his writing. What fits anywhere is composed to go nowhere in particular. Accordingly, what matters is not whether a writing fits one document or another, but whether, as the author or authorship has composed a piece of writing, that writing meets the requirements of any document we now have or can even imagine. If it does not, then we deal with a literary period in which the main kind of writing was ad hoc and episodic, not sustained and documentary.

The upshot is simple: whether the classification of writing be given a temporal or merely taxonomic valence, the issue is the same: have these writers done their work with documentary considerations in mind? In these cases it is clear that they have not. Then where did they expect their work to makes its way? Anywhere it might, because, so they assumed, fitting in nowhere in particular, it found a suitable locus everywhere it turned up. But I think temporal, not merely taxonomic, considerations pertain.

Now extra- and non-documentary kinds of writing derive from either [1] a period prior to the work of the making of Midrash-compilations and the two Talmuds alike; or [2] a labor of composition not subject to the rules and considerations that operated in the work of the making of Midrash-compilations and the two Talmuds. As a matter of hypothesis, non-documentary writing is more likely to come prior to making any kind of documents of consequence, and extra-documentary writing comes prior to the period in which the specificities of the documents we now have were defined. That is to say, writing that can fit anywhere or nowhere is to be situated at a time prior to writing that can fit somewhere but does not fit anywhere now accessible to us, and both kinds of writing are prior to the kind that fits only in the documents in which it is now located.

And given the documentary propositions and theses that we can locate in all of our compilations, we can only assume that the non-documentary writings enjoyed, and were assumed to enjoy, ecumenical acceptance. That means, very simply, when we wish to know the consensus of the entire textual (or canonical) community, we turn not to the distinctive perspective of documents, but the (apparently universally acceptable) perspective of the extra-documentary compositions.

Non-documentary compositions took shape not only separated from, but in time before, the documentary ones did. Non-documentary writings in general focus on matters of very general interest. These matters may be assembled into two very large rubrics: virtue, on the one side, reason, on the other. Stories about sages fall into the former category; all of them set forth in concrete form the right living that sages exemplify. Essays on right thinking, the role of reason, the taxonomic priority of Scripture, the power of analogy, the exemplary character of cases and precedents in the expression of general and encompassing rules — all of these intellectually coercive writings set forth rules of thought as universally applicable, in their way, as are the rules of conduct contained in stories about sages, in theirs. A great labor of generalization is contained in both kinds of non-documentary and extra-documentary writing. And the results of that labor are then given concrete expression in the documentary writings in hand; for these, after all, do say in the setting of specific passages or problems precisely what, in a highly general way, emerges from the writing that moves hither and yon, never with a home, always finding a suitable resting-place.

Now, admittedly, that rather general characterization of the non-documentary writing is subject to considerable qualification and clarification. But it does provide a reason to assign temporal priority, not solely taxonomic distinction, to the non-documentary compositions. We can have had commentaries of a sustained and systematic sort on Psalms or Chronicles, which we do not in fact have from late antiquity, on the one side, or treatises on virtue, such as Torah-study or the master-disciple-relationship, which we also do not have, on the second, or biographies ("gospels") on the third — to complete the triangle. The materials that can have comprised such documents are abundant in the Rabbinic literature. But we do not have these kinds of books.

The books we do have not only preserve the evidences of the possibility of commentaries and biographies. More than that, they also bring to rich expression the messages that such books will have set forth. And most important, they also express in fresh and unanticipated contexts those virtues and values that commentaries and biographies ("gospels") meant to bring to realization, and they do so in accord with the modes of thought that sophisticated reflection on right thinking has exemplified in its way as well. So when people went about the work of making documents, they did something fresh with something familiar. They made cogent compositions, documents, texts enjoying integrity and autonomy. But they did so in such a way as to form of their distinct documents a coherent body of writing, of books a canon, of documents a system. And this they did in such a way as to say, in distinctive and specific ways, things that, in former times, people had expressed in general and broadly-applicable ways. Now that we have examined the canon as a whole and identified its principal parts, let us turn to the differentiation of those parts: the criteria that distinguish one document from all others.

## ENDNOTES

[1]With the possible exception of those Targumim that exhibit the definitive traits of origin in Rabbinic circles, e.g., Onqelos.

[2]But that does not characterize Sifré to Numbers.

[3]This is the way taken by Strack-Stemberger, which devotes to "the Rabbis" half of the general introduction to biographies (sixty-two out 118 pages), pp. 62-118.

# 2

## The Documentary Foundation of Rabbinic Culture

### I. How do we Recognize a Document When We See One?

A distinct document is signified by the intersection of defining traits of rhetoric, topic, and logic of coherent discourse. The forms, the program, and the principle of cogency characterize a document and distinguish it from all other documents in some or another aspect, or in all aspects. The Rabbinic writings come to us in free-standing books or documents — large-scale cogent composites made up of a number of compositions, complete units of thought — by definition exist on their own. These books clearly differentiate themselves, each from all the others. The criteria are formal, logical, and topical.

The Mishnah clearly differs in formal as well as substantive ways from every other writing; the same may be said of Sifra, the two Sifrés, Genesis Rabbah, Leviticus Rabbah, and the like. If we took the two Talmuds and asked how they are comprised, we should have no difficulty on formal bases alone in distinguishing a passage drawn from the Mishnah from one deriving from the Talmud, or Gemara, that serves as a sustained and systematic commentary to the Mishnah. The documents, moreover, explicitly signal when they cite an external book, e.g., always indicating the citation of a verse of Scripture by a marking ("as it is said" or "as it is written"), a citation of a sentence of the Mishnah or of an official formulation of a rule bearing the status or authority of a sentence of the Mishnah (e.g., with TNY or TNN or variations thereof). Nearly the whole of the contents of the canonical books are unique to the books in which they occur. True, some sayings and stories — a negligible fraction of the whole documents in which they occur — float from document to document, these form a negligible proportion of any given document, only one of which appears at present to constitute little more than a scrapbook, a compilation of this and that. All the others exhibit traits of purpose and coherent conception.[1]

It is the simple fact that the canonical documents, without exception, may be readily distinguished from one another and, more to the point, except for the rare passages that float from writing to writing,[2] cannot be confused with one another. Presented with a passage of, let us say, a thousand words, we could readily assign it a place in its one particular home, with the proviso that said passage conforms to the definitive traits that in general characterize that home (again taking note of the few items that float hither and yon). It follows that, in the canon of Rabbinic Judaism, the building block is the free-standing document, and that fact derives not from the conventions of copyists or printers but from the internal evidences of the writings themselves.

So much for a concrete definition of the books or documents of the Rabbinic canon. A more abstract definition will serve as well. A document is a cogent composite of cogent compositions and through the compilation of those compositions into composites and composites into an entire collection makes a set of cogent statements. A document forms an artifact of a social culture, and that in diverse dimensions. The most important, in the Rabbinic canon, is that the document is anonymous and therefore represented by its writers as not sectarian but the statement of consensus;[3] where a name intrudes, it signals the sectarian status of the opinion. It follows that a particular group produced the document, finds it intelligible, preserves and transmits it; a document sets forth a sponsored, social statement. Its cogency depends on shared rhetoric, logic of intelligible discourse that is by definition public, and a topic and program that the sponsors of the document deem urgent. These traits will characterize the principal building blocks of the document — the composites — and perhaps even the compositions.

All of these traits of mind, of culture, moreover coalesce in the formation of a document: someone writes a document, someone buys it, an entire society sustains the labor of literature. Hence we place any document into its culture and society. And, in the context of the Judaism of the dual Torah represented by the score of compilations known as the Mishnah, two Talmuds, Midrash-compilations, and related writings, documents all are public, anonymous, official, and authoritative. That Judaism produced and preserved no writings that are not public in sponsorship, that are signed by individual names and, more to the point, bear the marks of personal, idiosyncratic authorship, that bear authority and the stamp of office.[4] Documents in that context therefore form building blocks of that culture, statements in behalf of the collectivity of "our sages of blessed memory," and since the entire testimony in our hands concerning the religious system or Judaism of those sages takes the form of writings that conform to the definition just now given, it follows, Rabbinic culture is to be studied solely and exhaustively in the setting of its documentary statements.

I have formulated the documentary method in the reading of the canonical writings of Rabbinic Judaism, on the one side, and in the study of the history of the formation of that Judaism, on the other. That method for historical purposes requires

[1] the systematic reading of the canonical writings one by one, and

[2] then the sequential reading of those same writings one after the other; the former yields rules of reading in context, the latter, rules of interpreting, the writings in their nourishing matrix.

Prior approaches to the history of the formation of Rabbinic Judaism identified as their building blocks singleton sayings or stories read atomistically and not in the larger context defined by the book that conveys them. Sayings, stories, and other compositions were deemed to circulate independent of all larger context and to be unaffected by the document that now conveys them.[5] Hence the documentary reading of canonical writings, that is, the insistence that context defines a critical dimension of contents, was dismissed as needless.[6]

A further obstacle to the documentary and contextual reading of writings arose in the premise that sayings were taken to represent things really said or done by those to whom the sayings were attributed. Since the absolute givens, the irreducible minima of facticity, in such a view of matters reach us in the form of authentic transcriptions of *ipsissima verba*, why ask the entirety of a writing to form the starting point of inquiry, when the document contains much more fundamental evidence than its own material traits? That uncritical and fundamentalist approach to historical and literary study has yielded dubious results, because all results rest on undemonstrated premises as to the facticity of attributions and the historical reliability of narratives, and also because the way in which these sayings and stories reach us has not been traced and verified as well. By sidestepping the received approach and starting fresh with the analysis of the traits of the media by which sayings and stories reach us, which is the document that conveys sayings and stories, I have redefined the work to be done; I also have done a great part of the earliest stages of that same work of literary description and historical analysis and religions-historical interpretation.

It follows that relationships between and among documents matter for two distinct reasons.

[1] The intrinsic relationships, which are formal, guide us to traits of intelligibility, teaching us through our encounter with one document how to read some other of its type or class. If we know how to read a document of one type, we may venture to read another of the same type, but not — without instruction — one of some other type altogether.

[2] The extrinsic relationships, which derive from context and are relative to community, direct us to how to understand a document as an artifact of culture and society. Traits not of documents but of doctrines affecting a broad range of documents come into play. The document, whatever its contents, therefore becomes an instrument of social culture, e.g., theology and politics, a community's public policy. A community then expresses itself through its choice of documents, the community's canon forming a principal mode of such self-definition.

So, as I said, through intrinsic traits a document places itself within a larger community of texts. Extrinsic traits, imputed to a document by not its authorship but its audience, select the document as canonical and make of the document a mode of social definition. The community through its mode of defining itself by its canonical choices forms a textual community — a community expressed through the books it reads and values.

### II. AUTONOMY = TEXT, CONNECTION = CONTEXT, CONTINUITY = MATRIX

The relationships among the documents produced by the sages of Judaism may take three forms, two extremes and a middle: [1] complete dependence, [3] complete autonomy, and [2] intersection in diverse manner and measure. All three relationships stand for a valid perspective on the distinct documents, from the Mishnah through the Talmud. Each document, whether the Mishnah or the Talmud or the Tosefta or Sifra, exhibits traits that distinguish it from all others. Hence its compilers anticipated that it would be read in its own terms. Each document finds a place in the larger canon of this Judaism, being valued as holy or part of the Torah. Hence all documents join together, each depending upon the others. And, finally, at specific points, documents intersect, either because the compilers utilize materials that occur elsewhere, or because one document will address a prior one and formulate its statement as a commentary to that prior one.

While it is the first, not the second, dimension that in the minds of critics of mine takes priority, still, it is the second dimension that provokes considerable debate and presents a remarkably unclear perspective. For while the dimensions of autonomy and continuity take the measure of acknowledged traits — books on their own, books standing in imputed, therefore socially verified, relationships — the matter of connection hardly enjoys the same clear definition. On the one side, so I claim at any rate, intrinsic traits permit us to assess theories of connection. On the other, confusing theological and social judgments of continuities and literary and heuristic ones of connection, people present quite remarkable claims as to the relationships between and among documents, alleging, in fact, that the documents all have to be read as a single continuous document: the Torah. Some maintain that the connections between and among documents are such that each has to be read in the light of all others. So the documents assuredly do form a canon, and that is a position adopted not in some distant past or alien society but among contemporary participants to the cultural debate.

The Rabbinic canon is comprised by a set of writings produced by sages of Judaism from about 200 to about 600 A.D. These writings rest on two base-documents, the Scriptures of ancient Israel (to Christianity, the Old Testament, to Judaism, the Written Torah), and the Mishnah (in Judaism, the first component of the Oral Torah ultimately encompassing all the literature at hand). All of the writings of Judaism in late antiquity copiously cite Scripture. Some of them serve (or are presented and organized) as commentaries on the former, others as amplifications of the latter. Since Judaism treats all of these writings as a single, seamless Torah, the one whole Torah revealed by God to Moses, our Rabbi, at Mount Sinai, the received hermeneutic naturally does the same. All of the writings are read in light of all others, and words and phrases are treated as autonomous units of tradition, rather than as components of particular writings, e.g., paragraphs — units of discourse — and books — composite units of sustained and cogent thought.

Describing documents — the building blocks of the Judaism at hand — in their context forms the first step in tracing the history of the system as a whole. That work, now completed in considerable measure, allows us to limn distinct stages in the formation of the system. Determining the relationship of document to document forms the necessary second step. Finding out what changed and what remained the same in the unfolding of the system as a whole tells us the history of the system as its canonical writings contain that history. Seeing the documents as a continuous and final statement, we shall understand the direction and goal of the history at hand and turn back to see how, from the viewpoint of the end, the system took shape: a history that emerges from a dialectical process of study and restudy. Relationships seen in general terms may take three forms: continuous, connected, and autonomous. In a continuous relationship, there is no boundary between one thing and something else; in a connected relationship, one thing may intersect with some other, while remaining free-standing, and in an autonomous setting, one thing will not relate to the other at all. And so it is with the documents, which stand on their own, interrelate, and also form a whole, that is, the canon.

[1] AUTONOMY: if a document comes down to us within its own framework, exhibiting its own distinctive traits of rhetoric, topic, and logic, as a complete book with a beginning, middle, and end, in preserving that book, the canon presents us with a document on its own and not solely as part of a larger composition or construct. So we too see the document as it reaches us, that is, as autonomous.

[2] CONNECTION: if, second, a document contains materials shared verbatim or in substantial content with other documents of its classification, or if one document refers to the contents of other documents, then the several documents that clearly wish to engage in conversation with one another have to address one another. That is to say, we have to seek for the marks of connectedness, asking for the meaning of those connections.

[3] CONTINUITY: finally, since the community of the faithful of Judaism, in all of the contemporary expressions of Judaism, concur that documents held to be authoritative constitute one whole, seamless "Torah," that is, a complete and exhaustive statement of God's will for Israel and humanity, we take as a further appropriate task the description of the whole out of the undifferentiated testimony of all of its parts. In other words, continuity among documents yields a theological system that encompasses all the documents.7 These components in the theological context are viewed, as is clear, as equally authoritative for the composition of the whole: one, continuous system. In taking up such a question, we address a problem not of theology alone, though it is a correct theological conviction, but one of description, analysis, and interpretation of an entirely historical order.

The several documents that make up Rabbinic literature relate to one another in yet three other important ways.

[1] All of them refer to the same basic writing, the Hebrew Scriptures. Many of them draw upon the Mishnah and quote it. So the components of the canon join at their foundations.

[2] As the documents reached closure in sequence, the later authorship can be shown to have drawn upon earlier, completed documents. So the writings of the Rabbis of the Talmudic corpus accumulate and build from layer to layer.

[3] Among two or more documents some completed units of discourse, and many brief, discrete sayings, circulated, for instance, sentences or episodic homilies or fixed sayings (e.g., moral maxims) of various kinds.

So in some (indeterminate) measure the several documents draw not only upon one another, as we can show, but also upon a common corpus of materials that might serve diverse editorial and redactional purposes. The extent of this common corpus of floating sayings can never be fully known. We know only what we have, not what we do not have. So we cannot say what has been omitted, or whether sayings that occur in only one document derive from materials available to the editors or compilers of some or all other documents. That is something we never can know.

## III. Describing the Literature — Analyzing the History of the Religion

These steps in the documentary history of Judaism correspond to steps in the documentary analysis of the canon of that same Judaism:

| Describing the Literature | Analyzing the History |
|---|---|
| 1. AUTONOMY: the text on its own | 1. TEXT: the Judaic system adumbrated thereby |
| 2. CONNECTION: the text in context | 2. CONTEXT: the system of texts of roughly the same age |
| 3. CONTINUITY: the canon whole | 3. MATRIX: the end product: the system seen whole |

The history of the formation of Judaism comprises these steps: [1] a stage (context), then [2] a stage (context) beyond, fully described in their sequential relationship: the given — the document — and how it changed.

[3] Then comes the third dimension in the history of the system, besides the ones measured by each document in its own context and two or more documents in their sequential and even temporal relationships. We take the measure of that third dimension through a labor of interpretation, which takes its perspective from a distance and encompasses all of the documents: the system as a whole. It sees the documents as continuous not from one to the next but all in all, all together, all at once. That, sum and substance is the scholarly program that precipitated the debate addressed in this book.

Is there a contrary view of matters and can we identify its elements? The three key-words of the inherited hermeneutic of Rabbinic literature are *continuity, uniqueness,* and *survival.* Scholars who view the texts as continuous with one another seek what is unique in the system formed by the texts as a whole. With the answer to what is unique, they propose to explain the survival of Israel, the Jewish people. Hence: continuity, uniqueness, survival.

The words to encapsulate the hermeneutic I espouse are these: *description, analysis,* and *interpretation.* I am trying to learn how to describe the constituents of the canon, viewed individually, each in its distinctive context. I wish to discover appropriate *analytical* tools, questions to lead me from description of one text to comparison and contrast between two or more texts of the canon. Only at the end do I address the question of *interpretation:* how do all of the texts of the canon at hand flow together into a single continuous statement, a "Judaism." That is the question of theology, not literature, history, and religion.

Within the inherited hermeneutic of continuity, survival, and uniqueness, the existence of the group defines the principal concern, an inner-facing one, hence the emphasis on uniqueness in quest, in continuities, for the explanation of survival. Within the proposed hermeneutic of description, analysis, and interpretation, by contrast, the continued survival of a "unique" group does not frame the issue. For my purposes, it is taken for granted, for the group is not the main thing at all. That is an insider's question. The problematic emerges from without. What I want to know is how to describe the society and culture contained within, taken as a given, how to interpret an enduring world-view and way of life, expressed by the artifacts in hand. How did, and does, the group work? That is an issue of benign curiosity.

## IV. Gaining Perspective: Comparing the Literatures of Judaism and Christianity

The traits of the documents of Rabbinic Judaism differ from those that characterize the counterpart religious system, earliest Christianity. While some of the formative documents share the traits of anonymity and public sponsorship, many of them bear the signatures of specific individuals, e.g., the letters of Paul; they speak for persons, not for institutions or even systems of a social and public character. And, to the contrary, the Christian documents, one and all, differ from the Rabbinic ones in that they do not homogenize statements by a great number of named persons. To understand the problems that are addressed in the documentary study of formative Judaism, readers will find useful a brief comparison between the Judaic and the Christian writings of the formative age.

That is what I undertook to do at the Society of Biblical Literature meeting in New York City in 1979. In order to explain to colleagues in the adjacent field of formative Christianity the shape and structure of the authoritative writings of Judaism, I translated into Christian terms the traits of the writings that convey the

Judaism of the dual Torah in its initial phase. I did so in such a way as to underscore the completely different character of those writings, which, I held, defined a quite fresh set of problems awaiting solution. A brief review of the main points will set the stage for the debates recorded in these pages, because only when I have defined the methodological problems I face in my inquiry into the history of the formative age of Judaism, and the solutions I have put forth to deal with those problems, will the context of debate clearly emerge. My presentation took the form of "Imagine if...." To advance my argument here, I briefly recapitulate the main points.

Specifically, if Christianity were written down in the way in which Judaism is, what should we know about Christianity, and how should we know it? What I now do is paint a picture of our problem in studying early Christianity, if the sources of early Christianity had reached us in the way, and in the condition, in which those of early Rabbinic Judaism come down to us. That is to say, what should we know, and how should we know it, if the records of early Christianity were like the Rabbinic literature of late antiquity? Answers to these questions afford perspective on the problem of the literary and religions-historical study of the Rabbinic canon.

(1) Imagine if all the statements of the principal founders of Christianity were put together into anonymous, public collections, not authored by any one individual (or sponsored by some one community)! What could we know, if all the literature of early Christianity had reached us in a fully homogenized and intellectually seamless form? Not only the New Testament, but all the works of the church fathers, from Justin to Augustine, now would be represented as expressions of one communal mind, dismembered and built into a single harmonious logical structure on various themes. True, they would be shown constantly to disagree with one another. But the range of permissible disagreement would define a vast area of consensus on all basic matters, so that a superficial contentiousness would convey something quite different: one mind on most things, beginning to end. The names of the fathers would be attached to some of their utterances. But all would have gone through a second medium of tradents and redactors — the editors of the compendium (the Patristic Talmud, so to speak, and these editors picked and chose what they wanted of Justin, and what of Origen, what of Tertullian, and what of Augustine, in line with what the editors themselves found interesting. In the end, the picture of the first six centuries of early Christianity would be the creation of people of the sixth century, out of the shards and remnants of people of the first five. Our work then would be to uncover what happened before the end through studying a document which portrays a timeless world.

Not only would the document be so framed as implicitly to deny historical development of ideas, but the framers also would gloss over diverse and contradictory sources of thought. I do not mean only that Justin, Irenaeus, and Tertullian would be presented as individual authors in a single, timeless continuum. I mean that all Gnostic and Catholic sources would be broken up into sense-units and their fragments rearranged in a structure presented as representative of a single

Christianity, with a single, unitary theology. This synthesized ecumenical body of Christian thought would be constructed so as to set out judgments on the principal theological topics of the day, and these judgments would have been accepted as normative from that day to this. So the first thing we must try to imagine is a Christianity which reaches us fully harmonized and whole — a Christianity of Nicaea and Chalcedon, but not of Arians, Nestorians, monophysites and the rest, so there is no distinctive Justin nor Augustine, no Irenaeus and no Gnostics, and surely no Nag Hammadi, but all are one "in Christ Jesus," so to speak.

(2) Imagine if no saying or story or disquisition yielded the marks of an individual's authorship. For, let me emphasize, this would be not merely a matter of early Christian literature's reaching us without the names of the authors of its individual documents. The thing we must try to imagine is that there would be no individual documents at all. Everything would have gone through a process of formation and redaction which obliterated the marks of individuality. Just as the theology would be one, so would the form and style of the documents which preserved it. Indeed, what would be striking about this picture of Christianity would be not that the tractate of Mark lacks the name of Mark, but that all of the tractates of the Gospels would be written in precisely the same style and resort to exactly the same rhetorical and redactional devices. Stylistic unity so pervasive as to eliminate all traces of individual authorship, even of most preserved sayings, would now characterize the writings of the first Christians. The sarcasm of Irenaeus, the majesty of Augustine, and the exegetical ingenuity of Origen, the lucid historicism of Aphrahat — all are homogenized. Everyone talks in the same way about the same things.

(3) And now to come to a principal task of the study of early Christianity: what should we know about Jesus, and how should we know it, if sayings assigned to Jesus in one book were given to Paul in a second, to John in a third, and to "They said," or, "He said to them," in a fourth. Can we imagine trying to discover the historical Jesus on this turf? If even the provenance of a saying could not be established on the basis of all those to whom it is attributed, if, often, even a single *Vorlage* and *Urtext* could not be postulated? Then what sort of work on the biography and thought of any of the early figures of Christianity would be credible?

(4) This brings me to the most difficult act of imagination which I must ask readers to perform: a supererogatory work of social imagination. Can we imagine a corner of the modern world in which this state of interpretation — of total confusion, of harmonies, homologies, homogenies, is not found confusing but reassuring? Can we mentally conjure up a social setting for learning in which differentiation is avoided and credulity rewarded? in which analysis is heresy, dismissed as worthless or attacked as "full of mistakes"? Can we conceive of a world in which repetition, in one's own words, of what the sources say is labeled scholarship, and anthologizing is labeled learning? In New Testament scholarship, we must imagine, the principal task now is to write harmonies of the Gospels, and,

in Patristic studies, to align the Catholic with the Gnostic, the second century with the fifth, the Arian and the Athanasian, Monophysite and Nestorian. In a word, we speak of a world in which the Diatesseron is the last word in scholarship, and in which contentiousness about trivial things masks a firm and iron consensus. In this imagined world, scholars further hold that all the sources are historical, and merely alluding to them suffices to establish facts of history.

If readers can envision such a state of affairs, then we have entered the world of sources and scholarly orthodoxies confronted by us who study the ancient Judaism emergent from the Rabbinic literature. And, it follows, scholars of New Testament history and exegesis will grasp the fact that Rabbinic literature is simply not homologous to the writings on which they work and cannot be used in anything like the same way. Not only so, but that literature deals with different types of problems and answers altogether different questions, with the result that we cannot present to Rabbinic literature questions deemed appropriate for address to another kind of writing altogether. A life of Jesus or of Augustine is plausible; a life of Aqiba or Hillel is not. An account of the intellectual biography of Paul and his theology is entirely a propos, the sources answering precisely the questions that are asked. A counterpart picture of Judah the Patriarch, who wrote up the Mishnah, or of Rabbah, Abbayye or Raba, the greatest geniuses of the Talmud, is not.

(l) I can spell out matters now very simply and very rapidly. First, as to the axioms of scholarship, all the Rabbinic sources are treated as representatives of a single, seamless world view and as expressions of a single, essentially united group, either the views as a whole, or, among the enlightened, *the* Rabbis as a group. While some more critical souls concede there may have been distinctions between the first century Rabbis' thought and that of the fourth, the distinctions make no material difference in accounts of "the Rabbis" and their thought. Whether anthologies or anthological essays (Moore, Montefiore and Loewe, Bonsirven, Urbach), *the* Rabbis are represented in their views on God, world, and redemption, as though all Rabbis for seven hundred ears had the same thing to say as all others.

Now this representation of the Rabbis is subject to an important, commonplace qualification. Everyone knows that the Talmuds abound in the recognition of differences between the teachings of different Rabbis in different periods on different points in discussions of which traditions or source was followed by the proponent of this or that opinion. But the recorded differences are about particular, trivial points. The Talmudic discussion, moreover, is directed normally towards reconciling them. What is particularly lacking in available accounts of "the Rabbinic mind" is, first, recognition and delineation of different general positions or basic attitudes, of the characteristic make-up, and backgrounds of different schools; second, what is lacking is anything like adequate reporting of the change of teachings over the course of time and in relation to historical changes. Obviously, there is plenty of speculation on how an individual or group reacted to a particular historical situation or event. But these random speculations are unsystematic and appear to be made up for the occasion. So these apparent exceptions to what I say have to be recognized — because they prove the accuracy of my description of the prevailing consensus.

(2) Second, as to the sources, the documents of earlier Rabbinic Judaism attempt to exhibit an internally uniform quality of style. So the scholars who represent a seamless world accurately replicate a superficial impression of the literary traits of the sources of the portrait. It is exceedingly difficult to differentiate on formal or stylistic grounds among the layers of the Mishnah, which is the document of Rabbinic Judaism first brought to redaction. The two Talmuds then so lay matters out as to represent themselves as the logical continuity from the Mishnah. They do so by breaking up the Mishnah into minute units and then commenting on those discrete units of thought. Consequently, the Mishnah as a document, a document which presents its own world view and its own social system, is not preserved and confronted. Nor do the Talmuds present themselves as successive layers, built upon, but essentially distinct from the Mishnah. Rather, the Talmuds aim at completely harmonizing their own materials both with the Mishnah and among themselves, despite the self-evidently contradictory character of the materials. Once more we observe, there are limits to disagreement.

The continuing contentiousness of the documents, their preservation of diverse viewpoints on single issues, underline the rigidly protected limits of permissible disagreement. Intense disagreement about trivialities powerfully reinforces basic unities and harmonies. The fact that, out there, were Jews who decorated synagogues in ways the Talmuds cannot have led us to anticipate, is mentioned only in passing, as if it is of no weight or concern. What matters to this literature is not how the Jews lived, nor even how they worshipped, but only the discussions of the Rabbinical schools and courts. What the documents say is what we are supposed to think, within the range of allowed difference. Consequently, the intellectually unitary character of the sources is powerfully reinforced by the total success of the framers and redactors of the sources in securing stylistic unity within documents and in some measure even among them.

## v. How Has the Documentary Method Changed Learning?

We have come a long way from that mental experiment I performed just now, to imagine what we should know about the first Christians, and how we should know it, if New Testament and Patristic literature, indeed all of the literary remains of the first five or six Christian centuries, reached us in the form of the Talmudic and Midrashic literature. So let me turn toward my conclusion by referring once more to the state of the field.

(1) No longer is it possible to treat the diverse corpus of Rabbinical literature as a uniform whole. Once one document, a principal one, such as the Mishnah, is shown to bear its distinctive formal and intellectual characteristics as I

have shown in the case of the Mishnah, then all others must be subjected to appropriate analysis, to determine the characteristics of each.

(2) No longer are the anonymity and the collective character of documents to be allowed to prevent differentiation and discrimination within a document and between documents. The work of harmonization is in ruins. The work of history may begin.

(3) No longer are we left to cope with all sayings, whatever document contains them, and to treat each as of equivalent weight to all others. Diverse attributions of a given saying in different documents are to be examined in the context of the preferences and tendencies of the several documents themselves.

To conclude, I revert, for one last time, to the point of departure. At the outset I emphasized the importance of trying to allow the literary and historical situation of early Christianity to serve as a metaphor for the problem of nascent Rabbinic Judaism. At the end I must construct the opposite of a simile, for at the foundations, the two are essentially opposite to one another The study of Judaism requires the differentiation of documents, the deconstruction of cogent statements into their constituents. The work of studying early Christianity requires us to put together distinct individuals, systems of thought, institutions, and to find out how these diverse expressions of Christian experience form something coherent and say something cogent. In a word, the work of Nicaea and Chalcedon also defines the labor of learning. The task of studying nascent Rabbinic Judaism is the opposite. In the Talmuds and Midrash-compilations we have the result of centuries of harmonization and cogent construction. But understanding these documents and the world which they portray requires us to unpack them and see how they function. It is as if from the Nicene Creed, we had to find our way back into the intellectual and theological issues of the earlier generations of Christians.

For in the end, knowing what people thought, without understanding the world about which they reflected, does not help us either to understand the people who did the thinking or to interpret the result of their reflection. While, without such understanding, we may take the results of their thinking — their theology, their exegesis of Scripture, and their law — and we may build on it for one purpose or another, we essentially know nothing of the inner structure of that building which we ourselves propose to construct. Not knowing the points of stress and places of tension in the building, not knowing the main lines of the foundation of the structure, not knowing the places at which the builder put the strongest joints and beams, we add to the building in total ignorance. It is not building. It is destruction — making things up as we go along. To state matters more generally, in front of us is a labor of description and interpretation, establishing context and providing exegesis. We have a sizable corpus of texts which clearly express a world view and propose to create a society and a way of life for a distinctive group of people. In order to describe that world view and to understand the society and way of life shaped by the ancient Rabbis, we have to interpret texts. In order to interpret those texts, we have to do three things.

First, we have to read the texts one by one, which work of systematic and uniform description I have now done. Second, we have establish context and setting. This work of documentary comparison and contrast is well under way, with only the Bavli and Yerushalmi awaiting sustained attention, beyond that already given. We have to describe the world in which the texts took shape and to offer a theory of the questions which seemed urgent and compelling to the people who made the texts as they are and not in some other way. So the work of exegesis depends upon establishing the appropriate context of exegesis. At the same time, to describe the context we have to read the texts. Third, we have to move from description and analysis, now complete so far as I am concerned, to the work of synthesis and interpretation of the whole. Once we have read the documents one by one, we have the further task of reading them all together. This should tell us, first, what they take for granted — the Judaism behind the texts that remains to be critically investigated; second, how they fit together, the Judaism that holds the texts together that, in the end, will show us what was truly normative and definitive, therefore theological.

If we ask ourselves why people should want to know about these things, we need not fall back upon the bankrupt claim that they merely are intrinsically interesting. The formation of Judaism by itself is a compelling social and intellectual phenomenon, for among other such phenomena, it teaches us how to describe and interpret the interplay between the historical situation of a distinct society, on the one side, and the world view brought into being to explain and shape that historical situation, on the other. That is what forms Rabbinic culture. When we can relate the religious world view and way of life of the ancient Talmudic Rabbis to the society whose vision they chose to shape and whose conduct and institutions they wished to govern, we can report much about what it is that religion, as a mode of constructing reality and explaining the world, is and what religion does.

## ENDNOTES

[1]I refer to Mekhilta and have spelled this out in my *Mekhilta Attributed to R. Ishmael. An Introduction to Judaism's First Scriptural Encyclopaedia.* Atlanta, 1988: Scholars Press for Brown Judaic Studies. My thinking on Mekhilta is guided by the approach of Guenter Stemberger.

[2]Here too a qualification is in order. The Tosefta often presents counterparts to formulations in the Mishnah. But a close examination shows that by reformulating the Mishnah's rules — putting into the mouths of the Mishnah's authorities opinions that the Mishnah has not assigned to them — the Tosefta's compositions' framers have refined the law under discussion or introduced issues other than those on which the Mishnah's version has those authorities comment. A passage in which we find an explicit reformulation, e.g., they disputed not about this but about that, will always belong to the Tosefta and never to the Mishnah. So even where compositions float from document to document, we can make good progress in identifying the correct point of origin of a fair proportion of that rather small section of the canon.

[3]The Rabbinic document forms the counterpart to the Christian Church Council.

[4]I presently draw a contrast between the condition of the Rabbinic canon and that of the Christian counterpart.
[5]The first premise can be validated, the second, falsified.
[6]I suspect that that dismissal out of hand also responded to the sheer volume of the canon; it was much easier to posit at the outset that sayings stand on their own, unaffected by context, than to study sayings in their broader documentary context and inquire about the interplay of context and contents. Since all study of canonical writings is exegetical, involving a sentence by sentence reading, the education of students and preparation of teachers reinforce the atomistic reading of all writing. That contrary task — seeing things whole — simply was not done in a systematic or comprehensive way before my undertaking, and to date I have not seen anyone else contest my results by doing the same work on their own, beginning to end, and producing contrary results. Episodic criticisms of my reading of discrete documents, to be sure, have reached print. I have collected and reprinted several volumes of negative reviews of my books. One interesting example of those who have adopted the documentary approach is David Kraemer, *Responses to Suffering in Classical Rabbinic Literature* (N.Y., 1994: Oxford University Press), where a quite different reading of the Bavli is set forth. But, as noted, in the same place Kraemer adopts and makes his own every principle of documentary study of Rabbinic literature and the documentary history of ideas, and his results can be read solely in the context I have defined, as he himself says. Other independent exercises in the documentary method have come from Maren Niehoff. But the documentary theory places an insuperable obstacle in the path of history-writers, who ask questions that presuppose the Rabbinic canon sets forth facts of things really said and done. Their work therefore lacks all critical standing and fabricates fictitious narratives. I document that fact in *Reading and Believing: Ancient Judaism and Contemporary Gullibility*. Atlanta, 1986: Scholars Press for Brown Judaic Studies. Now: Lanham, University Press of America.
[7]Much of my work from the mid 1990s to the present has devoted itself to the theological description of the Rabbinic canon and the interplay of the Halakhah and the Aggadah.

# 3

## How Documents Relate and Why It Matters

### I. How Documents Relate

Documents – cogent compositions made up of a number of complete units of thought – by definition exist on their own. That is to say, by invoking as part of our definition the trait of cogency of individual units as well as of the entire composite, we complete a definition of what a document is and is not.

A document is a cogent composite of cogent statements. But, also by definition, none of these statements is read all by itself. A document forms an artifact of a social culture, and that in diverse dimensions. Cogency depends on shared rhetoric, logic of intelligible discourse, topic and program – all of these traits of mind, of culture. Someone writes a document, someone buys it, an entire society sustains the labor of literature. Hence we place any document into its culture and society.

Each document therefore exists in both a textual and literary context, and also takes the measure of a social dimension of culture and even of politics. As to the former, documents may form a community whose limits are delineated by shared conventions of thought and expression. Those exhibiting distinctive, even definitive traits, fall within the community, those that do not, remain without. These direct the author to one mode of topic, logic, and rhetoric, and not to some other. So much for intrinsic traits. As to the extrinsic ones, readers bring to documents diverse instruments of intelligibility, knowledge of the grammar of not only language but also thought. That is why they can read one document and not some other. So one relationship derives from a literary culture, which forms the authorship of a document, and the other from a social culture. The literary bond links document to document, and the essentially social bond links reader to document – and also document (through the authorship, individual or collective) to reader. The one relationship is exhibited through intrinsic traits of language and style, logic, rhetoric, and topic, and the other through extrinsic traits of curiosity, acceptance and authority. While documents find their place in their own literary world and also in a larger social one, the two aspects have to remain distinct, the one textual, the other contextual.

It follows that relationships between and among documents also matter for two distinct reasons. The intrinsic relationships, which are formal, guide us to traits of intelligibility, teaching us through our encounter with one document how to read some other of its type or class. If we know how to read a document of one type, we may venture to read another of the same type, but not – without instruction – one of some other type altogether. The extrinsic relationships, which derive from context and are relative to community, direct us to how to understand a document as an artifact of culture and society. Traits not of documents but of doctrines affecting a broad range of documents come into play. The document, whatever its contents, therefore becomes an instrument of social culture, e.g., theology and politics, a community's public policy. A community then expresses itself through its choice of documents, the community's canon forming a principal mode of such self-definition. So, as I said, through intrinsic traits a document places itself within a larger community of texts. Extrinsic traits, imputed to a document by not its authorship but its audience, select the document as canonical and make of the document a mode of social definition. The community through its mode of defining itself by its canonical choices forms a textual community – a community expressed through the books it reads and values.

If I now may invoke the suggestive word, intertextuality, we then treat the relationships in which a given document stands as one expressed in the prepositions *between* and *among*. That is to say, in its intellectual traits a document bears relationship, to begin with, to some other, hence we describe relationships *between* two documents. These constitute formal and intrinsic matters: traits of grammar, arrangements of words and resonances as to their local meaning, structures of syntax of expression and thought. But in its social setting a document finds bonds *among* three or more documents, with all of which it is joined in the imagination and mind of a community. These range widely and freely, bound by limits not of form and language, but of public policy in behavior and belief. Documents because of their traits of rhetoric, logic, and topic form a community of texts. Documents because of their audience and authority express the intellect of a textual community.

The principal issue worked out in establishing a community of texts is hermeneutical, the chief outcome of defining a textual community, social and cultural. The former teaches us how to read the texts on their own. The latter tells us how to interpret texts in context. When we define and classify the relationships between texts, we learn how to read the components – words, cogent thoughts formed of phrases, sentences, paragraphs – of those texts in the broader context defined by shared conventions of intellect: rhetoric, logic, topic. More concretely, hermeneutical principles tell me how, in light of like documents I have seen many times, to approach a document I have never before seen at all. Hermeneutics teaches me the grammar and syntax of thought.

Let me give one example of the role of hermeneutics in an inductive inquiry into form. Memorizing a passage of a complex text will teach me the rhythms of expression and thought, for instance, that make of the sounds of some other document an intelligible music. Not only so, but documents joined into a common classification may share specific contents, not only definitive traits of expression – meaning and not solely method. So when I know how to assess the relationships between documents, I also come to a better way of sorting out the effects of those relationships: the intersections, the repetitions.

The upshot of defining a textual community, by contrast, is quite other. It is not hermeneutical, since at issue is not the reading and interpretation of texts but their social utility, their status as cultural indicators. When I know the choices a community has made for its canon, I find my way deep into the shared viewpoint of that community, moving from the contents of the texts to the contexts in which those texts bear meaning. And that brings us back to the basic matter: a text exists in diverse contexts, on its own, among other texts, and as part of a much larger social canon, e.g., a library or a court of appeal for authoritative judgments such as proof-texts supply. It is important now to help us sort out the most basic matters for discussion.

So far I have framed matters as if I planned to present a treatise on rather abstract matters, e.g., the definition of intertextuality, without specific reference to a particular document, set of documents, or canon. But the reader knows the truth, which is the opposite, since this book addresses a very particular set of writings. My intent at the outset is to explain why the particularities before us exemplify much broader issues of literature and culture. In this way the writings that concern me may provide a set of valuable instances, exempla gratia, for broader and more public discourse. Let me then backtrack and specify how, in particular, the documents on which we concentrate provide an ideal case-study of the problem of intertextuality viewed both formally and socially. For as to the debate on reading documents all by themselves and only as statements of a social group, the writings at hand present unusually suggestive examples of an entirely concrete character. And I believe our task requires us to read them both as exercises of a sophisticated formal character, and also as documents of a social culture, once more, as both a community of texts and testimonies to a textual community.

The relationships among the documents produced by the sages of Judaism may take three forms: complete dependence, complete autonomy, intersection in diverse manner and measure. That second dimension provokes considerable debate and presents a remarkably unclear perspective. For while the dimensions of autonomy and continuity take the measure of acknowledged traits – books on their own, books standing in imputed, therefore socially verified, relationships – the matter of connection hardly enjoys the same clear definition. On the one side, intrinsic traits permit us to assess theories of connection. On the other, confusing theological and social judgments of continuities and literary and heuristic ones of connection, people present quite remarkable claims as to the relationships between and among documents, alleging, in fact, that the documents all have to be read as a single continuous document: the Torah. As we shall now see, some maintain that the connections between and among documents are such that each has to be read in the light of all others. So the documents assuredly do form a canon, and that is a position adopted not in some distant past or alien society but among contemporary participants to the cultural debate.

While I take up a community of texts and explore those intrinsic traits that link book to book, my inquiry rests on the premise that the books at issue derive from a textual community, one which, without reference to the intrinsic traits of the writings, deems the set of books as a group to constitute a canon. My question is simple but critical:

If in advance I did not know that the community of Judaism treats the writings before us (among others) as a canon, would the traits of the documents have told me that the writings at hand are related?

The inquiry is inductive, concerns intrinsic traits, and therefore pursues the matter of connection between document and document. I work within literary categories, later on within social and ultimately theological ones. In order to clarify the task I have taken for myself, I have now to portray the state of opinion on the corpus of writings at hand. Only then will the reader appreciate not only what is at stake, but also why the issues transcend the boundaries of the documents before us.

## II. What Is at Stake

The issue of connection is legitimate to the data. But the outcome transcends these particular data. The stakes for public discourse about matters of general intelligibility are considerable, for when we can describe the relationships between two documents and among three or more, we shall know what a given group of editors or authorities contributed on its own, and also how that authorship restated or reworked what it received from a prior group. Determining that relationship further guides us to principles of exegesis of documents, allegations and formulations of ideas and rules. If a document depends on some other, prior one, then what we find in the later writing is to be read in light of the earlier (but, of course, never vice versa). If there is no clear evidence of dependence, then the later document demands a reading in essentially its own terms.

But what is at stake for the system in describing relationships transcends the matter of hermeneutics. Describing documents – the building blocks of the Judaism at hand – in their context forms the first step in tracing the history of the system as a whole. That work, now completed in considerable measure, allows us to limn distinct stages in the formation of the system. Determining the relationship of document to document forms the necessary second step. Finding out what changed and what remained the same in the unfolding of the system as a whole tells us the history of the system as its canonical writings contain that history. Later on, seeing the documents as a continuous and final statement, we shall understand the direction and goal of the history at hand and turn back to see how, from the viewpoint of the end, the system took shape: a history that emerges from a dialectical process of study and restudy. But for now, the history of the formation of Judaism comprises only these two steps: a stage, then a stage beyond, fully described in their sequential relationship: the given – the document – and how it changed. But we even now keep in mind the third dimension in the history of the system, besides the ones measured by each document in its own context and two or more documents in their sequential and even temporal relationships. That third dimension takes its perspective from a distance and encompasses all of the documents: the system as a whole. It sees the documents as continuous not from one to the next but all in all, all together, all at once. That, sum and substance is the scholarly program of which the present book forms a critical component.

The outcome for theoretical discourse is best determined by the parties to it. I believe that the framing of matters – a community of texts, spun out from within, as against a textual community, created from beyond the intellect of an authorship – may prove suggestive. For the conception of a community of texts forms the center of inquiry in this book. So before proceeding, let me make certain the conception is absolutely clear. Individual texts form a community when their internal traits indicate that they have been composed in relationship to one another. Such traits include a shared program of inquiry, e.g., into a single document; a common set of formal preferences; a single sort of substantive inquiries. That definition brings us to the particular writings of Judaism. To begin with the documents come to us as a group, that is, as important components of "the Oral Torah" of the Judaism of the dual Torah that took shape in late antiquity. But what if they had not come down bearing a single imprimatur, that of Judaism? Would we have imagined that these books form a community of interrelated documents? Only internal evidence allows us to form an answer to that question. Accordingly, I want to know how texts important in the canon of Judaism in its formative age form a community, that is to say, relate to one another not adventitiously or casually, by mere accidents of coincidence in a canon, but – let me say with due emphasis – through deliberation of authorships to participate, in their work, in constituting a communion through documents, a community of texts. And that matter seems to me to tell us something about literature: about how writers write.

I have in mind indications of a quite objective and material character, such as decisions of an authorship to refer to or not to refer to Scripture, to compose an intersecting set of agenda or to talk about essentially diverse things, to cite a prior text or not to cite one, to make ample use of materials common among a number of prior texts or to use only materials not earlier used, to imitate the rhetoric and redaction of earlier writings or to strike out in unexplored directions, and on and on. These matters of fact tell us whether, and how, autonomous documents connect with one another and so form a communion of authorships and give expression in textual form to a community. The connections include materials used in common, formal preferences dominant in two or more documents, substantive inquiries into topics interesting to two or more authorships, modes of intelligibility that characterize two or more sets of writers. In a word, we deal with rhetoric, topic, and logic. We take up such considerations as symmetrical or asymmetrical plans of logic and rhetoric, programs of topic and proposition about a given topic, sharing materials, not sharing materials, and other perfectly objective and factual criteria.

While we commonly hear about *The* Rabbinic Mind or intellect, or even about The (ethnic) *Jewish* Imagination, I doubt that these either naive or purely racist categories need detain us. I make no appeal to some inchoate "spirit" that I discern in two or more documents but not in one or five others, nor do I concede that by instinct we know something we cannot show through the application and testing of stated criteria of connection. Anyone who cares to can replicate my procedures and so test my results: matters of fact, not judgment, as to the intersection of texts and the sharing of premises among texts.

# THE DOCUMENTARY APPROACH IN PRACTICE

# 4

# Documents and their Traits. Form Analysis and the Documentary History of Ideas

## I. The Question that I ask

We now turn from theoretical to concrete topics, beginning with the most important. The impasse on historical critical use of the Rabbinic sources outlined in the Preface shows why I required a different starting point for all future work. I could no longer commence at the one provided by the attribution of a saying to a named authority, on the one side, or the telling of a story about him, on the other. There could be no more paraphrasing of uncriticized narratives. And no consistent and coherent principle of criticism presented itself to me.

A simple fact clearly formed an insuperable obstacle in the road that I had taken for more than a decade. It may be simply stated. I could neither validate nor falsify the attributions of sayings to named authorities, upon which all historical work had rested. Nor could I devise a means of distinguishing true from false narratives. Israeli Talmudic-historical scholars fatuously spoke of "the sound of truth," which they heard in some stories and not in others. They still do, but to less effect. I did not know how to replicate their results. Accordingly, I had not met the simple test: how do you know that what you say is so, on the basis of the sources in hand and the way you read them?

*What we cannot show, we do not know.*

So I asked myself, what are the facts we really do have in hand? The simplest is, the facticity of the documents, one by one — their traits, their messages. The documents form the irreducible givens, the corpus of evidence in its elementary form.[1] While the wordings may vary from one textual witness to the next, while the repertoire of materials may shift from one manuscript to another, the various documents viewed whole, one by one, for all the textual variation, do exhibit their distinctive, differentiating traits. These distinctive documentary patterns awaited discovery and elucidation, and that is what I determined I had to do.

It is the simple fact that everything we have received from Rabbinic Judaism in late antiquity comes to us in the documents of Rabbinic canon. There is no other body of information confidently attributed to Rabbinic sponsorship. These documents then required description, one by one, analysis, in comparison of one to the next, and interpretation, when viewed whole. A massive enterprise of the study of text, context, and matrix awaited. So all future study depended upon the systematic characterization of the Rabbinic canonical documents: the documentary hypothesis.

In the earlier 1970s, as I said in the Preface, I started with the first of these, which is the Mishnah, studied in constant dialogue with the Tosefta, and, two decades later, I concluded with the last, which is the Talmud of Babylonia. In the interim, I translated for the first time approximately a third of the sheer volume of that literature — the Tosefta, the Talmud of the Land of Israel, Sifra, and some other documents — and retranslated all the others. For all of them for the first time I provided a form-analytical presentation. That explains why I have now translated and introduced every document that with confidence is assigned to late antiquity's Rabbis. This corpus I treated as distinct from antiquity's other-than-Rabbinic sources, on the one side, or the Rabbinic writings that came to closure after the Muslim conquest marked the end of antiquity and the beginning of the Middle Ages, on the other. Each has now been systematically translated and fully analyzed as to rhetoric, logic of coherent discourse, and topical and propositional program, by me. I did the work twice, once for translation and description, a second time for analysis. That is the *oeuvre* that is partially summarized here in a systematic and succinct way in the pages of this book.

How did I propose to describe the components of the canon one by one? A brief reprise will clarity matters. Each document sets forth its own, unique combination of indicative traits: rhetoric, logic of coherent discourse, and topic. Now, some overlap in rhetorical pattern (Mishnah, Tosefta), others in logic of coherent discourse (the Rabbah-Midrash-compilations of late antiquity, e.g., Leviticus Rabbah, Lamentations Rabbah), and most pursue distinctive topical programs (exemplified by the contrast between Sifra and Leviticus Rabbah, both devoted to the book of Leviticus). Three definitive traits permit differentiating one document from another in Rabbinic literature, and the correct translation of a Rabbinic document makes possible the identification of these traits:[2]

[1] the rhetoric or formal preferences of a piece of writing, which dictate, without respect to meaning, how sentences will be composed; thus, the patterning of language characteristic of a given document, which, in combination with the two other facts that follow differentiate that document from all others;

[2] the logic of coherent discourse, which determines how one sentence will be joined to others in context; and how groups of sentences will cohere and form completed units of thought, and, finally, how said units of thought agglutinate or are otherwise held together in large-scale components of complete documents;

[3] the topical program of the writing, which indicates the subject and may also indicate the problematic — what we wish to know about the subject — of that same writing.

By invoking these three criteria in combination, which are entirely familiar in the analysis of literature in antiquity, we may distinguish each document from all others and establish a clear definition for every piece of writing in the literature. The reason is simple. A received discipline of thought and expression governed all writing that has survived in Rabbinic literature.

[1] RHETORIC: Writers in this literature followed formal conventions, making choices rarely particular to a given author but always set forth, to begin with, by a repertoire of commonly-understood fixed arrangements of words. These fixed arrangements, transcending particular meanings, signaled the purpose and even the context of a given set of sentences; following one form, rather than another, therefore dictated to the reader of a passage the character and intent of that passage: its classification. Correct translation will underscore the regularities of form and formulation.

[2] LOGIC OF COHERENT DISCOURSE: Since the Rabbinic writings ordinarily set forth not discrete sentences — aphorisms that stand, each in lapidary splendor — but cogent sets of sentences forming whole units of coherent thought ("paragraphs") in our language, we also have to identify the principles of logic that connect one sentence to another. That logic of coherent discourse has the power to make of a group of sentences a whole that is greater than the sum of the parts. Proper translation will point up the distinct small whole units of thought ("sentences") and further show how these units of thought coalesce in completed units of thought (paragraphs), and how sets of paragraphs hold together to make coherent statements ("chapters" or major parts thereof).

[3] TOPIC, PROPOSITION: Every document treats a specific topic. Moreover, many documents set forth sustained exercises in the analysis of a concrete problem pertinent to a given topic (which I call, the generative problematic). Some entire documents, early and late in the formation of the literature, are so set forth as to demonstrate propositions we are able to identify and define (exemplified by the Mishnah and Sifra). Few books in Rabbinic literature aim merely at collecting and arranging information (exemplified, so it seems to me, by Mekhilta attributed to R. Ishmael). Nearly all documents, to the contrary, work on not a topic in general but a specific problem concerning that topic, that is, as I said, a problematic; most of the documents set forth propositions that emerge out of masses of detail and may come to concrete expression through diverse details.

The governing protocols served because no document in Rabbinic literature ever accommodated idiosyncratic preference. Not a single one comes to us from an individual writer or author (e.g., Paul, Josephus, Philo); none collects the sayings or composites formulated in a single school (e.g., Matthew). All documents enjoy the sponsorship of sages as a group, whether we call the group an authorship, or redactors or compilers or editors. Not only so, but the compositions of which the composites are comprised themselves follow rigid rules of formulation and expression. When, therefore, we identify those rules, we can classify documents by differentiating among a limited repertoire of available choices.

Each document requires close analysis within its own limits, then comparison with other documents, first, those of its species, then, those not of its species. When compared as to rhetoric, topic, and logic of coherent discourse, nearly all of the documents will yield ample evidence that a restricted formal repertoire dictated to writers how they were to formulate their ideas if those ideas were to find a place in this particular document. Some forms appear in more than one document, others are unique to the writings in which they appear. Two examples of the former are the exegetical form and the dispute.

[1] EXEGETICAL FORM: The exegetical form requires two elements only: citation of a phrase of Scripture or a clause of the Mishnah, followed by a few words of paraphrase or other explanation.

[2] THE DISPUTE: The dispute form requires the presentation in a single syntactic pattern of two or more conflicting opinions on a given problem. The form will commonly have a topic sentences that implicitly conveys a problem and two or more elliptical solutions to the problem, each bearing attribution to a named authority. An alternative will have a problem and solution assigned to one authority, or given anonymously, followed by, And Rabbi X says..., with a contrary opinion.

Dominant in the Midrash-compilations but paramount also in the two Talmuds' treatment of the Mishnah, the exegetical form commonly defines the smallest whole unit of thought ("sentence") in a larger composition or composite ("paragraph," "chapter," respectively). No Midrash-compilation relies solely on the exegetical form for the formulation of its materials; every one of them uses that form as a building block. The dispute-form serves both legal and exegetical writers, the Mishnah and Talmuds and Midrash-compilations as well. It proves definitive in some documents, the Mishnah and Tosefta in particular, subordinate in others, Midrash-compilations, the two Talmuds.

These two forms exemplify the character of rhetoric of Rabbinic literature as a whole, showing us how a limited repertoire of syntactical conventions governed throughout. Fixed patterns of rhetoric, for example, the arrangement of words in recurrent syntactic patterns chosen out of a much larger repertoire of possibilities, provide the clues on distinguishing one document from another, since preferences of one set of writers and compositors differed from those of another, and explaining the basis for choices leads us deep into the definition of the respective documents as a whole. In section iii I shall explain the importance of documentary description.

## II. The Answer that I Set Forth

My answer to the question of the formalization of documents and their distinctive traits is in two parts, first, the translation and exegesis and literary analysis of a given document, second, an account of the single most important result, which was the description, analysis, and interpretation of the religious system that animates the Mishnah.

Let us consider form-analysis as an exegetical tool. How are we to transform the texts into their own best commentaries? Here is the answer, fully instantiated: I have made the technique of form-analysis into a tool for the exegesis of Rabbinic texts. Identifying the patterns of language can serve to distinguish primary from secondary elements in a composition. The patterns place in evidence the building blocks and allow us to define what is at hand and what is at stake. They signal the meaning, the intent, the emphases and proportions. The formulaic patterning of language — repetition of sound, form, and proposition — constitutes the first sustained commentary to the document itself. Form-analysis therefore can reveal the meaning of compositions to the document's framers: the original intent.

Form-analysis thus is the identification of recurrent syntactic patterns in the formulaic language of the Mishnah and the use of those patterns for literary-critical and exegetical purposes. The earliest exegetes of the Mishnah recognized that the language of the document follows disciplined patterns. They knew full well that these patterns at times may serve to indicate the meaning to be assigned to given lemmas. What has been grasped only in current studies is that the formal and formulaic patterning of language in the Mishnah constitutes the first and most important sustained commentary to the Mishnah itself. Form-analysis is the guide to the original meaning of the framers of the document as we now know it.

One principal contribution of form-analysis is to indicate what issues do, and what issues do not, inhere in the fundamental structure of a pericope. Because of the long history of the use of the Mishnah as a source for law far beyond its clear and explicit language, excluding what does not belong is probably the more important of the two exercises. But when we recognize the care with which the framers of the Mishnah have constructed their lists, laid out their triplets culminating in disputes, set forth contrasts between one proposition and its linguistically and conceptually matched opposite, and otherwise expressed their ideas with exquisite care, we grasp the proposition at hand.

I have chosen one of the most difficult units in the entire Mishnah, Mishnah Tohorot 2:2-8. In this example of how I believe the document must be interpreted, I indicate how the Mishnah's linguistic and syntactic patterns supply the key to its primary meaning. For the present purpose, the Tosefta is mostly ignored, since at only one point is it essential for the interpretation of the corresponding pericope of the Mishnah. I begin with an overview of the entire text and then turn to an analysis of its components. In parentheses I signal manuscript variants, these make no difference in the meaning.

## The Text
### Mishnah Tohorot 2:2-8

M.2:2 A. R. Eliezer [C: Leazar] says, "(1) He who eats food unclean in the first remove is unclean in the first remove;
"(2) [he who eats] food unclean in the second remove is unclean in the second remove;
"(3) [he who eats] food unclean in the third remove is unclean in the third remove."

B. R, Joshua says, "(1) He who eats food unclean in the first remove and food unclean in the second remove is unclean in the second remove.
"(2) [He who eats food] unclean in the third remove is unclean in the second remove so far as Holy Things are concerned,
"(3) and is not unclean in the second remove so far as heave-offering is concerned.

C. "[We speak of] the case of [N, P, K. Katsh #117. C, Maimonides' text lack:] unconsecrated food

D. "which is prepared in conditions appropriate to heave-offering."

M. 2:3 A. *Unconsecrated food:*
in the first remove is unclean and renders unclean;

B. in the second remove is unfit, but does not convey uncleanness;

C. and in the third remove is eaten in the pottage of heave-offering.

M. 2:4 A. *Heave-offering:*
in the first and in the second remove is unclean and renders unclean;

B. in the third remove is unfit and does not convey uncleanness;

C. and in the fourth remove is eaten in a pottage of Holy Things.

M. 2:5 A. *Holy Things:*
in the first and the second and the third removes are susceptible to uncleanness and render unclean;

B. and in the fourth remove are unfit and do not convey uncleanness;

C. and in the fifth remove are eaten in a pottage of Holy Things.

M. 2:6 A. *Unconsecrated food:*
in the second remove renders unconsecrated liquid unclean and renders foods of heave-offering unfit.

B. *Heave-offering:*
in the third remove renders unclean [the] liquid of Holy Things, and renders foods of Holy Things unfit,

C. if it [the heave-offering] was prepared in the condition of cleanness pertaining to Holy Things.

D. But if it was prepared in conditions pertaining to heave-offering, it renders unclean at two removes and renders unfit at one remove in reference to Holy Things.

M. 2:7 A. R. Eleazar *[Eliezer:* GRA, Rosh, V,N,M; *Eleazar* (Leazar): MA, K, Katsh #117, C, P, PB] says, "The three of them are equal:

B. "*Holy Things* and *heave-offering,* and *unconsecrated food:* "which are at the first remove of uncleanness render unclean at two removes and unfit at one [further] remove in respect to Holy Things;
"render unclean at one remove and spoil at one [further] remove in respect to heave-offering;
"and spoil unconsecrated food.

C. "That which is unclean in the second remove in all of them renders unclean at one remove and unfit at one [further] remove in respect to Holy Things;
"and renders liquid of unconsecrated food unclean;
"and spoils foods of heave-offering.

D. "The third remove of uncleanness in all of them renders liquids of Holy Things unclean,
"and spoils food of Holy Things."

M. 2:8 A. He who eats food unclean in the second remove should not work olive press [since he will render the oil unclean].

B. And unconsecrated food which is prepared in accord with the rules pertaining to Holy Things-lo, this is like unconsecrated food.

C. R. Eleazar b. R. $Sadoq says, "Lo, it is like heave-offering,

D. "conveying uncleanness at two removes and rendering unfit at one [further] remove."

## Overview

M. Tohorot 2:2-8 presupposes knowledge of the Rabbinic system of ritual purity. A review of some of its essential elements is necessary for an understanding of the arguments and analyses that follow. In the Rabbinic system, ritual impurity is acquired by contact with either a primary or a secondary source of uncleanness, called a "Father" or a "Child" or "Offspring" of uncleanness, respectively. In the first category are contact with a corpse, a person suffering a flux, a leper, and the like. Objects made of metal, wood, leather, bone, cloth, or sacking become Fathers of uncleanness if they touch a corpse.

Foodstuffs and liquids are susceptible to uncleanness, but will not render other foodstuffs unclean in the same degree or remove of uncleanness that they themselves suffer. Foodstuffs furthermore will not make vessels or utensils unclean. But liquids made unclean by a Father of uncleanness will do so if they touch the inner side of the vessel. That is, if they fall into the contained space of an earthenware vessel, they make the whole vessel unclean.

Food or liquid that touches a Father of uncleanness becomes unclean in the *first* remove (that is, remove from the original source). If food touches a person or vessel made unclean by a primary cause of uncleanness, he or it is unclean in the *second* remove. Food that touches what is unclean in the *second* remove uncleanness enters the *third* remove uncleanness, and food that touches what is in the *third* remove of uncleanness enters into the *fourth* remove of uncleanness, and so on. But liquids touching either a primary source of uncleanness (Father) or something unclean in the first or second remove (Offspring) are regarded as unclean in the first remove. They are able to make something else unclean. If, for example, the outer side of a vessel is made unclean by a liquid-thus unclean in the second remove- and another liquid touches the outer side, the other liquid enters not the second, but the first remove uncleanness.

Heave-offering (a.k.a., priestly rations, that is, food raised up for priestly use only) unclean in the third remove of uncleanness, and Holy Things (that is, things belonging to the cult) unclean in the fourth remove, do not make other things, whether liquids or foods, unclean. The difference among removes of uncleanness is important. What is unclean in the first remove of uncleanness in common food will convey uncleanness. But, although food unclean in the second remove will be unacceptable, it will not convey uncleanness, that is, third remove of uncleanness. But it will render heave-offering *unfit.*

Further considerations apply to heave-offering and Holy Things. Heave-offering can be made unfit and unclean by a first, and unfit by a second, remove of uncleanness. If it touches something unclean in the third remove, it is made unfit, but itself will not impart fourth remove uncleanness. A Holy Thing that suffers uncleanness in the first, second, or third remove is unclean and conveys uncleanness. If it is unclean in the fourth remove, it is invalid for the cult but does not convey uncleanness to what it touches, that is, to a fifth remove from the original source of uncleanness or corpse. It is much more susceptible than are non-cultic things. Thus, common food that suffers second remove uncleanness will render heave-offering invalid. We already know that it makes liquid unclean in the first remove. Likewise, heave-offering unclean in the third remove will make Holy Things invalid and put them into a fourth remove of uncleanness.

Complications in the system will arise if common food is prepared in conditions of cleanness appropriate for either heave-offering or Holy Things. In that case it will be necessary to determine the status of the food and its susceptibility to uncleanness. This matter is raised in the pericopae discussed below.

With these data firmly in hand, let us turn to a general discussion of M. Toh. 2:2-8.

M. 2:2 introduces the removes of uncleanness. Our interest is in the contaminating affect, upon a person, of eating unclean food. Does the food make the person unclean in the same remove of uncleanness as is borne by the food itself? Thus if one eats food unclean in the first remove, is he unclean in that same remove? This is the view of Eliezer. Joshua says he is unclean in the second remove. We note that they concur on all the primary conceptions and differ on a detail. If we could validate the attributions, we should assign to the period before the two masters beyond 70 C.E. the main principles of the law at hand. But verification of attributions is not readily accomplished.

The dispute, M. 2:2A-B, at M. 2:2C-D is significantly glossed. The further consideration is introduced as to the sort of food under discussion. Joshua is made to say that there is a difference between the contaminating affects upon the one who eats heave-offering, on the one side, and unconsecrated food prepared in conditions of heave-offering, on the other. This matter, the status of unconsecrated food prepared as if it were heave-offering, or as if it were Holy Things, and heave-offering prepared as if it were Holy Things, forms a substratum of our chapter, added to several primary items and complicating their exegesis. T. 2:1 confirms, however, that primary to the dispute between Eliezer and Joshua is simply the matter of the affects of food unclean in the first remove upon the person who eats such food. The gloss, M. 2:2C-D, forms a redactional-thematic link between Joshua's opinion and the large construction of M. 2:3-7.

M. 2.3:5, expanded and glossed by M. 2:6, follow a single and rather tight form. The sequence differentiates unconsecrated food, heave-offering, and Holy Things each at the several removes from the original source of uncleanness.

Eleazar, M. 2:7, insists that, at a given remove, all three are subject to the *same* rule. The contrary view, M. 2:3-6, is that unconsecrated food in the first remove makes heave-offering unclean and at the second remove spoils heave-offering; it does not enter a third remove and therefore has no affect upon Holy Things. Heave-offering at the first two removes may produce contaminating effects, and at the third remove spoils Holy Things, but is of no effect at the fourth. Holy Things in the first three removes produce uncleanness, and at the fourth impart unfitness to other Holy Things. M. 2:6 then goes over the ground of unconsecrated food at the second remove, and heave-offering at the third. The explanation of M. 2:6C is various; the simplest view is that the clause glosses M. 2:6B by insisting that the heave-offering to which we refer is prepared as if it were Holy Things, on which account, at the third remove, it can spoil Holy Things.

At M. 2:7, as I said, Eleazar restates matters, treating all three — Holy Things, heave-offering, and unconsecrated food — as equivalent to one another at the first, second, and third removes, with the necessary qualification for unconsecrated food that it is like the other, consecrated foods in producing effects at the second and even the third removes. Some commentators read *Eliezer.* They set the pericope up against Joshua's view at M. 2:2, assigning to Joshua M. 2:3ff. as well. My picture of the matter is significantly different from the established exegesis.

M. 2:8 is a singleton. First, we go over the matter on which Joshua and Eliezer agree at M. 2:2, which is that one who eats food unclean in the second remove is unclean in that same remove. Accordingly, he can make liquid unclean, and it is unclean in the first remove. Therefore he should not work in the olive press, since he will make the oil unclean. Then we raise the issue which, as we have seen, recurs in the earlier pericopae but never is wholly spelled out in one place as an integrated problem: What is the rule if we prepare unconsecrated food as if it were Holy Things? M. 2:8B says it remains in the status of unconsecrated food. Eleazar b. R. Sadoq says it is classified in the category of heave-offering. Our chapter does not contain the view that it indeed is classified as, or like, Holy Things. Yet one way of harmonizing M. 2:7 with M. 2:3-6 would be to assert that Eleazar holds the unconsecrated food of which he speaks has, in fact, been prepared as if it were Holy Things, which accounts for the fact that it produces the same effects as do Holy Things.

Thus, one persistent exercise – a variable, really — in our chapter is the introduction of the differentiation between unconsecrated food, on the one hand, and unconsecrated food prepared in accord with the rules of cleanness applicable to heave-offering, and, further, to Holy Things, on the other. The issue is intruded, in particular, at M. 2:2, 6, and 8. At M. 2:2, it is surely secondary to the dispute between Eliezer and Joshua, as shown both by form-critical considerations and by T.'s version of the problem under discussion. As to the former, Eliezer says that which is unclean in the first remove makes a person who eats it unclean in the first remove, and so with the second and third. Joshua's theory matches Eliezer's in formal articulation. If one eats something unclean in the first remove, he himself becomes unclean in the second. To be sure, he agrees that if one eats something unclean in the second remove, he too is unclean in the second remove. But, T. explains, that is because what is unclean in the second remove makes the spit in his mouth-liquid-unclean in the first remove, and that in turn makes *him* unclean in the second. Then comes the intrusion, "in respect to unconsecrated food prepared in accord with the rules of cleanness applicable to heave-offering." MSS variants give, further, "*heave-offering* prepared in accord, etc.," that is, omitting *unconsecrated food.* On the face of it, this formal issue is secondary, as I said, and T. knows nothing of it. But reading it as part of Joshua's saying, we have then to interpret the whole pericope to deal with two problems.

The second of these problems is the preparation of food in accord with rules of cleanness not applicable to it, *unconsecrated food* as heave-offering, M. 2:6; *heave-offering* prepared as Holy Things; and, M. 2:8, *unconsecrated food* prepared as Holy Things — the three possibilities. The three are not assembled in a single pericope, rather, added as a layer to the several primary rulings and disputes. The point is, the householder undertakes to protect secular food ("unconsecrated food") in accord with the rules of uncleanness that apply to heave offering, or heave-offering as though it were Holy Things, or, finally, secular food as if it were Holy Things. These procedures, respectively, involve obeying in the domestic household the rules that govern in the Temple, and pretending that food at home is consecrated as if it were in the Temple. The upshot is, the householder and his family live as though they were priests in the Temple.

Let us return to the exegesis of the language at hand. Naturally, the further exegetical problem will be raised, in the Talmuds, about whether we regard the unconsecrated food prepared as it were heave-offering, or the heave-offering prepared as if it were Holy Things, as *wholly* subject to the rules applicable to the higher degree of sanctity, or as only *partially* subject to those rules. It remains to ask, Is it possible that the issue of unconsecrated food prepared in conditions of cleanness required for heave-offering, and heave-offering prepared in conditions of cleanness required for Holy Things, has been intruded because of some sort of difficulty in the process of transmission of the primary pericopae to which it is attached?

A comparison of M. 2:2 and M. 2:6 makes this seem unlikely. The relationship between the segments is unmistakable, and each item means what it says. M. 2:2C-D speaks of *unconsecrated food* prepared under the conditions of cleanness required for *heave-offering,* and M. 2:6 clearly wishes to speak of *heave-offering* prepared under the rules of cleanness required for *Holy Things.* There is no repetition of the same words in the two pericopae, which might lead to the conclusion that they do not belong in one or the other unit. The issue is clearly secondary in both pericopae, but is formulated with precision.

To which strata shall we assign the several pericopae of the chapter?

Let us begin with M. 2:2. Here Joshua and Eliezer debate a fundamental point, the affect of eating unclean food upon the person who eats the food. Is he in the same remove of uncleanness as is the food he eats? Shall we assign to that same stratum the issue of the rules for unconsecrated food prepared *as if* it were heave-offering? It is difficult to know. Since Eleazar b. R. Sadoq treats the parallel matter — unconsecrated food prepared as if it were Holy Things — it is hardly a matter whose status was settled before Ushan times.

Moreover, the issue is secondary to, and a logical development of, the matter under dispute between Joshua and Eliezer. Why? Once we ask about whether unclean food produces an equivalent, or a diminished, level of uncleanness upon the person who eats it, we have then to ask about the parallel question of unclean food that naturally belongs in one category (unconsecrated), but which has been placed into another more sensitive category (heave-offering), by the owner's intent. Is this treated, for purposes of imparting contamination, as if it were in the category into which it has been raised? So we ask first about how ordinary food imparts uncleanness, and then about how extraordinary food imparts uncleanness. The logical connection to the former issue is tight.

What about the complex at M. 2:3-6+7, the removes of uncleanness applicable to unconsecrated food, heave-offering, and Holy Things? M. 2:3 allows two removes for unclean unconsecrated food, and M. 2:5 reinforces that rule; Eleazar rejects it, allowing for three removes of unclean unconsecrated food, saying it affect Holy Things. 'Aqiba, in a quite separate pericope, is explicit on the matter. While we cannot be sure which Eleazar is before us, not knowing whether it is a Yavnean or an Ushan Eleazar or Eliezer (b. Hyrcanus, as at M. 2:2), 'Aqiba tells us that the issue is live at Yavneh, ca. 90. He takes up a position contrary to that of M. 2:3-6, and, it *follows,* the topic under dispute is to be assigned to Yavneh, in the theory that what we have are several opinions formed (if not formulated) at the time that the issue was current.

M. 2:2 is Yavnean; M. 2:3-7 concern rather basic questions about the removes of uncleanness for unconsecrated food, heave-offering, and Holy Things, evidently under discussion in the later Yavnean and Ushan (ca. 140 C.E.) circles. Overall, the impression left by the chapter is that the differentiation among the several removes of uncleanness, as these pertain to various sorts of food to which uncleanness is imparted, as well as the differentiation of the contaminating affects upon such foods of various *sources* of uncleanness, was accomplished primarily at Yavneh and Usha, upon the basis of remarkably little tradition from the period before 70.

Let us now turn to a closer reading of the chapter's components.

## Analysis

### M.2:2

A. R. Eliezer [C: Leazar] says, "(1) He who eats food unclean in the first remove is unclean in the first remove;
"(2) [he who eats] food unclean in the second remove is unclean in the second remove;
"(3) [he who eats] food unclean in the third remove is unclean in the third remove."

B. R. Joshua says, "(1) He who eats food unclean in the first remove and food unclean in the second remove is unclean in the second remove.
"(2) [He who eats food] unclean in the third remove is unclean in the second remove so far as Holy Things are concerned,
"(3) and is not unclean in the second remove so far as heave-offering is concerned,

C. "[We speak of] the case of [N, P, K, Katsh #117, C, Maimonides' text lack:] unconsecrated food

D. "which is prepared in conditions of cleanness appropriate to heave-offering."

The dispute formally is complete and balanced in A-B. C-D then introduce a complication to gloss the terms of the dispute. So far as Joshua and Eliezer are concerned, the issue is the affect, upon a person, of eating unclean food.

Eliezer's view is that the person enters the same remove of uncleanness as that of the food he has eaten. If he ate food unclean in the first remove, he too is unclean in the first remove and produces equivalent effects, so too second and third.

This simple ruling is rejected by Joshua. His view is that a person who eats food unclean in the first remove is not unclean in the same remove, but only in the second remove; he concurs as to eating food in the second remove. In both cases, the person makes heave-offering unfit if he touches it. Why not lower the person who eats unclean food in the second remove to the status of the third remove? Because, as Rosh and Sens say, following T. 2:1 = b. Hul. 33b, the food he eats makes the spit in his mouth unclean, and, as liquid, it is unclean in the first remove and makes him unclean in the second remove. Clearly, therefore, Joshua's ruling is based upon a somewhat more complex picture.

This further affects his view of a person who eats food unclean in the third remove. Will he make the liquid in his mouth unclean, which food then is unclean in the first remove and places him into the second remove? With respect to Holy Things, he will. With respect to heave-offering, he will not. Why? Because in the former, the man unclean in the third remove produces a fourth remove, and, accordingly, the liquid too is affected (GRA). But in the latter, there is no further remove of uncleanness, so the liquid too cannot be affected.

C-D form a problem because of the MS variants that omit *unconsecrated food.* If we read C-D as given here, the point is that the *fore*going dispute (B) about food unclean in the third remove concerns not heave-offering but unconsecrated food prepared within the discipline applying to heave-offering. The point of the gloss then is that a third remove now applies to unconsecrated food. If we do not read *unconsecrated food,* then C-D refer back to B's "is not unclean in the second remove so far as heave-offering is concerned." The point is that the third remove applies to Holy Things but not to heave-offering prepared in conditions of cleanness that apply to heave-offering (and not to Holy Things). But if the heave-offering is prepared in conditions applying to *Holy Things,* it is subject to the rules of Holy Things, and he who eats food unclean in the third remove places it into the third or fourth remove, as specified.

In any event, on the surface C-D qualify only Joshua's saying. Since Eliezer makes reference neither to Holy Things nor to heave-offering, the qualification and the problem solved by it are not pertinent to his opinion.

A. Said R. Joshua to R. Eliezer, "where do we find a form of uncleanness in the Torah which produces another uncleanness which is like it [at the same remove, and not at one remove of diminished virulence], that you say, 'It produces [uncleanness at] the first, remove'?"

B. He said to him, "Also you say, 'it [that which is unclean in the second remove] produces something unclean in the second remove'!"

C. He said to him, "We find that that which is unclean in the second remove renders liquid unclean to produce uncleanness at the first remove, and the liquid renders food unclean to produce uncleanness at the second remove.

D. "But we do not find something unclean in the first remove which makes something else unclean in the first remove in any instance."

T. Toh. 2:1

T. treats only M. 2:2A-B, omitting reference to the third and fourth removes and to the matter of Holy Things and heave-offering. This strongly suggests that the essential dispute is at M. 2:2A-Bl-2. Eliezer does not answer Joshua's question. He simply points out that Joshua has to answer the same question. At C Joshua does, and it is in accord with T. that we interpreted M. D simply repeats Joshua's opinion in M., in more elaborate language.

**M.2:3-7**

2:3 A. *Unconsecrated food:*
in the first remove is unclean and renders unclean;
B. in the second remove is unfit, but does not convey uncleanness;
C. and in the third remove is eaten in the pottage of heave-offering.

2:4 A. *Heave-offering:*
in the first and second removes is unclean and renders unclean;
B. in the third remove is unfit and does not convey uncleanness;
C. and in the fourth remove is eaten in a pottage of Holy Things.

2.5 A. *Holy Things:*
in the first and the second and the third removes are susceptible to uncleanness and render unclean;
B. and in the fourth removes are unfit and do not convey uncleanness;
C. and in the fifth remove are eaten in a pottage of Holy Things.

2.6 A. *Unconsecrated food:*
in the second remove renders unconsecrated liquid unclean, and renders foods of heave-offering unfit.
B. *Heave-offering:*
in the third remove renders unclean [the] liquid of Holy Things, and renders foods of Holy Things unfit,
C. if it [the heave-offering] was prepared in the condition of cleanness pertaining to Holy Things.
D. But if it was prepared in conditions pertaining to heave-offering, it renders unclean at two removes and renders unfit at one remove in reference to Holy Things.

2.7 A. R. Eleazar *[Eliezer:* GRA, Rosh, V, N, M; *Eleazar* (Leazar): MA, K, Katsh #117, C, P, PB] says, "The three of them are equal:
B. "*Holy things and heave-offering and unconsecrated food:* "which are at the first remove of uncleanness render unclean at two removes are unfit at one [further] remove in respect to Holy Things,
"render unclean at one remove and spoil at one [further] remove in respect to heave-offering,
"and spoil unconsecrated food.
C. "That which is unclean in the second remove in all of them renders unclean at one remove and unfit at one [further] remove in respect to Holy Things,
"and renders liquid of unconsecrated food unclean,
"and spoils foods of heave-offering.

D. "The third remove of uncleanness in all of them renders liquids of Holy Things unclean,
"and spoils foods of Holy Things."

If we had no prepared agendum of questions and no preconceptions, formed on the basis of other rules, what should we understand by the present set of rules? The first, M. 2:3, tells us that unconsecrated food in the first remove from the original source of uncleanness is unclean and renders unclean. That language seems to me to mean exactly what is says, which is that unconsecrated food in the first remove is capable of a further affect of contamination, so that what touches unclean unconsecrated food in the first remove, thus in the second remove, is unclean — unclean, and unfit. Unconsecrated food in the second remove is unfit but does not convey uncleanness. Does heave-offering appear? Obviously not. The simple meaning, therefore, is that unconsecrated food in the second remove is unfit for consumption, presumably by people who wish to keep the laws of cleanness. Unconsecrated food in the third remove produces no contamination. The entire interest of the pericope, therefore, is in unconsecrated food. M. 2:4 then speaks of heave-offering and tells us that heave-offering in the first and second removes are unclean and impart uncleanness. To what do they impart uncleanness? To heave-offering, in the third remove. And that heave-offering is unfit, as we know. The same is to be said of Holy Things. They impart uncleanness at three removes. Accordingly, unconsecrated food produces not two further removes of contamination, but three.

The first remove at M. 2:3 makes something it touches unclean. What it touches should be that which is unclean-in the second remove. But we are told, explicitly, that what is unclean in the second remove is *unfit,* but does not convey uncleanness. The difficult point, therefore, is the second remove. What we should want, for M. 2:3B, if dictated by M. 2:3A, should make provision for the uncleanness referred to at M. 2:3A, and we should have:

Unconsecrated food which is unclean in the first remove is unclean
*and conveys uncleanness*
Unconsecrated food which is in the second remove is unclean
*but does not convey uncleanness*
That which is unclean in the third remove. . .

Why has the model of M. 2:3A been abandoned at B? For the contrast clearly is between *unclean/renders unclean* and *unclean/does not render unclean.* Why substitute *unfit* for *unclean* at B and not at A? The question applies to M. 2:7, *render unclean* at two removes and *unfit* at one [third] remove. This bears the same redundancy. If we said only, *render unclean at two removes,* it would follow that what is at the third remove does not *render* unclean-but it is unclean. In other words, at the foundation of the shift in language is the evident purpose of marking the end of a chain of contaminating contacts with *unfit,* rather than *unclean,* thus *mtm'. . . pswl . . .*, rather than M. 2:3A's *tm'. . . mtm'.* Maimonides uses both word choices *(Other Fathers of Uncleanness* 11:2B) "And whence do we learn that food stuff suffering *second remove uncleanness* is *invalid. . .* ?" I cannot imagine why, except for mnemonic reasons, someone should have shifted the usage, but it is done consistently.

Let us now ask a much more important question: Do M. 2:3-6 continue the opinion of Joshua at M. 2:2? He says that one who eats food unclean in the first and second remove is unclean in the second remove. Will he agree with M. 2:3, assuming we speak of unconsecrated food? Of course he will, because M. 2:3 is of the view that unconsecrated food at the second remove is unfit/unclean. But what do we gain — for Eliezer, M. 2:2A2, says exactly the same thing. Only if we insist that Eleazar at M. 2:7 is Eliezer of M. 2:2 shall we assume that there is disagreement between Eliezer and Joshua on the issues of the present pericope. This brings us to the main point I here contribute. The disagreement is between. M. 2:3-6 and M. 2:7, as follows:

<table>
<tr><th>M.2:3</th><th>M. 2:7</th></tr>
<tr><td>Unconsecrated food unclean in the first remove:<br>Contact 1: Unclean, imparts uncleanness<br>at<br>Contact 2: Unfit (= unclean, but does not impart uncleanness; there is no contact 3)</td><td>Unconsecrated food unclean at the first remove:<br>Contact 1: Unclean, imparts uncleanness<br>at<br>Contact 2: Unclean, imparts uncleanness<br>at<br>Contact 3: Unfit<br>in *respect to Holy Things*<br>Contact 1: Unclean, imparts uncleanness<br>at<br>Contact 2: Unfit (= unclean, etc.)<br>in *respect to heave-offering*<br>Contact 1: Spoils *unconsecrated food* (=makes it unclean,<br>but it does not impart uncleanness; there is no contact 2)</td></tr>
</table>

If we assume that M. 2:3-6 are talking, at M. 2:3, about the affects of unconsecrated food *upon* unconsecrated food, then the difference between M. 2:3 and M. 2:7 (Eleazar) is very clear. Eleazar is of the view that unconsecrated food in the first remove does not impart uncleanness at all. It may become unclean, but it has no affect upon other food. What sort of food does have an impact upon other food? Only heave-offering and Holy Things. They indeed do produce the affect of uncleanness/unfitness, and may further produce the affect of such severe contamination that a further stage of contamination is possible.

If that indeed is Eleazar's view, then to whom will it be important to insist that, when unconsecrated food does have the capacity to impart uncleanness, it is in fact unconsecrated food which has been prepared under conditions of cleanness required for heave-offering — to whom, if not to Eleazar! The gloss of M. 2:2C-D in fact brings Joshua into conformity with Eleazar's quite separate point, by making him say that, when he speaks of food in the first, second, and third removes producing uncleanness, it is specifically unconsecrated food prepared under conditions of cleanness required for heave-offering. But why should Joshua alone be made to say so? For Eliezer of M. 2:2 has told us that he who eats food unclean in the first remove is unclean in the first remove — which is to say, unclean food imparts uncleanness. So C-D must in fact be read as (Eleazar's) glosses of both Eliezer's and Joshua's total and completed dispute.

What about the equivalent gloss at M. 2:6? There we are told that heave-offering prepared in conditions of cleanness required for Holy Things when in the third remove produces uncleanness — that is, it makes fluids of Holy Things unclean and renders food of Holy Things unfit. (To put it otherwise, the liquid falls into the first remove and so has the capacity to render other things unclean, but the solid food does not, so is merely unclean itself, without further contaminating capacity.) What is Eleazar's view of the capacity of heave-offering to render something unclean? At M. 2:7D, he speaks of the third remove of "the three of them" (including heave-offering). What does it do? It renders unclean liquids of Holy Things and renders unfit food of Holy Things (!). Does Eleazar disagree with M. 2:6? Of course not — that is, *if* we include the gloss of M. 2:6C: heave-offering at the third remove renders liquid of Holy Things unclean and foods of Holy Things unfit.

What is it that the glosses accomplish?

First, they eliminate the dispute (?) between Eleazar and Joshua and Eliezer of M. 2:2, on the one side.

Second, they force M. 2:6 to concur with Eleazar.

And what is Eleazar's position in these matters? In his view, the unconsecrated food not prepared as if it were heave-offering and the heave-offering not prepared as if it were Holy Things has precisely the same contaminating power as if it were prepared in accord with the more strict set of rules, respectively.

At issue, then, is nothing other than the (unstated) agendum of our chapter,

*the capacity to raise food to a higher order of sensitivity to uncleanness by subjecting it to rules of cleanness not ordinarily required, unconsecrated food to heave-offering, heave-offering to Holy Things.*

That which is not essential at M. 2:2, 6, (and 8) in fact has shaped the articulation of the whole set, M. 2:2-8. If the fact is that M. 2:2C-D serve as a gloss, to bring that set into relationship to Eleazar's opinion, then what shall we isolate as the equivalent gloss to the set M. 2:3-6? The answer is obvious: the whole of M. 2:6 serves to gloss M. 2:3-5 in much the same way as M. 2:2C-D revise M. 2:2A-B.

Who is this Eleazar, who holds that it makes no difference whether we prepare unconsecrated food as unconsecrated food, or whether we prepare it as heave-offering, and whether we prepare heave-offering as such, or whether we prepare it as Holy Things? It is none other than the authority of M. 2:8B, who tells us that if we prepare unconsecrated food as if it were Holy Things, it has exactly the same capacity to impart uncleanness as other unconsecrated food. Eleazar b. R. Sadoq, who holds that unconsecrated food prepared as if it were Holy Things produces the contaminating affects of heave-offering, will differ. And we have, in fact, an Ushan construction, between Eleazar b. R. Sadoq and an Ushan Eleazar (or Eliezer, it hardly matters among Ushans) on exactly the same point.

*And why is it that Eleazar takes this position? Because, so far as he is concerned, what is important is not the source of contamination — the unclean foods — but that which* is subject to *contamination, the unconsecrated food, heave-offering, and Holy Things.*

He could not state matters more clearly than he does when he says that the three of them are exactly equivalent. And they are, because the differentiations will emerge in the food affected, or contaminated, by the three. So at the root of the dispute is whether we gauge the contamination in accord with the source — unconsecrated food, or unconsecrated food prepared as if it were heave-offering, and so on — or whether the criterion is the food which is contaminated. M. 2:3-5 are all wrong, Eleazar states explicitly at M. 2:7 A, because they differentiate among uncleanness imparted by unclean unconsecrated food, unclean heave-offering, and unclean Holy Things, and do not differentiate among the three sorts of food *to which* contamination is imparted.

It is surely a logical position, for the three sorts of food do exhibit differentiated capacities to receive uncleanness; one sort *is* more contaminable than another. And so too is the contrary view logical: *what* is *more sensitive to uncleanness also will have a greater capacity to impart- uncleanness.* The subtle debate before us clearly is unknown to Eliezer and Joshua at M. 2:2. To them the operative categories are something unclean in first, second, or third *removes,* without-distinction as to the relative sensitivities of the several types of food which may be unclean.

The sequence thus begins with Eliezer and Joshua, who ask about the contaminating power of that which is unclean in the first and second removes, without regard to whether it is unconsecrated food, heave-offering, or Holy Things. To them, the distinction between the capacity to impart contamination, or to receive contamination, of the several sorts of food is unknown. Once, however, their question is raised — in such general terms — it will become natural to ask the next logical question, one which makes distinctions not only among the several removes of uncleanness, but also among the several sorts of food involved in the processes of contamination. That step is not before us. Only the still further, logical extension of the issue *is* before us, the third dimension in our three-dimensional construction:

(1) removes, three; (2) types of food, three; and, finally, (3) whether the important aspect of the types of food is its susceptibility to *receive* uncleanness or its capacity to *impart* uncleanness, three respectively. Each system — Eleazar's and the authority of M. 2:3-5's — bears twenty-seven possibilities, therefore, with the difference in the systems coming in at the 18th through 27th cases, so to speak. Our picture of the matter will intersect with the inherited one, but also come into conflict, for fairly obvious reasons.

**M.2:8**

A. He who eats food unclean in the second remove should not work in the olive press, [since he will render the oil unclean].
B. And unconsecrated food which is prepared in accord with the rules pertaining to Holy Things — lo, this is like unconsecrated food.
C. R. Eleazar b. R. Sadoq says, "Lo, it is like heave-offering,
D. "conveying uncleanness at two removes and rendering unfit at one [further] remove."

A is separate from B-C. Why should a person who has eaten food unclean in the second remove not work in the olive press? Because the olive oil will emerge. The person is unclean in the second remove, as both Eliezer and Joshua will agree, and he will render the liquid unclean in the first remove. This will render the press unclean (T. 1:7C).

B now returns to the issue of M. 2:2C-D. There we are told that unconsecrated food which is prepared in accord with the rules of the cleanness of heave-offering produces a third remove, just as does heave-offering. B now adds that unconsecrated food prepared in accord with the rules pertaining to the cleanness of Holy Things is unchanged and remains adjudged in accord with the rules, for the cleanness and removes from uncleanness, of unconsecrated food, and with those alone. That matter is not raised at M. 2:2C-D, nor does it occur at M. 2:6. The former tells us about unconsecrated food prepared as if it were heave-offering. The latter speaks of heave-offering prepared as if it were Holy Things. So we can raise each level by one: (1) unconsecrated food *to* heave-offering; (2) heave-offering *to* Holy Things. But (3) we cannot raise the first to the third level.

Eleazar b. R. Sadoq says that if we treat unconsecrated food as if it were Holy Things, to be sure it does not fall into the category of Holy Things. But it *does* fall into the category of heave-offering and becomes subject to its rules of contamination, the other possible position. What is curious is that these matters are not put together into a single pericope but scattered among the several as glosses — so much for form-analytical exegesis.[3]

The close reading of the Mishnah with the Tosefta took many years, from 1972 into the earlier 1980s. When I began, I did not imagine I would ever finish the work; required were patience and determination to persist. But my goal was never narrowly exegetical. I was looking for patterns, not for exegetical novellae. So I began with the Division of Purities, the sixth of the Mishnah's six divisions, because this was the largest and conceptually the most difficult. As my bibliography shows, it took twenty-two volumes. I proceeded to the fifth division, Holy Things, then Women, Appointed Times, and Damages. My graduate students of the later 1970s and earlier 1980s took up the tractates of the first division. By 1985 the entire project was complete and publication was concluded in 1986. At first I permitted myself the luxury of extended discussions of particular problems, as illustrated in this presentation of Mishnah-tractate Tohorot 2:2-8. Later on I concluded that so elaborate a spelling out of each transaction was not needed; the pattern was established, and a few signals of what was to be done sufficed. Hence the later divisions of were set forth in a kind of shorthand, readily comprehensible by those who followed from the beginning.

With the Mishnah and the Tosefta in hand, I turned to the Talmud of the Land of Israel (Yerushalmi). For that Talmud only a preliminary translation was feasible, because we have nothing like a critical text and a definitive commentary, such as we do have for the Mishnah and the Tosefta. My preliminary translation aimed to provide an account of the forms and traits of the document and to make possible systematic comparative work, with attention to the Yerushalmi's rhetoric, logic, and topical program. I proceeded to the Midrash-compilations, Sifra, the two Sifrés, and Mekhilta, and then the Rabbah-Midrash-compilations, Genesis Rabbah, Leviticus Rabbah, and those for Song of Songs, Lamentations, Ruth, and Esther (I); along the way I conducted form-analytical studies and translations of tractate Abot and Abot deR. Natan. The work on the Talmud of Babylonia, the Bavli, concluded the project. Then I retranslated the two Talmuds to stress their formal traits — marking what is primary and what is appended, indicating the use of Hebrew and Aramaic by different type faces, marking off the unfolding of a coherent exposition. So I proposed to identify their primary components, then I compared the two Talmuds' treatment of the second, third, and fourth divisions of the Mishnah. This work took many years and filled many volumes. In the end I made it possible to describe, analyze and interpret each of the components of the Rabbinic canon.

The second outcome concerns the systemic reading of complete documents, viewed on their own, one by one. For that purpose, I present my reading of the Mishnah, which will form the foundation for what follows.

THE MISHNAH: The Mishnah is a philosophical law code, covering topics of both a theoretical and practical character. It was produced at about 200 C.E. under the sponsorship of Judah, Patriarch (*nasi*) or ethnic ruler of the Jews of the Land of Israel. It comprises sixty-two tractates (plus the prolegomenon, tractate Abot), divided by topics among six divisions, as follows:

1. AGRICULTURE (Zera'im): Berakhot (Blessings); Peah (the corner of the field); Demai (doubtfully tithed produce); Kilayim (mixed seeds); Shebi'it (the seventh year); Terumot (heave offering or priestly rations); Ma'aserot (tithes);

Maaser Sheni (second tithe); Hallah (dough offering); Orlah (produce of trees in the first three years after planting, which is prohibited); and Bikkurim (first fruits).

2. APPOINTED TIMES (Moed): Shabbat (the Sabbath); Erubin (the fictive fusion meal or boundary); Pesahim (Passover); Sheqalim (the Temple tax); Yoma (the Day of Atonement); Sukkah (the festival of Tabernacles); Besah (the preparation of food on the festivals and Sabbath); Rosh Hashanah (the New Year); Taanit (fast days); Megillah (Purim); Moed Qatan (the intermediate days of the festivals of Passover and Tabernacles); Hagigah (the festal offering).

3. WOMEN (Nashim): Yebamot (the levirate widow); Ketubot (the marriage contract); Nedarim (vows); Nazir (the special vow of the Nazirite); Sotah (the wife accused of adultery); Gittin (writs of divorce); Qiddushin (betrothal).

4. DAMAGES or civil law (Neziqin): Baba Qamma, Baba Mesia, Baba Batra (civil law, covering damages and torts, then correct conduct of business, labor, and real estate transactions); Sanhedrin (institutions of government; criminal penalties); Makkot (flogging); Shabuot (oaths); Eduyyot (a collection arranged on other than topical lines); Horayot (rules governing improper conduct of civil authorities);

5. HOLY THINGS (Qodoshim): Zebahim (every day animal offerings); Menahot (meal offerings); Hullin (animals slaughtered for secular purposes); Bekhorot (firstlings); Arakhin (vows of valuation); Temurah (vows of exchange of a beast for an already consecrated beast); Keritot (penalty of extirpation or premature death); Me'ilah (sacrilege); Tamid (the daily whole offering); Middot (the layout of the Temple building); Qinnim (how to deal with bird offerings designated for a given purpose and then mixed up);

6. PURITY (Tohorot): Kelim (susceptibility of utensils to uncleanness); Ohalot (transmission of corpse-uncleanness in the tent of a corpse); Negaim (the uncleanness described at Lev. 13-14); Parah (the preparation of purification-water); Tohorot (problems of doubt in connection with matters of cleanness); Miqvaot (immersion-pools); Niddah (menstrual uncleanness); Makhshirin (rendering susceptible to uncleanness produce that is dry and so not susceptible); Zabim (the uncleanness covered at Lev. 15); Tebul-Yom (the uncleanness of one who has immersed on that self-same day and awaits sunset for completion of the purification rites); Yadayim (the uncleanness of hands); Uqsin (the uncleanness transmitted through what is connected to unclean produce).

In volume, the sixth division covers approximately a quarter of the entire document. Topics of interest to the priesthood and the Temple, such as priestly fees, conduct of the cult on holy days, conduct of the cult on ordinary days and management and upkeep of the Temple, and the rules of cultic cleanness, predominate in the first, second, fifth, and sixth divisions. Rules governing the social order form the bulk of the third and fourth. Of these tractates, only Eduyyot is organized along other than topical lines, rather collecting sayings on diverse subjects attributed to particular authorities. The Mishnah as printed today always includes Abot (sayings of the sages), but that document reached closure about a generation later than the Mishnah. While it serves as its initial apologetic, it does not conform to the formal, rhetorical, or logical traits characteristic of the Mishnah overall.

MAIN POINTS OF STRESS IN THE MISHNAH: The stress of the Mishnah throughout on the priestly caste and the Temple cult point to the document's principal concern, which centered upon sanctification, understood as the correct arrangement of all things, each in its proper category, each called by its rightful name, just as at the creation as portrayed in the Priestly document, and just as with the cult itself as set forth in Leviticus. Further, the thousands of rules and cases (with sages' disputes thereon) that comprise the document upon close reading turn out to express in concrete language abstract principles of hierarchical classification. These define the document's method and mark it as a work of a philosophical character. Not only so, but a variety of specific, recurrent concerns, for example, the relationship of being to becoming, actual to potential, the principles of economics, the politics, correspond point by point to comparable ones in Graeco-Roman philosophy, particularly Aristotle's tradition. This stress on proper order and right rule and the formulation of a philosophy, politics, and economics, within the principles of natural history set forth by Aristotle, explain why the Mishnah makes a statement to be classified as philosophy, concerning the order of the natural world in its correspondence with the supernatural world.

THE MISHNAH'S PHILOSOPHY: METHOD AND PROPOSITIONS: The system of philosophy expressed through concrete and detailed law presented by the Mishnah, consists of a coherent logic and topic, a cogent worldview and comprehensive way of living. It is a worldview which speaks of transcendent things, a way of life in response to the supernatural meaning of what is done, a heightened and deepened perception of the sanctification of Israel in deed and in deliberation. Sanctification thus means two things, first, distinguishing Israel in all its dimensions from the world in all its ways; second, establishing the stability, order, regularity, predictability, and reliability of Israel in the world of nature and supernature in particular at moments and in contexts of danger. Danger means instability, disorder, irregularity, uncertainty, and betrayal. Each topic of the system as a whole takes up a critical and indispensable moment or context of social being. Through what is said in regard to each of the Mishnah's principal topics, what the system expressed through normative rules as a whole wishes to declare is fully expressed. Yet if the parts severally and jointly give the message of the whole, the whole cannot exist without all of the parts, so well joined and carefully crafted are they all. The details become clear in our survey of the document's topical program.

To understand the complete system set forth by the Mishnah, we review the six divisions as they were finally spelled out.

THE DIVISION OF AGRICULTURE treats two topics, first, producing crops in accord with the scriptural rules on the subject, second, paying the required offerings and tithes to the priests, Levites, and poor. The principal point of the Division is that the Land is holy, because God has a claim both on it and upon what it produces. God's claim must be honored by setting aside a portion of the produce for those for whom God has designated it. God's ownership must be acknowledged by observing the rules God has laid down for use of the Land. In the temporal context in which the Mishnah was produced, some generations after the disastrous defeat by the Romans of Bar Kokhba and the permanent closure of Jerusalem to Jews' access, the stress of the division brought assurance that those aspects of the sanctification of Israel — land of Israel, Israel itself and its social order, the holy cycle of time — that survived also remained holy and subject to the rules of Heaven.

THE DIVISION OF APPOINTED TIMES carried forward the same emphasis upon sanctification, now of the high points of the lunar-solar calendar of Israel. The second division forms a system in which the advent of a holy day, like the Sabbath of creation, sanctifies the life of the Israelite village through imposing on the village rules on the model of those of the Temple. The purpose of the system, therefore, is to bring into alignment the moment of sanctification of the village and the life of the home with the moment of sanctification of the Temple on those same occasions of appointed times. The underlying and generative logic of the system comes to expression in a concrete way here. We recall the rule of like and opposite, comparison and contrast. What is not like something follows the rule opposite to that pertaining to that something. Here, therefore, since the village is the mirror image of the Temple, the upshot is dictated by the analogical-contrastive logic of the system as a whole. If things are done in one way in the Temple, they will be done in the opposite way in the village. Together the village and the Temple on the occasion of the holy day therefore form a single continuum, a completed creation, thus awaiting sanctification. The village is made like the Temple in that on appointed times one may not freely cross the lines distinguishing the village from the rest of the world, just as one may not freely cross the lines distinguishing the Temple from the world. But the village is a mirror image of the Temple. The boundary lines prevent free entry into the Temple, so they restrict free egress from the village. On the holy day what one may do in the Temple is precisely what one may not do in the village.

So the advent of the holy day affects the village by bringing it into sacred symmetry in such wise as to effect a system of opposites; each is holy, in a way precisely the opposite of the other. Because of the underlying conception of perfection attained through the union of opposites, the village is not represented as conforming to the model of the cult, but of constituting its antithesis. The world thus regains perfection when on the holy day heaven and earth are united, the whole completed and done: the heaven, the earth, and all their hosts. This moment of perfection renders the events of ordinary time, of "history," essentially irrelevant. For what really matters in time is that moment in which sacred time intervenes and effects the perfection formed of the union of heaven and earth, of Temple, in the model of the former, and Israel, its complement. It is not a return to a perfect time but a recovery of perfect being, a fulfillment of creation, which explains the essentially ahistorical character of the Mishnah's Division on Appointed Times. Sanctification constitutes an ontological category and is effected by the creator.

This explains why the division in its rich detail is composed of two quite distinct sets of materials. First, it addresses what one does in the sacred space of the Temple on the occasion of sacred time, as distinct from what one does in that same sacred space on ordinary, undifferentiated days, which is a subject worked out in Holy Things. Second, the Division defines how for the occasion of the holy day one creates a corresponding space in one's own circumstance, and what one does, within that space, during sacred time. The division as a whole holds together through a shared, generative metaphor. It is the comparison, in the context of sacred time, of the spatial life of the Temple to the spatial life of the village, with activities and restrictions to be specified for each, upon the common occasion of the Sabbath or festival. The Mishnah's purpose therefore is to correlate the sanctity of the Temple, as defined by the holy day, with the restrictions of space and of action which make the life of the village different and holy, as defined by the holy day.

THE DIVISION OF WOMEN defines the women in the social economy of Israel's supernatural and natural reality. As we shall see in Chapter Three, women acquire definition wholly in relationship to men, who impart form to the Israelite social economy. The status of women is effected through both supernatural and natural, this-worldly action. Women formed a critical systemic component, because the proper regulation of women — subject to the father, then the husband — was deemed a central concern of Heaven, so that a betrothal would be subject to Heaven's supervision (Qiddushin, sanctification, being the pertinent tractate); documents, such as the marriage-contract or the writ of divorce, drawn up on earth, stand also for Heaven's concern with the sanctity of women in their marital relationship; so too, Heaven may through levirate marriage dictate whom a woman marries. What man and woman do on earth accordingly provokes a response in heaven, and the correspondences are perfect. So women are defined and secured both in heaven and here on earth, and that position is always and invariably relative to men.

The principal interest for the Mishnah is interstitial, just as, in general, sanctification comes into play at interstitial relationships, those that require decisive classification. Here it is the point at which a woman becomes, and ceases to be, holy to a particular man, that is, enters and leaves the marital union. These transfers of women are the dangerous and disorderly points in the relationship of woman to man, therefore, the Mishnah states, to society as well. The division's systemic statement stresses the preservation of order in transactions involving women and (other) property. Within this orderly world of documentary and procedural concerns a place is made for the disorderly conception of the marriage not formed by human volition but decreed in heaven, the levirate connection. Mishnah-tractate *Yebamot* states that supernature sanctifies a woman to a man (under the conditions of the levirate connection). What it says by indirection is that man sanctifies too: man, like God, can sanctify that relationship between a man and a woman, and can also effect the cessation of the sanctity of that same relationship.

Five of the seven tractates of the Division of Women are devoted to the formation and dissolution of the marital bond. Of them, three treat what is done by man here on earth, that is, formation of a marital bond through betrothal and marriage contract and dissolution through divorce and its consequences. The Division and its system therefore delineate the natural and supernatural character of the woman's role in the social economy framed by man: the beginning, end, and middle of the relationship. The whole constitutes a significant part of the Mishnah's encompassing system of sanctification, for the reason that heaven confirms what men do on earth. A correctly prepared writ of divorce on earth changes the status of the woman to whom it is given, so that in heaven she is available for sanctification to some other man, while, without that same writ, in heaven's view, should she go to some other man, she would be liable to be put to death. The earthly deed and the heavenly perspective correlate. That is indeed very much part of larger system, which says the same thing over and over again.

THE DIVISION OF DAMAGES comprises two subsystems, which fit together in a logical way. One part presents rules for the normal conduct of civil society. These cover commerce, trade, real estate, and other matters of everyday intercourse, as well as mishaps, such as damages by chattels and persons, fraud, overcharge, interest, and the like, in that same context of everyday social life. The other part describes the institutions governing the normal conduct of civil society, that is, courts of administration, and the penalties at the disposal of the government for the enforcement of the law. The two subjects form a single tight and systematic dissertation on the nature of Israelite society and its economic, social, and political relationships, as the Mishnah envisages them. The main point of the first of the two parts of the Division is that the task of society is to maintain perfect stasis, to preserve the prevailing situation, and to secure the stability of all relationships. To this end, in the interchanges of buying and selling, giving and taking, borrowing and lending, it is important that there be an essential equality of interchange. No party in the end should have more than what he had at the outset, and none should be the victim of a sizable shift in fortune and circumstance. All parties' rights to, and in, this stable and unchanging economy of society are to be preserved. When the condition of a person is violated, so far as possible the law will secure the restoration of the antecedent status.

The goal of the system of civil law is the recovery of the prevailing order and balance, the preservation of the established wholeness of the social economy. This idea is powerfully expressed in the organization of the three tractates that comprise the civil law, which treat first abnormal and then normal transactions. The framers deal with damages done by chattels and by human beings, thefts and other sorts of malfeasance against the property of others. The civil law in both aspects pays closest attention to how the property and person of the injured party so far as possible are restored to their prior condition, that is, a state of normality. So attention to torts focuses upon penalties paid by the malefactor to the victim, rather than upon penalties inflicted by the court on the malefactor for what he has done. When speaking of damages, the Mishnah thus takes as its principal concern the restoration of the fortune of victims of assault or robbery. Then the framers take up the complementary and corresponding set of topics, the regulation of normal transactions. When we rapidly survey the kinds of transactions of special interest, we see from the topics selected for discussion what we have already uncovered in the deepest structure of organization and articulation of the basic theme.

The other half of this same unit of three tractates presents laws governing normal and routine transactions, many of them of the same sort as those dealt with in the first half. At issue are deposits of goods or possessions that one person leaves in safe-keeping with another. Called bailments, for example, cases of such transactions occur in both wings of the triple tractate, first, bailments subjected to misappropriation, or accusation thereof, by the bailiff, then, bailments transacted under normal circumstances. Under the rubric of routine transactions are those of workers and householders, that is, the purchase and sale of labor; rentals and bailments; real estate transactions; and inheritances and estates. Of the lot, the one involving real estate transactions is the most fully articulated and covers the widest range of problems and topics. The three tractates of the civil law all together thus provide a complete account of the orderly governance of balanced transactions and unchanging civil relationships within Israelite society under ordinary conditions.

The character and interests of the Division of Damages present probative evidence of the larger program of the philosophers of the Mishnah. Their intention is to create nothing less than a full-scale Israelite government, subject to the administration of sages. This government is fully supplied with a constitution and bylaws. It makes provision for a court system and procedures, as well as a full set of laws governing civil society and criminal justice. This government, moreover, mediates between its own community and the outside ("pagan") world. Through its system of laws it expresses its judgment of the others and at the same time defines, protects, and defends its own society and social frontiers. It even makes provision for procedures of remission, to expiate its own errors. The (then non-existent) Israelite government imagined by the second-century philosophers centers upon the (then non-existent) Temple, and the (then forbidden) city, Jerusalem. For the Temple is one principal focus. There the highest court is in session; there the high priest reigns.

The penalties for law infringement are of three kinds, one of which involves sacrifice in the Temple. (The others are compensation, physical punishment, and death.) The basic conception of punishment, moreover, is that unintentional infringement of the rules of society, whether "religious" or otherwise, is not penalized but rather expiated through an offering in the Temple. If a member of the people of Israel intentionally infringes against the law, to be sure, that one must be removed from society and is put to death. And if there is a claim of one member of the people against another, that must be righted, so that the prior, prevailing status may be restored. So offerings in the Temple are given up to appease heaven and restore a whole bond between heaven and Israel, specifically on those occasions on which without malice or ill will an Israelite has disturbed the relationship. Israelite civil society without a Temple is not stable or normal, and not to be imagined. And the Mishnah is above all an act of imagination in defiance of reality.

The plan for the government involves a clear-cut philosophy of society, a philosophy that defines the purpose of the government and ensures that its task is not merely to perpetuate its own power. What the Israelite government, within the Mishnaic fantasy, is supposed to do is to preserve a perfect, steady-state society. That state of perfection which, within the same fantasy, the society to begin with everywhere attains and expresses forms the goal of the system throughout: no change anywhere from a perfect balance, proportion, and arrangement of the social order, its goods and services, responsibilities and benefits. This is in at least five aspects:

First of all, one of the ongoing principles of the law, expressed in one tractate after another, is that people are to follow and maintain the prevailing practice of their locale.

Second, the purpose of civil penalties is to restore the injured party to his prior condition, so far as this is possible, rather than merely to penalize the aggressor.

Third, there is the conception of true value, meaning that a given object has an intrinsic worth, which, in the course of a transaction, must be paid. In this way the seller does not leave the transaction any richer than when he entered it, or the buyer any poorer (parallel to penalties for damages).

Fourth, there can be no usury, a biblical prohibition adopted and vastly enriched in the Mishnaic thought, for money ("coins") is what it is. Any pretense that it has become more than what it was violates, in its way, the conception of true value.

Fifth, when real estate is divided, it must be done with full attention to the rights of all concerned, so that, once more, one party does not gain at the expense of the other.

In these and many other aspects the law expresses its obsession with the perfect stasis of Israelite society. Its paramount purpose is in preserving and ensuring that that perfection of the division of this world is kept inviolate or restored to its true status when violated.

THE DIVISION OF HOLY THINGS presents a system of sacrifice and sanctuary. The division centers upon the everyday and rules always applicable to the cult: the daily whole offering, the sin offering and guilt-offering which one may bring any time under ordinary circumstances; the right sequence of diverse offerings; the way in which the rites of the whole-, sin-, and guilt-offerings are carried out; what sorts of animals are acceptable; the accompanying cereal offerings; the support and provision of animals for the cult and of meat for the priesthood; the support and material maintenance of the cult and its building. We have a system before us: the system of the cult of the Jerusalem Temple, seen as an ordinary and everyday affair, a continuing and routine operation. That is why special rules for the cult, both in respect to the altar and in regard to the maintenance of the buildings, personnel, and even the whole city, will be elsewhere — in Appointed Times and Agriculture. But from the perspective of Holy Things, those divisions intersect by supplying special rules and raising extraordinary (Agriculture: land-bound; Appointed Times: time-bound) considerations for that theme which Holy Things claims to set forth in its most general and unexceptional way: the cult as something permanent and everyday.

THE DIVISION OF PURITIES presents a very simple system of three principal parts: sources of uncleanness, objects and substances susceptible to uncleanness, and modes of purification from uncleanness. So it tells the story of what makes a given sort of object unclean and what makes it clean. Viewed as a whole, the Division of Purities treats the interplay of persons, food, and liquids. Dry inanimate objects or food are not susceptible to uncleanness. What is wet is susceptible. So liquids activate the system. What is unclean, moreover, emerges from uncleanness through the operation of liquids, specifically, through immersion in fit water of requisite volume and in natural condition. Liquids thus deactivate the system. Thus, water in its natural condition is what concludes the process by removing uncleanness. Water in its unnatural condition, that is, deliberately affected by human agency, is what imparts susceptibility to uncleanness to begin with. The uncleanness of persons, furthermore, is signified by body liquids or flux in the case of the menstruating woman and the *zab* (the person suffering from the form of uncleanness described at Lev. 15:1ff.). Corpse uncleanness is conceived to be a kind of effluent, a viscous gas, which flows like liquid. Utensils for their part receive uncleanness when they form receptacles able to contain liquid.

In sum, we have a system in which the invisible flow of fluid-like substances or powers serve to put food, drink, and receptacles into the status of uncleanness and to remove those things from that status. Whether or not we call the system "metaphysical," it certainly has no material base but is conditioned upon highly abstract notions. Thus in material terms, the effect of liquid is upon food, drink, utensils, and man. The consequence has to do with who may eat and drink what food and liquid, and what food and drink may be consumed in which pots and pans. These loci are specified by tractates on utensils and on food and drink.

The human being is ambivalent. Persons fall in the middle, between sources and loci of uncleanness, because they are both. They serve as sources of uncleanness. They also become unclean. The *zab*, suffering the uncleanness described in Leviticus Chapter 15, the menstruating woman, the woman after childbirth, and the person afflicted with the skin ailment described in Leviticus Chapters 13 and 14 — all are sources of uncleanness. But being unclean, they fall within the system's loci, its program of consequences. So they make other things unclean and are subject to penalties because they are unclean. Unambiguous sources of uncleanness never also constitute loci affected by uncleanness. They always are unclean and never can become clean: the corpse, the dead creeping thing, and things like them. Inanimate sources of uncleanness and inanimate objects convey uncleanness ex opere operato; their status of being unclean never changes; they present no ambiguity. Systemically unique, man and liquids have the capacity to inaugurate the processes of uncleanness (as sources) and also are subject to those same processes (as objects of uncleanness).

OMITTED DIVISIONS: When we listen to the silences of the system of the Mishnah, as much as to its points of stress, we hear a single message. It is a message of a system that answered a single encompassing question, and the question formed a stunning counterpart to that of the sixth century B.C.E. The Pentateuchal system addressed one reading of the events of the sixth century, highlighted by the destruction of the Jerusalem Temple in 586 B.C.E. At stake was how Israel as defined by that system related to its land, represented by its Temple, and the message may be simply stated: what appears to be the given is in fact a gift, subject to stipulations. The precipitating event for the Mishnaic system was the destruction of the Jerusalem Temple in 70 C.E., the question turned obsession with the defeat of Bar Kokhba and the closure of Jerusalem to Jews. The urgent issue taken up by the Mishnah was, specifically, what, in the aftermath of the destruction of the holy place and holy cult, remained of the sanctity of the holy caste, the priesthood, the holy land, and, above all, the holy people and its holy way of life? The answer was that sanctity persists, indelibly, in Israel, the people, in its way of life, in its land, in its priesthood, in its food, in its mode of sustaining life, in its manner of procreating and so sustaining the nation.

The Mishnah's system therefore focused upon the holiness of the life of Israel, the people, a holiness that had formerly centered on the Temple. The logically consequent question was, what is the meaning of sanctity, and how shall Israel attain, or give evidence of, sanctification. The answer to the question derived from the original creation, the end of the Temple directing attention to the beginning of the natural world that the Temple had embodied. For the meaning of sanctity the framers therefore turned to that first act of sanctification, the one in creation,. It came about when, all things in array, in place, each with its proper names, God blessed and sanctified the seventh day on the eve of the first Sabbath. Creation was made ready for the blessing and the sanctification when all things were very good, that is to say, in their rightful order, called by their rightful name. An orderly nature was a sanctified and blessed nature, so dictated Scripture in the name of the Supernatural. So to receive the blessing and to be made holy, all things in nature and society were to be set in right array. Given the condition of Israel, the people, in its land, in the aftermath of the catastrophic war against Rome led by Bar Kokhba in 132-135, putting things in order was no easy task. But that is why, after all, the question pressed, the answer proving inexorable and obvious. The condition of society corresponded to the critical question that obsessed the system-builders.

## III. Why It Matters

Defining documents through a fresh form-analytical exegesis of their contents clearly requires a massive, detailed rereading of the entire canon. Why does defining documents matter? It shows that each document represents a coherent and purposive statement and speaks for itself. That forms the documents into distinct building blocks, each in its place in sequence.

What I did first was to show the particularity of the Mishnah, distinct from the Tosefta, and I proceeded then — in the 1980s through the mid-1990s — to broaden the range of analysis and identify the unique or at least distinctive character of each document or group of documents. That yielded the conclusion that documents represented coherent systems and made cogent statements, and their contents attested to the convictions of those responsible for their respective programs. First, the Mishnah emerged as a systematic statement, a coherent construction that said the same thing about many things. Then work on the subsequent compilations yielded coherent accounts of matters, not mere collections of episodic data. The upshot was not only a fresh approach to the exegesis of the documents, Halakhic and Aggadic alike, but a different approach to the historical problem, one that did not rely on attributions for the ordering of data. This came to fruition in *Transformation of Judaism. From Philosophy to Religion.*

Once I was able to characterize the documents one by one, I could follow the unfolding of the Rabbinic system by following the assumed, but occasionally demonstrable, sequence of documentary treatments of a given conception, thus recovering the documentary history of ideas. The approach via documents, their systems and contexts, provided a mode of relating writing to religion through history through close attention to the circumstance in which writing reached closure. It has been accomplished, specifically, by assessing shifts exhibited by a sequence of documents and appealing to the generally accepted dates — for instance, 200 for the Mishnah, 600 for the Talmud of Babylonia — assigned to writings in explaining those shifts. In this way I propose to confront questions of the cultural order, social system and political structure, to which the texts respond explicitly and constantly.

If we are to trace the unfolding, in the sources of formative Judaism, of a given theme or ideas on a given problem, the order in which we approach the several books, that is, components of the entire canon, gives us the sole guidance on sequence, order, and context, that we are apt to find. As is clear, we have no way of demonstrating that the authorities to whom, in a given composition, ideas are attributed really said what is assigned to them. The sole fact in hand therefore is that the framers of a given document included in their compilation sayings imputed to named authorities. Are these dependable? Unlikely on the face of it. Why not? Since the same sayings will be imputed to diverse authorities by different groups of editors, of different books, we stand on shaky ground indeed if we rely for chronology upon the framers' claims of who said what. More important, attributions by themselves cannot be shown to be reliable. And, it goes without saying, assuming without corroboration that we have *ipsissima verba* merely because a saying is attached to a name simply contradicts the basic premises of all contemporary historical scholarship.

We return to the critical point: *What we cannot show we do not know.*[4] Lacking firm evidence in a sage's own, clearly assigned writings, or even in writings redacted by a sage's own disciples and handed on among them in the discipline of their own community, we have for chronology only a single fact. It is that a document, reaching closure at a given time, contains the allegation that Rabbi X said statement Y. So we know that people *at the time the document reached closure* took the view that Rabbi X said statement Y. Rabbi X can have made that statement in his own place and time; what we cannot show we do not know. But we build on the firm foundation of fact: what we know for sure, that irreducible fact supplied by the document itself, its particular rhetoric, logic of coherent discourse, and topical (sometimes: propositional) program.

The consequence is simple. We may then assign to statement Y a position, in the order of the sequence of sayings, defined by the location of the document in the order of the sequence of documents. The several documents' dates, as is clear, all constitute guesses. But the sequence explained in the prologue, Mishnah, Tosefta, Yerushalmi, Bavli for the exegetical writings on the Mishnah is absolutely firm and beyond doubt. The sequence for the exegetical collections on Scripture Sifra, the Sifrés, Mekhilta Attributed to R. Ishmael, Genesis Rabbah, Leviticus Rabbah, the Pesiqtas and beyond is not entirely sure. Still the position of the Sifra and the two Sifrés at the head, followed by Genesis Rabbah, then Leviticus Rabbah, then Pesiqta deR. Kahana and Lamentations Rabbati and some related collections, seems likely.

What are the canonical main-beams that sustain the history of ideas as I propose to trace that history?

Three principal periods presently delineate the canonical sequence, the Mishnah's, in the first two centuries; the Yerushalmi's, in the next, ca. 200-400; and the Bavli's, in the third, ca. 400-600. The formative age of Judaism is the period marked at the outset by the Mishnah, taking shape from sometime before the Common Era and reaching closure at ca. 200 C.E., and at the end by the Talmud of Babylonia, ca. 600 C.E. In between these dates, two streams of writings developed, one legal, explaining the meaning of the Mishnah, the other theological and exegetical, interpreting the sense of Scripture. The high points of the former come with tractate Abot which is the Mishnah's first apologetic, the Tosefta, a collection of supplements ca. 300 C.E., the Talmud of the Land of Israel ca. 400 C.E., followed by the Babylonian Talmud. The latter set of writings comprise compositions on Exodus, in Mekilta attributed to R. Ishmael and of indeterminate date, Sifra on Leviticus, Sifre on Numbers, and another Sifre, on Deuteronomy at a guess to be dated at ca. 300 C.E., then Genesis Rabbah ca. 400 C.E., Leviticus Rabbah ca. 425 C.E., and at the end, Pesiqta de Rab Kahana, Lamentations Rabbati, and some other treatments of biblical books, all of them in the fifth or sixth centuries. The so-called Tannaitic Midrashim, Mekhilta, Sifra, the two Sifrés, form transitional documents, between the Mishnah and the Yerushalmi and its Midrash-companions, Genesis Rabbah, Leviticus Rabbah, and Pesiqta deRab Kahana. Alongside the Bavli are its Midrash-associates, Lamentations Rabbah, Song of Songs Rabbah, Esther Rabbah I, and Ruth Rabbah. These books and some minor related items together form the canon of Judaism as it had reached its definitive shape by the end of late antiquity.

If we lay out these writings in the approximate sequence in which — according to the prevailing consensus — they reached closure beginning with the Mishnah, the Tosefta, then Sifra and its associated compositions, followed by the Talmud of the Land of Israel, and alongside Genesis Rabbah and Leviticus Rabbah, then Pesiqta de Rab Kahana and its companions, and finally the Talmud of Babylonia, we gain what I have called "documentary history." This is, specifically, the order of the appearance of ideas when the documents, read in the outlined sequence, address a given idea or topic. The consequent history consists of the sequence in which a given statement on the topic at hand was made (early, middle, or late) in the unfolding of the canonical writings.

To illustrate the process: what does the authorship of the Mishnah have to say on the theme? Then how does the compositor of Abot deal with it? Then the Tosefta's compositor's record comes into view, followed by the materials assembled in the Talmud of the Land of Israel, alongside those now found in the earlier and middle ranges of compilations of scriptural exegeses, and as always, the Talmud of Babylonia at the end. The results, for the history of ideas, of the documentary method are set forth in various monographs of mine, and now are fully put together into a single account as well.[5]

The program represents a minimalist claim of historical knowledge. I do not maintain that the documents represent the state of popular or synagogue opinion. I do not know whether the history of the idea in the unfolding official texts corresponds to the history of the idea among the people who stand behind those documents. Even less do I claim to speak about the history of the topic or idea at hand outside of Rabbinic circles, among the Jewish nation at large. The reason is that the evidence at hand is of a particular sort and hence permits us to investigate one category of questions and not another. The category is defined by established and universally held conventions about the order in which the canonical writings reached completion. Therefore we trace the way in which matters emerge in the sequence of writings.

We trace the way in which ideas were taken up and spelled out in these successive stages in the formation of the canon. Let the purpose of the exercise be emphasized.

*When we follow this procedure, we discover how, within the formation of the Rabbinic canon of writings, the idea at hand came to literary expression and how it was then shaped to serve the larger purposes of the nascent canonical system as a whole.*

That exercise then defines the first task in trying to understand the relationship between the history of the ideas of a Judaism — a Judaic religious system, represented by a cogent canon and its community — and the social history of that same Judaism in late antiquity. By knowing the place and uses of the topic under study within the literary evidences of the Rabbinic system, we gain a better understanding of the formative history of that system. What do we not learn? Neither the condition of the people at large nor the full range and power of the Rabbinic thinkers' imagination comes to the fore. About other larger historical and intellectual matters we have no direct knowledge at all. Consequently we claim to report only what we learn about the canonical literature of a system evidenced by a limited factual base. No one who wants to know the history of a given idea in all the diverse Judaisms of late antiquity, or the role of that idea in the history of all the Jews in all parts of the world in the first seven centuries of the Common Era will find it here.

In order to understand the documentary method and its promise for social and intellectual history we must again underline the social and political character of the documentary evidence that is presented. These are public statements, preserved and handed on because people have adopted them as authoritative. The sources constitute a collective, and therefore official, literature. All of the documents took shape and attained a place in the canon of the Rabbinic movement as a whole. None was written by an individual in such a way as to testify to personal choice or decision. Accordingly, we cannot provide an account of the theory of a given individual at a particular time and place. We have numerous references to what a given individual said about the topic at hand. But these references do not reach us in the authorship of that person, or even in his language. They come to us only in the setting of a *collection* of sayings and statements, some associated with names, other unattributed and anonymous. The collections by definition were composed under the auspices of Rabbinic authority — a school or a circle. They tell us what a group of people wished to preserve and hand on as authoritative doctrine about the meaning of the Mishnah and Scripture. The compositions reach us because the larger Rabbinic estate chose to copy and hand them on. Accordingly, we know the state of doctrine at the stages marked by the formation and closure of the several documents.

This protracted account carries us to the documentary history of ideas, which got under way in the later 1980s and accomplished its goals in about a decade. In that approach we follow what references we find to a topic in accord with the order of documents just now spelled out. In this sort of study we learn the order in which ideas came to expression in the canon. We begin any survey with the Mishnah, the starting point of the canon. We proceed systematically to work our way through tractate Abot, the Mishnah's first apologetic, then the Tosefta, the Yerushalmi, and the Bavli at the end. In a single encompassing sweep, we finally deal with the entirety of the compilations of the exegeses of Scripture, arranged, to be sure, in that order that I have now explained. The reason for that stress is simple. We have to ask not only what documents viewed whole and all at once ("Judaism") tell us about our theme. In tracing the order in which ideas make their appearance, we ask about the components in sequence ("history of Judaism") so far as we can trace the sequence. Then and only then shall we have access to issues of *history*, that is, of change and development. If our theme makes its appearance early on in one form, so one set of ideas predominate in a document that reached closure in the beginnings of the cannon and then that theme drops out of public discourse or undergoes radical revision in writings in later stages of the canon, that fact may make considerable difference. Specifically, we may find it possible to speculate on where, and why a given approach proved urgent, and also on the reasons that that same approach receded from the center of interest.

In knowing the approximate sequence of documents and therefore the ideas in them (at least so far as the final point at which those ideas reached formal expression in the canon), a second possibility emerges. What if — as is the case — we find pretty much the same views, treated in the same proportion and for the same purpose, yielding the same message, early, middle, and late in the development of the canon? Then we shall have to ask why the literature remains so remarkably constant. Given the considerable shifts in the social and political condition of Israel in the land of Israel as well as in Babylonia over a period of more than four hundred years, that evident stability in the teachings for the affective life will constitute a considerable fact for analysis and interpretation. History, including the history of religion, done rightly thus produces two possibilities, both of them demanding sustained attention. Things change. Why? Things do not change. Why not? We may well trace the relationship between the history of ideas and the history of the society that holds those same ideas. We follow the interplay between society and system — world view, way of life, addressed to a particular social group — by developing a theory of the relationship between contents and context, between the world in which people live and the world which people create in their shared social and imaginative life. When we can frame a theory of how a system in substance relates to its setting, of the interplay between the social matrix and the mode and manner of a society's world-view and way of life, then we may develop theses of general intelligibility, theories of why this, not that, of why, and why no and how come.

The story of continuity and change rests upon the notion that we can present the history of the treatment of a topical program in the canonical writings of that Judaism. I repeat: *I certainly do not claim that the documents represent the state of popular or synagogue opinion.* I do not know whether the history of the idea in the unfolding official texts corresponds to the history of the idea among the people who stand behind those documents. Even less do I claim to speak about the history of the topic or idea at hand outside of Rabbinic circles, among the Jewish nation at large. All these larger dimensions of the matter lie wholly beyond the perspective of research to date. The reason is that the evidence at hand is of a particular sort and hence permits us to investigate one category of questions and not another. The category is defined by established and universally held conventions about the order in which the canonical writings reached completion.

Therefore we trace the way in which matters emerge in the sequence of writings. We trace the way in which ideas were taken up and spelled out in these successive stages in the formation of the canon. When we follow this procedure, we discover how, within the formation of the Rabbinic canon of writings, the idea at hand came to literary expression and how it was then shaped to serve the larger purposes of the nascent canonical system as a whole — a different approach to the study of the history of Rabbinic Judaism in the formative age, but one that has produced interesting results. Throughout at issue is a single problem, the interplay between the ideas that people hold and the social world in which they live, or, as in the present case, in which they imagine that they live.

## ENDNOTES

[1] Variant textual traditions do not affect the definitive logic of coherent discourse, topical program, and rhetoric of a given document but confirm them. The manuscript traditions of the Mishnah, for example, and of the Tosefta set forth diverse readings of clauses, sentences, and paragraphs, but do not call into question the governing traits of those documents overall.

[2]The other introductions to Rabbinic literature, besides my *Introduction to Rabbinic Literature*. N.Y., 1994: Doubleday. The Doubleday Anchor Reference Library, do not address the matters of rhetoric, logic, and topic. For further reading and bibliography on the form-analysis of Rabbinic literature, see my *A History of the Mishnaic Law of Purities*. Leiden, 1977: Brill. XXI. *The Redaction and Formulation of the Order of Purities in the Mishnah and Tosefta.* That is where I lay out the basic definitions and inquiries pursued throughout. The explanation of the necessity of form-analytical translation is given in *Translating the Classics of Judaism. In Theory and in Practice*. Atlanta, 1989: Scholars Press for Brown Judaic Studies.

[3] See *Form Analysis and Exegesis: A Fresh Approach to the Interpretation of Mishnah.* Minneapolis, 1980: University of Minnesota Press for a more elaborate presentation of the same approach to the exegesis of the Mishnah and the Tosefta, not to mention the History of Mishnaic Law, where the work is gone for the second through sixth divisions of the Mishnah.

[4] See *What We Cannot Show, We Do Not Know: Rabbinic Literature and the New Testament.* Philadelphia, 1993: Trinity Press International, and *Judaic Law from Jesus to the Mishnah. A Systematic Reply to Professor E. P. Sanders.* Atlanta, 1993: Scholars Press for South Florida Studies in the History of Judaism.

[5] Two such monographs are *Judaism and its Social Metaphors. Israel in the History of Jewish Thought.* and *The Incarnation of God: The Character of Divinity in Formative Judaism,* cited above. My summaries of the documents as a whole and the history of Judaism are in my *Introduction to Rabbinic Literature* (N.Y., 1994), *Rabbinic Judaism. The Documentary History of the Formative Age.* Bethesda, 1994: CDL Press and *Rabbinic*

*Judaism. Structure and System.* Minneapolis, 1996: Fortress Press. I mean the latter two items to answer the same question as does Moore's *Judaism,* Urbach's *The Sages,* Sanders's *Paul and Palestinian Judaism* and his *Judaism. 63 B.C.E. E.-67 C.E.,* respectively.

# 5

# Extra- and Non-Documentary Writing in the Rabbinic Canon of Late Antiquity

## I. Defining Terms

The Rabbinic compilations in the canon of Rabbinic Judaism, from the Mishnah through the Bavli, ca. 200-600 C.E., are comprised by two classifications of writing, [1] documentary (which I have defined at length) and [2] extra- (including non-) documentary. Documentary writing conforms to a protocol paramount in, and particular to, a given text, extra-documentary writing ignores the distinctive preferences of that same text. It may match the protocol of some other document than the one in which it appears, in which case it is classified as extra-documentary.[1] Or it may correspond to no documentary protocol in the extant canon, which I call "non-documentary."

To spell this out: A subset of extra-documentary writing is formed by non-documentary writing. That is writing of a sort that not only does not fit into the protocol of the document in which it occurs, but that does not conform to the protocol of any other extant canonical document of Rabbinic Judaism (or indeed, of any other document of any late antique Judaism).[2] Non-documentary writing can show us how Rabbinic sages committed thought to permanent form for transmission and preservation in other than the extant (or comparable) canonical compilations. At stake is whether non-documentary writing conveys a system or program distinct from documentary writing. Does it afford access to thought or attitudes otherwise inaccessible to us in the canonical compilations. In other words, in the extra-documentary compositions do we possess a window into a Judaism beyond the texts that conform to the documentary protocols of the canon?

Why does the answer matter? The issue arises out of a contemporary debate on how we know about Rabbinic Judaism in its formative age: the sources and their implications. Many claim to know *a priori* data about Judaism, or about Rabbinic Judaism, that the sources do not transmit to us. They make allegations as to the beliefs and character of that Judaism, or of "Judaism in general," for which no sources account. Here is an occasion to ask for evidence within the framework of the texts that constitute all of our evidence of Rabbinic Judaism. Specifically, do anomalous or asymmetric compositions or composites attest to thought that takes place beyond the limits of the documents subject to the rules and symmetry of the canon? Here I set forth the results of a systematic analysis of the asymmetrical writing preserved in canonical documents with a view to describing the extra- and non-documentary texts that have survived in them.[3]

By "texts without boundaries," then, I mean, writing that ignores the protocols of the document(s) in which it is preserved. But as I said, in that body of evidence what concerns me in particular is extra- and especially non-documentary writing, which attests to a corpus of thought beyond the canonical limits of the Rabbinic corpus, Mishnah through Bavli. At issue is whether non-documentary writing exhibits readily-discernible patterns of form and meaning as does documentary writing. If so, what are these patterns and how are we to classify and to interpret them? And finally, what, if anything, do we learn, from the two classifications of writing, that which is characteristic of the canonical compilations and that which ignores all of the paramount protocols, about the processes at work in Rabbinic Judaism?

Since by these processes otherwise-idiosyncratic opinion or thought can have been, and manifestly was, recorded, preserved, and compiled in public documents that make up the formative canon, the ultimate issue concerns itself with the formative history of Rabbinic Judaism. From form-analysis of literature, we move to history and thence to religion. Thus the question answered in this project: What evidence, exactly, do the documents yield about the realm of thought and sensibility beyond the boundaries of their authors and compilers of the canonical documents?

At this time we do not know whether there are formal differences between the two classifications of writing, the documentary and the non-documentary, and, if there are, what they are. We also do not know, even as a matter of hypothesis, whether the distinction in types of writing makes any difference in our understanding of the formation of the writing of the distinct types and of the documents that accommodate them both. I cannot say what were the rules that governed writing things down in permanent form for each of the two purposes that pertained, the preservation of opinion on its own, the formation of opinion for preservation in large conglomerates, each with its distinctive features of logic, rhetoric, and topic.

## II. What Is at Stake?

What is at stake is, first, understanding the processes of formulating, out of a mass of opinion and tradition, the religious system and structure, that is constituted as a Judaism, the Rabbinic Judaism. It is, second, characterizing the processes that yielded the formalization and preservation of that Judaism in books bearing corporate consensus such as now constitute the sole source of that system. Stated simply: Rabbinic Judaism makes its entire statement in the medium of writing, encompassing Scripture as mediated by the canonical books from the Mishnah through the Bavli. How, precisely, did that massive corpus take shape in the realization, for all time, of the Torah as contemplated by the Rabbinic sages? The history of the formation of Judaism is embodied in the story of the writing down of rules and opinions.

The upshot is, in Rabbinic Judaism, history, literature, and religion can be differentiated but never wholly separated. The history is the process, the literature is the documents at hand, and the religion is the statement that they make. The documents come at the end of a process that yielded the concretization of Rabbinic Judaism, which made its normative statement in writing compiled in large aggregates of a particular order. The study begins with literature, proceeds to history (of ideas) and comes to its fulfillment in religion, its system and structure in its particular aesthetic and social contexts. From my *History of the Mishnaic Law*,[4] I have asked literary and form-analytical study to yield the history of the ideas of the religion, Judaism, which deems those documents authoritative and representative. Here, it follows, I continue that same inquiry. Working backward, from the end-product to the prior formations thereof, I hope to discern steps in that process.

At this time we are at an elementary stage in tracing the pre-documentary processes and stages. All we can do with certainty is what I do here: distinguish types of processes, but not their ordinal, temporal stages. We cannot define the rules that guided the process that moved thought from its initial stages in the mind of a particular authority or corporate consensus to the final formulation of the outcome. I mean, the steps from [1] opinion on a given topic to [2] formalization of opinion in fixed wording to [3] preservation of opinions on a topic commonly accepted as constitutive and consequential, said opinions deriving from a number of sources to [4] conglomeration of diverse opinions within a single authoritative statement on a topic that all concur matters. That logically such a sequence of steps makes sense does not obscure dismal reality: we have no clue on how matters actually unfolded. We have not got models of such a process of homogenization, e.g., within another Judaism besides the Rabbinic one. To be sure, the history of the formation of Christianity as orthodox and catholic, or as Gnostic, has been definitively recovered, and we can say how individual opinion was taken over and homogenized in Church councils and creeds. But the Rabbinic documents vastly differ from the Christian counterparts of the same age, and the history of Christianity supplies only suggestive analogies, that is, perspective, not parallels.

But some progress registers. Now we do have a fairly comprehensive picture of the final stages in the process: what people had to do to turn publicly accepted thought into a formally correct composition for preservation. But — to approach the problem at hand — that picture of matters serves only so far as writing destined for the respective documents was concerned. As to the classification of Rabbinic writing under study here, texts without boundaries, we do not know the corresponding patterns that indicate a governing protocol for writing not destined for determinate documents. That is what this project will help us to understand that we do not now know.

## III. Where Do We Stand?

In line with the process just now outlined, we possess half of the facts that we need to frame a theory on the story behind our documents, viewed whole and complete. That is, protocols of documentary writing that govern in one document but in no other by definition permit us to identify writing undertaken for one documentary purpose and no other. Unique congeries of these three indicators join together to differentiate one canonical document from some other and indeed from all others. Some compilations, e.g., the Rabbah-Midrash-compilations or the Mishnah and the Tosefta, may share rhetorical traits. All compilations select from a severely-limited repertoire of logics of coherent discourse. Some few go over a common topic, e.g., the exposition of the same biblical book, Leviticus, by Sifra and Leviticus Rabbah. But these are differentiated by rhetoric and logic of coherent discourse. To be sure, all of the Aggadic and Halakhic ones participate in a single theological structure and system, such as I have designed in *Theology of the Oral Torah*[5] and *Theology of the Halakhah*.[6] But in all cases, the combination of the three classes of indicative traits exhibited by a given document is unique to that document. Given a piece of writing that conforms to the protocol of a given document, we should have little difficulty in identifying its source.

But — as this project makes clear — that characterization of documentary coherence in writing is not true of the entirety of the several compilations, only (by definition) of those components that conform to the determinate documentary protocol. These predominate in proportion and permit us to differentiate one document from all others, as I just said. The extra- and non-documentary writing, present everywhere as well, for its part may occupy a small proportion of the compilation, as in the Mishnah and Sifra. We have yet to come across a document, the greater part of which ignores what the component that adheres to the documentary protocol and defines it — but that is by definition. But the upshot is: the presence of both documentary- and extra- and non-documentary writing in the canonical books analyzed within the present program constitutes an established fact.

Now, while we have a systematic account of the types and forms of documentary writing in the entire formative canon, no prior effort to my knowledge has gone into the systematic description of the traits of other-than-documentary writing in those same compilations, severally, then jointly. So that is why I ask, how, if at all, are we to characterize the corpus of Rabbinic extra- and non-documentary writing, first within the framework of the document in which it occurs, then viewed all together as a large corpus of writing outside documentary bounds? Are we able to discern patterns of language and formulation — rhetoric, logic, topic — that prove distinctive to writing of this other classification of composition now situated in compilations with their well-exposed documentary preferences of expression?

Situating the current, rather sizable project within my larger oeuvre therefore presents no puzzle. Beyond my form-analytical translation of, and academic commentary on, the entire formative canon, this is the logical next step, building as it does on results already in hand. I have already spelled out the initial, theoretical foundations of the work. In *The Three Questions of Formative Judaism: History, Literature, and Religion*, Chapter Three, "The Question of Literature," I found these particular, still-fundamental, questions awaiting attention. That is why I chose the present project to follow upon *The Three Questions*. I hope and plan to move forward, from this project, to engage with questions of the history of Rabbinic Judaism that inquiry into the history of its formulation permits me to raise.

The collateral implications — those that pertain the exegesis of the canonical documents of late antiquity — strike me as formidable. Form-analysis has redefined the framework within which exegesis of words and phrases takes place, insisting that the context defined by the formal limits of a composition govern. But out-of-context exegesis of free-standing sentences, even discrete phrases, continues to predominate — indeed, work on words and phrases in preference to sense-units made up of sets of sentences and paragraphs. At this time, much exegetical work that takes up free-standing sentences deals with their hypothetical meaning out of all literary context. Entire theoretical histories of the wording and meaning of such sentences, even complete compositions, are fabricated. A theory of how the literature took shape, such as is required to sustain the prevailing style of exegesis, will place the enterprise on a firmer foundation — or redefine the exegetical possibilities entirely. But I have never worked on exegetical problems and do not now propose to invent the New Exegesis.

## IV. Distinguishing Documentary from Extra- and Non-Documentary Writing: The Starting Point

Documentary writing is defined for each Rabbinic document, respectively, by a combination of indicative traits that, all together, are unique to that document. These traits represent choices as to [1] form or rhetoric, [2] topic or problem or proposition, and [3] logic of coherent discourse and analysis (terms explained presently). In each document the bulk of the compositions and composites conform to the governing protocol, tiny numbers and negligible proportions of the compositions do not. These paltry representations of writing that ignores the documentary protocol fall into two divisions, extra- and non-documentary. The extra-documentary type of writing simply ignores the indicative documentary traits of the document in which it occurs but coheres to the traits of some other document, extant or readily conceived within the Rabbinic canon. Non-documentary writing ignores the protocols that define any and all Rabbinic canonical compilations. It thereby crosses the boundaries that separate one text document another, indeed a given canonical compilation from all others.

I collect and characterize those compositions and composites[7] that [1] come to us within the well-crafted canonical documents of Rabbinic Judaism but that [2] do not respond to the documentary boundaries that characterize those compilations. They ignore one or another of the components of the documentary protocol(s). These are defined by the particular congeries of rhetoric, topic, and logic, such as otherwise prevail. Once we establish the regularities characteristic of the rhetoric, topic, and logic of a given compilation, we confidently define the protocol that governs writing for that document — and thereby, also, the extra-documentary writing contained therein.

This is not an exercise in taste and judgment, only in sifting large volumes of data. In fact each of the canonical documents sets forth its own protocol in its own way, generating what fits, clearly indicating what does not. They thereby indicate writing that is not particular to that document. Once we identify documentary writing, therefore, in the same act we willy-nilly recognize the extra- and also the non-documentary sort. As is clear, what is extra-documentary does not belong to the document in which it occurs, but can fit well into a document the like of which we do possess in the extant canon. We have models of commentaries, supplied, e.g., by Sifra and Leviticus Rabbah for Leviticus. When in Sifra or Leviticus Rabbah we come across a snippet of a systematic commentary to Proverbs or Qohelet, we can readily imagine the realization of a commentary to those books of Scripture in the model of available counterparts. But some writing not only does not cohere to the protocol of the document in which it occurs, it also points to a type of compilation that the canon does not possess, e.g., collections of stories about sages, compilations of theological propositions, and the like. These canonically-unthinkable compilations are defined for us by that subset of extra-documentary writing that I classify as non-documentary altogether.

To explain the analytical terms just now introduced, let me start with the three established facts concerning texts within boundaries, then identify the opposite, texts without boundaries. There are three indicators of documentary preferences, rhetoric, logic, and topic:

[1] the rhetoric or formal preferences of a piece of writing, which dictate, without respect to meaning, how sentences will be composed;

[2] the logic of coherent discourse, which determines how one sentence will be joined to others in context; and how groups of sentences will cohere and form completed units of thought, and, finally, how said units of thought agglutinate or are otherwise held together in large-scale components of complete documents;

[3] the topical program of the writing, which indicates the subject and may also indicate the problematic — what we wish to know about the subject — of that same writing.

To apply these classifications of indicators to documentary analysis in particular:

[1] DOCUMENTARY RHETORIC: in each canonical writing from the Mishnah to the Bavli, a selection of a particular type of patterned language[8] governs syntax and sentence-structure.[9]

[2] DOCUMENTARY LOGIC: Subject to a particular logic of coherent discourse, sentences cohere to form cogent propositions in one way, rather than in some other. This is amplified for Leviticus Rabbah in Chapter one.

[3] DOCUMENTARY TOPIC: A given agendum of topics dictates what belongs, and what does not belong, in the compilation.

Documents may utilize the same patterns; they may connect statements through a logic that operates in many compilations; they may even treat a topic common to two or more documents. But each document, without exception, differs from all others in how it combines the possibilities. These three indicators — rhetoric, logic, topic, — join together in a unique combination to characterize a given document, so that that particular combination governs in no other. In some important way or other, the Mishnah is readily distinguished from the two Talmuds that organize their presentations as commentaries to the Mishnah; Genesis Rabbah cannot be confused with Abot; the Tosefta manifests its differences from Song of Songs Rabbah; and so too Sifra and Leviticus Rabbah, sharing a common topic, Leviticus, can *never* be confused with one another.

But compositions and composites following conventions particular to documents comprise only part — though as we shall once again see, by far the largest part — of the contents of the several canonical documents. The other component of the respective documents is made up of texts without boundaries, which I have called, also, "extra-" and "non-documentary writing." Such writing differs from the documentary writing in the same compilation. That is because it dismisses as null the particular set of indicators of rhetoric, logic, and topic, that all together govern in that compilation. Extra- and non-documentary writing may ignore the manifest formal traits of the document in which it occurs, as in the Mishnah. It may take up its own topical program, as in the writing in Genesis Rabbah or Leviticus Rabbah that is devoted to the exegesis of other books of Scripture altogether. It may ignore the tight logical cogency otherwise characteristic of the document at hand, as in Leviticus Rabbah. In one or another of the definitive characteristics of its documentary setting, therefore, extra- and non-documentary writing will mark itself as anomalous in context.

Such extra- and non-documentary compositions, moreover, may appear in more than a single document, not being limited by indicative traits to any one compilation.[10] But even singletons, occurring uniquely in one compilation but violating that compilation's formal, logical, and topical rules, fall into the category of Rabbinic writing under study here. Among these extra- and non-documentary types of writing, for example, we find compositions and composites that circulate in two or more documents and therefore by definition are non- and extra-documentary. A sample of several documents suggests that these peripatetic passages form a very small portion of any one document, therefore of the canon as a whole.[11]

More to the point: the extra- and non-documentary compositions simply do not play a critical role in delivering the documentary messages of the respective documents in which they occur. In context they are subordinated and clearly secondary in their function and formal position. In the Rabbah-Midrash-compilations, for example, the extra- and non-documentary components invariably position themselves as interpolations. The composite in which they find a place commonly assigns to extra- and non-documentary writing the task of illustration or amplification. Or that writing appears parachuted down, out of all local context. It is very rare for a peripatetic composition or a extra- and non-documentary composite to take a primary role in the propositional exposition of the document in which it occurs. That is to say, the composition that ignores the formal preferences will not take a principal part in expounding the topical program, in registering the proposition, that is at issue and that imparts cogency to the composite at hand. These matters will return in due course as we systematically examine all occurrences of extra- and non-documentary writing from the Mishnah forward. So much for distinguishing documentary- from extra- and non-documentary writing in the canon of formative Judaism.

## v. Other Approaches to the Same Problem

To this point I have written as though the analytical program outlined here is universally affirmed. But it competes with a contrary approach. Specifically, the distinction between documentary and extra- and non-documentary writing derives from a particular approach to the analysis of the canon, one that focuses on whole documents and their definitive, recurrent patterns and traits and works back to the parts. But why not start from the parts and build toward the whole? That represents a plausible option too. Indeed, for characterizing the writing of the Rabbinic canon, two starting points present themselves, and both have their advocates:

[1] the whole document, its definitive traits viewed in large aggregates, distinguished by large-scale patterns, which is the position taken by the documentary hypothesis and its advocates;

or

[2] the smallest irreducible pieces of writing, words, phrases, sentences that constitute entire and complete statements of meaning, which is the implicit position of those that deem documentary lines to bear no signals of intent or meaning at all.

The former starting point seizes upon patterns and regularities exhibited through a given compilation. That is what generates the distinction between documentary and extra- and non-documentary writing.

The latter stand-point, by addressing the smallest whole units of discourse (sentences, not paragraphs, let alone chapters) does not, and cannot, discern patterned writing or, if it sees patterns, by definition cannot deem regularities to bear consequence. That is because it does not recognize documentary boundaries or the autonomy of documents at all. It treats everything as interchangeable with everything else, each as undifferentiated from all others, and dismisses as null the literary context of texts and the massive regularities demonstrably in play. The canon is comprised not by a score of huge, purposeful compilations — statements, really — but of tens of thousands of compositions and composites that stand each on its own, an inchoate composite of this and that and whatever. Rather, starting from the smallest whole unit and focusing upon the overall matrix calls into play all the components of a compilation, all at once. These are homogenized into a whole canon, and then, as I said, differentiated only by individual sense-units. These smallest whole units of discourse form the sole point of intersection and synergy. The intermediate units of the canon that documents define signify nothing and contain no signals as to intent and meaning.

Both approaches serve. The only question is, which of the two approaches serves better? The criterion must be, which differentiates data with greater perspicacity? That is indicated by which forms the data into intelligible patterns, and which obscures points of distinction altogether.

Compare the two analytical models. We consider first of all starting from the whole and working inward. In this approach we commence from a completed document and unpeel its layers, from the ultimate one of closure and redaction, to the penultimate one of joining two or more distinct pieces of writing into a coherent whole, and onward into the innermost formation of the smallest whole units of thought of which a document is comprised. The whole defines the context of the parts, and the whole is defined — as already explained — by its unique congeries of topic, logic, and rhetoric. In seeing the patterns indicated by the whole, we read singleton-texts in their formal *and intellectual* context (rhetorical indicators assure the former, topical and logical ones the latter). As a matter of hypothesis, therefore, we treat the entire writing as a coherent document, one that has come to closure intentionally, at some fixed point, and through the intellection of purposeful framers or redactor.

We start the analytical process by asking what those framers — that authorship of the whole — have wanted their document to accomplish *as a whole* and by pointing to the means by which that authorship achieved its goals. The tangible, accessible patterns of prevailing rhetoric and logic of coherent discourse, as well as of the topical program of the whole, guide us in our definition of the document as a whole. The parts then come under study under the aspect of the whole. Knowing the intent of the framers, we ask whether, and how, materials they have used have been shaped in response to the program of the document's authorship. That is how the reading of the parts will take place in the light of the program of the whole. We define the norm on the base-line of the whole and ask about variables: where, how, and why the parts diverge from the norm. That is the mode of comparison and contrast that will generate our hypotheses of literary history and purpose — and also, therefore our hermeneutics.[12]

The alternative point of entry, second, is to begin with the smallest building block of any and all documents, which is the free-standing sentence or irreducible minimum of completed thought, and working upward and outward from the innermost layer of the writing. That point of entry ignores the boundaries of discrete documents and, in focusing upon what rarely exhibits documentary markers, asks what we find in common within and among all documents. The norm is defined by the traits of the singleton-saying as it moves from here to there. Within this atomistic theory of the construction of the literature, the boundary-lines of documents do not demarcate important classifications of data, not even of topic or proposition, even when uniformities prove blatant. Boundaries bear no meanings and signify nothing. Those between documents, or, within documents, between and among coherent expositions, are inert and formal. So we may snatch a sentence from here and match it to one from there, ignoring the context at both points.[13]

The stress then lies not on the differentiating traits of documents, but the points shared in common among them; these points are the same free-floating sayings out of context that occur in two or more places. Literary history then consists in the inquiry into the fate of sayings, undifferentiated as to context and origin, as they move from one place to another. The hermeneutics will focus upon the saying all by itself and its theoretical history, rather than on the program and plan of documents that encompass, also, the discrete saying. Exegesis of verses is deemed a function of the traits of the verses subject to exegesis. A larger hermeneutical theory is unthinkable. The advantage of this approach, of course, is that it takes account of what is shared among documents, on the one side, and also of what exhibits none of the characteristic traits definitive of given documents, on the other.

In my view, first asking questions of large-scale coherence and only then securing answers based on large aggregates of like data define the better way to approach the texts. For that procedure matches the character of the evidence, shaped as it is into large formal aggregates. That then predetermines the program of inquiry, and for a simple reason, already suggested. It is in the document viewed whole, in its largest aggregates, that patterns to begin with manifest themselves. By definition, no patterns are to be discerned in the singleton-sentences from which the contrary analytical program commences its inquiry. That is why, I maintain, an approach that obscures the indicative traits of the writing cannot serve.

While the documentary hypothesis of the formative Rabbinic canon has provoked a fair amount of controversy, it does not lack precedents in the received tradition. Explicit comments on formalized rhetoric in the canonical sources themselves as well as their exegetes underscore that the indicators important in the documentary hypothesis are familiar. Indeed, that hypothesis, while intensely controversial at this time, rests on a well-established view of the character of the Rabbinic writing. From antiquity, the Rabbinic sages have recognized and commented upon formal patterns in the wording of received traditions, e.g., positioning authority A before authority B in nearly all appearances of the two together, and similar blatant formalizations of data. They further recognized that documents bear their own autonomy, asking why, for example, two documents go over the same topic or problem, or how documents are rationally ordered. And from the beginning, in the early nineteenth century, of the *Wissenschaft des Judenthums* patterns of other kinds, e.g., the proem in Midrash-compilations, were recognized and interpreted. True, I have moved beyond that program. But that is mainly through doing systematically what earlier was done haphazardly. That is, for the entire formative canon I have conduced the systematic identification of the patterns in large aggregates and evaluation of their meaning in the differentiation of whole documents from one another. I have re-presented that entire canon form-analytically, preserving its traits in translation. But in all this, I have built upon solid foundations in the received tradition of learning. But I have built on the still more solid foundations of radical empiricism: the data are everything, their regularities determinative.

So, as between the two approaches, starting at the smallest or at the largest whole and complete units of meaning,[14] the documentary hypothesis rests on sound precedent and furthermore makes the choice that matches the character of the evidence. The ubiquity of dominant forms and patterns by definition requires that work commence with the whole compilation in hand. The contrary view — the one that concentrates on the smallest whole sense-units, words, phrases, sentences — obscures the data and misses the point. Seen from this other approach, these minimal sense-units on their own present few regularities and yield no laws.

Equally significant: the critics of the documentary hypothesis have in no case produced a form-analytical translation and commentary to a single document set forth by me within my hypothesis. Since they have not actually done the work, they have yet to call into question the regularities I discern. To shed doubt on the points of differentiation to which I call attention, they have only impressions and opinions to offer. When they have met the challenge that documentary description presents — dealing with vast documents and confronting their patterns and presenting them in a systematic way — *and* demonstrated that I have missed the correct patterns, or, more to the point, have imputed regularities and order that do not inhere, then they will provoke debate. For at that point, the work having been done, the critics of the documentary hypothesis will have established a claim upon a serious hearing. Episodic remarks about this and that, not to mention out-of-hand, unreasoned and arbitrary dismissals, do not constitute weighty criticism, absent the hard work of systematic engagement with the actual traits of the writing.[15]

In the end what will settle matters is the outcome: do people judge that the data are better differentiated, accounted for and accommodated within one model or the other? Indeed, are there data that we discern *only* by following one model and not the other — discern and also understand? Stated concretely: do we find consequential the formal-rhetorical, topical, and logical traits that manifestly distinguish one compilation from another, the Mishnah from Genesis Rabbah, for example? Or are these mere formalities and inert conventions, bearing no significance beyond themselves? Where atomistic exegesis and lexical hermeneutics (if there can be such) have prevailed,[16] it is at a heavy price in comprehension of the Judaic system embodied in the texts subjected to that exegesis and that generative hermeneutics. For details do accumulate, we do notice points of difference in rhetoric, topic, and logic, that differentiate one document from another — and what are we to make of those details? The documentary hypothesis can respond to those questions, the contrary model cannot — or, at least, to date has not.

Each model claims its own strengths. I have already stated those of the documentary hypothesis of the Rabbinic canon. The atomistic approach finds its strength at the exegetical level, and none denies the results are engaging. Close atomistic exegesis yields important lexical outcomes. The readings of words and phrases have enriched the exegetical tradition, changing our grasp of numerous interesting details. I cannot point to a single significant contribution made by the documentary hypothesis to the solution of lexical problems, which rarely register at the documentary level. As to solving problems of the exegesis of phrases and sentences, establishing a rhetorical or logical or topical context (how does subject A intersect with subject Q?) occasionally clarifies what atomistic exegesis does not address, but not often.

So the reading from smallest details outward and upward has much to offer. But as an approach to the comprehension of Rabbinic Judaism, at what cost! The ad hoc, episodic reading of words, phrases, and sentences out of context bears within itself a massive flaw, ignoring as it does the context that imparts sense to the text. For in denying a vision of the wholes that comprise the canon, those who start with the details end up drowning in details. The result of missing those formal conventions of rhetoric, topic, and logic that characterize one document and no other is to misconstrue the very context of Rabbinic discourse. It is to deem random what is demonstrably purposeful and to treat as chaotic what is in fact coherent. That is to say, it is to ignore the messages that the documents were composed to convey to begin with. An exegesis of words and phrases on its own obscures the presence of Rabbinic Judaism, structure and system, which in fact animates every line and phrase of the texts but makes its statement first through the whole, then through the parts: whole, cogent, complete.

Still, we do stand at the elementary stage of a large enterprise. The burden lies on the documentary hypothesis to show that its distinction between documentary and extra- and non-documentary writing makes a difference, and to specify what that difference is. Let us proceed to what I have underscored as the building blocks of the documentary hypothesis: the *contexts* of the canonical compositions, and the relationships between and among those compositions, severally and jointly.

### vi. The Documentary Context: Autonomy, Connection, Continuity

In documentary context the respective Rabbinic compilations from the Mishnah through the Bavli are viewed as free-standing and autonomous of one another. They are treated as separate literary entities. That is so except where a document later in sequence explicitly and systematically cites one that came to closure earlier, whether that is the Tosefta citing the Mishnah, or the Midrash-compilations citing Scripture. From such a perspective each document, complete in itself and distinct from all others with the stated exception, requires its own systematic description, analysis, and interpretation. Simple examples suffice to make the point. The Mishnah viewed whole, in line with recurrent formal traits of rhetoric, topic, and logic of coherent discourse, is manifestly different in its indicative traits from Leviticus Rabbah, which by its rhetorical, topical, and logical traits, defined by a program pertinent to all documents, is blatantly different from the Talmud of Babylonia. No one can confuse a chapter of tractate Abot with a chapter of Song of Songs Rabbah — and so throughout. A comparison of the Talmud of the Land of Israel and the Talmud of Babylonia produced comparable points of systematic differentiation of a global order.[17]

To show through a mental experiment that that is self-evident, I venture to claim a simple fact. A random, unassigned sample of completed units of exposition, e.g., 500 or 1,000 word coherent statements conforming to the distinctive traits of one document can seldom be confused with a random, unassigned sample of completed units of exposition of the same order from some other document(s). Once we have deciphered the key to the formal rules of composition of all documents, we can use that key to assign one piece of writing to one compilation, and another to its right and proper venue. And we have deciphered the key and use it all the time. Once more, in concrete terms, take a paragraph out of the Mishnah and a paragraph out of Genesis Rabbah and try to imagine confusing the one with the other. It cannot be imagined.

But by this point it is obvious that that claim bears within itself an important qualification. Some compositions and composites in a given document do not conform to the documentary protocol that otherwise pertains. These extra- and non-documentary compositions and composites fit anywhere and belong nowhere. A counterpart mental experiment comes to the fore. Take two pieces of non-documentary writing at random from two different documents and ask where each originates. Without the indicative data, the key to documentary location, one should rarely guess right as to the abstract's point of origin.[18]

With these facts in hand, let us turn to the details. The most important is simple: once we recognize the autonomy of documents and also the complexity of their components, how, in accord with the documentary hypothesis of the Rabbinic canon, do documents relate? First, as the language just now used indicates, they form components of a canon, defined by the Rabbinic consensus to be constituted by the Mishnah, Tosefta, Talmuds, and designated Midrash-compilations. But — so the hypothesis maintains — they form distinct literary entities as well. And — and this point is critical — they furthermore overlap. Accordingly, documents are to be perceived in three relationships, first, as autonomous writings, second, as writings connected with others of the same class, and, finally, as parts of a complete and continuous corpus deemed unitary and coherent: autonomy, connection, continuity beyond the key words to portray perspective. The labor is one of description, analysis, and interpretation, and it involves study of the text, its literary context, and its intellectual matrix. A brief recapitulation of these matters suffices, with the key-words autonomy/text, connection/context, and continuity/matrix.

### A. Autonomy: Description of the Text on its Own

At this point a document is set on display in its own terms, in an exercise of examining the text in particular and in its full particularity and immediacy. The text will be described in accord with the three now-familiar distinct, differentiating traits, those of rhetoric, logic, and topic: the formal traits of the writing, the principles of cogency that dictate how one sentence will link up with another, and the topical, and even propositional, program that the entire document addresses.

### B. Connection: Analysis of the Text in Context through Comparison and Contrast with Intersecting Affines

A document connects with others in two ways, first and less important, through shared sayings or stories or entire components, e.g., Leviticus Rabbah, Pesiqta deRab Kahana, Pesiqta Rabbati. Second and far more important, connection of documents is effected through recurrent points of emphasis found in a number of documents or through intersection upon a prior compilation. That is, a set of documents may address a single shared writing, Midrash-compilations facing Scripture, the Tosefta and two Talmuds addressing the Mishnah. They may, further, pursue a single exegetical program or take up a common question, deemed urgent in two or more compilations. They may intersect in other ways. Groups of documents may take shape out of an inductive examination of points of differentiation and aggregation. That notion presents no surprises, since the so-called Tannaite Midrashim — Sifra, the two Sifrés, possibly also Mekhilta attributed to R. Ishmael — are deemed a subset of the Midrash-compilations, as are the Rabbah-Midrash-compilations (neither set for compelling reasons to be sure).

### C. Continuity: Interpretation of the Matrix that Forms of the Canonical Texts a Coherent Statement

The examination of the entire corpus of Rabbinic writings (or the writings found in the library at Qumran, or other groups of writings deemed by common consensus to form a textual community), finally, leads outward toward that shared matrix in which a variety of texts finds its place. Here description moves from the interior world of intellectuals and their logic to the exterior world they proposed to shape and create, the theology that animates the entire canon, for example, and imparts coherence to it. That inquiry defines as its generative question how the social world formed by the texts as a whole proposes to define and respond to a powerful and urgent question.

To spell this out: I read the canonical writings as response to critical and urgent questions. A set of questions concerning the formation of the social order — its ethics, ethos, and ethnos — for example will turn out to produce a single set of answers from a variety of writings. If that is the case, then we may describe not only documentary cogency and the coherence of two or more writings but the matrix in an intellectual system that the continuity among many documents permits us to outline. These represent intellectually ambitious problems. They concern a complex agenda. Solving them involves a dense corpus of data. Constructing a coherent theology that pervades the whole represents one such exercise in identifying the sustaining matrix of the documents viewed all together, as a coherent statement start to finish. Such theological exercises in canonical coherence are represented by the names of Schechter, Moore, Urbach, and the like. My own systematic theology based on the formative canon is in print as well.[19]

## VII. Imagining the Rabbinic Canon: Toward a General Theory

The upshot is, the Rabbinic canon is comprised by a community of texts, related in three ways ("dimensions"): autonomy, connection, and continuity. Documents stand on their own. They intersect at specific points with other documents, e.g., through peripatetic compositions. And they constitute a continuity — in form and in substance — with all other documents. In that way they constitute a canon, clearly indicating what does not belong by markers of what does. That is, just as we should readily assign to a given document a piece of writing bearing documentary markers, so if presented with entire documents produced by diverse Judaic systems in antiquity — Rabbinic, Hellenistic-Jewish (e.g., Philonic), Qumranian, Judaeo-Christian — we should sort out the lot of them with facility. What marks a text as belonging to the Rabbinic canon also explains why another text belongs somewhere else. Random intersections of documents, Rabbinic and otherwise, do not cause confusion. Points on which all documents concur prove episodic, not systemic, formal, rarely substantive, notional and occasional, never consequential and theological.

To clarify this perspective, let us consider the analogy of a library. Books brought together form a library. Each title addresses its own program and makes its own points. But books produced by a cogent community constitute not merely a library but a canon: a set of compositions each of which embodies a common norm and each of which contributes to a statement that transcends its own pages. The books exhibit intrinsic traits that make of them all a community of texts. We should know on the basis of those characteristics that the texts form a community even if we knew nothing more than the texts themselves. In the Judaic writings, moreover, the documents at hand are held by Judaism to form a canon.

How in this context are we to imagine the canon viewed whole and in its documentary parts? Once more, as before, I conceive of two models, the scrapbook as against the reasoned collection, the one random, the other purposive.

One theory is that a document serves solely as a convenient repository of ready-made sayings and stories, available materials that will have served equally well (or poorly) wherever they took up their final residence. Such a theory of the literature validates an atomistic hermeneutics and yields an ad hoc, episodic approach to exegesis of words and phrases and sentences — rarely of paragraphs or compositions. In accord with that theory documentary boundaries demarcate nothing. Their lines of structure and order are null. We deal with atoms, not molecules.

The other theory is that in its active constitutive elements a document exhibits a viewpoint, a purpose of authorship distinctive to its framers or collectors and arrangers. Such a characteristic, literary purpose — by this other theory — is so powerfully particular to one authorship that much of the writing at hand can be shown to have been (re)shaped to conform to the ultimate purpose of the authorship at hand. In accord with this other theory context and circumstance form the prior condition of inquiry, the result, in exegetical terms, the contingent one. The implications for hermeneutics and consequent exegesis are self-evident: context imposes itself on text, paragraphs on sentences, sentences on words and phrases.

But the documentary hypothesis readily recognizes in any given document a component of other-than-documentary writing. That is writing that does not conform to the program of the document before us, also writing that does not conform to any documentary program at all. So the documentary hypothesis recognizes the complexity of the Rabbinic documents, made up, as they are, of writing undertaken for a given document in particular, and writing utterly unresponsive to the conventions and protocol of a documentary venue of any known kind. Within the documentary hypothesis, therefore, a complementary hermeneutics must function, yielding an exegetics that responds not only to contextual considerations but also to their absence, as the case requires.

## ENDNOTES

[1] I originally spelled out these matters in *Making the Classics in Judaism: The Three Stages of Literary Formation.* Atlanta, 1990: Scholars Press for Brown Judaic Studies. Now: Lanham, MD: University Press of America.

[2] I wonder whether proponents of the theory of a single, unitary, incremental, harmonistic Judaism have fully appreciated the uniqueness of the canonical documents of Rabbinic Judaism in the context of all Judaic writing from Scripture forward to the end of late antiquity. While philological work moves from one Judaic canon to another, and while episodic points of intersection in Halakhic and Aggadic data are well established, massive differences in law and theology differentiate Rabbinic documents from all other writings attributed to Judaic authorship in antiquity.

[3] The monographic project summarized here is as follows: *Texts without Boundaries. Protocols of Non-Documentary Writing in the Rabbinic Canon*, Binghamton, 2002: Global Publications. Academic Studies in Ancient Judaism series. Volume One. *The Mishnah, Tractate Abot, and the Tosefta;* Volume Two. *Sifra and Sifré to Numbers*; Volume Three. *Sifré to Deuteronomy and Mekhilta Attributed to R. Ishmael;* Volume Four. *Leviticus Rabbah.*

[4] Leiden, 1974-1986: E. J. Brill, in forty-three volumes.

[5] *The Theology of the Oral Torah. Revealing the Justice of God.* Kingston and Montreal, 1999: McGill-Queens University Press and Ithaca, 1999: Cornell University Press.

[6] Leiden, 2002: E. J. Brill.

[7] I spell out the difference between composition and composite and why it matters in my *The Rules of Composition of the Talmud of Babylonia. The Cogency of the Bavli's Composite.* Atlanta, 1991: Scholars Press for South Florida Studies in the History of Judaism.

[8] That is blatant not only in the Hebrew but in the close-to-literal form-analytical translation in English such as I have set forth for all components of the canon.

[9] My form-analytical work includes, but is not limited to, the following monographs: *The Bavli's One Voice: Types and Forms of Analytical Discourse and their Fixed Order of Appearance.* Atlanta, 1991: Scholars Press for South Florida Studies in the History of Judaism. *Form-Analytical Comparison in Rabbinic Judaism. Structure and Form in* The Fathers *and* The Fathers According to Rabbi Nathan. Atlanta, 1992: Scholars Press for South Florida Studies in the History of Judaism. *The Documentary Form-History of Rabbinic Literature.* I. *The Documentary Forms of the Mishnah.* Atlanta, 1998: Scholars Press for USF Academic Commentary Series. *The Documentary Form-History of Rabbinic Literature* II. *The Aggadic Sector: Tractate Abot, Abot deRabbi Natan, Sifra, Sifré to Numbers, and Sifré to Deuteronomy.* Atlanta, 1998: Scholars Press for USF Academic Commentary Series. *The Documentary Form-History of Rabbinic Literature* III. *The Aggadic Sector: Mekhilta Attributed to R. Ishmael and Genesis Rabbah.* Atlanta, 1998: Scholars Press for USF Academic Commentary Series. *The Documentary Form-History of Rabbinic Literature* IV. *The Aggadic Sector: Leviticus Rabbah, and Pesiqta deRab Kahana.* Atlanta, 1998: Scholars Press for USF Academic Commentary Series. *The Documentary Form-History of Rabbinic Literature* V. *The Aggadic Sector: Song of Songs Rabbah, Ruth Rabbah, Lamentations Rabbati, and Esther Rabbah I.* Atlanta, 1998: Scholars Press for USF Academic Commentary Series. *The Documentary Form-History of Rabbinic Literature.* VI. *The Halakhic Sector. The Talmud of the Land of Israel.* A. *Berakhot and Shabbat through Taanit.* Atlanta, 1998: Scholars Press for USF Academic Commentary Series. *The Documentary Form-History of Rabbinic Literature.* VI. *The Halakhic Sector. The Talmud of the Land of Israel.* B. *Megillah*

*through Qiddushin.* Atlanta, 1998: Scholars Press for USF Academic Commentary Series. *The Documentary Form-History of Rabbinic Literature.* VI. *The Halakhic Sector. The Talmud of the Land of Israel.* C. *Sotah through Horayot and Niddah.* Atlanta, 1998: Scholars Press for USF Academic Commentary Series. *The Documentary Form-History of Rabbinic Literature.* VII. *The Halakhic Sector. The Talmud of Babylonia.* A. *Tractates Berakhot and Shabbat through Pesahim.* Atlanta, 1998: Scholars Press for USF Academic Commentary Series. *The Documentary Form-History of Rabbinic Literature.* VII. *The Halakhic Sector. The Talmud of Babylonia.* B. *Tractates Yoma through Ketubot.* Atlanta, 1998: Scholars Press for USF Academic Commentary Series. *The Documentary Form-History of Rabbinic Literature.* VII. *The Halakhic Sector. The Talmud of Babylonia.* C. *Tractates Nedarim through Baba Mesia.* Atlanta, 1998: Scholars Press for USF Academic Commentary Series. *The Documentary Form-History of Rabbinic Literature.* VII. *The Halakhic Sector. The Talmud of Babylonia.* D. *Tractates Baba Batra through Horayot.* Atlanta, 1998: Scholars Press for USF Academic Commentary Series. *The Documentary Form-History of Rabbinic Literature.* VII. *The Halakhic Sector. The Talmud of Babylonia.* E. *Tractates Zebahim through Bekhorot.* Atlanta, 1998: Scholars Press for USF Academic Commentary Series. *The Documentary Form-History of Rabbinic Literature.* VII. *The Halakhic Sector. The Talmud of Babylonia.* F. *Tractates Arakhin through Niddah. And Conclusions.* Atlanta, 1998: Scholars Press for USF Academic Commentary Series.

[10] Documentary writing for its part also may occur in more than a single compilation, e.g., in Leviticus Rabbah and in Pesiqta deRab Kahana, or in Genesis Rabbah and in Leviticus Rabbah. When a composition occurs in more than a single document, in some instances we can discern to the protocol of which of the two documents the composition conforms. That is, we ordinarily are able to identify the document in which such compositions take a primary place, and the one(s) to which they are secondary. I have shown that fact for the single blatant case in the entire formative canon, the one involving Leviticus Rabbah, Pesiqta deRab Kahana, and Pesiqta Rabbati. See *From Tradition to Imitation. The Plan and Program of Pesiqta deRab Kahana and Pesiqta Rabbati.* Atlanta, 1987: Scholars Press for Brown Judaic Studies. But see also, for Genesis Rabbah and Leviticus Rabbah, *Comparative Midrash: The Plan and Program of Genesis Rabbah and Leviticus Rabbah.* Atlanta, 1986: Scholars Press for Brown Judaic Studies. We rarely find difficulty in identifying the primary locus of a passage shared by Genesis Rabbah and Leviticus Rabbah. But most of the peripatetic compositions and composites of the formative canon — those that occur in more than a single document — ignore all documentary protocols of the documents that contain them.

[11] See *Extra- and Non-Documentary Writing in the Canon of Formative Judaism.* II. *Paltry Parallels. The Negligible Proportion and Peripheral Role of Free-Standing Compositions in Rabbinic Documents.* Binghamton 2001: Global PublicationsAcademic Studies in the History of Judaism Series.

[12] I claim to understand the hermeneutics of the Halakhic documents in the definitive aspect of their category-formations. That is spelled out in my systematic work, *The Hermeneutics of the Rabbinic Category-Formations: An Introduction.* Lanham, 2000: University Press of America. Studies in Judaism series; *The Comparative Hermeneutics of Rabbinic Judaism.* Volume One. *Introduction. Berakhot and Seder Mo'ed.* Binghamton, 2000: Global Publications. Academic Studies in Ancient Judaism series; *The Comparative Hermeneutics of Rabbinic Judaism.* Volume Two. *Seder Nashim.* Binghamton, 2000: Global Publications. Academic Studies in Ancient Judaism series; *The Comparative Hermeneutics of Rabbinic*

*Judaism.* Volume Three. *Seder Neziqin.* Binghamton, 2000: Global Publications. Academic Studies in Ancient Judaism series; *The Comparative Hermeneutics of Rabbinic Judaism.* Volume Four. *Seder Qodoshim.* Binghamton, 2000: Global Publications. Academic Studies in Ancient Judaism series; *The Comparative Hermeneutics of Rabbinic Judaism.* Volume Five. *Seder Tohorot.* Part *Kelim through Parah.* Binghamton, 2000: Global Publications. Academic Studies in Ancient Judaism series; *The Comparative Hermeneutics of Rabbinic Judaism.* Volume Six. *Seder Tohorot. Tohorot through Uqsin.* Binghamton, 2000: Global Publications. Academic Studies in Ancient Judaism series; *The Comparative Hermeneutics of Rabbinic Judaism.* Volume Seven *The Generic Hermeneutics of the Halakhah. A Handbook.* Binghamton, 2000: Global Publications. Academic Studies in Ancient Judaism series; *The Comparative Hermeneutics of Rabbinic Judaism.* Volume Eight. *Why This, Not That? Ways Not Taken in the Halakhic Category-Formations of the Mishnah-Tosefta-Yerushalmi-Bavli.* Binghamton, 2000: Global Publications. Academic Studies in Ancient Judaism series. By contrast, I cannot claim to account for the hermeneutics of the Aggadic documents, because I cannot explain the counterpart-category-formations. I cannot define them, let alone account for their working, in the way in which I can and do for the Halakhic ones. I should regard the Aggadic hermeneutics as embodied in the Aggadic category-formations as a critical unsolved problem of Rabbinic Judaism in its formative, canonical statement.

[13] Questions of hermeneutics are generated by exegetics, as though exegetics produced hermeneutics, rather than vice versa. That is why, also, the Aggadic category-formations prove beyond all contemplation.

[14] I cannot conceive of a starting point in-between the entirety of documents and the smallest whole units of comprehensible formulations. That is an invitation to chaos.

[15] For further discussion, see my *The Documentary Foundation of Rabbinic Culture. Mopping Up after Debates with Gerald L. Bruns, S. J. D. Cohen, Arnold Maria Goldberg, Susan Handelman, Christine Hayes, James Kugel, Peter Schaefer, Eliezer Segal, E. P. Sanders, and Lawrence H. Schiffman.* Atlanta, 1995: Scholars Press for South Florida Studies in the History of Judaism. There I survey the critics of the documentary hypothesis and systematically address what they have had to say. My sense is some of them simply have gone on to other issues, for in the six years since this work was published, they have not engaged with the issue in heavy-weight scholarly exercises. Indeed, more than a few of them have simply fallen silent and ceased to participate in public debate at all; they have stopped publishing.

[16] In the most recent past, that exegetical atomism, focused on words and phrases and occasionally whole sentences, marks the work of David W. Halivni and Shamma Friedman, the only systematic exegetes of an academic venue who have actually produced important exercises of textual interpretation. In the academic world no one else comes close as systematic exegetes of Rabbinic writings. For discussion of Halivni's hermeneutics and exegetical exercises based there on, see my *The Formation of the Babylonian Talmud. Studies on the Achievements of Late Nineteenth and Twentieth Century Historical and Literary-Critical Research.* Leiden, 1970: Brill. Reprint: Binghamton, 2002: Global Publications Classics in Judaic Studies Series; *The Modern Study of the Mishnah.* Leiden, 1973: Brill. Reprint: Binghamton, 2002: Global Publications Classics in Judaic Studies Series, and *Sources and Traditions. Types of Composition in the Talmud of Babylonia.* Atlanta, 1992: Scholars Press for South Florida Studies in the History of Judaism. and, on Halivni and Friedman, *Law as Literature.* Chico, 1983: Scholars Press. = *Semeia. An Experimental Journal for Biblical*

*Criticism* Volume 27. I devoted my doctoral seminar for several semesters to the close reading of Halivni and Friedman, yielding the cited works. Halivni's ignoring of his critics and their constructive propositions has been remarked upon by third-party reviewers more than once.

[17] The work is done systematically in *The Bavli's Unique Voice. A Systematic Comparison of the Talmud of Babylonia and the Talmud of the Land of Israel.* Volume One. *Bavli and Yerushalmi Qiddushin Chapter One Compared and Contrasted.* Atlanta, 1993: Scholars Press for South Florida Studies in the History of Judaism' *The Bavli's Unique Voice. A Systematic Comparison of the Talmud of Babylonia and the Talmud of the Land of Israel.* Volume Two. *Yerushalmi's, Bavli's, and Other Canonical Documents' Treatment of the Program of Mishnah-Tractate Sukkah Chapters One, Two, and Four Compared and Contrasted. A Reprise and Revision of* The Bavli and its Sources. Atlanta, 1993: Scholars Press for South Florida Studies in the History of Judaism' *The Bavli's Unique Voice. A Systematic Comparison of the Talmud of Babylonia and the Talmud of the Land of Israel.* Volume Three. *Bavli and Yerushalmi to Selected Mishnah-Chapters in the Division of Moed. Erubin Chapter One, and Moed Qatan Chapter Three.* Atlanta, 1993: Scholars Press for South Florida Studies in the History of Judaism; *The Bavli's Unique Voice. A Systematic Comparison of the Talmud of Babylonia and the Talmud of the Land of Israel.* Volume Four. *Bavli and Yerushalmi to Selected Mishnah-Chapters in the Division of Nashim. Gittin Chapter Five and Nedarim Chapter One. And Niddah Chapter One.* Atlanta, 1993: Scholars Press for South Florida Studies in the History of Judaism; *The Bavli's Unique Voice. A Systematic Comparison of the Talmud of Babylonia and the Talmud of the Land of Israel.* Volume Five. *Bavli and Yerushalmi to Selected Mishnah-Chapters in the Division of Neziqin. Baba Mesia Chapter One and Makkot Chapters One and Two.* Atlanta, 1993: Scholars Press for South Florida Studies in the History of Judaism; *The Bavli's Unique Voice. A Systematic Comparison of the Talmud of Babylonia and the Talmud of the Land of Israel.* Volume Six. *Bavli and Yerushalmi to a Miscellany of Mishnah-Chapters. Gittin Chapter One, Qiddushin Chapter Two, and Hagigah Chapter Three.* Atlanta, 1993: Scholars Press for South Florida Studies in the History of Judaism; *The Bavli's Unique Voice.* Volume Seven. *What Is Unique about the Bavli in Context? An Answer Based on Inductive Description, Analysis, and Comparison.* Atlanta, 1993: Scholars Press for South Florida Studies in the History of Judaism.

[18] That is so even in blind differentiation of compositions of the two Talmuds, which in any event bear formal markers unique to each, respectively. This I showed in *The Two Talmud's Compared* and in *The Talmud's Unique Voice.*

[19] *The Theology of the Oral Torah. Revealing the Justice of God.* Kingston and Montreal, 1999: McGill-Queens University Press and Ithaca, 1999: Cornell University Press. For the Halakhah, the counterpart is in *The Halakhah: An Encyclopaedia of the Law of Judaism.* Volume I. *Between Israel and God.* Part A. *Faith, Thanksgiving, Enlandisement: Possession and Partnership.* Leiden, 1999: E. J. Brill. The Brill Reference Library of Ancient Judaism; *The Halakhah: An Encyclopaedia of the Law of Judaism.* Volume II. *Between Israel and God.* Part B. *Transcendent Transactions: Where Heaven and Earth Intersect.* Leiden, 1999: E. J. Brill. The Brill Reference Library of Ancient Judaism; *The Halakhah: An Encyclopaedia of the Law of Judaism.* Volume III. *Within Israel's Social Order.* Leiden, 1999: E. J. Brill. The Brill Reference Library of Ancient Judaism; *The Halakhah: An Encyclopaedia of the Law of Judaism.* Volume IV. Inside the Walls of the Israelite Household. Part A. *At the Meeting of Time and Space. Sanctification in the Here and Now: The Table and the Bed.*

*Sanctification and the Marital Bond. The Desacralization of the Household: The Bed.* Leiden, 1999: E. J. Brill. The Brill Reference Library of Ancient Judaism; *The Halakhah: An Encyclopaedia of the Law of Judaism.* Volume V. *Inside the Walls of the Israelite Household.* Part B. *The Desacralization of the Household: The Table. Foci, Sources, and Dissemination of Uncleanness. Purification from the Pollution of Death.* Leiden, 1999: E. J. Brill. The Brill Reference Library of Ancient Judaism; and *The Theology of the Halakhah.* Leiden, 2001: E. J. Brill. Brill Reference Library of Ancient Judaism.

# 6

# The Mishnah's Extra-Documentary Forms and its Unpatterned Discourses

## I. Do We Identify in the Mishnah Extra-Documentary Forms or Idiosyncratic Prose?

When sages wrote for the Mishnah, they wrote within a highly-restricted set of patterns, matched by an equally-economical repertoire of logics of coherent discourse. The list and its ancillary forms, the logic of comparison and contrast, analogy and polarity, governed. The thesis that the Mishnah comprises a highly-patterned piece of writing, and that we can identify the handful of language-patterns, or forms, that define the document's protocol, requires the testing of a null hypothesis. This is in two parts. First, if the Mishnah conforms to a handful of formal patterns, then we should find little writing of a random, unpatterned character. Second, if the repertoire of forms (inclusive of logics) I have defined truly serves, then we should find little evidence of the formalization of language outside of the specified repertoire of forms, the list and its companions.

The first null-hypothesis presents its own problem. It requires that we both identify a pattern and also show that that pattern does not characterize the document as a whole. Discerning a recurrent pattern is easier than identifying as a pattern arrangements of language (e.g., syntax) that occur seldom. But we deal not with writing in general, or even with Rabbinic writing, but with the Mishnah, and the Mishnah defines for us what its framers mean by patterns or forms. What characterizes them all will then mark as a pattern an arrangement of words in forms extrinsic to meaning (e.g., formal, not idiosyncratic prose) even in the case of patterns that the document overall utilizes seldom. In the Mishnah a pattern produces rhythm, order, balance, matching of phrases and clauses, appeal to stereotype language, proportion, and a clear mark of closure. Most of the Mishnah's patterned language occurs in sets, e.g., in lists. So in the present instance, if we find writing that exhibits balance, rhythm, matching syllables, and that recapitulates in a sequence of thoughts that same balance and the rest, we shall have a pattern. If that pattern does not exhibit the traits of a list (resort to polarity or analogy to impart coherence to the items arranged in order), then we have an extra-documentary form for the Mishnah.

The second null-hypothesis — the Mishnah's language is not patterned at all, and the writers of its compositions and compilers of its composites could follow their own idiosyncratic preferences in producing their statements — requires testing. To construct a null-hypothesis, let us now ask the Mishnah to supply its own evidence against the thesis that the document adheres to strict rules of syntactical and other patterning of language. For that purpose, we raise the question, to what extent, exactly, does the corpus of compositions and composites of the Mishnah adhere to a strict and ubiquitous convention of the patterning of language? We have now to collect and consider all the Mishnah's unpatterned compositions and composites, on the one side, and also seek in the Mishnah any instances of clearly-patterned language that does not replicate the dominant patterns of the Mishnah, on the other.

## II. The Mishnah's Miscellaneous Compositions: A Complete Repertoire

### I. Abodah Zarah

As before, we examine each composition of Mishnah-tractate Abodah Zarah. By the criteria of formalization of rhetoric set forth in the companion-study, I cannot find evidence that a rhetorical convention has intervened in the formulation of the following entries in Mishnah-tractate Abodah Zarah:

**M. A.Z. 2:5**

A. Said R. Judah, "R. Ishmael asked R. Joshua as they were going along the road.

[1] B. "He said to him, 'On what account did they prohibit cheese made by gentiles?'

C. "He said to him, 'Because they curdle it with rennet from carrion.'

D. "He said to him, 'And is not the rennet from a whole offering subject to a more stringent rule than rennet from carrion, and yet they have said, 'A priest who is not squeamish sucks it out raw?'

E. (But they did not concur with him and ruled, "It is not available for [the priests'] benefit, while it also is not subject to the laws of sacrilege."

F. "He went and said to him, 'Because they curdle it with rennet of calves sacrificed to idols,

G. "He said to him, 'If so, then why have they not also extended the prohibition affecting it to the matter of deriving benefit from it?'

[2] H. "He moved him on to another subject.

I. "He said to him, 'Ishmael, my brother, How do you read the verse: For your [masculine] love is better than wine, or, Your [feminine] love is better than wine (Song 1:2)?'

J. "He said to him, 'For your [feminine] love is better than wine.'

K. "He said to him, 'The matter is not so. For its neighbor teaches concerning it, 'Your [masculine] ointments have a goodly fragrance' (Song 1:3)."

I discern in this narrative-conversation not a single mark of formalization. Without A, it is not even a narrative, just an account of two question-answer exchanges. I see no balance in the language of the paired exchanges. It is a list in no meaningful Mishnaic sense, there being nothing that joins the problem of No. 1 to that of No. 2; it is simply a catalogue of two items that X asked Y: not a pattern, certainly not an extra-documentary form.

The next item follows suit, that is, X asked Y in circumstance A. No balance governs what is attributed, and the subsequent exchanges utilize only "he said to him...he said to him..." for structure.

**M. A.Z. 3:4**

A. Peroqlos b. Pelosepos asked Rabban Gamaliel in Akko, when he was washing in Aphrodite's bathhouse, saying to him, "It is written in your Torah, And there shall cleave nothing of a devoted thing to your hand (Dt. 13:18). How is it that you're taking a bath in Aphrodite's bathhouse?"

B. He said to him, "They do not give answers in a bathhouse."

C. When he went out, he said to him, "I never came into her domain. She came into mine. They don't say, 'Let's make a bathhouse as an ornament for Aphrodite.' But they say, 'Let's make Aphrodite as an ornament for the bathhouse.'

D. "Another matter: Even if someone gave you a lot of money, you would never walk into your temple of idolatry naked or suffering a flux, nor would you piss in its presence.

E. "Yet this thing is standing there at the head of the gutter and everybody pisses right in front of her."

F. It is said only, ". . . their gods" (Dt. 12:3) — that which one treats as a god is prohibited, but that which one treats not as a god is permitted.

The setting is narrated in both description and dialogue, and the statements are framed in accord with a natural, not a patterned, rhetoric, as the contrast between the innumerable instances of X says/Y says, followed by matching apodoses shows.

The final item yields an equally random formulation. The only limiting detail of the colloquy, "in Rome," corresponds to "when they were going...."

**M. A.Z. 4:7**

A. They asked sages in Rome, "If [God] is not in favor of idolatry, why does he not wipe it away?"

B. They said to them, "If people worshipped something of which the world had no need, he certainly would wipe it away.

C. "But lo, people worship the sun, moon, stars, and planets.
D. "Now do you think he is going to wipe out his world because of idiots?"
E. They said to them, "If so, let him destroy something of which the world has no need, and leave something which the world needs!"
F. They said to them, "Then we should strengthen the hands of those who worship these [which would not be destroyed], for then they would say, 'Now you know full well that they are gods, for lo, they were not wiped out!' "

The narrative consists of "they asked...they said to them...they said to them...." The colloquy then is made up of conversational prose formed into challenges and responses, which are worded in accord with the requirements of the argument, not those of an extrinsic rhetorical pattern other than that of standard grammar. By my definition of a debate, we have no debate. That is to say, none of the stock-logics comes into play, merely a debater's riposte, "if so, then...," which takes account of the stated explanation and accommodates it with a case.

None of these items supplied by Mishnah-tractate Abodah Zarah falls within the range of formalized prose; in each case the narrative consists in "they said to him...he said to them..." and counterparts; what is attributed is formally miscellaneous. These compositions, the only ones in the tractate we have analyzed start to finish, fail to yield evidence of careful formalization of language. It suffices to note, further, that they form a negligible proportion of the whole.

What this complete account of the non-patterned compositions of the tractate yields is three hypotheses for further examination:

[1] a negligible proportion of the Mishnah is in other-than-patterned prose

[2] other-than-patterned prose is likely to occur in a (pseudo-)narrative setting.

[3] If we do not regard as a form "he asked him in such and such a location," then we find no extra-documentary forms in the Mishnah.

From this point forward, I itemize each entry in which I find no clear-cut formalization of prose, and give a few illustrations to show precisely what I mean and why I classify a given item as I do.

## II. Arakhin

**M. 6:5**
**M. 7:1**

6:5 A. All the same are the one who sanctifies his property and the one who pledges his own Valuation:
B. he has no claim either on his wife's garment, or on his children's garment, or on dyed clothes which he dyed for them, or on new shoes which he bought for them.
C. Even though they have said: Slaves are sold with their clothing to improve their value,

D. so that if for him [the slave] a garment should be purchased for thirty denars, it improves his value by a maneh,

E. and so in the case of a cow: if they keep it for sale in a market place, it fetches a better price,

F. and so in the case of a pearl: if they bring it up to a city, it fetches a better price-

G. the sanctuary [nonetheless] has a claim only in its own place and in its own time.

7:1 A. They do not declare [the field of possession] sanctified less than two years before the year of Jubilee.

B. And they do not redeem it less than a year after the year of Jubilee.

C. [In redeeming the field] they do not reckon the months against the sanctuary.

D. But the sanctuary reckons the months [to its own advantage].

E. He who sanctifies his field at the time of the Jubilee's [being in effect] [compare M. 8:1]

F. pays the fifty shekels of silver [for every part of a field that suffices for] the sowing of a homer of barley.

G. [If] there were there crevices ten handbreadths deep or rocks ten hand- breadths high, they are not measured with it.

H. [If they were in height] less than this, they are measured with it.

I. [If] one sanctified it two or three years before the Jubilee, he gives a sela and a pondion for each year.

J. If he said, "Lo, I shall pay for each year as it comes," they do not pay attention to him.

K. But: He pays the whole at once.

While the "all the same" formula continues, linking M. 6:5A to M. 7:2, the composite before us exhibits no marks of formalization I can discern. If we itemize the entries, we also find no list. That is, M. 6:5A-B deal with what is not subjected to the householder's act of sanctification. C-G contains another item pertinent to that subject, but in no way formulated to provide a single pattern. M. 7:1A-B opens a new subject, declaring a field of possession sanctified. C-D deals with redeeming the field. E-F, G-I, and J-K present three rules pertinent in theme but in no way framed in a pattern to form a list. So I classify the entire set as unpatterned in any sense that I can make out.

**M. 8:7.**

### III. Baba Batra

**M. 2:4**

**M. 2:8**

2:7 A. They keep a tree twenty-five cubits from a town,

B. and in the case of a carob or a sycamore, fifty cubits.

C. Abba Saul says, "In the case of any sort of tree which produces no fruit, fifty cubits."

**I.** D. If the town was there first, one cuts down the tree and pays no compensation.
**II.** E. And if the tree came first, one cuts down the tree but pays compensation.
**III.** F. [If it is a matter of] doubt whether this came first or that came first,
G. one cuts down the tree and pays no compensation.
2:8 A. They set a permanent threshing floor fifty cubits from a town.
B. A person should not build a permanent threshing floor on his own property,
C. unless he owns fifty cubits of space in all directions.
D. And he sets it some distance away from the crops of his fellow and from his ploughed land,
E. so that it will not cause damage.

The contrast between the acute patterning of M. 2:7 — dispute, then an exquisitely-composed list — and M. 2:8 shows the difference between patterned and unpatterned language. The latter sets forth three sentences of a random character, with no manifest effort to balance the formulation of one rule with that of the next.

**M. 3:3**
**M. 6:3**
**M. 7:4**
**M. 8:3-4**

### IV. Baba Mesia

**M. 2:5**
**M. 2:7**
**M. 2:8**
**M. 4:3**

4:3 A. Fraud [overreaching] is an overcharge of four pieces of silver out of twenty-four pieces of silver to the sela —
B. (one-sixth of the purchase price).
C. For how long is it permitted to retract [in the case of fraud]?
D. So long as it takes to show [the article] to a merchant or a relative.
E. R. Tarfon gave instructions in Lud:
F. "Fraud is an overcharge of eight pieces of silver to a sela
G. "one-third of the purchase price."
H. So the merchants of Lud rejoiced.
I. He said to them, "All day long it is permitted to retract."
J. They said to him, "Let R. Tarfon leave us where we were."
K. And they reverted to conduct themselves in accord with the ruling of sages,

I see nothing more than a sequence of simple declarative sentences, A-B, C-D, then the little narrative at E-K. The narrative, for its part, does not follow the formal requirements of the ma'aseh, not only because it lacks the particle, but because the tale follows its own plan, not the fixed plan of action/ruling, characteristic of the primary component of every ma'aseh. Here the tale establishes tension and resolves it, E-H, I-K, and it makes its own point, not in the service of the context in which it is inserted.

**M. 4:6**
**M. 4:11**
**M. 6:6**
**M. 9:13**

### V. BABA QAMMA

**M. 2:6**
**M. 4:8**
**M. 7:1**
**M. 8:2**
**M. 8:5**
**M. 8:7**
**M. 9:5**
**M. 9:9**
**M. 9:10**

9:9 A. He who steals from his father and takes an oath to him, and then [the father] dies-
B. lo, this one pays back the principal and an added fifth to his [father's other] sons or brothers [and brings the guilt offering].
C. But if he does not want to do so or does not have what to pay back,
D. he takes out a loan,
E. and the creditors come along and collect what is owing.

9:10 A. He who says to his son, "Qonam! You will not derive benefit from anything that is mine!"-
B. if the father died, the son may inherit him.
C. [But if he had specified that the vow applied] in life and after death, if the father died, the son may not inherit him.
D. And he must return [what he has of the father's] to his sons or to his brothers.
E. And if he does not have that to repay, he takes out a loan, and the creditors come along and collect what is owing.

The two compositions stand alone, with no relationship either to one another or to what stands fore or aft. But both build on the formal foundation of apocopation, he who — lo, this one, and he who...if..., the son... That is why, while at first glance the entries appear unformed, in fact they are listed in the catalogue of compositions that utilize for form the familiar apocopated sentences.

### VI. BEKHOROT

**M. 3:2**
**M. 3:3**
**M. 5:1**
**M. 5:6**

**M. 8:8**
**M. 9:7**

### VII. BERAKHOT

**M. 2:4**
**M. 4:2**
**M. 5:1**
**M. 5:4**

#### M. BERAKHOT 5:5

A. One who prays and errs-it is a bad sign for him.
B. And if he is a communal agent, [who prays on behalf of the whole congregation], it is a bad sign for them that appointed him.
C. [This is on the principle that] a man's agent is like [the man] himself.
D. They said concerning R. Haninah b. Dosa, "When he would pray for the sick he would say 'This one shall live' or 'This one shall die.'"
E. They said to him, "How do you know?"
F. He said to them, "If my prayer is fluent, then I know that it is accepted [and the person will live].
G. "But if not, I know that it is rejected [and the person will die."

The opening units, A-C, give two cases and a general rule — a typical list. But the second item does not conform to the pattern of the ma'aseh, because it does not contain the action/ruling we expect. Rather, it is a narrative setting for a saying — a different form altogether.

#### M. BERAKHOT 9:5

A. A man is obligated to recite a blessing over evil just as he recites a blessing over good.
B. As it is said, "And you shall love the Lord your God with all your heart, with all your soul and with all your might" (Dt. 6:5).
C. With all your heart — [this means] with both of your inclinations, with the good inclination and with the evil inclination.
D. And with all your soul-even if He takes your soul.
E. And with all your might-with all of your money.

The exegetical construction constitutes another extra-documentary form that the Mishnah presents. It is used seldom, but, when used, it follows a standard pattern: proposition, proof-text, exposition of the proof-text.

### VIII. BESAH

**M. 4:1A-D**

### IX. BIKKURIM

**M. 1:5A-E**
**M. 1:9 HOW DO WE KNOW + SCRIPTURAL SOURCE & EXEGESIS**
**M. 3:1 (NARRATIVE)**
**M. 3:2-6 (NARRATIVE)**

3:2 A. How do they bring the firstfruits up [to the Temple]?
B. [The male inhabitants of] all the towns in the priestly course gather in the [main] town of the priestly course [M. Ta. 4:2],
C. and they sleep [outside] in the open area of the town
D. and they would not enter the houses [in the town, for fear of contracting corpse uncleanness].
E. And at dawn, the officer would say,
F. "Arise, and let us go up to Zion, to [the house of] the Lord our God (Jer. 31:6)."

3:3 A. Those [who come] from nearby bring figs and grapes,
B. but those [who come] from afar bring dried figs and raisins.
C. And an ox walks before them,
D. its horns overlaid with gold,
E. and a wreath of olive [leaves] on its head.
F. A flutist plays before them until they arrive near Jerusalem.
G. [Once] they arrived near Jerusalem, they sent [a messenger] ahead of them [to announce their arrival], and they decorated their firstfruits.
H. The high officers, chiefs, and treasurer [of the Temple] come out to meet them.
I. According to the rank of the entrants, they would [determine which of these officials would] go out.
J. And all the craftsmen of Jerusalem stand before them and greet them, [saying],
K. "Brothers, men of such and such a place, you have come in peace."

3:4 A. A flutist plays before them, until they reach the Temple mount.
B. [Once] they reached the Temple mount,
C. Even Agrippa the King puts the basket [of firstfruits] on his shoulder, and enters, [and goes forth] until he reaches the Temple court.
D. [Once] he reached the Temple court, the Levites sang the song,
E. "I will extol thee, 0 Lord, for thou hast drawn me up, and hast not let my foes rejoice over me" (Ps. 30:1).

3:5 A. The pigeons that [were] on top of the baskets were [sacrificed as] burnt offerings,
B. but [the pigeons] which are in their hands are given [as a gift] to the priests.

3:6 A. While the basket is still on his shoulder, he recites [the entire confession of firstfruits, beginning] from the words "I declare this day to the Lord your God" (Dt. 26:3),
B. [and proceeding] until he finishes the entire passage.
C. R. Judah says, "[While the basket is on his shoulder, he recites only] up to [the second part of the confession, which begins with the words,] 'A wandering Aramean was my father' (Dt. 26:6)."
D. "[Once] he [has] reached [the words] 'A wandering Aramean was my father,'

E. he takes the basket down from his shoulder, and holds it by its rim,
F. and a priest puts his hand beneath [the basket], and waves it [before the altar].
G. And [then the Israelite] recites [the second part of the confession, beginning] from [the words], 'A wandering Aramean was my father,' [and proceeding] until he finishes the entire passage."
H. And [then] he places [the basket] beside the altar, and he bows down and departs.

The narrative follows no pattern I can discern, nor do I see rules that dictate the way in which the rite is described, other than that rather short clauses and phrases predominate. The narrative passages of the Mishnah recur in the setting of Temple rites, which are described in language that otherwise plays little or no role in our document.

### x. Demai

**M. 2:4**
**M. 3:3A-D**
**M. 4:4**
**M. 5:8**
**M. 7:1**
**M. 7:2**

7:1 A. He who invites his friend to eat with him [on the Sabbath],
B. and he [the friend] does not trust him [the host] in the matter of tithing-
C. he [the friend] says [stipulates] on the eve of the Sabbath [before the Sabbath begins],
D. "That which I shall separate tomorrow [one hundredth part of the whole],
E. "behold, it is [made first] tithe,
F. "and the remainder of the [first] tithe is adjacent to it.
G. "That which I have made [first] tithe is [now] made heave offering of the tithe for it [for the remainder of the first tithe, nine hundredths of the whole, adjacent to the specified hundredth part] ,
H. "and second tithe is to the north of it, or to the south of it [of the designated remainder of the first tithe], and is redeemed with coins."

7:2 A. They mixed for him a cup [of wine] —
B. he says,
C. "That which I shall leave at the bottom of the cup,
D. "behold, it is [made first] tithe,
E. "and the remainder of the [first] tithe is adjacent to it.
F. "That which I have made [first] tithe is [now] made heave offering of the tithe for it [for the remainder of the first tithe],
G. "and second tithe is at its mouth [at the mouth of the cup], and is redeemed with coins."

The formulaic quality of the recitation does not impart that same character to the whole.

**M. 7:6**

XI. EDUYYOT

**M. 5:6-7**

I. He would say, "They do not administer bitter water [to test the woman accused of adultery] in the case of a proselyte woman or in the case of a freed slave girl.
J. And sages say, "They do administer the test."
K. They said to him, M'SH B: "Karkemit, a freed slave girl, was in Jerusalem, and Shemaiah and Abtalion administered the bitter water to her."

The ma'aseh follows the standard form, act/decision. The passage then shades off into a protracted narrative, with no counterpart in the rest of the Mishnah. I indent the components as they unfold, item by item. At any point of indentation the narrative can have come to a suitable conclusion without loss of meaning.

L. He said to them, "They administered it to her to make her into an example."
M. They excommunicated him, and he died while he was subject to the excommunication, so the court stoned his bier.
N. Said R. Judah, "God forbid that Aqabiah was excommunicated!
O. "For the courtyard is never locked before any Israelite of the wisdom and fear of sin of a man like Aqabiah b. Mehalalel.
P "But whom did they excommunicate? It was Eliezer b. Hanokh, who cast doubt on [the sages' ruling about] the cleanness of hands.
Q. "And when he died, the court sent and put a stone on his bier."
R. This teaches that whoever is excommunicated and dies while he is subject to the excommunication — they stone his bier.
5:7 A. When he was dying, he said to his son, "My son, retract in the four rulings which I had laid down."
B. He said to him, "And why do you retract now?"
C. He said to him, "I heard the rulings in the name of the majority, and they heard them in the name of the majority, so I stood my ground on the tradition which I had heard, and they stood their ground on the tradition they had heard.
D. "But you have heard the matter both in the name of an individual and in the name of the majority.

E. "It is better to abandon the opinion of the individual and to hold with the opinion of the majority."

F. He said to him, "Father, give instructions concerning me to your colleagues."

G. He said to him, "I will give no instructions."

H. He said to him, "Is it possible that you have found some fault with me?"

I. He said to him, "No. It is your deeds which will bring you near, or your deeds which will put you off [from the others]."

**M. 8:7**

**M. Eduyyot 8:7**

A. Said R. Joshua, "I have a tradition from Rabban Yohanan b. Zakkai, who heard it from his master, and his master from his master, as a law revealed to Moses at Sinai,

B. "that Elijah is not going to come to declare unclean or to declare clean, to put out or to draw near,

C. "but only to put out those who have been brought near by force, and to draw near those who have been put out by force."

The saying is in no way patterned, and the context does not help.

**xii. Erubin**

**M. Erubin 2:6**

A. Said R. Ilai, "I heard from R. Eliezer, 'Even if it is a kor's space [seventy-five thousand square cubits] .,

B. "And so did I hear from him, 'The inhabitants of a courtyard, one of whom forgot and did not prepare an erub —

C. "'as to his house, it is prohibited for him to bring in [something] or take [it] out.

D. "'But for them it is permitted.'

E. "And so did I hear from him, 'They fulfill their obligation [to eat bitter herbs] through hart's tongue on Passover.'

F. "And I made the rounds of all his disciples, and I looked for a partner for myself [in holding these traditions] but found none."

The triplet (and so did I hear) joins unrelated items. The Mishnah's lists are topical and propositional, rarely joined merely by the name of the authority behind them.

**M. Erubin 3:9**

A. R. Dosa b. Harkinas says, "He who goes before the ark on the first day of the New Year says,

B. "'Give us strength, Lord our God, on this first day of the month,

C. "'whether it is today or tomorrow.'

D. "On the next day he says, 'If it is today or yesterday."'

E. And sages did not concur with him.

Many of the unpatterned compositions set forth singleton rules, such as the foregoing.

**M. 5:3**
**M. 5:4**
**M. 5:5**
**M. 6:7**

### XIII. Gittin

**M. 3:7**
**M. 3:8**
**M. 5:7**
**M. 7:4**
**M. 9:3**

### M. Gittin 9:3

A. The text of the writ of divorce [is as follows]:
B. "Lo, you are permitted to any man."
C. R. Judah says, "[In Aramaic]: Let this be from me your writ of divorce, letter of dismissal, and deed of liberation, that you may marry anyone you want."
D. The text of a writ of emancipation [is as follows]:
E. "Lo, you are a free girl, lo, you are your own [possession]" [cf. Dt. 21:14].

The difference between patterned and unpatterned language is clear in the foregoing; the Mishnah's formulaic language does not affect the recorded texts of legal documents.

**M. 9:9**

### XIV. Hagigah

### M. Hagigah 1:6

A. He who did not make a festal offering on the first festival day of a festival makes festal offerings throughout the entire festival, including the last festival day of the Festival [of Tabernacles].
B. [But if] the festival passed and he did not make a festal offering, he is not liable to make it good.
C. Of such a person it is said, That which is crooked cannot be made straight, and that which is wanting cannot be reckoned (Qoh. 1:15).

1:7 A. R. Simeon b. Menasia says, "What is that which is crooked which cannot be made straight?
B. "This is one who has sexual relations with woman in a forbidden relationship and produces a mamzer from her.
C. "If you should claim that it applies to a thief or a robber, he can make restitution and be made straight."

D. R. Simeon b. Yohai says, "They call that which is crooked only one who was straight to begin with and who became crooked. What is such a person? It is a disciple of a sage who took his leave of the Torah."

The additional language — Scripture and its exegesis — is uncommon for the Mishnah.

### xv. Hallah

**M. 3:1**
**M. 3:2**
**M. 4:6**

4:6 A. [Even though he intends to set a batch of dough aside for later use (M. 4:6B),] a person must [immediately] remove the requisite amount [of dough as] dough offering [from the batch of] dough, the dough offering of which has not [yet] been removed, in order to make [separate] it [the dough offering] in [a state of] cleanness.

B. [This is the case even though he intends to set the dough aside] until it rots [so that he can] continue separating it [from that batch of dough] dough offering on behalf of dough about which there is a doubt whether or not dough offering [already] has been separated from it.

C. For dough offering on behalf of dough about which there is a doubt whether or not dough offering had [already] been separated from it may be removed from a clean [batch to fulfill the liability] for an unclean [batch], and [also may be removed] from [a batch that is] not nearby [connected].

I simply do not know how to classify this singleton.

### xvi. Horayyot

I find nothing pertinent.

### xvii. Hullin

**M. 5:5**
**M. 12:5**

### xviii. Kelim

**M. 3:6**
**M. 7:6**
**M. 15:5**

### xix. Keritot

**M. Keritot 3:7**

A. Said R. Aqiba, "I asked Rabban Gamaliel and R. Joshua in the meat-market of Emmaus, where they had gone to buy a beast for the banquet of Rabban Gamaliel's son:

B. "He who has sexual relations with his sister, with his father's sister, and with his mother's sister in one spell of inadvertence [M. 1:IE9, 10, 11] — what is the rule?

C. "Is he liable once for all of them, or once for each and every action?

D. "They said to me, 'We have not heard [the rule on that case], but we have heard the rule, He who has sexual relations with his five wives when they are menstruating, in a single spell of inadvertence, that he is liable for each and every act of sexual relations.

E. "'And we regard the matters [in the former case] as subject to a proof by an argument a fortiori [from the latter case]., "

3:8 A. And further did R. Aqiba ask them:

B. "A limb is dangling from a beast-what is the rule?"

C. They said to him, "We have not heard the rule [for that particular case]. But we have heard the rule concerning a limb which is dangling from a man, that it is deemed clean.

D. "For so did the people afflicted with boils do in Jerusalem:

E. "He goes on the eve of Passover to a physician, and he [the physician] cuts [the boil] until he leaves on it a hair's breadth. And he sticks it onto a thorn. And he [the patient] pulls away from it.

F. "And this one would prepare his Passover. And the physician likewise would prepare his Passover.

G. "And we regard the matters as subject to a proof by an argument a fortiori."

3:9 A. And further did R. Aqiba ask them:

B. "He who slaughters five animal sacrifices outside [the Temple courtyard] in a single spell of inadvertence, what is the law?

C. "Is he liable for one [single] offering for all of them, or for one [offering] for each and every act of slaughter?"

D. They said to him, "We have not heard."

E. Said R. Joshua, "I heard [the rule which applies] in the case of him who eats from a single animal sacrifice in five dishes, that he is liable on account of each and every act for violation of the laws of sacrilege.

F. "And I regard the matters as subject to proof by an argument a fortiori."

G. Said R. Simeon, "Not in this way did R. Aqiba interrogate them but in the case of:

H. "One who eats remnant from five animal sacrifices in a single act of inadvertence-what is the law?

I. "Is he liable for a single offering for all of them, or is he liable for an offering for each and every one?

J. "They said to him, 'We have not heard.'

K. "Said R. Joshua, 'I heard that in the case of:

L. "'One who eats from a single animal sacrifice in five dishes in a single act of inadvertence, that he is liable to bring an offering for each and every one on account of violation of the laws of sacrilege.

M. "'And I regard the matters as subject to proof by an argument a fortiori.'
N. "Said R. Aqiba, 'If it is law, we shall accept it. But if it is for purposes of argument, there is an answer.'
O. "He said to him, 'Answer.'
P. "He said to him, 'No. If you have so stated in the case of the laws of sacrilege, in which instance the one who gives something to someone else to eat is equivalent to the one who eats, and the one who causes another to enjoy benefit is equivalent to the one who derives benefit himself, joining together a quantity sufficient to be subject to the laws of sacrilege over a long period of time, will you say so in the case of remnant, to which none of all of these things apply?'"

Here we have a pattern that is not familiar in the Mishnah, a triplet, M. 3:7B-E, M. 34:8B-G, and M. 3:9B-F, as well as a supplementary set of materials. That each entry of the triplet is carefully patterned is obvious. Here is a form that is extra-documentary to the Mishnah: it lists diverse rulings in the name of a single authority, rather than observing the Mishnah's list-making of topically coherent items. But the sentence-formations and the logic — the qol vehomer and its anomaly — are absolutely standard for our document.

**M. 6:3**
**M. 6:5**

## XX. Ketubot

**M. 1:5**
**M. 2:1**
**M. 3:5**
**M. 4:6**
**M. 6:2**

6:2 A. He who agrees to pay over money [as a dowry] to his son-in-law, and his son-in-law dies-
B. sages have said, "He can claim, 'To your brother was I willing to give [money], but to you [the levir] I am not willing to give money.'"

If we remove the attributive language, B, we have "He who agrees...can claim...." This is a simple sentence and in context not part of a list or exemplary of a pattern.

**M. 6:5**
**M. 8:2**
**M. 10:6**
**M. 11:1**

## XXI. Kilayim

**M. 3:2**

**M. 3:5**
**M. 4:3**
**M. 9:8**

9:8 A. Nothing is prohibited on account of [the laws of] diverse kinds except [wool and flax which are] spun or woven [together],
B. as it is written, You shall not wear sha'atnez (Dt. 22:11)-something which is hackled, spun, or woven.
C. R. Simeon b. Eleazar says, "It is turned away, and turns his Father in Heaven against him."

The citation of a rule + "as it is written" + proof-text follows a pattern in no way characteristic of the Mishnah.

### XXII. Maaserot

**M. 5:2**

### XXIII. Makhshirin

**M. 4:8**
**M. 5:9**

### XXIV. Makkot

**M. 1:6**
**M. 2:4**
**M. 2:5**
**M. 3:12-14**

3:12 [A] How do they flog him?
[B] One ties his two hands on either side of a pillar,
[C] and the minister of the community grabs his clothing —
[D] if it is torn, it is torn, and if it is ripped to pieces, it is ripped to pieces —
[E] until he bares his chest.
[F] A stone is set down behind him, on which the minister of the community stands.
[G] And a strap of cowhide is in his hand, doubled and redoubled, with two straps that rise and fall [fastened] to it.

3:13 [A] Its handle is a handbreadth long and a handbreadth wide,
[B] and its end must reach to his belly button.
[C] And he hits him with a third of the stripes in front and two-thirds behind.
[D] And he does not hit [the victim] while he is either standing or sitting, but bending low,
[E] as it is said, And the judge will cause him to lie down (Dt. 25:2).
[F] And he who hits him hits with one hand, with all his might.

3:14 [A] And a reader reads: If You will not observe to do . . . the Lord will have your stripes pronounced, and the stripes of your seed (Dt. 28:58ff.) (and he goes back to the beginning of the passage). And you will observe the words of this covenant (Dt. 29:9), and he finishes with, But he is full of compassion and forgave their iniquity (Ps. 78:38), and he goes back to the beginning of the passage.

[B] And if the victim dies under the hand of the one who does the flogging, the latter is exempt from punishment.
[C] [But if] he added even a single stripe and the victim died, lo, this one goes into exile on his account,
[D] If the victim dirtied himself, whether with excrement or urine, he is exempt [from further blows].
[E] R. Judah says, "In the case of man, with excrement; and in the case of a woman, with urine."

Here once more is the narrative of a rite as the Mishnah's framers present the narrative. This story-telling style (we cannot call it a "form") is common in the document. We note a little list at the end, concluding in a dispute, and the contrast to the foregoing is striking.

### XXV. MAASER SHENI

**M. 2:10**
**M. 4:4**
**M. 4:5**
**M. 5:2**
**M. 5:8**
**M. 5:10-13**

5:10 A. During the afternoon of the last festival day [of Passover during the fourth and seventh years of the Sabbatical cycle, the farmers] would recite the confession [Dt. 26:13-15, stating that they have properly distributed or destroyed all consecrated produce from their domain, cf. M. M.S. 5:6].
B. What was the confession?
C. I removed all holy [produce] from my house (Dt. 26:13f) —
D. this [refers to] second tithe and [produce from] a planting's fourth year [of growth].
E. I gave it to the Levite —
F. this [refers to] the tithe for the Levites [first tithe].
G. And I also gave it —
H. this [refers to] heave offering and heave offering of the tithe.
I. To the stranger, the orphan, and the widow —
J. this [refers to] poor man's tithe, gleanings, forgotten sheaves and what grows in the corner of the field [all of which are left for the poor];
K. even though [leaving] these is not a prerequisite for saying the confession.
L. From the house —
M. this [refers to] dough offering.

5:11 A. According to all the precepts you commanded me —
B. lo, if he separated second tithe before [he separated] first [tithe, i.e., out of order] he may not recite the confession.
C. I did not transgress your precepts —

D. [this means] I did not separate [agricultural gifts] from one kind [of food] on behalf of another kind, and not from harvested produce on behalf of unharvested produce, and not from unharvested produce on behalf of harvested produce and not from new produce [produce harvested after the current omer] on behalf of old produce [from before the current omer] and not from old produce on behalf of new produce [M. Ten 1:5].
E. And I did not forget anything —
F. I did not forget to praise you and to mention your name [in connection with my crop].

5:12 A. I did not eat of it while in mourning —
B. lo, if he ate [second tithe or produce of a planting's Fourth Year] while he was in a state of mourning before the burial, he may not recite the confession.
C. Nor did I separate unclean produce from it [as an agricultural gift]—
D. lo, if he separated it [the agricultural gift] when it was in a state of uncleanness, he may not recite the confession.
E. And I did not give [any of 'its value] for the dead —
F. I did not [use its value] to buy a coffin and shrouds for the dead.
G. And I did not give it —
H. to other mourners [whose dead are unburied].
I. I obeyed the Lord my God —
J. I brought it to the chosen Sanctuary [Jerusalem].
K. I did according to all you commanded me —
L. I was happy and made others happy [with the produce].

5:13 A. Look down from your holy dwelling place in heaven —
B. We did what you required of us, now ('p) you do what you promised us.
C. Look down from your holy dwelling place in heaven and bless your people Israel —
D. with sons and daughters.
E. And the earth which you gave us —
F. with dew and rain and with offspring of cattle,
G. As you vowed to our fathers [to give them] a land flowing with milk and honey —
H. in order to give the fruit a [sweet] taste.

The form is uncommon in the Mishnah, but the citation and glossing of a fixed text certainly conforms to a clear pattern, and that pattern is systematically executed here.

### XXVI. MEGILLAH

**M. 1:3**

### XXVII. MEILAH

I identify nothing pertinent.

### XXVIII. MENAHOT

**M. 4:5**
**M. 8:2**
**M. 10:2**
**M. 10:3-4**

10:3 A. How did they do it?
B. Agents of the court go forth on the eve of [the afternoon before] the festival [of Passover].
C. And they make it into sheaves while it is still attached to the ground, so that it will be easy to reap.
D. And all the villagers nearby gather together there [on the night after the first day of Passover],so that it will be reaped with great pomp.
E. Once it gets dark [on the night of the sixteenth of Nisan], he says to them, "Has the sun set?"
F. They say, "Yes."
G. "Has the sun set?"
H. They say, "Yes."
I. "[With] this sickle?"
J. They say, "Yes."
K. "[With] this sickle?"
L. They say, "Yes."
M. "[With] this basket?"
N. They say, "Yes."
O. "[With] this basket?"
P. They say, "Yes."
Q. On the Sabbath, he says to them, "[Shall I reap on] this Sabbath?"
R. They say, "Yes."
S. "[Shall I reap on] this Sabbath?"
T. They say, "Yes."
U. "Shall I reap?"
V. They say, "Reap."
W. "Shall I reap?"
X. They say, "Reap"-
Y. three times for each and every matter.
Z. And they say to him, "Yes, yes, yes."
AA. All of this [pomp] for what purpose?
BB. Because of the Boethusians, for they maintain, "The reaping of the [barley for] the omer is not [done] at the conclusion of the festival."

10:4 A. They reaped it,
B. and they put it into baskets,
C. They brought it to the court [of the Temple].
D. "They did parch it in fire, "so as to carry out the requirement that it be parched with fire [Lev.2:141," the words of R. Meir.
E. And sages say, "With reeds and with stems of plants do they [first] beat it [to thresh it],"so that it not be crushed.

F. "And they put it into a tube.
G. "And the tube was perforated, so that the fire affect all of it."
H. They spread it out in the court, and the breeze blows over it.
I. They put it into a grist mill and took out therefrom a tenth ephah, which is sifted through thirteen sieves [M. 6:7].
J. And the residue is redeemed and eaten by anyone. And it is liable for the dough offering, but exempt from tithes.
K. R. Aqiba declares it liable for both dough offering and tithes.
L. He came [on the sixteenth of Nisan] to the tenth [ephah of flour], and put in its oil and frankincense [M. 6:31.
M. He poured in [oil] and mingled it and waved it.
N. And he brought it near [M. 5:6] and took out the handful and offered it up.
O. And the residue is eaten by the priests.

Here is another fine example of the style governing narratives of rites — simple, brief sentences of clauses, which convey the actions and formulas of the procedure.

**M. 11:6-7**
**M. 12:4**

### XXIX. MIDDOT

**M. 1:2**

**M. MIDDOT 1:2**

A. The man in charge of the Temple mount would go around to every watch, and lighted torches were [flaring] before him.
B. And to any watch which was not standing did the man in charge of the Temple mount say, "Peace be with you."
C. [If] it was obvious that he was sleeping, he beats him with his staff.
D. And he had the right to burn his garment.
E. And they say, "What is the noise in the courtyard?"
F. "It is the noise of a Levite being smitten, and his clothing being burned, for he went to sleep at his post."
G. R. Eliezer b. Jacob says, "One time they found my mother's brother sleeping and burned his garment."

Here is another familiar style. No one could confuse these Temple-tales with the ma'aseh.

**M. 1:8**
**M. 1:9**
**M. 2:1**
**M. 2:2**

2:2 A. All those who enter the Temple mount enter at the right, go around, and leave at the left,

B. except for him to whom something happened, who goes around to the left.
C. "What ails you, that you go around to the left?"
D. "For I am a mourner."
E. "May he who dwells in this house comfort you."
F. "That I am excommunicated."
G. "'May he who dwells in this house put it into their heart that they draw you nigh again,' " the words of R. Meir.
H. Said to him R. Yosé, "You have treated the matter as if they have transgressed the law on his account.
I. "But: 'May he who dwells in this house put it into your heart that you listen to the opinion of your fellows, and they draw you nigh again.'"

The little dispute at the end, G-I, may yield a continuation of the narrative, if we simply choose between G and I and drop the rest.

**M. 3:1-8**
**M. 4:1**
**M. 4:3**
**M. 4:4**
**M. 4:5**

### XXX. MIQVAOT

**M. 2:9**
**M. 3:3**
**M. 6:4**
**M. 6:8**

### XXXI. MOED QATAN

I find nothing relevant.

### XXXII. NAZIR

**M. 6:6**
**M. 9:5**

### XXXIII. NEDARIM

**M. 5:5**
**M. 9:6**
**M. 9:9**

**M. NEDARIM 9:9**

A. They unloose a vow for a man by reference to his own honor and by reference to the honor of his children.
B. They say to him, "Had you known that the next day they would say about you, 'That's the way of so-and-so, going around divorcing his wives,'
C. "and that about your daughters they'd be saying, 'They're daughters of a divorcée! What did their mother do to get herself divorced' [would you have taken a vow]?"
D. And [if] he then said, "Had I known that things would be that way, I should never have taken such a vow"'

E. lo, this [vow] is not binding.

The illustrative material, B-E, is not patterned, and the base-sentence, A, is not part of a sequence, e.g., from M. 9:8 to 9:10. So we have nothing more than a singleton.

**M. 9:10**
**M. 10:4**
**M. 11:8**

### XXXIV. NEGAIM

**M. 2:3**

2:3 A. A priest blind in one of his eyes, or whose eyes are dim, should not examine the plagues, as it is said, In accord with the entire vision of the eyes of the priest (Lev. 13:12).

B. As to a dark house, they do not break open windows in it to examine its plague.

**M. 3:2**

3:2 A. A bridegroom on whom a plague appeared — they give him the seven days of the marriage feast [before inspecting him]-

B. him, and his house, and his garment.

C. And so with respect to the festival: they give him all the days of the festival.

Both items are singletons, standing by themselves out of all context with their neighbors. But both make use of familiar forms and do not belong here. I include them only to underscore the difference between unpatterned or extra-documentary forms and those that follow the Mishnah's program. M. 2:3 adopts one of the two standard commentary-forms (verse/meaning; proposition/proof-text). M. 3:2 utilizes apocopation.

**M. 7:4**

### M. NEGAIM 7:4

A. He who removes the tokens of uncleanness or cauterizes the quick flesh transgresses a negative rule.

B. And as to cleanness?

C. [If he does so] before he comes to the priest, he is clean.

D. [If he does so] after his certification [of uncleanness], he is unclean.

E. Said R. Aqiba, "I asked Rabban Gamaliel and R. Joshua, en route to Gadvad, '[If he does so] during his quarantine, what is the law?'

F. "They said to me, 'We have not heard. But we have heard, 'Before he comes to the priest, he is clean. After his certification, he is clean.'

G. "I began to bring proofs to them."

H. (1) Whether [one does so when he] stands before the priest, and

I. [whether one does so when he] is in the midst of his quarantine-he is clean, before the priest declares him unclean.

The narrative, E-I, is anomalous for the Mishnah, though not an unfamiliar form: setting, direct discourse, citation of sages, I-statements.

**M. 9:3**
**M. 11:7**

**M. Negaim 11:7**

A. (1) A summer garment which has colored and white checks- (2) they spread from one [white] to another [white square].
B. They asked R. Eliezer, "And lo, it is a distinctive check?"
C. He said to them, "I have not heard."
D. Said to him R. Judah b. Beterah, "May I teach concerning it?"
E. He said to him, "If to confirm the words of sages, yes."
F. He said to him, "Perhaps it will remain on it for two weeks, and that which stands on garments for two weeks is unclean."
G. He said to him, "You are a great sage, for you have confirmed the words of sages."

Here is another brief narrative, lacking both plot and all pretense at serving as a precedent, for that matter.

**M. 12:5-7**

**M. Negaim 12:5**

A. How is the inspection of the house [carried out]?
B. Then he who owns the house shall come and tell the priest, saying, 'There seems to me to be some sort of disease in my house' (Lev. 14:35).
C. Even a disciple of a sage, knowing that it certainly is a plague, will not decisively state, "A plague has appeared to me in the house," but, "Something like a plague has appeared to me in the house."
D. Then the priest shall command that they empty the house before the priest goes to examine the disease, lest all that is in the house be declared unclean: and afterward the priest shall go in to see the house (Lev. 14:36)-
  E. "and even bundles of wood, and even bundles of reeds," the words of R. Judah.
  F. R. Simeon says, "That is work in connection with emptying [the house] ."
    G. Said R. Meir, "And what of his property does it render unclean? If you say, his wooden objects and his clothing and his metal objects-he immerses them and they are clean,
    H. "For what has the Torah shown concern?
    I. "For his [clay] utensils, his cruse, and his ewer.
    J. "If thus the Torah has shown concern for his humble possessions, all the more so for cherished possessions.
    K. "If thus for his property, all the more so for the soul of his sons and his daughters.

L. "If thus for the evil person, how much the more so for the righteous person."

12:6 A. He does not go into his own house and [from there] shut up [the other house], nor into the house in which the plague is located and shut it up. But he stands at the door of the house in which the plague is located and shuts it up,

B. as it is said, Then the priest shall go out of the house to the door of the house, and shut up the house seven days (Lev. 14:38).

C. He comes at the end of the week and sees if it spread.

D. Then the priest shall command that they take out [dismantle] the stones in which is the disease and throw them into an unclean place outside the city (Lev. 14:40).

E. Then they shall take other stones and put them in the place of those stones. And he shall take other plaster and plaster the house (Lev. 14:40).

F. He does not take stones from this side and bring them to that side, and not dirt from this side and bring it to that side, and not lime from any place.

G. He does not bring one [stone] for [to replace] two, nor two for one, but he brings two for two, for three, for four.

H. On this basis have they said, "Woe to an evil person. Woe to his neighbor."

I. The two of them tear down the stones, the two of them scrape the walls, the two of them bring stones.

J. But he alone brings the dirt.

K. As it is said, And he shall take other plaster and plaster the house (Lev. 14:40).

L. His fellow does not join with him in the plastering.

12:7 A. He comes at the end of a week and sees if it returned:

B. And he shall break down [demolish] the house, its stones and timber and the plaster of the house, and he shall carry them forth out of the city to an unclean place (Lev. 14:45).

C. Spreading which is near-in any measure.

D. And that which is distant-the size of a split bean.

E. And that which returns in houses-two split beans.

Here is another narrative, built around verses of Scripture as in the one we noted at M. M.S. above. Excluding the interpolated dispute and homily, E-F, G-L, the narrative flows smoothly and moves forward without attributed statements or disputes.

**M. 14:1-3, 7-10**

14:1 A. How do they purify the leper?

B. (1) He would bring a new flask of clay, and (2) put in it a quarter-log of living water, and (3) bring two undomesticated birds.

C. He slaughtered one of them over the clay utensil and over the living water

D. He dug [a hole] and buried it before him [the leper].
E. He took cedar-wood and hyssop and scarlet wool and bound them together with the ends of the strip [of wool] and brought near to them the tips of the wings and the tip of the tail of the second [bird].
F. He dipped [them in the blood of the slaughtered bird] and sprinkled [the blood] seven times on the back of the hand of the leper.
G. There are some who say, "On his forehead."
H. And thus did he sprinkle on the lintel of the house on the outside.

14:2 A. He came to send forth the living bird.
B. He does not turn its face either to the sea or to the city or to the wilderness, as it is said, And he shall send forth the living bird out of the city into the open field (Lev. 14:53).
C. He came to shave the leper.
D. He passed a razor over all of his flesh.
E. And he washed his garments and immersed.
F. He is clean so far as rendering unclean through entry, and lo, he renders unclean like an insect.
G. He enters inside the wall,
H. is separated from his house seven days [Lev, 14:8],
I. and is prohibited from sexual intercourse.

14:3 A. On the seventh day he shaves the second shaving, as [in the manner of] the first shaving.
B. He washed his garments and immersed.
C. He is [now] clean so far as rendering unclean like an insect.
D. And lo, he is one who has immersed [on the selfsame day]: he eats [second] tithe.
E. [Once] his sun has set:
F. he eats heave offering.
G. [Once] he has brought his atonement offering [on the eighth day],
H. he eats holy things.
I. It comes out that there are three [stages of] purifications in regard to a leper,
J. and three [stages of] purifications in regard to one who gives birth.

These are further examples of the narrative concerning the conduct of a rite, in the model of the foregoing.

### xxxv. Niddah

**M. 4:1**

**M. Niddah 8:4**

A. "A testing rag which is placed under the pillow, and blood was found on it —
B. "if it is round it is clean."
C. "If it is elongated, it is unclean," the words of R. Eleazar b. R. Sadoq.

This item is a random singleton; it invites a dispute but I see none.

**M. Niddah 5:2**

A. [If] one was eating heave offering and felt his limbs tremble
B. he holds on to the penis and swallows the heave offering.
C. And they are made unclean by any amount [of discharge] at all,
D. even though it is like a grain of mustard,
E. and less than that.

This item is a random singleton.

**M. 8:4**

**xxxvi. Ohalot**

**M. 16:1**

**M. Ohalot 16:1**

A. All movables bring uncleanness [as Tents] when they are as thick as an ox goad.
  B. Said R. Tarfon, "May I ruin my sons, that this is a ruined law, which the hearer heard and erred, that:
  C. "the farmer passes [by the tomb] and the ox goad is on his shoulder, and one side of it overshadowed the tomb, and they declared him unclean,
  D. "because [of the rule governing] utensils which overshadow the corpse."
  E. Said R. Aqiba, "I shall repair it so that the words of sages may endure. Thus:
  F. "all movables bring the uncleanness on the man who carries them if they are thick as an ox goad,
  G. "and on themselves if they are of any measure at all,
  H. "and on another man and utensils if they are a square handbreadth."

The item is unique in context; but the law is framed at F-H as a standard list, that is, for inclusion in the Mishnah.

**xxxvii. Orlah**
**M. Orlah 2:5**

A. Dositheus of Kefar Yatmah was one of the disciples of the House of Shammai and he said, "I have heard [a tradition] from Shammai the Elder, who said,
B. "'It does not convey uncleanness unless it is an egg's bulk [in quantity].'"

What is odd is the elaborate attributive, in place of Shammai says....

**M. 2:12**

**M. Orlah 2:12**

A. Yoezer of the Birah was one of the disciples of the House of Shammai, and he said, "I asked Rabban Gamaliel the Elder who was standing at the Eastern Gate [about the rule of M. 2:11A-C], and he said, 'It does not render [the dough] prohibited unless there is enough of it to leaven [by itself].'"

As above, we have an odd and elaborate attributive, but the formulation of the law itself is, in context, well patterned.

**xxxviii. Parah**

**M. 2:2**
**M. 3:1-6**

**M. Parah 3:1**

A. Seven days before the burning of the cow, they separate the priest who burns the cow from his house, [bringing him] to the chamber which faces the northeast corner of the Temple building, and it was called the stone house.

B. And they sprinkle on him all seven days [with a mixture] from all the purification [waters] which were there.

C. R. Yosé says, "They sprinkled on him only on the third and seventh [days] alone."

D. R. Hananiah Prefect of the Priests says, "On the priest who burns the cow they sprinkle each of the seven days.

E. "And on the one of the Day of Atonement, they sprinkled only on the third and seventh [days] alone."

3:2 A. There were courtyards in Jerusalem, built on rock, and under them was a hollow, [which served as a protection] against a grave in the depths.

B. And they bring pregnant women, who give birth there, and who raise their sons there.

C. And they bring oxen, and on them are doors, and the youngsters sit on top of them, with cups of stone in their hands.

D. [When] they reached the Siloam, they descended and filled them, and mounted and sat on top of them.

E. R. Yosé says, "From his place did he let down and fill [the cup, without descending]."

3:3 A. They came to the Temple mount and dismounted.

(B. The Temple mount and the courtyards under them is a hollow against a grave in the depth.)

C. And at the door of the courtyard was set up a flask of [ashes of] purification [rites done in the past].

D. And they bring a male sheep, and tie a string between its horns, and they tie a stick or a bushy twig on the head of the rope, and one throws it into the flask.

E. And one hits the male, and it starts backward.

F. And one takes [the ashes spilled onto the stick] and mixes as much of it as could be visible on the surface of the water.

G. R. Yosé says, "Do not give the Sadducees an opportunity to cavil. But he takes it and mixes it."

3:4 A. They did not prepare one purification offering [by virtue of the preparations made] for another purification offering, nor one child for his fellow.

B. "And youngsters had to be sprinkled [and immersed]," the words of R. Yosé the Galilean.

C. R. Aqiba says, "They did not have to be sprinkled."

3:6 A. And they would make a causeway from the Temple mount to the Mount of Olives, arches upon arches, an arch directly above each pair,

B. because of the grave in the depths,

C. on which the priest who burns the cow, and the cow, and all those that assist it go forth to the Mount of Olives.

Here we have another instance of the cultic narrative style, and here too, we notice, a dispute remains within the limits of the governing style, so that if we remove the attributions and one or another opinion, the narrative continues uninterrupted. The basic narrative goes forward at the following item.

**M. 3:7-11**

### XXXIX. PEAH

**M. 4:4**
**M. 5:5**
**M. 5:6**

### XL. PESAHIM

**M. 1:2**
**M. 5:6-9**

5:6 A. An Israelite slaughtered [the Passover lamb] and a priest received the blood, hands it to his fellow, and his fellow to his fellow,

B. [each one] receiving a full basin and handing back an empty one.

C. The priest nearest the altar tosses [the blood] in a single act of tossing, toward the base.

5:7 A. The first group went out and the second group came in.

B. The second group went out and the third group came in.

C. In accord with the rite of the first group were the rites of the second and third.

D. [The Levites meanwhile] proclaimed the Hallel psalms [113-118].

E. If they completed [the recitation], they repeated it, and if they completed the second time, they repeated it for a third-

F. even though they never in all their days had to repeat it a third time.

G. R. Judah says, "In all the days of the third group they never even reached the verse, I love the Lord because he has heard my voice (Ps. 116:1),

H. "because its numbers were small."

5:8 A. In accord with the rite as conducted on an ordinary day, so was the conduct of the rite on the Sabbath.

B. And the priests mopped up the courtyard [on the Sabbath, just as on a weekday],

C. contrary to sages' wishes.

D. R. Judah says, "A cup was filled with the mingled blood [which had been spilled]. One tossed it with a single act of tossing on the altar."

E. And sages did not concur with him.

5:9 A. How do they hang up [the carcasses] and flay them?

B. Iron hooks were set into the walls and pillars, on which they would hang up and flay the carcasses [M. Mid. 3:5].

C. And for whoever did not have space for hanging and flaying his carcass,

D. there were thin smooth poles, and one would put one end on his shoulder and one on the shoulder of his fellow,

E. and [thereon] hang and flay the carcass.

F. R. Eliezer says, "On the fourteenth of Nisan which coincided with the Sabbath, he would put his hand on the shoulder of his fellow, and the hand of his fellow on his shoulder, and thereon suspend and flay the carcass."

Once more the simple narrative style sets forth the conduct of a rite in the cult.

**M. 7:10**
**M. 7:11**
**M. 8:3**

**M. Pesahim 8:3**

A. He who says to his children, "Lo, I shall slaughter the Passover offering in behalf of the one of you who will get up to Jerusalem first"

B. once the first [child] poked his head and the greater part of his body into the city, he has effected acquisition of his share and has furthermore effected acquisition in behalf of his brothers along with himself.

C. Under all circumstances do [people] register with [a Passover offering] so long as there is an olive's bulk of meat for each and every one of them.

D. They register and then withdraw their registration from it until the moment that one will slaughter it.

E. R. Simeon says, "Until one will toss the blood on his behalf."

M. 8:3A-B is listed under apocopated sentences. I do not see any patterning at the foregoing, but rather, free-standing singleton at C.

**M. 9:1**

9:1 A. [The Lord said to Moses, Say to the people of Israel, if any man of you or of your descendants] is unclean or is on a long journey (Num. 9:9-10)

B. and did not observe the first [Passover], let him keep the second Passover [on the fourteenth of Iyyar].

C. [If ] he inadvertently or under constraint failed to observe the first Passover, let him keep the second Passover.

D. If so, why is it said, Unclean . . . or on a long journey?

E. For these are exempt from punishment by extirpation, and those are liable to punishment by extirpation [if they deliberately refrain from observing the second Passover].

The citation of a verse followed by amplification is uncommon in the Mishnah, though the form is a familiar one in other documents.

**M. Pesahim 9:6**

A. Said R. Joshua, "I have heard:
"(1) that a beast declared to be substituted for an animal set aside for a Passover offering is offered,
"and (2) that a beast declared to be substituted for an animal set aside for a Passover offering is not offered.

B. "And I cannot explain [the contradiction between these two opinions] ."

C. Said R. Aqiba, "I shall explain [the two sayings].

D. "[In the case of a beast designated as a substitute for an animal set apart as a Passover offering which was lost], the [lost] Passover offering which turned up before the slaughtering of the [substituted] Passover offering is set out to pasture until it is blemished, then is sold, and peace offerings are to be purchased with the money received for it, and so too is the rule for the beast substituted for it.

E. "[But if the lost beast which had been set aside for a Passover offering was found] after the slaughtering of the Passover [substituted in its place], it is offered as peace offerings, and so too is the rule for the beast substituted for it."

We have already seen the model in which Aqiba explains what another sage cannot sort out, but it is difficult to find striking traits of formalization in this item.

**M. 10:1**
**M. 10:3**
**M. 10:4**
**M. 10:7**

All of these items cite liturgical passages.

### XLI. Qiddushin

**M. 2:6**
**M. 2:7**
**M. 2:10**

#### M. Qiddushin 4:14

F. R. Meir says, "A man should always teach his son a clean and easy trade. And let him pray to him to whom belong riches and possessions.
G. "For there is no trade which does not involve poverty or wealth.
H. "For poverty does not come from one's trade, nor does wealth come from one's trade.
I. "But all is in accord with a man's merit."
J. R. Simeon b. Eleazar says, "Have you ever seen a wild beast or a bird who has a trade? Yet they get along without difficulty. And were they not created only to serve me? And I was created to serve my Master. So is it not logical that I should get along without difficulty? But I have done evil and ruined my living."
K. Abba Gurion of Sidon says in the name of Abba Gurya, "A man should not teach his son to be an ass driver, a camel driver, a barber, a sailor, a herdsman, or a shopkeeper. For their trade is the trade of thieves."
L. R. Judah says in his name, "Most ass drivers are evil, most camel drivers are decent, most sailors are saintly, the best among physicians is going to Gehenna, and the best of butchers is a partner of Amalek."
M. R. Nehorai says, "I should lay aside every trade in the world and teach my son only Torah.
N. "For a man eats its fruits in this world, and the principal remains for the world to come.
O. "But other trades are not that way.
P "When a man gets sick or old or has pains and cannot do his job, lo, he dies of starvation.
Q. "But with Torah it is not that way.
R. "But it keeps him from all evil when he is young, and it gives him a future and a hope when he is old...."

This sequence of wise sayings exhibits no patterning that I can discern.

### XLII. Qinnim

The entire tractate is carefully formalized.

### XLIII. Rosh Hashanah

**M. 2:3**
**M. 2:4**
**M. 2:6**
**M. 2:7**
**M. 3:1**

**M. Rosh Hashanah 3:8**

A. Now it happened that when Moses held up his hand, Israel prevailed, and when he let his hand fall, Amalek prevailed (Ex. 17:11).
B. Now do Moses's hands make war or stop it?
C. But the purpose is to say this to you:
D. So long as the Israelites would set their eyes upward and submit their hearts to their Father in heaven, they would grow stronger. And if not, they fell.
E. In like wise, you may say the following:
E Make yourself a fiery serpent and set it on a standard, and it shall come to pass that every one who is bitten, when he sees it, shall live (Num. 21:8).
G. Now does that serpent [on the standard] kill or give life? [Obviously not.]
H. But: So long as the Israelites would set their eyes upward and submit to their Father in heaven, they would be healed. And if not, they would pine away.

Here is another homily lacking all traits of patterning.

**M. 4:7**

The Mishnah contains a handful of instances in which the precedent-particle, M'SH, occurs, but the standard form is violated. We expect an action and a ruling, and the requirement is met, more or less, at B-C. But the rest of the passage ignores the purpose of the precedent-form and goes its own way in an elaborate exposition. That is why, in my judgment, in the following, we have not a precedent but a narrative with its own inner logic.

**M. Rosh Hashanah 2:8**

A. A picture of the shapes of the moon did Rabban Gamaliel have on a tablet and on the wall of his upper room, which he would show ordinary folk, saying, "Did you see it like this or like that?"
B. M'SH S: Two witnesses came and said, "We saw it at dawn [on the morning of the twenty-ninth] in the east and at eve in the west."
C. Said R. Yohanan b. Nuri, "They are false witnesses."
D. Now when they came to Yabneh, Rabban Gamaliel accepted their testimony [assuming they erred at dawn].
E. And furthermore two came along and said, "We saw it at its proper time, but on the night of the added day it did not appear [to the court]."
F. Then Rabban Gamaliel accepted their testimony.
G. Said R. Dosa b. Harkinas, "They are false witnesses.
H. "How can they testify that a woman has given birth, when, on the very next day, her stomach is still up there between her teeth [for there was no new moon!]?"

I. Said to him R. Joshua, "I can see your position."

2:9 A. Said to him Rabban Gamaliel, "I decree that you come to me with your staff and purse on the Day of Atonement which is determined in accord with your reckoning."

B. R. Aqiba went and found him troubled.

C. He said to him, "I can provide grounds for showing that everything that Rabban Gamaliel has done is validly done, since it says, These are the set feasts of the Lord, even holy convocations, which you shall proclaim (Lev. 23:4) . Whether they are in their proper time or not in their proper time, I have no set feasts but these [which you shall proclaim] [vs. M. 2:7D]."

D. He came along to R. Dosa b. Harkinas.

E. He [Dosa] said to him, "Now if we're going to take issue with the court of Rabban Gamaliel, we have to take issue with every single court which has come into being from the time of Moses to the present day,

F. "since it says, Then went up Moses and Aaron, Nadab and Abihu, and seventy of the elders of Israel (Ex . 24:9).

G. "Now why have the names of the elders not been given? To teach that every group of three [elders] who came into being as a court of Israel-lo, they are equivalent to the court of Moses himself."

H. [Joshua] took his staff with his purse in his hand and went along to Yabneh, to Rabban Gamaliel, on the Day of Atonement which is determined in accord with his [Gamaliel's] reckoning.

I. Rabban Gamaliel stood up and kissed him on his head and said to him, "Come in peace, my master and my disciple —

J. "My master in wisdom, and my disciple in accepting my rulings."

### XLIV. SANHEDRIN

The following resorts to one of the two exegetical forms, proposition + proof-text, and the fixed particle, "how do we know," likewise marks the formalization of the passage.

#### M. SANHEDRIN 1:6

A. The great sanhedrin was [made up of] seventy-one members,

B. and the small one was [made up of] twenty-three.

C. And how do we know that the great sanhedrin was to have seventy-one members?

D. Since it is said, Gather to me seventy men of the elders of Israel.

E. Since Moses was in addition to them, lo, there were seventy-one.

F. R. Judah says, "It is seventy"

G. And how do we know that a small one is twenty-three?

H. Since it is said, The congregation shall judge, and The congregation shall deliver (Num. 35:24, 25)-

I. one congregation judges, and one congregation saves-thus there are twenty.

J. And how do we know that a congregation is ten? Since it is said, How long shall I bear with this evil congregation [of the ten spies] (Num. . 14:27)-excluding Joshua and Caleb.
K. And how do we know that we should add three more?
L. From the implication of that which is said, You shall not follow after the many to do evil (Ex. 23:20), I derive the inference that I should be with them to do good.
M. If so, why is it said, After the many to do evil?
N. Your verdict of acquittal is not equivalent to your verdict of guilt.
O. Your verdict of acquittal may be on the vote of a majority of one, but your vote for guilt must be by a majority of two. Since there cannot be a court of an even number of members [twenty-two], they add yet another-thus twenty-three.
P. And how many residents must there be in a town so that it may be suitable for a sanhedrin? One hundred and twenty
Q. R. Nehemiah says, "Two hundred and thirty, equivalent in number to the chiefs of groups of ten [Ex. 18:21]."

**M. 3:6-7**
**M. 4:3-4**
**M. 4:5**

**M. SANHEDRIN 4:5**

A. How do they admonish witnesses in capital cases?
B. They would bring them in and admonish them [as follows]: "Perhaps it is your intention to give testimony (1) on the basis of supposition, (2) hearsay, or (3) of what one witness has told another;
C. "[or you may be thinking], 'We heard it from a reliable person.'
D. "Or, you may not know that in the end we are going to interrogate you with appropriate interrogation and examination.
E. "You should know that the laws governing a trial for property cases are different from the laws governing a trial for capital cases.
F. "In the case of a trial for property cases, a person pays money and achieves atonement for himself. In capital cases [the accused's] blood and the blood of all those who were destined to be born from him [who was wrongfully convicted] are held against him [who testifies falsely] to the end of time,
G. "For so we find in the case of Cain who slew his brother, as it is said, The bloods of your brother cry (Gen . 4:10) .
H. "It does not say, 'The blood of your brother,' but, 'The bloods of your brother' — his blood and the blood of all those who were destined to be born from him." Another matter:-The bloods of your brother- for his blood was spattered on trees and stones.
  I. Therefore man was created alone, (1) to teach you that whoever destroys a single Israelite soul is deemed by Scripture as if he had destroyed a whole world.
  J. And whoever saves a single Israelite soul is deemed by Scripture as if he had saved a whole world.

K. And (2) it was also for the sake of peace among people, so that someone should not say to his fellow, "My father is greater than your father."

L. And (3) [it was also on account of the minim,] so that the minim should not say, "There are many domains in Heaven."

M. And (4) to portray the grandeur of the Holy One, blessed be He. For a person mints many coins with a single seal, and they are all alike one another. But the King of kings of kings, the Holy One, blessed be He, minted all human beings with that seal of his with which he made the first person, yet not one of them is like anyone else. Therefore everyone is obligated to maintain, "On my account the world was created. , ,

N. Now perhaps you [witnesses] would like now to say, "What business have we got with this trouble?"

O. But it already has been written, He being a witness, whether he has seen or known, if he does not speak it, then he shall bear his iniquity (Lev. 5:1).

P. And perhaps you might want to claim, "What business is it of ours to convict this man of a capital crime?"

Q. But has it not already been said, When the wicked perish there is rejoicing (Prov. 11:10).

This remarkable exposition sets forth a protracted homily, rich in proof-texts, and no aspect of the item conforms to anything otherwise paramount in the Mishnah's program of formalization of prose.

**M. 5:4-5**
**M. 6:1**

**M. Sanhedrin 6:2**

A. [When] he was ten cubits from the place of stoning, they say to him, "Confess," for it is usual for those about to be put to death to confess.

B. For whoever confesses has a share in the world to come.

C. For so we find concerning Achan, to whom Joshua said My son, I pray you, give glory to the Lord, the God of Israel, and confess to him, [and tell me now what you have done: hide it not from me.] And Achan answered Joshua and said, Truly have I sinned against the Lord, the God of Israel and thus and thus I have done (Josh. 7:19). And how do we know that his confession achieved atonement for him? For it is said, And Joshua said, Why have you troubled us? The Lord will trouble you this day (Josh. 7:25) — This day the Lord will trouble you, but you will not be troubled in the world to come.

D. And if he does not know how to confess, they say to him, "Say as follows: 'Let my death be atonement for all of my transgressions.'"

E. R. Judah says, "If he knew that he had been subjected to perjury, he says, 'Let my death be atonement for all my sins, except for this particular sin [of which I have been convicted by false testimony]!'

F. They said to him, "If so, then everyone is going to say that, so as to clear themselves."

Here if we omit C, we find a narrative of how a rite is conducted.

**M. 6:5**

**M. Sanhedrin 6:5**

A. Said R. Meir, "When a person is distressed, what words does the Presence of God say? As it were: 'My head is in pain, my arm is in pain.'

B. "If thus is the Omnipresent distressed on account of the blood of the wicked when it is shed, how much the more so on account of the blood of the righteous!"

C. And not this only, but whoever allows his deceased to stay unburied overnight transgresses a negative commandment.

D. But [if] one kept [a corpse] overnight for its own honor, [for example,] to bring a bier for it and shrouds, he does not transgress on its account.

E. And they did not bury [the felon] in the burial grounds of his ancestors. But there were two graveyards made ready for the use of the court, one for those who were beheaded or strangled, and one for those who were stoned or burned.

Once more, a homily ignores all rules of formalization to which we are accustomed. The remainder strikes me as miscellaneous.

**M. 6:6**
**M. 7:2**
**M. 8:1**
**M. 10:5**
**M. 11:3**

xlv. Shabbat

**M. 13:3**
**M. 13:4**

**M. Shabbat 19:1**

A. R. Eliezer says, "If one did not bring a utensil [used for circumcision] on the eve of the Sabbath, he brings it openly on the Sabbath."

B. And in the time of the danger, one covers it up in the presence of witnesses.

C. And further did R. Eliezer state, "They cut wood to make coals to prepare an iron utensil [for circumcision]."

D. An operative principle did R. Aqiba state, "Any sort of labor [in connection with circumcision] which it is possible to do on the eve of the Sabbath does not override [the restrictions of] the Sabbath, and that which it is not possible to do on the eve of the Sabbath does override [the prohibitions of] the Sabbath."

I see no coherence in these three entries (A-B, C, D) but a set, A-C, then D. These ought to constitute a dispute, but are not formed into the usual pattern for such a presentation. Eliezer gives examples that would yield a rule framed in opposition to Aqiba's, but the anticipated process of reformalization for dispute-purposes has not taken place.

### XLVI. Shabuot

**M. 2:4**
**M. 4:2**
**M. 6:4**

### XLVII. Shebiit

**M. 3:4**
**M. 3:5**
**M. 10:3**
**M. 10:4**

### M. Shebiit 10:3

A. [A loan against which] a prosbol [has been written] is not cancelled [by the Sabbatical year].
B. This is one of the things which Hillel the Elder ordained.
C. When he saw that people refrained from lending one another money [on the eve of the Sabbatical year]
D. and [thereby] transgressed that which is written in the Torah, Beware lest you harbor the base thought [ . . and so you are mean to your kinsman and give him nothing (Dt. 15:9)],
E. Hillel ordained the prosbol [whereby the court, on behalf of the creditor, may collect unpaid debts otherwise cancelled by the Sabbatical year].

10:4 A. This is the substance of the prosbol:
B. "I declare to you, Messrs. X and Y, judges in such — and — such a place, that every debt which I have [which is owed to me] I may collect [the money owed me] anytime I wish."
C. And the judges sign below or the witnesses.

I see no elements of patterning in this presentation; the substance of the legal document responds to its own formal requirements, not those of the Mishnah.

### XLVIII. Sheqalim

**M. 1:2, 4**
**M. 2:1**
**M. 3:2-4**

**M. Sheqalim 3:3**

A. A member of the household of Rabban Gamaliel would go in and take his sheqel between his fingertips and throw it in front of the one who takes up the heave offering [of the sheqels, so as to make sure his coin would be used for the purchase of the public sacrifices].

B. And the one who takes up the heave offering intentionally pushes it into the basket.

C. The one who takes up the heave offering does not do so until he says to them, "Shall I take up the heave offering?" And they say to him, "Take up heave offering, take up heave offering, take up heave offering," three times.

3:4 A. He took up [heave offering] the first time and covered [the residue] with coverings.

B. [He took up the heave offering] a second time and covered [the residue] with covers.

C. But the third time he did not cover [it up].

D. [He covered the first two times], lest he forget and take up heave offering from those sheqels from which heave offering already had been taken.

E. He took up the heave offering the first time in behalf of the Land of Israel, the second time in behalf of cities surrounding it, and the third time in behalf of Babylonia, Media, and the more distant communities.

What we have is another instance of the narrative style — short, simple declarative sentences, arranged as subject-verb-object. Much of this tractate is set forth in this same style, which I do not allege constitutes a form.

**M. 4:5**
**M. 4:8**
**M. 5:2**
**M. 5:4**
**M. 5:5**
**M. 7:5**
**M. 8:5**

### xlix. Sotah

**M. 1:4-6**

1:4 A. They would bring her up to the high court which is in Jerusalem and admonish her as they admonish witnesses in a capital crime.

B. They say to her, "My daughter, much is done by wine, much is done by joking around, much is done by kidding, much is done by bad friends. For the sake of the great Name which is written in holiness, do it so that it will not be blotted out by water [Num. 5:23]."

C. And they tell her things which neither she nor the family of her father's house should be hearing.

1:5 A. [Now] if she said, "I am unclean," she gives a quittance for her marriage contract [which is not paid over to her], and goes forth [with a writ of divorce].

B. And if she said, "I am clean," they bring her up to the eastern gate, which is at the entrance of Nicanor's Gate.

C. There it is that they force accused wives to drink the bitter water,

D. and they purify women after childbirth and purify lepers.

E. And a priest grabs her clothes-if they tear, they tear, and if they are ripped up, they are ripped up-until he bares her breast.

F. And he tears her hair apart [Num. 5:18].

G. R. Judah says, "If she had pretty breasts, he did not let them show. And if she had pretty hair, he did not pull it apart."

1:6 A. [If] she was clothed in white clothing, he puts black clothes on hen

B. [If] she had gold jewelry, chains, nose rings, and finger rings on, they take them away from her to put her to shame.

C. Then he brings a rope made out of twigs and ties it above her breasts.

D. And whoever wants to stare at her comes and stares, except for her boy slaves and girl slaves, since in any case she has no shame before them.

E. And all women are allowed to stare at her, since it is said, That all women may be taught not to do after your lewdness (Ezek. 23:48).

The narrative style takes over to present the rite of the accused wife. We note that where verses of Scripture are available, the narrator will insert them, now with the intent of showing how their requirements are met in a concrete way. The same trait marks the composition at M. Sotah 8:1, below.

**M. 2:2-3**
**M. 3:1**
**M. 3:4**
**M. 8:1**

### M. Sotah 8:1

A. The anointed for battle, when he speaks to the people, in the Holy Language did he speak,

B. as it is said, And it shall come to pass when you draw near to the battle, that the priest shall approach (this is the priest anointed for battle) and shall speak to the people (in the Holy Language) and shall say to them, Hear, 0 Israel you draw near to battle this day (Dt. 20:2-3)-

C. against your enemies (Dt. 20:3)-and not against your brothers,

D. not Judah against Simeon, nor Simeon against Benjamin.

E. For if you fall into their [Israelites'] hand, they will have mercy for you,

F. as it is said, And the men which have been called by name rose up and took the captives and with the spoil clothed all that were naked among them and arrayed them and put shoes on their feet and gave them food to eat and something to drink and carried all the feeble of them upon asses and brought them to Jericho, the city of palm trees, unto their brethren, Then they returned to Samaria (II Chron. 28:15).
G. Against your enemies do you go forth.
H. For if you fall into their hand, they will not have mercy upon you.
I. Let not your heart be faint, fear not, nor tremble, neither be afraid (Dt. 20:3).
J. Let not your heart be faint-on account of the neighing of the horses and the flashing of the swords.
K. Fear not-at the clashing of shields and the rushing of the tramping shoes.
L. Nor tremble-at the sound of the trumpets.
M. Neither be afraid-at the sound of the shouting.
N. For the Lord your God is with you (Dt. 20:4)-
O. they come with the power of mortal man, but you come with the power of the Omnipresent.
P The Philistines came with the power of Goliath. What was his end? In the end he fell by the sword, and they fell with him.
Q. The Ammonites came with the power of Shobach [II Sam. 10:161. What was his end? In the end he fell by the sword, and they fell with him.
R. But you are not thus: For the Lord your God is he who goes with you to fight for you
S. (-this is the camp of the ark).

Once more we find ourselves far from the Mishnah's ordinary cadences and rhythms.

**M. 8:6**
**M. 9:1**
**M. 9:5-6**

### L. Sukkot

**M. 2:9**
**M. 3:10**
**M. 4:6, 7, 9**
**M. 5:2-4**

5:2 A. At the end of the first festival day of the Festival [the priests and Levites] went down to the women's courtyard.
B. And they made a major enactment [by putting men below and women above].
C. And there were golden candle holders there, with four gold bowls on their tops, and four ladders for each candlestick.

D. And four young priests with jars of oil containing a hundred and twenty logs, [would climb up the ladders and] pour [the oil] into each bowl.

5:3 A. Out of the worn-out undergarments and girdles of the priests they made wicks,

B. and with them they lit the candlesticks.

C. And there was not a courtyard in Jerusalem which was not lit up from the light of bet hashshoebah.

5:4 A. The pious men and wonder workers would dance before them with flaming torches in their hand,

B. and they would sing before them songs and praises.

C. And the Levites beyond counting played on harps, lyres, cymbals, trumpets, and [other] musical instruments,

D. [standing, as they played] on the fifteen steps which go down from the Israelites' court to the women's court-

E. corresponding to the fifteen Songs of Ascents which are in the Book of Psalms-

F. on these the Levites stand with their instruments and sing their song.

G. And two priests stood at the upper gate which goes down from the Israelites' court to the women's court, with two trumpets in their hands.

H. [When] the cock crowed, they sounded a sustained, a quavering, and a sustained note on the shofar

I. [When] they got to the tenth step, they sounded a sustained, a quavering, and a sustained blast on the shofar

J. [When] they reached the courtyard, they sounded a sustained, a quavering, and a sustained blast on the shofar

K. They went on sounding the shofar in a sustained blast until they reached the gate which leads out to the east.

L. [When] they reached the gate which goes out toward the east, they turned around toward the west,

M. and they said, "Our fathers who were in this place turned with their backs toward the Temple of the Lord and their faces toward the east, and they worshipped the sun toward the east (Ez. 8:16).

N. "But as to us, our eyes are to the Lord."

O. R. Judah says, "They said it a second time, 'We belong to the Lord, our eyes are toward the Lord.'"

Once more, the narrative of a rite shifts into the familiar style. The inserted schismatic opinion at the end adheres to the same form.

## LI. Taanit

**M. 2:1-2**

### M. Taanit 2:1

A. The manner of fasting: how [was it done]?

B. They bring forth the ark into the street of the town and put wood ashes on (1) the ark, (2) the head of the patriarch, and (3) the head of the court.
C. And each person puts ashes on his head.
D. The eldest among them makes a speech of admonition: "Our brothers, concerning the people of Nineveh it is not said, 'And God saw their sackcloth and their fasting,' but, And God saw their deeds, for they repented from their evil way (Jonah 3:10).
E. "And in prophetic tradition it is said, Rend your heart and not your garments (Joel 2:13)."

2:2 A. They arise for prayer.
B. They bring down before the ark an experienced elder, who has children, and whose cupboard [house] is empty, so that his heart should be wholly in the prayer.
C. And he says before them twenty-four blessings:
D. the eighteen said every day, and he adds six more to them.

This item presents no surprises: how was it done? They do this, they do that. The rich repertoire of homily joins with appropriate proof-texts.

**M. 2:7**
**M. 3:8**
**M. 3:9**
**M. 4:2**
**M. 4:8**

**M. Taanit 3:8**

A. On account of every sort of public trouble (may it not happen) do they sound the shofar,
B. except for an excess of rain.
C. M'SH S: They said to Honi, the circle drawer, "Pray for rain."
D. He said to them, "Go and take in the clay ovens used for Passover, so that they not soften [in the rain which is coming]."
E. He prayed, but it did not rain.
F. What did he do?
G. He drew a circle and stood in the middle of it and said before Him, "Lord of the world! Your children have turned to me, for before you I am like a member of the family. I swear by your great name-I'm simply not moving from here until you take pity on your children!"
H. It began to rain drop by drop.
I. He said, "This is not what I wanted, but rain for filling up cisterns, pits, and caverns."
J. it began to rain violently.
K. He said, "This is not what I wanted, but rain of good will, blessing, and graciousness."
L. Now it rained the right way, until Israelites had to flee from Jerusalem up to the Temple Mount because of the rain.

M. Now they came and said to him, "Just as you prayed for it to rain, now pray for it to go away."

N. He said to them, "Go, see whether the stone of the strayers is disappeared."

O. Simeon b. Shatah said to him, "If you were not Honi, I should decree a ban of excommunication against you. But what am I going to do to you? For you importune before the Omnipresent, so he does what you want, like a son who importunes his father, so he does what he wants.

P. "Concerning you Scripture says, Let your father and your mother be glad, and let her that bore you rejoice (Prov. 23:25)."

This tale is close to unique in the Mishnah; only the story about Aqabiah at M. Ed. 5:6-7 competes for drama and intensity. The ma'aseh-particle is a false friend, signaling what is not present. The style of the story cannot be compared with that of the style of the rites, since much of the story here is worked out through dialogue, and the tensions and resolutions that make this story move find no counterpart in the laconic and one-dimensional narratives of rites.

### LII. Tamid

**M. 1:1-4**

1:2 A. He who wants to take up [the ashes] from the altar gets up early,

B. and immerses before the superintendent comes by.

C. And at what time does the superintendent come by?

D. Not all the times are the same.

E. Sometimes he comes at cockcrow, or near then, earlier or later.

F. The superintendent came and knocked on their door.

G. And they opened it to him.

H. He said to them, "Let him who has immersed come and cast lots."

I. They cast lots.

J. Whoever won won.

1:3 A. He took the key and opened the door and entered via the room of the hearth into the Temple courtyard.

B. And they entered after him with two lighted torches in their hands.

C. And they divided into two parties.

D. These go along the colonnade eastward, and those go along the colonnade westward.

E. They would go along and inspect [to make sure everything was in order], until they reach the place where they make the baked cakes.

F. These met up with those.

G. They said, "Is it in order?"

H. "All is in order."

I. They had those who make the baked cakes begin to make baked cakes.

This tractate consists of a narrative of the Temple rites in connection with the daily whole offering. A brief sample suffices to show the character of the whole.

**M. 2:1-5**
**M. 3:2, 4-7, 9**
**M. 4:1-3**
**M. 5:1-6**
**M. 7:1**

### LIII. TEBUL YOM

I find nothing that lacks formalization.

### LIV. TEMURAH

All the compositions exhibit familiar traits of formalization.

### LV. TERUMOT

**M. 3:7**

#### M. TERUMOT 3:7

A. And from where [do we know] that firstfruits should be separated before heave offering,
B. for this [heave offering] is called heave offering [Num. 18:111 and first [Num. 18:12],
C. and this [firstfruits] is called heave offering [Dt. 12:6] and first [Ex. 23:19].
D. Still firstfruits should be separated first, since they are the firstfruits of all [produce].
E. And [they should separate] heave offering before first [tithe],
F. since it [heave offering] is [called] 'first.'
G. And [they should separate] first tithe before second [tithe],
H. since it has in it [an offering called] 'first.'

The appeal to Scripture as the formal basis for the composition marks the passage as outside the documentary program of the Mishnah.

**M. 7:1**

### LVI. TOHOROT

I find nothing pertinent.

### LVII. UQSIN

**M. 3:7**

#### M. UQSIN 3:7

A. The palm sprout-
B. lo, it is like wood in every respect,
C. except that it is purchased with money of [second] tithe.
D. Unripened dates are food, but are free of tithes,

This is a singleton in two parts, A-C, D, and I see no traits of a list either within the passage or in its redactional setting.

### LVIII. YADAYIM

I find nothing relevant.

### LIX. YEBAMOT

**M. 8:4**

8:4 A. Said R. Joshua, "I have heard that:
B. "The eunuch performs the rite of halisah, and they perform the rite of halisah with his wife.
C. "And: The eunuch does not perform the rite of halisah, and they do not perform the rite of halisah with his wife.
D. "And I cannot explain [the conflict between the two sayings]."
E. Said R. Aqiba, "I shall explain [the conflict between the two sayings]. A eunuch castrated by man performs the rite of halisah, and they perform the rite of halisah with his wife,
F. "because there was a time in which he was valid [as a husband].
G. "A eunuch by nature does not perform the rite of halisah, and they do not perform the rite of halisah with his wife, because there was never a time in which he was valid.
H. Eliezer says, "Not so, but:
I. "A eunuch by nature performs the rite of halisah, and they perform the rite of halisah with his wife, because he may be healed.
J. "A eunuch castrated by man does not perform the rite of halisah, and they do not perform the rite of halisah with his wife, because he may never be healed."
K. Testified R. Joshua b. Beterah concerning Ben Megusat, who was in Jerusalem, a eunuch castrated by man, and they subjected his wife to levirate marriage- thus confirming the opinion of R. Aqiba.

Here is a familiar kind of composition, but it cannot be offered as an example of a broad, documentary form; it demonstrably follows a pattern, but not a documentary one.

**M. 12:6**

12:6 A. The proper way to carry out the rite of halisah [is as follows]:
B. He and his deceased childless brother's widow come to court.
C. And they offer him such advice as is appropriate for him,
D. since it says, Then the elders of the city shall call him and speak to him (Dt. 25:8).
E. And she shall say, My husband's brother refuses to raise up for his brother a name in Israel. He will not perform the duty of a husband's brother to me (Dt. 25:7).
F. And he says, I do not want to take her (Dt. 25:7).
G. And [all of this] was said in the Holy Language.
H. Then his brother's wife comes to him in the presence of the elders and removes his shoe from his foot and spits in his face (Dt. 25:9)- spit which is visible to the judges.
I. And she answers and says, "So shall it be done to the man who does not build up his brother's house."

J. Thus far did they pronounce [the words of Scripture].
K. And when R. Hyrcanus pronounced [the words of Scripture] under the terebinth tree in Kefar Etam and completed the reading of the entire pericope, they became accustomed to complete the entire pericope.
L. And his name shall be called in Israel: The house of him who has had his shoe removed (Dt. 25:9)-it is the duty of the judges, and not the duty of the disciples [so to name him].
M. R. Judah says, "It is the duty of all bystanders to say, 'The man whose shoe has been removed! The man whose shoe has been removed! The man whose shoe has been removed!' "

Predictably, a composition that sets forth a rite follows the narrative style and appeals to pertinent verses of Scripture.

**M. 14:2**

**M. 16:7**

16:7 A. Said R. Aqiba, "When I went down to Nehardea to intercalate the year, Nehemiah of Bet Deli came upon me. He said to me, 'I heard that only R. Judah b. Baba permits a wife in the Land of Israel to remarry on the evidence of a single witness [to her husband's death].'
B. "I stated to him, 'That is indeed so.'
C. "He said to me, 'Tell them in my name-
D. "'you know that the country is alive with ravaging bands-
E. "'I have a tradition from Rabban Gamaliel the Elder that:
F. "'They permit a wife to remarry on the testimony of a single witness [to her husband's death].'
G. "And when I came and laid the matters out before Rabban Gamaliel, he was overjoyed at my report and said, "We now have found a pair for R. Judah b. Baba.'
H. "And in the same discourse Rabban Gamaliel recalled that men were slain at Tel Arza, and Rabban Gamaliel the Elder permitted their wives to remarry on the evidence of a single witness."
I. And they confirmed in the practice of permitting [the wife to] remarry (1) on the evidence of a single witness, (2) on the evidence of a slave, (3) on the evidence of a woman, (4) on the evidence of a slave girl.
J. R. Eliezer and R. Joshua say, "They do not permit a woman to remarry on the evidence of a single witness."
K. R. Aqiba says, "Not on the evidence of a woman, nor on the evidence of a slave [12], nor on the evidence of a slave girl [14], nor on the evidence of relatives."
L. They said to him, M'SH B: "The Levites went to Soar, the date town, and one of them got sick on the road, and they left him in an inn.

M. “And upon their return, they said to the inn hostess, ‘Where is our buddy?’”
N. “She said to them, ‘He died, and I buried him.’
O. “And they permitted his wife to remarry [on the strength of her evidence].”
P. They said to him, “And should not a priest girl be equivalent to an inn hostess?”
Q. He said to them, “When she [the priest girl] will be an inn hostess, she will be believed.
R. “The inn hostess had produced for them his staff, his pouch, and the Torah scroll which he had had in hand.”

Here we have a composite that encompasses a rare mode of formulation, the first-person report, which, as we have noted, is not widely utilized but also not unknown. But the extensive character of the report, the narrative embedded within it, the amplification and even run-on quality of the whole — these mark the composite as unique in the Mishnah. Within the composite, the underlined portion of the ma’aseh follows the required form: action/ruling. I should point to this entry as the Mishnah’s single richest example of the combination of formalization and free-hand writing.

## lx. Yoma

**M. 1:1-8, 2:1**

### M. Yoma 1:1

A. Seven days before the Day of Atonement they set apart the high priest from his house to the councilors’ chamber.
B. And they [also] appoint another priest as his substitute,
C. lest some cause of invalidation should overtake him.
D. R. Judah says, “Also: they appoint another woman as a substitute for his wife,
E. “lest his wife die.
F. “Since it says, *And he shall make atonement for himself and for his house* (Lev. 16:6).
G. “*His house* — this refers to his wife.”
H. They said to him, “If so, the matter is without limit.”

1:2 A. All seven days he tosses the blood, offers up the incense, trims the lamp, and offers up the head and hind leg [of the daily whole offering],
B. But on all other days, if he wanted to offer it up he offers it up.
C. For a high priest offers up a portion at the head and takes a portion at the head [of the other priests].

1:3 A. They handed over to him elders belonging to the court, and they read for him the prescribed rite of the day [of atonement].
B. And they say to him, “My lord, high priest, you read it with your own lips,

C. "lest you have forgotten — or never [even] learned it to begin with."

D. On the eve of the Day of Atonement at dawn they set him up at the eastern gate and bring before him bullocks, rams, and sheep,

E. so that he will be informed and familiar with the service.

**M. 3:1-2**

**M. Yoma 3:1**

A. The supervisor said to them, "Go and see whether the time for slaughtering the sacrifice has come."

B. If it has come, he who sees it says, "It is daylight!"

C. Matithiah b. Samuel says, "[He says], 'Has the whole east gotten light?'

D. "'To Hebron?'

E. "And he says, 'Yes.' "

3:2 A. And why were they required to do this?

B. For once the moonlight came up, and they supposed that the eastern horizon was bright, and so they slaughtered the daily whole offering and had to bring it out to the place of burning.

C. They brought the high priest down to the immersion hut.

D. This governing principle applied in the Temple: Whoever covers his feet [and defecates] requires immersion, and whoever urinates requires sanctification [the washing] of hands and feet.

These entries conform to what is now a familiar pattern.

**M. 3:4**
**M. 3:6**
**M. 3:8-9**
**M. 4:1-3**

**M. Yoma 4:1**

A. He shook the box [with the lots] and brought up the two lots.

B. On one was written, "For the Lord," and on one was written, "For Azazel."

C. The prefect was at his right, and the head of the ministering family [father's house] at his left.

D. If the lot "for the Lord" came up in his right hand, the prefect says to him, "My lord, high priest, raise up your right hand."

E. If the one "for the Lord" came up in his left hand, the head of the ministering family says to him, "My lord, high priest, raise up your left hand."

F. He put them on the two goats and says, "For the Lord, a sin offering."

G. R. Ishmael says, "He did not have to say, 'Sin offering,' but only 'For the Lord.' "

H. And they respond to him, "Blessed is the name of the glory of his kingdom forever and even"

4:2 A. He tied a crimson thread on the head of the goat which was to be sent forth,
B. and set it up towards the way by which it would be sent out.
C. And on that which was to be slaughtered [he tied a crimson thread] at the place at which the act of slaughter would be made [the throat].
D. And he came to his bullock a second time [M. 3:8A] and put his two hands on it and made the confession.
E. And thus did he say, "O Lord, I have committed iniquity, transgressed, and sinned before you, I and my house and the children of Aaron, your holy people. "O Lord, forgive, I pray, the iniquities, transgressions, and sins which I have committed, transgressed, and sinned before you, 1, my house, and the children of Aaron, your holy people,
F. "as it is written in the Torah of Moses, your servant, For on this day shall atonement be made for you to cleanse you. From all your sins shall you be clean before the Lord (Lev. 16:30)."
G. And they responded to him, "Blessed is the name of the glory of his kingdom forever and ever."

**M. 5:1-6**
**M. 6:2**

6:2 A. He comes to the goat which is to be sent forth and lays his two hands on it and makes the confession.
B. And thus did he say, "O Lord, your people, the house of Israel, has committed iniquity, transgressed, and sinned before you. Forgive, 0 Lord, I pray, the iniquities, transgressions, and sins, which your people, the house of Israel, have committed, transgressed, and sinned before you,
C. "as it is written in the Torah of Moses, your servant, For on this day shall atonement be made for you to clean you. From all your sins shall you be clean before the Lord (Lev. 16:30)."
D. And the priests and people standing in the courtyard, when they would hear the Expressed Name [of the Lord] come out of the mouth of the high priest, would kneel and bow down and fall on their faces and say, "Blessed be the name of the glory of his kingdom forever and ever.""

When public rites and liturgies are set forth, the rules of formalization that govern writing for the Mishnah no longer apply. The counterpart is found in the liturgies of Mishnah-tractate Taanit.

**M. 6:3-8**
**M. 7:1-4**
**M. 8:4**

### LXI. Zabim

The tractate is comprised by lists, and no miscellanies form a composition of consequence.

### LXII. ZEBAHIM

I find nothing that is either unpatterned or patterned in accord with a form not characteristic of Mishnah-writing.

## III. WHEN SAGES WROTE FOR THE MISHNAH, THEY WROTE WITH THE MISHNAH'S PLAN IN MIND

We have found very few compositions that violate the forms that govern throughout the Mishnah, and among these, the few that are not simply odd singletons prove if not disciplined within a rigid pattern then at least highly stylized. For while within the definition given here we cannot classify the narrative style is a form, we also cannot ignore that it is a style that applies to a restricted topical repertoire. So the style worked as a form does, to limit the possibilities of free expression and to signal, through how something was said, the standing and character of what was said. When the framers of the materials that comprise the Mishnah wished to describe rites of the Temple and other rituals, they resorted to that very particular narrative style of brief and unadorned sentences — continuous tense, laconic, with practically monosyllabic dialogue — that otherwise does not occur in the document at all. Functionally, therefore, what we have called "narrative style" corresponds to a form, even though the language is not patterned and balanced in the way in which the language of law is.

That leaves a handful of singletons, none of them imparting to a sizable composite the miscellaneous character that, individually, all of them exhibit. That is why the Mishnah emerges from this complete form-analysis as a remarkably well-crafted document, one in which powerful conventions of order and syntax, logic and argument, secured for the whole a single voice.

Not only so, but the document's restrictive, penetrating protocol extends even to the ritualization of argument, defining the acceptable character of debate, which may be carried on in one way, not in another. The result is that a point may be demonstrated only in an accepted way, and refuted only within the framework of the same conventions of reasoning: analogy and anomaly forming the poles of argument, matching the list-maker's logic of analogy and polarity. If, as I have argued in *Judaism as Philosophy. The Method and Message of the Mishnah,* 1 the Mishnah says the same thing about nearly everything, we now see that its framers also speak about nearly everything in pretty much the same way. The list, augmented by the dispute, predominates.

Some much-repeated oddities of sentence-structure do find their way into the writing and thus reinforce the Mishnah's character as a highly formalized piece of writing: the apocopated sentence, other matched sentences, and the precedent. In this final catalogue, we note, rules of formulation and composition even extended to the correct style for use in dealing with a given subject-matter, much as the apocopated sentence turns out mainly to set up a problem for solution.

What of extra-documentary forms? These are two, story-telling and exegetical. In the entire document, only a few important compositions ignore the main lines of rhetorical expression that dictate the shape and structure of discourse throughout, and these involve stories in which sages figure not as partners to a dispute but prominently and idiosyncratically, e.g., Aqabiah and Aqiba. Formal patterns familiar in later documents, such as the commentary-form in its variations, do occur but only rarely and then in odd compositions, outside the main lines of Mishnah-discourse, as in the cases given above from Mishnah-tractate Sotah. We have a sufficient number of instances of commentary-form to validate the judgment that we do indeed deal with an established pattern, but not enough instances to treat the form as integral to the Mishnah. More to the point: the form violates the Mishnah's basic character as a set of lists animated by a taxonomic logic that generates disputes within the principle of analogy and provokes debates carried on within the logic of polarity (anomaly, that is, what looks alike really is not alike because...).

In the Rabbinic canon the Mishnah sets the standard for formal cogency. To trace the form-history of that canon from this starting point, we now define the issues that await.

First, is a piece of writing a document, defined by a coherent program of rhetoric, logic of coherent discourse, and topic or proposition; or is it a collection of miscellaneous compositions and composites that exhibit few important traits in common? Our criterion for a document has now come to full definition and instantiation, a piece of writing that holds together in so coherent a way that we find ample evidence of rules of rhetoric and logic operative throughout. A document is so set forth that nearly everything it contains can be shown to have been written with the requirements of that particular document in mind — and for no other purpose.

Second, if a piece of writing constitutes a document, then what are its paramount forms and what logic of coherent discourse operates throughout? Stated in simple terms: what rules instructed those writing compositions and composites intended for inclusion in a given document on how to do their work?

Third, how do the forms of later documents relate to those of earlier ones — the documentary form-history that this project promises to set forth in complete detail? Do earlier forms govern later on? If not, what new forms have come forward, and how do they serve in a way that the received ones did not? And if earlier forms do play a role later on, are these merely copied or recast and revised for new purposes?

As is our way, we have also to formulate a null-hypothesis. For the present project, it is simply: what would a piece of writing look like that is not highly formalized and expressed in stereotype and conventional patterns? In other words, what kind of writing do sages do when a document does not instruct them on how to express their ideas? For that purpose, I point first of all to tractate Abot, which typifies a formally-random collection of sayings, a scrapbook, just as the Mishnah typifies a formally-disciplined formulation of statements, a document. In tractate Abot we discern the traits of writing not with a particular document in mind, free-standing singletons lacking all formal coherence. In the contrast we assess the full measure of success attained by those who wrote the Mishnah, start to finish — the Mishnah, not only the compositions and composites assembled in the Mishnah, but the whole Mishnah, in nearly every part.

## ENDNOTES

[1]Columbia, 1991: University of South Carolina Press

# 7

# The Documentary Dimensions of Talmudic Phenomenology

## I. What Do We Mean by a Document? The Problem of Contextualizing the Free-Standing Saying or Composition

Since a Rabbinic text such as the Talmud is a document, meaning, a well-crafted and cogent text, one possessing integrity, and not merely a random and purposeless compilation of this and that, and, furthermore, since we now know in acute detail precisely the aesthetic, formal, and logical program followed by each of those texts, I am able to move to the logical next step. It is to define the context ("contextualizing") in which we conduct the study of the free-standing compositions or composites or even singleton-sayings out of which the document takes shape.

This I accomplish in a simple way. It is to show that in the background of the documents is to be identified three classes of writing, each with its own traits. Then we classify the writing that comprises a document among these three classes and determine the character of the document's paramount components. The classification is as follows:

[1] writing that is entirely formed within the rules of the documents that now present that writing.

[2] writing that is not shaped by documentary requirements of the text before us but by some other document of the canon;

[3] writing that is not shaped by the documentary requirements of the canonical compilations we now have.

It follows that — as a matter of hypothesis — in the Rabbinic texts are [2, 3] some writings that were formed independent of the plan of using them in a given compilation, alongside [1] the other writings that were formed in response to the program of the authorship of a given compilation. And that fact makes it possible to address the problem of the origin of writing that does not conform to the requirements of a particular document. In the present case, we take up writing that is in the Talmud but not of the Talmud.

The broader class of such writing encompasses those floating materials that progress from one document to another — some bearing names of authorities, some anonymous. Because they may serve any and all documents equally well (or poorly), these extra-documentary cognitive units and even whole compositions will guide us to that prior ("a priori") system that underlay all of the discrete documents of the canon of the Judaism of the dual Torah. And, within the framework of this monograph, that will constitute the answer to the question of where the Talmud comes from, besides its own compilers and the writers of its characteristic and necessary compositions.

To expand on this point: each of the score of documents that make up the canon of Judaism in late antiquity exhibits distinctive traits in logic, rhetoric, and topic, so that we may identify the purposes and traits of form and intellect of the authorship of that document. It follows that documents that exhibit coherent traits possess integrity and are not merely scrapbooks, compilations made with no clear purpose or aesthetic plan. But, as is well known, some completed units of thought — propositional arguments, sayings, and stories for instance — travel from one document to another. It further follows that the several documents intersect through shared materials. Furthermore, writings that peregrinate *by definition* do not carry out the rhetorical, logical, and topical program of a particular document. If they can fit in as well or as poorly wherever they end up, then they have not been composed with a particular document's definition in mind. Free-standing units of discourse then have to be classified in relationship to the document in which they appear, and it is that criterion, as I said, that dictates the context in which these compositions or composites are to be examined.

In framing a theory to accommodate the facts that documents are autonomous but also connected through such shared materials, therefore, we must account for the history of not only the documents in hand but also the completed pieces of writing that move from here to there. In fact documents stand in three relationships to one another and to the system of which they form part, that is, to Judaism, as a whole. The specification of these relationships constitutes the principal premise of this inquiry and validates the approach to the formation of compositions and composites that I offer here.

[1] Each document is to be seen all by itself, that is, as autonomous of all others.

[2] Each document is to be examined for its relationships with other documents universally regarded as falling into the same classification, as Torah.

[3] And, finally, in the theology of Judaism every canonical writing is equally and undifferentiatedly part of the Torah. That is to say, each document is to be allowed to take its place as part of the undifferentiated aggregation of documents that, all together, constitute the canon of, in the case of Judaism, the "one whole Torah revealed by God to Moses at Mount Sinai."

Simple logic makes self-evident the proposition that, if a document comes down to us within its own framework, as a complete book with a beginning, middle, and end, a book with its own logic in the ordering of materials, a logic we can identify, then, in preserving that book, the canon presents us with a document on its own and not solely as part of a larger composition or construct. So we too see the document as it reaches us, that is, as autonomous. If, second, a document contains materials shared verbatim or in substantial content with other documents of its classification, or if one document refers to the contents of other documents, then the several documents that clearly wish to engage in conversation with one another have to address one another. That is to say, we have to seek for the marks of connectedness, asking for the meaning of those connections. It is at this level of connectedness that we labor. For the purpose of comparison is to tell us what is like something else, what is unlike something else. To begin with, we can declare something unlike something else only if we know that it is like that other thing. Otherwise the original judgment bears no sense whatsoever. So, once more, canon defines context, or, in descriptive language, the first classification for comparative study is the document, brought into juxtaposition with, and contrast to, another document.

Finally, since the community of the faithful of Judaism, in all of the contemporary expressions of Judaism, concur that documents held to be authoritative constitute one whole, seamless "Torah," that is, a complete and exhaustive statement of God's will for Israel and humanity, we take as a further appropriate task, if one not to be done here, the description of the whole out of the undifferentiated testimony of all of its parts. These components in the theological context are viewed, as is clear, as equally authoritative for the composition of the whole: one, continuous system.

Some of these same documents draw upon materials that have been composed with the requirements of the respective documents in mind. The present monograph rests on the acknowledged fact that Rabbinic documents in some measure also draw upon a fund of completed compositions of thought that have taken shape without attention to the needs of the compilers of those documents. These constitute those free-standing cognitive units or composites of which we speak. Within the distinction between writing that serves a redactional purpose and writing that does not, we see four types of completed compositions of thought. Each type may be distinguished from the others by appeal to a single criterion of differentiation, that is to say, to traits of precisely the same sort. The indicative traits concern relationship to the redactional purpose of a piece of writing, viewed overall. This permits us to review the basic scheme:

[1] Some writings in a given compilation clearly serve the redactional program of the framers of the document in which those writings occur. In the case of the Talmud, defined as a Mishnah-commentary and amplification, that covers the great part of the document, most of which is given over to the document's definitive purpose.

[2] Some writings in a given compilation serve not the redactional program of the document in which they occur, but some other document, now in our hands. There is no material difference, as to the taxonomy of the writing of the classics in Judaism, between the first and second types; it is a problem of transmission of documents, not their formation. In the Talmud, we find abstracts of other documents, e.g., the Tosefta, the Sifra, and so on, and, when we do, these present themselves as distinctive in their indicative traits, so that we can always pick out what is primary to the Tosefta from what is primary to the Talmud, so too to Sifra or Sifré to Deuteronomy or the other documents upon which the compilers draw from time to time.

[3] Some writings in a given compilation serve not the purposes of the document in which they occur but rather a redactional program of a document, or of a type of document, that we do not now have, but can readily envision. One example would be, commentaries to passages of Scripture, read in sequence. In this category we find the possibility of imagining compilations that we do not have, but that can have existed but did not survive; or that can have existed and were then recast into the kinds of writings that people clearly preferred (later on) to produce.

[4] Some writings now found in a given compilation stand autonomous of any redactional program we have in an existing compilation or of any we can even imagine on the foundations of said writings. An example, out of the Talmud, is the formation of a theological demonstration or an ethical proposition, for the compilation of neither one of which we have any extant document.

The distinctions upon which these analytical taxonomies rest are objective, since they depend upon the fixed and factual relationship between a piece of writing and a larger redactional context.

[1] We know the requirements of redactors of the several documents of the Rabbinic canon, because I have already shown[1] what they are in the case of a large variety of documents.[2] When, therefore, we judge a piece of writing to serve the program of the document in which that writing occurs, it is not because of a personal impulse or a private and incommunicable insight, but because the traits of that writing self-evidently respond to the documentary program of the book in which the writing is located. Enough systematic work on the Talmud makes unnecessary any further discussion of this point.

[2] When, further, we conclude that a piece of writing belongs in some other document than the one in which it is found, that too forms a factual judgment.

[3] A piece of writing that serves no where we now know may nonetheless conform to the rules of writing that we can readily imagine and describe in theory. For instance, a propositional composition, that runs through a wide variety of texts to make a point autonomous of all of the texts that are invoked, clearly is intended for a propositional document, one that (like the Mishnah) makes points autonomous of a given prior writing, e.g., a biblical book, but that makes points that for one reason or another cohere quite nicely on their own. Authors of propositional

compilations self-evidently can imagine that kind of redaction. We have their writings, but not the books that they intended to be made up of those writings. Another example is a collection of stories about a given authority, or about a given kind of virtue exemplified by a variety of authorities. These and other types of compilations we can imagine but do not have are dealt with in the present rubric.

[4] And, finally, where we have utterly hermetic writing, sealed off from any broader literary context and able to define its own limits and sustain its point without regard to anything outside itself, we know that here we are in the presence of authorships that had no larger redactional plan in mind, no intent on the making of books out of their little pieces of writing.

I therefore offer public and accessible criteria for the classification of the data, and anyone is able to test my judgments against the actualities of the documents, their compositions and composites. My results are readily tested and reproduced. Since no subjective judgment limits their use, these data of a wholly phenomenological character bear implications for both literary and intellectual description. First, this theory on the literary formation of the Rabbinic canon in general posits three stages in the formation of writing. Moving ordinally, not temporally, from the latest to the earliest,[3] one stage is marked by the definition of a document, its topical program, its rhetorical medium, its logical message. The document as we know it in its basic structure and main lines therefore comes at the end. It follows that writings that clearly serve the program of that document and carry it the purposes of its authorship were made up in connection with the formation of *that* document. What I have already said about the Talmud suffices to make this point clear.

Another, and I think, prior stage is marked by the preparation of writings that do not serve the needs of a particular document now in our hands, but can have carried out the purposes of an authorship working on a document of a *type* we now have. The existing documents then form a model for defining other kinds of writings worked out to meet the program of a documentary authorship.

But there are other types of writings that in no way serve the needs or plans of any document we now have, and that, furthermore, also cannot find a place in any document of a type that we now have. These writings, as a matter of fact, very commonly prove peripatetic, traveling from one writing to another, equally at home in, or alien to, the program of the documents in which they end up. These writings therefore were carried out without regard to a documentary program of any kind exemplified by the canonical books of the Judaism of the dual Torah. They form what I conceive to be the earliest in the three stages of the writing of the units of completed thought that in the aggregate form the canonical literature of the Judaism of the dual Torah of late antiquity.

That proposed order in the formation of the distinct types of writing explains why, when we wish to find out where the Talmud comes from, we turn to the free-standing components of the document, as those items that come from persons outside of the circle of writers of the Talmud's own materials or prior to the work of writing the Talmud's materials. It further explains why, when we want to describe layers of thought autonomous of, and arguably prior to, the thought represented by the Talmud, we turn to those same writings.[4]

## II. Redaction and Writing. The Extreme Case of the Mishnah

My example of a document that is written down essentially in its penultimate and ultimate stages, that is, a document that takes formal, written-out shape[5] within the redactional process and principally there, is, of course, the Mishnah. In that writing, the patterns of language, e.g., syntactic structures, of the apodosis and protasis of the Mishnah's smallest whole units of discourse are framed in formal, mnemonic patterns. They follow a few simple rules. These rules, once known, apply nearly everywhere and form stunning evidence for the document's cogency. They permit anyone to reconstruct, out of a few key phrases, an entire cognitive unit, and even complete intermediate units of discourse. Working downward from the surface, therefore, anyone can penetrate into the deeper layers of meaning of the Mishnah. Then and at the same time, while discovering the principle behind the cases, one can easily memorize the whole by mastering the recurrent rhetorical pattern dictating the expression of the cogent set of cases. For it is easy to note the shift from one rhetorical pattern to another and to follow the repeated cases, articulated in the new pattern downward to its logical substrate. So syllogistic propositions, in the Mishnah's authors' hands, come to full expression not only in *what* people wish to state but also in *how* they choose to say it. The limits of rhetoric define the arena of topical articulation. Now to state my main point in heavy emphasis:

*The Mishnah's dominant formal traits of rhetoric indicate that the document has been formulated all at once, and not in an incremental, linear process extending into a remote (mythic) past, (e.g., to Sinai).*

These traits, common to a series of distinct cognitive units, are redactional, because they are imposed at that point at which someone intended to join together discrete (finished) units on a given theme. The varieties of traits particular to the discrete units and the diversity of authorities cited therein, including masters of two or three or even four strata from the turn of the first century to the end of the second, make it highly improbable that the several units were formulated in a common pattern and then preserved, until, later on, still further units, on the same theme and in the same pattern, were worked out and added. The entire indifference, moreover, to historical order of authorities and concentration on the logical unfolding of a given theme or problem without reference to the sequence of authorities, confirm the supposition that the work of formulation and that of redaction go forward together.

The principal framework of formulation and formalization in the Mishnah is the intermediate division rather than the cognitive unit. The least-formalized formulary pattern, the simple declarative sentence, turns out to yield many examples of acute formalization, in which a single distinctive pattern is imposed upon two or more (very commonly, groups of three or groups of five) cognitive units. While an intermediate division of a tractate may be composed of several such conglomerates of cognitive units, it is rare indeed for cognitive units formally to stand wholly by themselves. Normally, cognitive units share formal or formulary traits with others to which they are juxtaposed and the theme of which they share. It follows that the principal unit of formulary formalization is the intermediate division and not the cognitive unit.

And what that means for our inquiry, is simple: we can tell when it is that the ultimate or penultimate redactors of a document do the writing. Now let us see that vast collection of writings that exhibit precisely the opposite trait: a literature in which, while doing some writing of their own, the redactors collected and arranged available materials. The Mishnah provides a fine, extreme case of how the compositions and composites of a document may formally cohere, beginning to end, with the document's requirements and purpose. But no other Rabbinic document proves so uniform as a work of composition in the process of redaction, though the Talmud comes closer than most.

## III. When the Document Does Not Define the Literary Protocol: Stories Told But Not Compiled

Can I point to a kind of writing that in no way defines a document now in our hands or even a type of document we can now imagine, that is, one that in its particulars we do not have but that conforms in its definitive traits to those that we do have? Indeed I can, and it is the writing of stories about sages and other exemplary figures. To explain: The Bavli as a whole and through nearly the whole of its parts lays itself out as a commentary to the Mishnah. So the framers wished us to think that whatever they wanted to tell us would take the form of Mishnah commentary. But a second glance indicates that the Bavli is made up of enormous composites, themselves closed prior to inclusion in the Bavli. Some of these composites — the estimate of around 35% to 40% of Bavli's in initial sample is exaggerated, for in the larger tractates, the proportion is substantially lower[6] — were selected and arranged along lines dictated by a logic other than that deriving from the requirements of Mishnah commentary.

The components of the canon of the Judaism of the dual Torah prior to the Bavli had encompassed amplifications of the Mishnah, in the Tosefta and in the Yerushalmi, as well as the same for Scripture, in such documents as Sifra to Leviticus, Sifré to Numbers, another Sifré, to Deuteronomy, Genesis Rabbah, Leviticus Rabbah, and the like. But there was no entire document, now extant, organized around the life and teachings of a particular sage. Even The Fathers According to Rabbi Nathan, which contains a good sample of stories about sages, is not so organized as to yield a life of a sage, or even a systematic biography of any kind. Where events in the lives of sages do occur, they are thematic and not biographical in organization, e.g., stories about the origins, as to Torah-study, of diverse sages; death-scenes of various sages. The sage as such, whether Aqiba or Yohanan ben Zakkai or Eliezer b. Hyrcanus, never in that document defines the appropriate organizing principle for sequences of stories or sayings. And there is no other in which the sage forms an organizing category for any material purpose.[7] Accordingly, the decision that the framers of the Bavli reached was to adopt the two redactional principles inherited from the antecedent century or so and to reject the one already rejected by their predecessors, even while honoring it. [1] They organized the Bavli around the Mishnah. But [2] they adapted and included vast tracts of antecedent materials organized as scriptural commentary. These they inserted whole and complete, not at all in response to the Mishnah's program. But, finally, [3] while making provision for small-scale compositions built upon biographical principles, preserving both strings of sayings from a given master (and often a given tradent of a given master) as well as tales about authorities of the preceding half millennium, they *never* created redactional compositions, of a sizable order, that focused upon given authorities. But sufficient materials certainly lay at hand to allow doing so.

To show what might have been, I point to the simple fact that the final organizers of the Talmud of Babylonia had in hand a tripartite corpus of inherited materials awaiting composition into a final, closed document.

[1] The first type of material, in various states and stages of completion, addressed the Mishnah or took up the principles of laws that the Mishnah had originally brought to articulation.

[2] These the framers of the Bavli organized in accord with the order of those Mishnah-tractates that they selected for sustained attention. Second, they had in hand received materials, again in various conditions, pertinent to Scripture, both as Scripture related to the Mishnah and also as Scripture laid forth its own narratives. These they set forth as Scripture-commentary. In this way, the penultimate and ultimate redactors of the Bavli laid out a systematic presentation of the two Torahs, the oral, represented by the Mishnah, and the written, represented by Scripture.

[3] And, third, the framers of the Bavli also had in hand materials focused on sages. These in the received form, attested in the Bavli's pages, were framed around twin biographical principles, either as strings of stories about great sages of the past or as collections of sayings and comments drawn together solely because the same name stands behind all the collected sayings. These can easily have been composed into biographies. But the compilers failed to do so, and, in due course, we shall find reason to reclassify these compositions and composites as not biography at all but as the narrative presentation of (examples of) virtue. In the context of Christianity and of Judaism, it is appropriate to call the biography of a holy man or woman, meant to convey the divine message, a gospel. This is writing that is utterly outside of the documentary framework in which it is now preserved; nearly all

narratives in the Rabbinic literature, not only the biographical ones, indeed prove remote from any documentary program exhibited by the canonical documents in which they now occur.

For the writings that wholly carry out a redactional purpose the Mishnah is our prime example. Some writings ignore all redactional considerations we can identify. The stories about sages in the Fathers According to Rabbi Nathan for instance show us kinds of writing that are wholly out of phase with the program of the document that collects and compiles them. We further identify writings that clearly respond to a redactional program, but not the program of any compilation we now have in hand. There is little speculation about the identification of such writings. They will conform to the redactional patterns we discern in the known-compilations, but presuppose a collection other than one now known to us. Finally, we note that there are pieces of writing that respond to no redactional program known to us or susceptible to invention in accord with the principles of defining compilation known to us.

## IV. Pericopes Framed for the purposes of the Particular Document in which They Occur

This brings us back to our original classification-scheme. We have now to examine it in some detail. My analytical taxonomy of the writings now collected in various compilations point to not only three stages in the formation of the classics of Judaism. It also suggests that writing went on outside of the framework of the editing of documents, and also within the limits of the formation and framing of documents. Writing of the former kind then constituted a kind of literary work to which redactional planning proved irrelevant. But the second and the third kinds of writing responds to redactional considerations. So in the end we shall wish to distinguish between writing intended for the making of books — compositions of the first three kinds listed just now — and writing not response to the requirements of the making of compilations.

The distinctions upon which these analytical taxonomies rest are objective and no way subjective, since they depend upon the fixed and factual relationship between a piece of writing and a larger redactional context.

[1] We know the requirements of redactors of the several documents of the Rabbinic canon, because I have already shown what they are in the case of a large variety of documents. When, therefore, we judge a piece of writing to serve the program of the document in which that writing occurs, it is not because of a personal impulse or a private and incommunicable insight, but because the traits of that writing self-evidently respond to the documentary program of the book in which the writing is located.

[2] When, further, we conclude that a piece of writing belongs in some other document than the one in which it is found, that too forms a factual judgment.

My example is a very simple one: writing that can serve only as a component of a commentary on a given scriptural book has been made up for the book in which it appears. My example may derive from any of the ten Compilations of late antiquity. Here is one among innumerable possibilities.

**Sifré to Numbers I:VII.1**

A. "[The Lord said to Moses, 'Command the people of Israel that they put out of the camp every leper and every one having a discharge, and every one that is unclean through contact with the dead.] You shall put out both male and female, putting them outside the camp, that they may not defile their camp, in the midst of which I dwell'" (Gen. 5:1-4)

B. I know, on the basis of the stated verse, that the law applies only to male and female [persons who are suffering from the specified forms of cultic uncleanness]. How do I know that the law pertains also to one lacking clearly defined sexual traits or to one possessed of the sexual traits of both genders?

C. Scripture states, "...putting *them* outside the camp." [This is taken to constitute an encompassing formulation, extending beyond the male and female of the prior clause.]

D. I know, on the basis of the stated verse, that the law applies only to those who can be sent forth. How do I know that the law pertains also to those who cannot be sent forth?

E. Scripture states, "...putting them outside the camp." [This is taken to constitute an encompassing formulation, as before.]

F. I know on the basis of the stated verse that the law applies only to persons. How do I know that the law pertains also to utensils?

G. Scripture states, "...putting *them* outside the camp." [This is taken to constitute an encompassing formulation.]

**I:VII.2.**A. [Dealing with the same question as at 1.F,] R. Aqiba says, "'You shall put out both male and female, putting them outside the camp.' Both persons and utensils are implied."

B. R. Ishmael says, "You may construct a logical argument, as follows:

C. "Since man is subject to uncleanness on account of *Negaim* ["plagues"], and clothing [thus: utensils] are subject to uncleanness on the same count, just as man is subject to being sent forth [ostracism], likewise utensils are subject to being sent forth."

D. No, such an argument is not valid [and hence exegesis of the actual language of Scripture, as at A, is the sole correct route]. If you have stated the rule in the case of man, who imparts uncleanness when he exerts pressure on an object used for either sitting or lying, and, on which account, he is subject to ostracism, will you say the same rule of utensils, which do not impart uncleanness when they exert pressure on an object used for sitting and lying? [Clearly there is a difference between the uncleanness brought about by a human being from that brought about by an inanimate object, and therefore the rule that applies to the one will not necessarily apply to the other. Logic by itself will not suffice, and, it must follow, the proof of a verse of Scripture alone will suffice to prove the point.]

E. [No, that objection is not valid, because we can show that the same rule does apply to both an inanimate object and to man, namely] lo, there is the case of the stone affected with a *nega*, which will prove the point. For it does not impart uncleanness when it exerts pressure on an object used for sitting or lying, but it does require ostracism [being sent forth from the camp, a rule that Scripture itself makes explicit].

F. Therefore do not find it surprising that utensils, even though they in general do not impart uncleanness when they exert pressure on an object used for sitting or lying, are to be sent forth from the camp." [Ishmael's logical proof stands.]

**I:VII.3** A. R. Yosé the Galilean says, "'You shall put out both male and female, putting them outside the camp, that they may not defile their camp, in the midst of which I dwell.'

B. "What marks as singular male and female is that they can be turned into a generative source of uncleanness [when they die and are corpses], and, it follows, they are to be sent forth from the camp when they become unclean [even while alive], so anything which can become a generative source of uncleanness will be subject to being sent forth from the camp.

C. "What is excluded is a piece of cloth less than three by three fingerbreadths, which in the entire Torah is never subject to becoming a generative source of uncleanness."

**I:VII.4** A. R. Isaac says, "Lo, Scripture states, '[And every person that eats what dies of itself or what is to torn by beasts, whether he is a native or a sojourner, shall wash his clothes and bathe himself in water and be unclean until the evening; they he shall be clean.] But if he does not wash them or bathe his flesh, he shall bear his iniquity' (Lev. 17:15-16).

B. "It is on account of failure to wash one's body that Scripture has imposed the penalty of extirpation.

C. "You maintain that it is on account of failure to wash one's body that Scripture has imposed the penalty of extirpation. But perhaps Scripture has imposed a penalty of extirpation only on account of the failure to launder one's garments.

D. "Thus you may construct the argument to the contrary [*su eipas*]: if in the case of one who has become unclean on account of corpse-uncleanness, which is a severe source of uncleanness, Scripture has not imposed a penalty merely because of failure to launder one's garments, as to one who eats meat of a beast that has died of itself, which is a minor source of uncleanness, it is a matter of reason that Scripture should not impose a penalty on the account of having failed to launder the garments."

The indentation signals a secondary amplification. Why do I maintain that the composition can serve only the document in which it occurs? The reason is that we read the verse in a narrow framework: what rule do we derive from the *actual* language at hand. No. 1 answers the question on the basis of an exegesis of the verse. No. 2 then provides an alternative proof. Aqiba provides yet another reading of the language at hand. Ishmael goes over the possibility of a logical demonstration. I find it difficult to see how Yosé's pericope fits in. It does not seem to me to address the problem at hand. He wants to deal with a separate issue entirely, as specified at C. No. 4 pursues yet another independent question. So Nos. 3, 4 look to be parachuted down. On what basis? No. 3 deals with our base verse. But No. 4 does not. Then what guided the compositors to introduce Nos. 1, 2, 3, and 4? Nos. 1, 2 deal with the exegesis of the limited rule at hand: how do I know to what classifications of persons and objects ostracism applies? No. 1 Answers to questions, first, the classifications, then the basis for the rule. No. 2 introduces the second question: on what basis do we make our rule? The answer, as is clear, is Scripture, not unaided reason. Now at that point the issue of utensils emerges. So Yosé the Galilean's interest in the rule governing a utensil — a piece of cloth — leads to the intrusion of his item. And the same theme — the rule governing utensils, garments — accounts for the introduction of I:VII.4 as well. In sum, the redactional principle is looks to be clear: treat the verse, then the theme generated by the verse. Then this piece of writing can have been formed only for the purpose of a commentary to the book of Numbers: Sifré to Numbers is the only one we have. QED

### v. Pericopes Framed for the purposes of a Particular Document But Not of a Type we Now Possess

A piece of writing that serves no where we now know may nonetheless conform to the rules of writing that we can readily imagine and describe in theory. For instance, a propositional composition, that runs through a wide variety of texts to make a point autonomous of all of the texts that are invoked, clearly is intended for a propositional document, one that (like the Mishnah) makes points autonomous of a given prior writing, e.g., a biblical book, but that makes points that for one reason or another cohere quite nicely on their own. Authors of propositional compilations self-evidently can imagine that kind of redaction. We have their writings, but not the books that they intended to be made up of those writings. In all instances, the reason that we can readily imagine a compilation for that will have dictated the indicative traits of a piece of writing will prove self-evident: we have compilations of such a type, if not specific compilations called for by a given composition. A single example suffices. It derives from Sifra.

If the canon of Judaism included a major treatise or compilation on applied logic and practical reason, then a principal tractate, or set of tractates, would be devoted to proving that reason by itself cannot produce reliable results. And in that treatise would be a vast and various collection of sustained discussions, which spread themselves across Sifra and Sifré to Numbers and Sifré to Deuteronomy, the Yerushalmi and the Bavli, as well as other collections. Here is a sample of how that polemic has imposed itself on the amplification of Lev. 1:2 and transformed treatment of that verse from an exegesis to an example of an overriding proposition. It goes without saying that where we have this type of proof of the priority of Scripture over logic, or of the necessity of Scripture in the defining of generative taxa, the discussion serves a purpose that transcends the case, and on that basis I maintain the proposition proposed here. It is that there were types of collections that we can readily imagine but that were not made up. In this case, it is, as is clear, a treatise on applied logic, and the general proposition of that treatise is that reliable taxonomy derives only from Scripture.

**Sifra Parashat Vayyiqra Dibura Denedabah Parashah 2=III.I.1.**

A. "Speak to the Israelite people [and say to them, 'When any [Hebrew: Adam] of you presents an offering of cattle to the Lord, he shall choose his offering from the herd or from the flock. If his offering is a burnt offering from the herd, he shall offer a male without blemish; he shall offer it at the door of the tent of meeting, that he may be accepted before the Lord;] he shall lay [his hand upon the head of the burnt offering, and it shall be accepted for him to make atonement for him]'" (Lev. 1:2):

B. "He shall lay his hand:" Israelites lay on hands, gentiles do not lay on hands.

C. [But is it necessary to prove that proposition on the basis of the cited verse? Is it not to be proven merely by an argument of a logical order, which is now presented?] Now which measure [covering the applicability of a rite] is more abundant, the measure of wavings or the measure of laying on of hands?

D. The measure of waving [the beast] is greater than the measure of laying on of hands.

E. For waving [the sacrifice] is done to both something that is animate and something that is not animate, while the laying on of hands applies only to something that is animate.

F. If gentiles are excluded from the rite of waving the sacrifice, which applies to a variety of sacrifices, should they not be excluded from the rite of laying on of hands, which pertains to fewer sacrifices? [Accordingly, I prove on the basis of reason the rule that is derived at A-B from the verse of Scripture.]

G. [I shall now show that the premise of the foregoing argument is false:] [You have constructed your argument] from the angle that yields waving as more common and laying on of hands as less common.

H. But take the other angle, which yields laying on of hands as the more common and waving as the less common.

I. For the laying on of hands applies to all partners in the ownership of a beast [each one of whom is required to lay hands on the beast before it is slaughtered in behalf of the partnership in ownership of the beast as a whole],

J. but the waving of a sacrifice is not a requirement that applies to all partners in the ownership of a beast.

K. Now if I eliminate [gentiles' laying on of hands] in the case of the waving of a beast, which is a requirement applying to fewer cases, should I eliminate them from the requirement of laying on of hands, which applies to a larger number of cases?

L. Lo, since a rule pertains to the waving of the sacrifice that does not apply to the laying on of hands, and a rule pertains to the laying on of hands that does not apply to the waving of the sacrifice, it is necessary for Scripture to make the statement that it does, specifically:

M. "He shall lay his hand:" Israelites lay on hands, gentiles do not lay on hands.

The basic premise is that when two comparable actions differ, then the more commonly performed one imposes its rule upon further actions, the rule governing which is unknown. If then we show that action A is more commonly performed than action B, other actions of the same classification will follow the rule governing A, not the rule governing B. Then the correct route to overturn such an argument is to show that each of the actions, the rule governing which is known, differs from the other in such a way that neither the one nor the other can be shown to be the more commonly performed. Then the rule governing the further actions is not to be derived from the one governing the two known actions. The powerful instrument of analytical and comparative reasoning proves that diverse traits pertain to the two stages of the rite of sacrifice, the waving, the laying on of hands, which means that a rule pertaining to the one does not necessarily apply to the other. On account of that difference we must evoke the specific ruling of Scripture. The polemic in favor of Scripture, uniting all of the components into a single coherent argument, then insists that there really is no such thing as a genus at all, and Scripture's rules and regulations serve a long list of items, each of them *sui generis,* for discovering rules by the logic of analogy and contrast is simply not possible.

### VI. Pericopes Framed for the purposes Not Particular to a Type of Document Now in Our Hands

Some writings stand autonomous of any redactional program we have in an existing compilation or of any we can even imagine on the foundations of said writings. Compositions of this kind, as a matter of hypothesis, are to be assigned to a stage in the formation of classics prior to the framing of all available documents. For, as a matter of fact, all of our now extant writings adhere to a single program of conglomeration and agglutination, and all are served by composites of one sort, rather than some other. Hence we may suppose that at some point prior to the decision to make writings in the model that we now have but in some other model people also made up completed units of thought to serve these other kinds of writings. These persist, now, in documents that they do not serve at all well. And we can fairly easily identify the kinds of documents that they can and should have served quite nicely indeed. These then are the three stages of literary formation in the making of the classics of Judaism.

Of the relative temporal or ordinal position of writings that stand autonomous of any redactional program we have in an existing compilation or of any we can even imagine on the foundations of said writings we can say nothing. These writings prove episodic; they are commonly singletons. They serve equally well everywhere, because they demand no traits of form and redaction in order to endow them with sense and meaning. Why not? Because they are essentially free-standing and episodic, not referential and allusive. They are stories that contain their own point and do not invoke, in the making of that point, a given verse of Scripture. They are sayings that are utterly ad hoc. A variety of materials fall into this — from a redactional perspective — unassigned, and unassignable, type of writing. They do not belong in books at all. By that I mean, whoever made up these pieces of writing did not imagine that what he was forming required a setting beyond the limits of his own piece of writing; the story is not only complete in itself but could stand entirely on its own; the saying spoke for itself and required no nurturing context; the proposition and its associated proofs in no way was meant to draw nourishment from roots penetrating nutriments outside of its own literary limits.

Where we have utterly hermetic writing, able to define its own limits and sustain its point without regard to anything outside itself, we know that here we are in the presence of authorships that had no larger redactional plan in mind, no intent on the making of books out of their little pieces of writing. We may note that, among the "unimaginable" compilations is not a collection of parables, since parables rarely[8] stand free and never are inserted for their own sake. Whenever in the Rabbinic canon we find a parable, it is meant to serve the purpose of an authorship engaged in making its own point; and the point of a parable is rarely, if ever, left unarticulated. Normally it is put into words, but occasionally the point is made simply by redactional setting. It must follow that, in this canon, the parable cannot have constituted the generative or agglutinative principle of a large-scale compilation. It further follows, so it seems to me, that the parable always takes shape within the framework of a work of composition for the purpose of either a large-scale exposition or, more commonly still, of compilation of a set of expositions into what we should now call the chapter of a book; that is to say, parables link to purposes that transcend the tale that they tell (or even the point that the tale makes). Let me now give one example of what I classify as a free-standing piece of writing, one with no place for itself in accord with the purposes of compilers either of documents we now have in hand or of documents we can readily envisage or imagine. My example again derive from Sifra, although, as a matter of fact, every document of the canon yields illustrative materials for all three types of writing.

The issue of the relationship between the Mishnah and Scripture deeply engaged a variety of writers and compilers of documents. Time and again we have evidence of an interest in the scriptural sources of laws, or of greater consequence in the priority of Scripture in taxonomic inquiry. We can show large-scale compositions that will readily have served treatises on these matters. But if I had to point to a single type of writing that is quite commonplace in the compilations we do have, but *wholly* outside of the repertoire of redactional possibilities we have or can imagine, it must be a sustained piece of writing on the relationship of the Mishnah to Scripture. Such a treatise can have been enormous, not only because, in theory, every line of the Mishnah required attention. It is also because, in practice, a variety of documents, particularly Sifra, the two Sifrés, and the Talmuds, contain writing of a single kind, meant to amplify the Mishnah by appeal to Scripture (but never to amplify Scripture by appeal to the Mishnah!). It is perfectly clear that no one imagined compiling a commentary to the Mishnah that would consist principally of proofs, of a sustained and well-crafted sort, that the Mishnah in general depends upon Scripture (even though specific and sustained proofs that the principles of taxonomy derive from Scripture are, as I said, susceptible of compilation in such treatises).

How do we know that fact? It is because, when people did compile writings in the form of sustained commentaries to the Mishnah, that is to say, the two Talmuds, they did not focus principally upon the scriptural exegesis of the Mishnah; that formed only one interest, and, while an important one, it did not predominate; it certainly did not define the plan and program of the whole; and it certainly did not form a center of redactional labor. It was simply one item on a list of items that would be brought into relationship, where appropriate, with sentences of the Mishnah. And even then, it always was the intersection at the level of sentences, not sustained discourses, let alone with the Mishnah viewed whole and complete.

And yet — and yet if we look into compilations we do have, we find sizable sets of materials that can have been joined together with the Mishnah, paragraph by paragraph, in such a way that Scripture might have been shaped into a commentary to the Mishnah. Let me now give a sustained example of what might have emerged, but never did emerge, in the canonical compilations of Judaism. I draw my case from Sifra, but equivalent materials in other Compilations as well as in the two Talmuds in fact are abundant. In bold face type are direct citations of Mishnah-passages. I skip Nos. 2-12, because these are not germane to this part of my argument.

**Sifra Parashat Behuqotai Parashah 3**

**CCLXX:I.1** A. ["The Lord said to Moses, Say to the people of Israel, When a man makes a special vow of persons to the Lord at your Valuation, then your Valuation of a male from twenty years old up to sixty years old shall be fifty shekels of silver according to the shekel of the sanctuary. If the person is a female, your Valuation shall be thirty shekels. If the person is from five years old up to twenty years old, your Valuation shall be for a male twenty shekels and for a female ten shekels. If the person is from a month old up to five years old, your Valuation shall be for a male five shekels of silver and for a female your Valuation shall be three shekels of silver. And if the person is sixty years old and upward, then your Valuation for a male shall be fifteen shekels and for a female ten shekels. And if a man is too poor to pay your Valuation, then he shall bring the person before the priest, and the priest shall value him; according to the ability of him who vowed the priest shall value him" (Lev. 27:1-8).]

B. **"Israelites take vows of Valuation, but gentiles do not take vows of Valuation [M. Ar. 1:2B].**

C. "Might one suppose they are not subject to vows of Valuation?

D. "Scripture says, 'a man,'" the words of R. Meir.

E. Said R. Meir, "After one verse of Scripture makes an inclusionary statement, another makes an exclusionary statement.

F. "On what account do I say that gentiles are subject to vows of Valuation but may not take vows of Valuation?

G. "It is because greater is the applicability of the rule of subject to the pledge of Valuation by others than the applicability of making the pledge of Valuation of others [T. Ar. 1:1A].

H. "For lo, a deaf-mute, idiot, and minor may be subjected to vows of Valuation, but they are not able to take vows of Valuation [M. Ar. 1:1F]."

I. R. Judah says, "Israelites are subject to vows of Valuation, but gentiles are not subject to vows of Valuation [M. Ar. 1:2C].

J. "Might one suppose that they may not take vows of Valuation of third parties?

K. "Scripture says, 'a man.'"

L. Said R. Judah, "After one verse of Scripture makes an inclusionary statement, another makes an exclusionary statement.

M. "On what account do I say that gentiles are not subject to vows of Valuation but may take vows of Valuation?

N. "It is because greater is the applicability of the rule of pledging the Valuation of others than the applicability of being subject to the pledge of Valuation by others [T. Ar. 1:1C].

O. "For a person of doubtful sexual traits and a person who exhibits traits of both sexes pledge the Valuation of others but are not subjected to the pledge of Valuation to be paid by others" [M. Ar. 1:1D].

13\. A. And how do we know that the sixtieth year is treated as part of the period prior to that year?

B. Scripture says, "from twenty years old up to sixty years old" —

C. **this teaches that the sixtieth year is treated as part of the period prior to that year.**

D. I know only that that is the rule governing the status of the sixtieth year. How do I know the rule as to assigning the fifth year, the twentieth year?

E. It is a matter of logic:

F. Liability is incurred when one is in the sixtieth year, the fifth year, and the twentieth year.

G. Just as the sixtieth year is treated as part of the period prior to that year,

H. so the fifth and the twentieth years are treated as part of the period prior to that year.

I. But if you treat the sixtieth year as part of the prior period, imposing a more stringent law [the Valuation requiring a higher fee before than after sixty],

J. shall we treat the fifth year and the twentieth year as part of the period prior to that year, so imposing a more lenient law in such cases [the Valuation being less expensive]?

K. Accordingly, Scripture is required to settle the question when it refers repeatedly to "year,"

L. thus establishing a single classification for all such cases:

M. just as the sixtieth year is treated as part of the prior period, so the fifth and the twentieth years are treated as part of the prior period.

N. And that is the rule, whether it produces a more lenient or a more stringent ruling [M. Ar. 4:4M-Q, with somewhat different wording].

14\. A. R. Eliezer says, "How do we know that a month and a day after a month are treated as part of the sixtieth year?

B. "Scripture says, 'up...:'

C. "Here we find reference to 'up...,' and elsewhere we find the same. Just as 'up' used elsewhere means that a month and a day after the month [are included in the prior span of time], so the meaning is the same when used here. **[M. Ar. 4:4R: R. Eleazar says, "The foregoing applies so long as they are a month and a day more than the years which are prescribed."]**

15\. A. I know only that this rule applies after sixty. How do I know that the same rule applies after five or twenty?

B. It is a matter of logic:

C. One is liability to pay a pledge of Valuation if the person to be evaluated is old than sixty, and one is liable if such a one is older than five or older than twenty.

D. Just as, if one is older than sixty by a month and a day, , the person is as though he were sixty years of age, so if the one is after five years or twenty years by a month and a day, lo, these are deemed to be the equivalent of five or twenty years of age.

16\. A. "And if a man is too poor to pay your Valuation:"

B. this means, if he is too impoverished to come up with your Valuation.

17. A. "then he shall bring the person before the priest:"
    B. this then excludes a dead person.
    C. I shall then exclude a corpse but not a dying person?
    D. Scripture says, "Scripture says, "then he shall bring the person before the priest, and the priest shall value him" —
    E. one who is subject to being brought is subject to being valuated, and one who is not subject to being brought before the priest [such as a dying man] also is not subject to the pledge of Valuation.
18. A. Might one suppose that even if someone said, "The Valuation of Mr. So-and-so is incumbent on me," and he died, the man should be exempt?
    B. Scripture says, "and the priest shall value him."
    C. That is so even if he is dead.
19. A. "and the priest shall value him:"
    B. This means that one pays only in accord with the conditions prevailing at the time of the Valuation.
20. A. "according to the ability of him who vowed the priest shall value him:"
    B. It is in accord with the means of the one who takes the vow, not the one concerning whom the vow is taken,
    C. whether that is a man, woman or child.
    D. In this connection sages have said:
    E. The estimate of ability to pay is made in accord with the status of the one who vows;
    F. and the estimate of the years of age is made in accord with the status of the one whose Valuation is vowed.
    G. And when this is according to the Valuations spelled out in the Torah, it is in accord with the status, as to age and sex, of the one whose Valuation is pledged.
    H. And the Valuation is paid in accordance with the rate prescribed at the time of the pledge of Valuation [M. Ar. 4:1A-D].
21. A. "the priest shall value him:"
    B. This serves as the generative analogy covering all cases of Valuations, indicating that the priest should be in charge.

The program of the Mishnah and the Tosefta predominates throughout, e.g., Nos. 1, 12, 13, 14-15. The second methodical inquiry characteristic of our authorship, involving exclusion and inclusion, accounts for pretty much the rest of this well-crafted discussion. Now we see a coherent and cogent discussion of a topic in accord with a program applicable to all topics, that trait of our document which so won our admiration. Thus Nos. 2-11, 17-20, involve inclusion, exclusion, or extension by analogy. I should offer this excellent composition as an example of the best our authorship has to give us, and a very impressive intellectual gift at that. The point throughout is simple. We know how the compilers of canonical writings produced treatments of the Mishnah. The one thing that they did not do was to create a scriptural commentary to the Mishnah. That is not the only type of writing lacking all correspondence to documents we have or can imagine, but it is a striking example.

## VII. The Three Stages of Literary Formation

We now are able to return to our starting point, namely, the problem of those sizable selections of materials that circulated from one document to another and why I tend to think they were formed earlier than the writings particular to documents. The documentary hypothesis affects our reading of the itinerant compositions, for it identifies what writings are extra-documentary and non-documentary and imposes upon the hermeneutics and history of these writings a set of distinctive considerations. The reason is that these writings serve the purposes not of compilers (or authors or authorships) of distinct compilations, but the interests of a another type of authorship entirely: one that thought making up stories (whether or not for collections) itself an important activity; or making up exercises on Mishnah-Scripture relationships; or other such writings as lie beyond the imagination of the compilers of the score of documents that comprise the canon. When writings work well for two or more documents therefore they must be assumed to have a literary history different from those that serve only one writing or one type of writing, and, also, demand a different hermeneutic.

My "three stages" in ordinal sequence correspond, as a matter of fact, to a taxic structure, that is, three types of writing.

[1] The first — and last in assumed temporal order — is writing carried out in the context of the making, or compilation, of a classic. That writing responds to the redactional program and plan of the authorship of a classic.

[2] The second, penultimate in order, is writing that can appears in a given document but better serves a document other than the one in which it (singularly) occurs. This kind of writing seems to me not to fall within the same period of redaction as the first. For while it is a type of writing under the identical conditions, it also is writing that presupposes redactional programs in no way in play in the ultimate, and definitive, period of the formation of the canon: when people did things this way, and not in some other. That is why I think it is a kind of writing that was done prior to the period in which people limited their redactional work and associated labor of composition to the program that yielded the books we now have.

[3] The third kind of writing seems to me to originate in a period prior to the other two. It is carried on in a manner independent of all redactional considerations such as are known to us. Then it should derive from a time when redactional considerations played no paramount role in the making of compositions. A brief essay, rather than a sustained composition, was then the dominant mode of writing.

My hypothesis is that people can have written both long and short compositions — compositions and composites, in my language — at one and the same time. But writing that does not presuppose a secondary labor of redaction, e.g., in a composite, probably originated when authors or authorships did not anticipate any fate for their writing beyond their labor of composition itself. If that reasoning be accepted, then we have grounds on which to suppose that writing exclusive of all redactional purpose and context would come not only separate from, but prior to, writing that acknowledges a redactional purpose and context.

The upshot is simple: whether the classification of writing be given a temporal or merely taxonomic valence, the issue is the same: have these writers done their work with documentary considerations in mind? I believe I have shown that they have not. Then where did they expect their work to makes its way? Anywhere it might, because, so they assumed, fitting in no where in particular, it found a suitable locus everywhere it turned up. But I think temporal, not merely taxonomic, considerations pertain.

Along these same lines of argument, this writing may or may not travel from one document to another. What that means is that the author or authorship does not imagine a future for his writing. What fits anywhere is composed to go nowhere in particular. Accordingly, what matters is not whether a writing fits one document or another, but whether, as the author or authorship has composed a piece of writing, that writing meets the requirements of any document we now have or can even imagine. If it does not, then we deal with a literary period in which the main kind of writing was ad hoc and episodic, not sustained and documentary.

Where does this leave us in our interest in finding out where the Talmud comes from? Extra- and non-documentary kinds of writing seem to me to derive from either [1] a period prior to the work of the making of compilations and the two Talmuds alike; or [2] a labor of composition not subject to the rules and considerations that operated in the work of the making of compilations and the two Talmuds. The second may be treated as a fact, beyond all question.

The first stands for a possibility and an opinion. If we ignore the attributions of sayings to named authorities from the beginning to the end of the sequence of the Talmud's sages' generations, then I should guess that non-documentary writing would come prior to making any kind of documents of consequence, and extra-documentary writing comes prior to the period in which the specificities of the documents we now have were defined. That is to say, writing that can fit anywhere or nowhere is prior to writing that can fit somewhere but does not fit anywhere now accessible to us, and both kinds of writing are prior to the kind that fits only in what documents in which it is now located. But just as we cannot validate attributions and so compose a history of the Talmud and of its sources that depends upon attributions, so we cannot demonstrate that they have no foundation in fact. We rely upon the fact in hand, but do not exclude other possibilities of description and analysis. So, for the moment, we are left to undertake an ahistorical picture of matters, even though that provides a less satisfying result than the historical one generally does.

# ENDNOTES

[1]One set of demonstrations has already been noted, *The Integrity of Leviticus Rabbah. The Problem of the Autonomy of a Rabbinic Document.* Chico, 1985: Scholars Press for Brown Judaic Studies; *Canon and Connection: Intertextuality in Judaism.* Lanham, 1986: University Press of America. *Studies in Judaism* Series; *Midrash as Literature: The Primacy of Documentary Discourse.* Lanham, 1987: University Press of America *Studies in Judaism* series.

[2]The entire repertoire is summarized in my *The Doubleday Anchor Reference Library Introduction to Rabbinic Literature.* N.Y., 1994: Doubleday, from which the Introduction to this book derives.

[3]I underscore that I use these terms not in a temporal but only in an ordinal sense. That is, mere logic suggests the order in which steps have to have been taken; but these steps can have been taken in one afternoon of hard work, as much as in a hundred years of labor. The document is logically the latest stage, writings for it falling in line with it; the free-standing units that can fit into a document but not the one in which they are located forms a second stage; and the first stage is represented by compositions and even composites that fit some document the like of which we now do not have at all. In a moment I offer the opinion — not a hypothesis — that the ordinal sequence may stand for a temporal, that is, a historical one; but the considerations I introduce do not settle the matter even of formulating a hypothesis.

[4]We return to this matter in the concluding unit.

[5]I do not mean, in referring to "written out," to take a position on whether the Mishnah was published in writing or only orally, that is, orally formulated and orally transmitted solely in mnemonic form. The considerations I have adduced to show that the Mishnah was orally formulated and orally transmitted, in memory, apply solely to the Mishnah and uniformly applied demonstrate that all other Rabbinic documents were produced in written form. These matters are spelled out in my *The Memorized Torah. The Mnemonic System of the Mishnah.* Chico, 1985: Scholars Press for Brown Judaic Studies, and *Oral Tradition in Judaism: The Case of the Mishnah.* N.Y., 1987: Garland Publishing Co. *Albert Bates Lord Monograph Series* of the journal, *Oral Tradition.*

[6]I compared Bavli and Yerushalmi tractates Sukkah, Sanhedrin, and Sotah, showing the proportion of what I call Scripture-units of thought to Mishnah-units of thought. See my *Judaism. The Classic Statement. The Evidence of the Bavli* (Chicago, 1986: University of Chicago Press).

[7]The occasion, in the history of Judaism, at which biography defines a generative category of literature, therefore also of thought, will therefore prove noteworthy. The model of biography surely existed from the formation of the Pentateuch, with its lines of structure, from Exodus through Deuteronomy, set forth around the biography of Moses, birth, call, career, death. And other biographies did flourish prior to the Judaism of the dual Torah. Not only so, but the wall of the Dura synagogue highlights not the holy people so much as saints, such as Aaron and Moses. Accordingly, we must regard as noteworthy and requiring explanation the omission of biography from the literary genres of the canon of the Judaism of the dual Torah.

[8]I should prefer to say "never," but even at the present, advanced stage of the work, it is still easier to say what is in the Rabbinic literature than what is not there.

# 8

## The Parable (*Mashal*) A Documentary Approach

The marker, *Mashal*, generally translated "parable," like the marker, *Ma'aseh,* "precedent," signals that certain distinctive rules of writing govern in a narrative composition in the Rabbinic canon of the formative age. What defines the parable is the announcement contained in that marker that a case or proposition or transaction, Halakhic or exegetical-Aggadic, may be approached through a static simile or a dynamic metaphor. It is an account of a transaction the components of which are comparable in character or relationship to the case or proposition that requires explanation.

### I. The Documentary Analysis of Parables

In the Rabbinic canon the marker, *Mashal*, travels from document to document, but it gives diverse signals — lays down different rules of writing — as it moves. Even within a single document, the marker signals more than a single function. Sometimes — particularly in Halakhic contexts — the word *Mashal* signifies a static simile, indicating a comparison of one thing to something else, without a trace of narrative exposition: "sages have devised this as a simile for that" is the governing language. Other times it is dynamic, marking the narrative evocation of the presence of a transaction, not merely describing a situation, even an action with consequences. And that requires narrative, a sequence of actions and responses thereto, with an implicit outcome. Then the parable, comparing one thing to something else, shades over into the replication of a pattern formed by one set of actions deemed to correspond to another set of actions. The narrative of the *Mashal* recapitulates, in other terms, the transaction, whether Halakhic or exegetical or theological, that is subject to clarification. In that case the governing language is, "a parable: to what is the matter comparable?" The sign, *Mashal,* like *Ma'aseh*, may signify a composition that clarifies a Halakhic ruling or it may be one that embodies in concrete, social terms an otherwise abstract theological conception or an exegesis of a verse of Scripture.

The *Mashal* as narrative parable requires differentiation from the *Ma'aseh*, which also involves narrative, that is, description of something said and/or done, and which also clarifies both Halakhic and theological cases. Is there nothing that characterizes *every* composition bearing the marker, *Mashal?* In all documents these traits are routinely present where the signal, *Mashal,* occurs. The parabolic narrative is totally abstract, asking for an act of imagination, [1] not mentioning specific authorities, [2] not placing the action in concrete time and a determinate, locative setting, and [3] not invoking an authoritative text (e.g., a proof-text of Scripture or a citation of the Mishnah). The *Ma'aseh* exhibits the opposite traits. It asks for an act of mimesis. For [1] it is concrete, involving determinate, named authorities, [2] it situates an event at a particular occasion, and [3] it takes for granted a Halakhic text and context, commonly but not invariably cited or at least supplied in the redactional placement of the *Ma'aseh* in the Mishnah or in the Tosefta. So the *Mashal* stands on its own, and the *Ma'aseh* is rarely autonomous of its redactional setting. This negative approach to definition both encompasses all compositions labeled *Mashal* and excludes most of those labeled *Ma'aseh.*

Documents make distinctive choices, and one may readily distinguish the *Mashal* as utilized in one from the same as utilized in another. The signal, *Mashal,* refers in the Mishnah to one kind of simile, in Song of Songs Rabbah to a different kind of narrative parable altogether. Documentary differentiation in the analysis of the *Mashal* is new.[1] Since, until now, studies of the *Mashal* have taken as their premise the uniformity of parables in canonical context[2] without regard to documentary programs and preferences, the eight documents briefly characterized here yield jarring results for established approaches to the *Mashal. The* parable cannot in this context be viewed as a coherent corpus of data uniform throughout the Rabbinic canon without regard to venue. Sometimes a static simile, sometimes a dynamic narrative, sometimes abbreviated, sometimes protracted, the *Mashal* produces evidence that is formally and functionally to be differentiated and classified, then compared from one document to another in its classifications.

Some suppose the opposite: first comes the parable, a narrative about the king who did such and so with the prince, for example, then comes its utilization for — adaptation to — a particular Halakhic or more commonly exegetical task. The existence of a ready-made corpus of conventional parables, articulated stories that stand on their own and possess characteristics in common, is taken for granted. Thus we have catalogues of parables that, as in folklore indices, are organized by theme but indifferent to documentary origin or venue. So studies of *The* Parable log in types of *Meshalim*, as types of folklore-narratives are classified, e.g., "the story of the king who…," "the story of the prince and the pedagogue…," "the householder and the workers…," "the king and the queen who…," and other fixed thematic or topical taxa. These catalogues then yield knowledge of how the given type of parable could be adapted for specific exegetical tasks. Circulating hither and yon, these parabolic stories — so this theory holds — were ready-made, not bespoke but off the rack. Available parabolic narratives were merely adapted to the requirements of a particular task of exposition.

## II. THE PRIORITY OF THE DOCUMENTARY TASK: THE *NIMSHAL* OVER THE *MASHAL*

To explain: the parabolic narrative — the *Mashal* proper — is ordinarily seen as defined prior to the utilization of said parable to clarify a particular situation or transaction. This may be expressed in the formal language of the matter, as between the *Mashal* (the parabolic narrative) and the *Nimshal* (the case subject to narrative exposition) — which comes first? To explain: the Hebrew word for parable, *Mashal,* yields a passive, [2] *Nimshal,* thus [1] the parable and [2] the base-pattern or situation or transaction or event or proposition that is replicated in the simile constructed by the parable, respectively. This is a bit abstract, so readers will be grateful for a concrete case. In the following composition, the exegetical task is defined at J-K, the *Mashal* is set forth at L, and the *Nimshal* — the explicit articulation of the point of the parable, at M.

### T. BERAKHOT 1:11

J. Similarly, "Remember not the former things, nor consider the things of old" (Is. 43:18). Remember not the former things — these are [God's mighty acts in saving Israel] from the [various] kingdoms; nor consider things of old — these are [God's mighty acts in saving Israel] from Egypt.

K. "Behold, I am doing a new thing; now it springs forth" (Is. 43:19) — this refers to the war of God and Magog [at the end of time].

L. <u>They drew a parable, to what may the matter be compared? To one who was walking in the way and a wolf attacked him, but he was saved from it. He would continually relate the incident of the wolf. Later a lion attacked him, but he was saved from it. He forgot the incident of the wolf and would relate the incident of the lion. Later still a serpent attacked him, but he was saved from it. He forgot the other two incidents and would continually relate the incident of the serpent.</u>

M. So, too is the case for Israel: the recent travails make them forget about the earlier ones.

Here the *Nimshal*, M, briefly articulates the point of the *Mashal,* L, but in many instances the *Nimshal* is detailed and elaborate. This analytical provocation for the introduction of the *Mashal*, the *Nimshal,* meaning "that to which the parable forms a narrative simile," "that pattern of actions or events to which the comparison is drawn," is commonly deemed secondary, notional, and occasional. Hence, for example, catalogues of types of ready-at-hand parables, e.g., the king and the prince who..., such as Thoma compiles, may be gleaned from the particularities of writing marked *Mashal*.

But in most cases, first comes the exegetical task, J-K, M, above, then, in response, comes the parable, L, responding to the assignment *detail by detail.* It is the exact match of the *Mashal* to the *Nimshal* that tells the tale: the *Nimshal* is generative, the *Mashal,* responsive. And — so I claim, furthermore — the exegetical-theological assignment is documentary, in that the authorships of the several entire documents, respectively, define the task assigned to parabolic writing, as much as to any other kind of writing. For the specified occasion the *Mashal* is made up to carry out the work of exposition and clarification dictated by the document and its encompassing program, whether the Mishnah or the Tosefta or tractate Abot or Sifra. Consequently, the traits, other than those specified at the outset, of the received corpus of ready-made narratives to be adapted for particular purposes prove difficult to identify and describe in detail, though apart from the fixed marker, *Mashal,* a few generic traits of mind and rhetoric do surface, already specified. And the traits take on meaning only in the contrast with the *Ma'aseh* and its variations.

To summarize: the hypothesis emerging from the probe of eight documents is, then, readily stated. The primary task of the *Mashal* is defined by the *Nimshal,* meaning, the Halakhic or exegetical problem governs the formation and functioning of the parable. To state the matter in extreme but defensible form: numerous cases show that *every single detail* of the *Mashal* captures a component of the Halakhic or the exegetical situation subject to exposition. And the parable succeeds when it is evaluated by the criterion: has the simile left out even one detail of that which is subjected to comparison? Or has it added a detail not generated by that which is subjected to comparison? That exact match in detail of *Mashal* to *Nimshal* is the key. Seldom does the *Mashal* give evidence of constituting a free-standing story or situational simile, exhibiting marks of adaptation of a ready-made narrative. Commonly, though not always, the *Mashal* in its rich detail shows itself to be the formation of a narrative made up for the distinctive purpose at hand.

This *ad hoc* theory of the *Mashal* — seeing the *Mashal* as contextually-driven and made up for the occasion, not drawn upon from a ready-made corpus of conventional, available narratives— yields a clear result. The task assigned to the *Mashal* is primary and generative. Thus first comes the transaction or the situation to be illuminated, then comes the formation of the parable, first the *Nimshal*, then the *Mashal.* The exegetical or Halakhic task of exposition defines the character of the parabolic narrative, which only rarely has a free-standing existence and seldom transcends the limits of the exegetical or Halakhic case subject to illumination.

### III. The *Mashal* in the Mishnah

True to its Halakhic focus, the Mishnah is the natural homeland of the disciplined, Halakhic *Ma'aseh.* The *Mashal,* which in later documents was found quite serviceable even for Halakhic exposition, appears only three times in the entire document. All fall into the category of Halakhic similes. Static, none tells a story. Then in the Mishnah *Mashal* marks an inert simile that clarifies a normative law. These are the three instances in which the marker, *Mashal,* occurs in the Mishnah:

### 1. Mishnah-tractate Sukkah 2:9

A. All seven days a person treats his Sukkah as his regular dwelling and his house as his sometime dwelling.
B. [If] it began to rain, at one point is it permitted to empty out [the Sukkah]?
C. From the point at which the porridge will spoil.
D. They made a parable: To what is the matter comparable?
E. To a slave who came to mix a cup of wine for his master, and his master threw the flagon into his face.

E on its own is curiously moot, making no point out of its Halakhic context, but slightly out of phase with that context. We do not know why the master threw the flagon in the slave's face, or what the slave did wrong. The Halakhic parable makes sense only in its context, B-C. Why choose as the moment at which it is permitted to empty out the Sukkah the point at which the porridge spoils? Because eating signifies dwelling in the Sukkah (in line with the conception of the Sabbath that where one eats his meal is what designates where he locates his domicile for the Sabbath). Then when the food is spoiling, it is a mark of rejection: the person for the dwelling. When the slave mixes the wine for the master, instead of drinking, the master throws the wine in his face. Now too, instead of eating, one is driven out. The Halakhic ruling to be clarified, C, then is more than closely tracked by the *Mashal*, D-E, it is required if D-E are not to be reduced to sheer gibberish.

### 2. Mishnah-tractate Niddah 2:5

A. The sages made a parable in connection with the woman:
B. (1) the room, (2) the front hall, and (3) the room upstairs.
C. Blood in the room is unclean.
D. If it is found in the front hall, a matter of doubt concerning it is deemed unclean, since it is assumed to come from the fountain [uterus].

C-D posit three spaces, to which the three areas, B, the downstairs room, the front hall, and the upstairs room, correspond. The Halakhic classification, C-D, then is clarified by the spatial relationships of the parable as not anecdote but simile. There is no pretense of a narrative here. It is self-evident that the simile is constructed in response to the data that the sages wish to clarify.

### 3. Mishnah-tractate Niddah 5:7

A. Sages have made a parable in regard to the woman: (1) an unripe fig, (2) a ripening fig, and (3) a fully ripe fig.
B. An unripe fig — she is still a little girl.
C. And a ripening fig — these are the days of her girlhood.
D. In both periods her father is entitled to whatever she finds and to her wages and to annul her vows.
E. A fully ripe fig — once she has grown up, her father has no further right over her.

The same pattern recurs, the simile/parable, A, which clarifies the three stages of the Halakhah, B, C, and E. Absent the *Nimshal,* B-E, the *Mashal,* A, is pointless. Once more, the parable stands for a comparison of a Halakhic classification-system and its rules to a familiar natural phenomenon, the state of a fig at various points in its development. Without the Halakhic facts of B, C, and E, the parable — unripe fig, ripening fig, fully ripe fig — forms a set of facts bearing no meaning beyond themselves.

The initial canonical document beyond Scripture, with its static, inert simile, lacking all narrative articulation, refers to a comparison of a Halakhic category to an arrangement of rooms or to a growth-process of nature. Anyone who has examined the parables in other Rabbinic documents will be struck by what the Mishnah does not present, which is the parable as a story, a narrative of a particular kind. The marker scarcely hints at the development in the Tosefta and beyond of an anecdotal aspect of the *Mashal*, a more complex articulation of the simile as a narrative. Only when the marker, *Mashal,* referred to a dynamic narrative, not only a static simile, did the signal encompass a Halakhic transaction or event.

## IV. The *Mashal* From the Mishnah to the Tosefta

Since that shift would surface in the Tosefta and not in the Mishnah we must wonder, why not? The answer is clear: it is a documentary choice deriving from the character of the compilation: the *Ma'aseh* yes, the *Mashal*, no! When the framers of the Mishnah wished to resort to narrative to clarify a Halakhic ruling, they invariably asked the *Ma'aseh*, precedent, to bear the burden of concretization. Indeed, as we realized in Volume One, most of the narratives of the Mishnah fall into the classification of Halakhic *Ma'aseh*. The framers of the Mishnah's compositions and composites think juridically, therefore seek precedents.

But the Tosefta served in part an exegetical purpose, the clarification of cited laws of the Mishnah, for example. It follows that exegetical thinking, focused not on the rule but on the case, would surface in the Tosefta alongside the other, the juridical mode of thought. In the exegetical-theological documents later on — self-evidently — exegetical thinking would predominate, to the near exclusion of the *Ma'aseh* as precedent and also, and concomitantly, of the *Mashal* as static simile. But it does not suffice to explain only, why not. Why does the writing of compositions for the Tosefta encompass exegetical, not only juridical writing, such as the Mishnah provoked? Within theory that the Tosefta contains not only free-standing writing, but also citation and gloss of Mishnah-rules the answer is clear. The Tosefta's compilers and authors and authorships undertook a subordinate, exegetical role, citing the Mishnah, not only setting forth Halakhic rulings in the manner of the Mishnah. So when they contemplated the *Mashal,* they asked of it service in the exegetical, not only in the juridical, labor, hence not only a simile to clarify a rule, but a narrative parable to make sense of a transaction, event, or activity.

### v. The *Mashal* in the Tosefta

A striking contrast between the inert simile and the parabolic narrative marks the move from the Mishnah to the Tosefta. Now the *Mashal* occurs not only as a static declaration, "sages have compared this to that," thus, in the rhetorical pattern, "this is like that...." The dynamic, narrative *Mashal*, which we meet in the Tosefta — "They drew a parable, to what is the matter compared? To the case of a king who did such-and-such, and so-and-so resulted...so when God/Israel does such-and-such, and so-and-so results..." — had struck no one writing for the Mishnah as a promising medium of thought and argument. The simile was built on comparison and contrast of things in a static relationship, one in which nothing happens. The *Mashal* now makes its appearance, mostly, but not wholly, in the Aggadic discourse of the Tosefta. It comes to the fore as a dynamic, protracted narrative, involving a series of paradigmatic transactions.

Stated simply: things happen, with the result that actions or events or transactions form a pattern, and juxtaposed patterns sustain comparison and contrast between one transaction and the other. Throughout, the *Nimshal* then defines the pattern, and the *Mashal* replicates that pattern in other categories altogether. The task of the parabolic narrative then is to capture the base-pattern in other terms. So the Tosefta produces a dynamic simile, so to speak, or, more really, transforms the inert simile into an active metaphorical narrative.

Predictably, the innovation occurs in writing that serves for the Tosefta's speaking on its own, not citing and glossing the Mishnah or amplifying its Halakhic rulings. It concerns mainly, but not exclusively, theological or exegetical problems. Then some authorship conceived that the *Mashal* might render not only a comparable situation, a simile, but a comparable activity or transaction, a pattern shaped in one transaction set forth in a narrative of a comparable transaction. The Tosefta's *Meshalim* are far more elaborate and more diverse than those of the Mishnah. In the unfolding of the Rabbinic canon document by document, with the Mishnah followed by the Tosefta, yielding Sifra, and so onward, the Tosefta comes forth as the first canonical document after Scripture to conceive of not just an inert simile but a dynamic narrative as a medium for comparison and contrast. But the Tosefta both depends upon the Mishnah in passages, and also goes its own way in other passages. Consequently, the Tosefta's *Meshalim* are divided in two: [1] the familiar inert similes, containing no action, replicating the traits of the Mishnaic *Mashal*, and [2] the new model of exegetical or theological narratives, characterized by sequences of actions or events, two patterns of which are compared. So the Tosefta both continues the Mishnah's pattern for the *Mashal* and innovates — a documentary trait replicated in many aspects.

The source of the idea for exegetical and theological discourse is surely Scripture, which in Prophecy and in Wisdom affords models of parabolic writing. That is a plausible explanation for the Aggadic parable that surfaces in the Tosefta. But how about the Halakhic parables of the Tosefta, two of which, we shall see, concur in the value of narrative for illuminating a transaction, a possibility not explored in the Mishnah? To explain the appearance of a proportionately insignificant population of dynamic narrative parables in the Halakhic exposition, I appeal to the development of the narrative for Aggadic parabolic discourse. The model of the Aggadic narrative *Mashal* triggered the formation of at least two Halakhic ones, giving promise of future exploitation of the narrative *Mashal* for Halakhic purposes as much as for exegetical and theological ones.

The Tosefta's other-than-static (and other-than-Halakhic!) kind of *Mashal* is represented by the following, first in the conventional order of the document.

**Tosefta-tractate Berakhot 1:11**

J. Similarly, "Remember not the former things, nor consider the things of old" (Is. 43:18). Remember not the former things — these are [God's mighty acts in saving Israel] from the [various] kingdoms; nor consider things of old — these are [God's mighty acts in saving Israel] from Egypt.

K. "Behold, I am doing a new thing; now it springs forth" (Is. 43:19) — this refers to the war of God and Magog [at the end of time].

L. <u>They drew a parable, to what may the matter be compared? To one who was walking in the way and a wolf attacked him, but he was saved from it. He would continually relate the incident of the wolf. Later a lion attacked him, but he was saved from it. He forgot the incident of the wolf and would relate the incident of the lion. Later still a serpent attacked him, but he was saved from it. He forgot the other two incidents and would continually relate the incident of the serpent.</u>

M. So, too is the case for Israel: the recent travails make them forget about the earlier ones.

Note the brevity of the *Nimshal*. M. But the narrative sequence, wolf/lion/serpent, is required to make the desired point that M expresses. So the narrative of the *Mashal* — the succession of travails — responds to its exegetical task, which is, to illustrate a case in which new travails obscure older ones.

What is important is two facts. First, the *Mashal* now portrays a series of events, happenings that form a pattern and bear meaning expressed in movement.

Second, the *Mashal* produces a coherent composition out of relationship with the exegetical task defined by Is. 43:18. So it is only M, the *Nimshal,* that has — that can have — generated each detail of L, the *Mashal*. The completed *Mashal-Nimshal,* L-M, forms an awry comment on J-K, pointing out that not only are God's more current mighty acts likely to make Israel forget the former ones, but God's "new thing" — a travail, the opposite of saving Israel from the kingdoms — does the same. So the completed parable with its lesson form a comment on the exegesis of the cited verse, Is. 43:18, and the whole constitutes an exegetical parable.

To classify the data systematically: the *Mashal* in the Tosefta falls into these three categories:

[1] a simile in the model of the Mishnah's;

[2] Halakhic parables; always spun out in dialogue with the Halakhic case or transaction; and

[3] exegetical (including theological) parables.

The exegetical ones are divided into those that respond to the task of explaining theological or moral or ethical situation that provokes the formation of the parable, and those that are utilized to illuminate a transaction but do not respond to the details of the transaction. The Tosefta's indicative trait, its dual relationship to the Mishnah, recapitulates itself in the matter of the *Mashal*: half the time in the model of the Mishnah's, half the time not. The Mishnaic *Mashal,* a static, inert simile serving Halakhic exposition, accounts for approximately half of the Tosefta's *Meshalim*. More to the point: when the Tosefta wishes to ask for a *Mashal* to help convey and clarify a Halakhic point, it ordinarily relies on the received definition of the matter. So the Mishnaic model persists in its original context: the resort to similes, lacking narrative initiatives, for Halakhic exposition. And no new model of Halakhic exposition complements the received one.

What is unexpected in the Tosefta therefore is the advent of the exegetical or theological parable, which (from the perspective of the Mishnah's record) is new both in its task and in its utilization of a kind of narrative (abstract, indeterminate in time, utopian in location) for carrying out that task. Where the task is exegetical or theological, the *Mashal* will take on a narrative quality, introducing sequences of actions with an indicated outcome. But the narrative *Mashal,* as distinct from the simile, also enters Halakhic discourse. So while the Halakhic *Meshalim* remain within the inert, Mishnaic model, still at some few points the exposition of Halakhic rules through the *Mashal* encompasses the utilization of narrative. These are precisely the results that the character of the Tosefta — recapitulating the Mishnah's Halakhic rules, also venturing to amplify and extend them, and furthermore setting forth compositions that do not intersect with the Mishnah at all — overall would lead us to anticipate.

So the program of the document's compilers has governed its repertoire of parables: types and functions. That is illustrated in a simple mental experiment. If we were given a random sample of Meshalim of the Tosefta together with a sample of those of the Mishnah, we should identify the Tosefta's items half of the time, and half of the time we should have no valid criterion for assigning an item to the Tosefta over the Mishnah. We shall now turn to a document, where none can mistake the *Mashal* — if it is a *Mashal* — that belongs there and no where else.

### VI. THE *MASHAL* IN TRACTATE ABOT

Tractate Abot is attached to, but topically, rhetorically, and logically distinct from, the Mishnah. The collection of wise sayings is put together in such a way as utterly to ignore the Mishnah's Halakhic topical program, its rhetorical plan, and the syllogistic logic of coherent discourse that govern in the Mishnah's other sixty-two tractates. I find in tractate Abot no compositions bearing the marker *Mashal*. But we have a number of similes, using the language of comparison ("to what is he/it to be likened?"). They all are inert similes, like the Halakhic similes of the Mishnah and the Tosefta, but they concern themselves with matters of wisdom, therefore representing the distinctive utilization of an established form for a new purpose. These are as follows:

**TRACTATE ABOT 3:17**

I. He would say, "Anyone whose wisdom is greater than his deeds — to what is he to be likened? To a tree with abundant foliage, but few roots.

J. "When the winds come, they will uproot it and blow it down,

K. "as it is said, 'He shall be like a tamarisk in the desert and shall not see when good comes but shall inhabit the parched places in the wilderness' (Jer. 17:6).

L. "But anyone whose deeds are greater than his wisdom — to what is he to be likened? To a tree with little foliage but abundant roots.

M. "For even if all the winds in the world were to come and blast at it, they will not move it from its place,

N. "as it is said, 'He shall be as a tree planted by the waters, and that spreads out its roots by the river, and shall not fear when heat comes, and his leaf shall be green, and shall not be careful in the year of drought, neither shall cease from yielding fruit' (Jer. 17:8)."

The form varies from the familiar *Mashal* of the Mishnah and the Tosefta in four ways, [1] the omission of the marker, Mashal; [2] the inclusion of proof-texts (K, N), which is unknown in the Mishnah's and the Tosefta's *Meshalim*; [3] the exposition of the point of the simile by J, M, as though conceding that the simile does not speak for itself. Finally, [4] the language is highly formalized and balanced, I matching L; the Mishnah's and the Tosefta's parables rarely exhibit concern for the formalization of prose. The subject-matter — not Halakhic, not exegetical, not theological — conforms to that which defines the document, Torah-study, inclusive of fulfillment of the teachings thereof.

**Tractate Abot 4:20**

A. Elisha b. Abbuyah says, "He who learns when a child — what is he like? Ink put down on a clean piece of paper.

B. "And he who learns when an old man — what is he like? Ink put down on a paper full of erasures."

**3. Tractate Abot 4:20**

C. R. Yosé b. R. Judah of Kefar Habbabli says, "He who learns from children — what is he like? One who eats sour grapes and drinks fresh wine.

D. "And he who learns from old men — what is he like? He who eats ripe grapes and drinks vintage wine."

The same distinguishing qualities noted above apply to these two *Meshalim* as well.

If we were given a collection of *Meshalim* without identification as to their sources, we should readily pick out those deriving from Abot. These obviously form a cogent set by reason of shared traits of rhetoric and topic, and clearly differ from those of the Mishnah and the Tosefta because of those same traits — beginning, after all, with the omission of the marker.

## vii. The *Mashal* in Sifra: The Halakhic Parable and the Exegetical Parable

What defines the parable in Sifra as in the Mishnah and the Tosefta is the announcement that a case or proposition may be approached through a simile, an account of a transaction the components of which are comparable in character or in relationship to the case or proposition at hand. That account, like the *Ma'aseh,* then may, but need not, report an anecdote, involving a transaction comparable to the one at hand but more readily accessible in its simplicity of detail than the one at hand.

Sifra's parable thus takes two forms. In the first, as with the Mishnah's similes, it simply sets up a situation comparable to the one under discussion, lacking all activity or movement. In the second, as in the Tosefta's exegetical and theological parables, it narrates a transaction or event deemed comparable to the one under discussion. In neither case does the logic of teleology, which characterizes authentic narratives, have to impart coherence to the composition. Rather, the context — the situation to be replicated in other, more accessible terms — does. In this document the parable serves two purposes, clarification of an exegesis of a verse of Sifra, or clarification of a Halakhic ruling set forth in Leviticus. Does the *Mashal* of either type stand on its own, or does it require the exegetical context to bear specific meaning? Ordinarily, but not always, the *Nimshal* governs the details of the *Mashal,* which details, on their own, do not present a coherent statement.

## VIII. THE HALAKHIC PARABLE

Ordinarily, like that of the Mishnah, the Halakhic parable of Sifra is so closely tied to, generated by, the case at hand that it is incomprehensible beyond that context. That is to say, removed from the case that is clarified, the Halakhic parable yields no sense whatsoever; it is incoherent and gibberish. The Halakhic parables before us involve descriptions of situations, rather than unfolding transactions or singular events. They are inert, not dynamic, and they scarcely qualify even as anecdotal. The economical, stripped-down description of what is said and done recalls the Halakhic *Ma'aseh*. The difference is, the Halakhic *Ma'aseh* frames a transaction or a circumstance on which sages make a ruling, while the Halakhic *Mashal* establishes a counterpart situation in which the outcome is implicit and requires no articulated ruling. The power of the simile therefore lies in its self-evident implication.

**SIFRA III:VI. 2**

A. Might one suppose that one should not bring an offering of a wild beast, but if one has brought a wild beast as an offering, it is valid?

B. The matter may be compared to the case of someone whose master said to him, "Go and bring me wheat," and he went and brought him both wheat and barley. ...

C. <u>Lo, to what may the matter be compared? To the case of someone whose master said to him, "Go and bring me only wheat."</u>

The paired parables match the case and have no autonomous standing, since out of context they bear no point I can discern. Here there is no unpacking of a transaction, only the description of the case, lacking an outcome. This is simile in the form of a situation, not a transaction with secondary amplification.

We see two facts concerning Sifra's Halakhic *Meshalim*. First, it is a fixed trait of the Halakhic parables of Sifra that the case dictate the simile; only one of the Halakhic parables can stand outside of its Halakhic context. Second, the Halakhic parables tend not to entail the protracted description of an anecdotal transaction, e.g., actions and reactions. They tend to serve to replicate the relationships of a Halakhic problem in another, neutral situation not particular to the details of the Halakhic rule at hand.

## IX. THE EXEGETICAL PARABLE

The task of the exegetical or theological parable is to clarify not a law but a statement of Scripture or the theology implicit therein. The link to Scripture is intimate, and ordinarily the parable bears no self-evident meaning or message out of exegetical context, as we shall now see. It is necessary to articulate this connection point by point, e.g., in the first entry, "So with Aaron...." None of these parabolic compositions has the capacity to stand on its own. Most of them, however, involve protracted transactions, e.g., action and reaction. The *Nimshal* then governs the *Mashal,* the document, the detailed illustrative materials utilized by the document. In a commentary to the book of Leviticus, then, the task of expounding the verses of that book dictates where parables are required and the form that they are to take.

**Sifra XCVIII:VI. 1**

A. "And Moses killed it and took the blood:" For all seven days of consecration, Moses served in the high priesthood. He would slaughter the beast, he would toss the blood, he would sprinkle the blood, he would perform the rite of purification, he would pour oil, he would atone.

B. There is then a parable: to what may the matter be compared? To a princess who was married when she was a minor, and they made an agreement with her mother that the mother would serve until her daughter would learn [what was required of her].

C. So with Aaron, at first he was a Levite, as it is said, "And is not Aaron, your brother, the Levite" (Ex. 4:14). But when he was chosen to serve as High Priest, the Holy One, blessed be He, said to Moses, "You will serve me until Aaron will learn."

The parable, "A princess was married as a minor" matches the case point by point, as the articulation of matters makes explicit. I cannot think of what the parable as articulated here can mean outside of this particular context. What we see is how the exegetical parable constructs a situation, rather than tells a tale of what was said or done in sequences. There are no stages of activity, no initiative with its consequences, just the construction of a situation, — a woman married under such-and-such stipulation, — deemed to illuminate Aaron's situation in the priesthood.

Sifra is classified as a Halakhic Midrash-compilation, and with good reason. But when it comes to the principal classification of parables, the document favors the exegetical over the Halakhic. Of the twelve parables that I have identified, eight are exegetical, four Halakhic. Of that same population nine are particular to the exegetical setting. Those that on the surface can serve for some purpose other than the specific one at hand involve a more elaborate transaction than those that are particular to the terms of the verse that is amplified or the Halakhic ruling that is clarified.

As to the particularity of the parable, the result is congruent with the Tosefta and the Mishnah. Both the Halakhic and the exegetical types of parable in Sifra tend to emerge from the particular setting and to respond to an exegetical assignment. That is to clarify a distinctive case or problem or ruling. The parables, whether Halakhic or exegetical, that predominate emerge from the details of particular cases, translated into readily accessible similes. Some, to be sure, bear an autonomous, internally cogent, narrative; the free-standing parables then require and receive an explicit statement showing how the simile applies to the particular case at hand.

The upshot of Mishnah-Tosefta-Abot-Sifra may be simply expressed. Overall, parables appear more likely to commence within the exegetical process than outside its limits, to respond to a particular exegetical task, rather than to define one. To this point, therefore, the parable forms a minor component of documentary writing. That proposition proves coherent with the use of parables in the Mishnah, where, if only for three times in a vast document, the signal, *Mashal,* always promises an inert simile, meaning, this is like that, rather than an active narrative establishing a paradigm of conduct and consequence, "the matter may be compared to the case of a king who...." In the Tosefta, the same kind of parable predominates, but the dynamic *Mashal*, bearing its own meaning out of exegetical/ Halakhic context, does occur. That represents a step beyond the Mishnah's rather sparse and casual utilization of the genre. And Sifra follows suit. But if the Halakhic parable appears to have enjoyed a secure position within the repertoire of documentary authorships, that surmise proves false. We shall now address an exegetical document, covering matter of both Halakhah and theology, that nearly abandons the Halakhic parable and exacts from the parable principally exegetical service.

### X. The *Mashal* in Sifré to Numbers

In Sifré to Numbers we find two Halakhic parables and twenty-nine exegetical parables. (We shall encounter the same remarkable disproportion in the companion, Sifré to Deuteronomy.) Since the book of Numbers is rich in Halakhic compositions, the disproportion is not to be predicted. And, by comparison to Sifra, Sifré to Numbers certainly finds more interest in parabolic writing than did the authorship of Sifra's compositions. But it is still an ancillary genre of writing, not principal to the documentary program.

In Sifré to Numbers nearly all of the parables take shape in close conversation with the verse subject to clarification, and the terms of the Halakhic simile too are particular to the context in which the simile serves. Rarely is a detail superfluous, a match other than exact between details of the parable and details of the verse clarified by the parable. Occasionally we find a component of a parable that is not commensurate, which marks the parable as not-particular to its exegetical task but adapted therefor.

The available, ready-made heritage of parables then consists of a literary convention available for articulation and particularization in response to the requirement of a distinctive context. Thus, while we commonly meet a king and a prince, a king and a queen, or a king and an ally, these take on meaning and significance only within the details modeled after the situation constructed by the base-verse, that is, God and Moses, or God and Israel. Allusion to "king/prince" or "king/ally" never leaves unclear the point of the parable *in all its specificity* — and most exegetical parables bear in their wake an explicit, wholly articulated message: so is it here, with God and Israel, or God and Moses, and so on throughout.

Sifré to Numbers' exegetical parables follow a simple form: citation of a verse and a comment on it, followed by a parable that embodies the relationships or terms, participants or transactions, of the base-verse. The parable sometimes involves action, other times requires only a static replication of the situation outlined by the base-verse. But that is now in other terms than Scripture's. The close correspondence comes to expression in many instances with an explicit exegesis of the parable, explaining how it is relevant to the base-verse and the situation portrayed therein. Consequently, the exegetical parable has no autonomous standing, being comprehensible only in exegetical context. And that is defined by the task of the document, as we have noted, now, time and again. The relationships or terms, participants or transactions, of the parable originate in, and form obvious counterparts to, those of the base-verse. The parables are constructed to form similes of an abstract, but wholly conventional, character, meant to treat as general the particularities of the base-verse and its participants and transactions. In some instances the parable augments the proposition or adds to the message of the base-verse, in many it simply recapitulates that message.

Has the exegetical task provoked the parable, or did the parable take shape independent of the exegetical circumstance? The governing criterion is the question: is the parable *in every last detail* particular to the exegetical context, or is it necessary to adjust the parable to that context? We know that such a necessity comes into play when a detail of a parable proves superfluous, playing no role in the exposition of the base-verse or context. Overall, then, the answer to the question is this: *in Sifré to Numbers, the exegetical task is primary, the construction of a pertinent, illuminating simile only secondary and derivative.* What, then, can have circulated beyond the limits of Sifré to Numbers? The conception that similes involving the king and the prince, the king and the queen, the king and the ally, could be constructed: the generative force derives not from the fixed conventions of the abstract players, the king, the prince (not King Herod or King Ardavan, not Queen Shelomsiyyon/Salome). Like chess pieces, these nameless kings and princes and queens are available to be moved hither and yon, to reconstitute a relationship or a transaction in terms analogous to mathematical symbols: purely abstract, very precise.

### XI. The *Mashal* in Sifré to Deuteronomy

In Sifré to Deuteronomy we find no Halakhic parables and forty-five exegetical ones. That on the face of it shows a documentary preference for this, not that. Can we explain why? On the one side, the character of the document, with its verse by verse exegesis, leads us to anticipate a bias in favor of the exegetical parable. On the other hand, given the Halakhic heart of Deuteronomy, formed by Chapters 12 through 26, and the systematic reading of those formidable chapters by Sifré to Deuteronomy's exegetes, the complete disinterest in the Halakhic parable is surprising. What we learn is that the *Mashal,* deemed illuminating for Halakhic as much as for Aggadic-theological discourse, in the purely-Halakhic documents, now loses its well-attested prior role, such as had been dominant in the Mishnah and important in the Tosefta.

Many, though not all, of the exegetical parables respond to the distinctive exegetical task at hand, and our friends, the king/queen/prince/ally on their own stand for nothing that transcends the limits of the case. Their persons, relationships, and transactions derive from the exegetical setting at hand. Only in the intersection with a particular verse of Deuteronomy do they take on specificity and become cogent *as parables.* It is a reciprocal process: the persons, relationships, and transactions depicted in the realized parables track those of the verse subject to clarification, and the parables reverse course and impart sense and meaning to their context as well. The formulaic quality of the parable now is such that given the problem, we can predict the course of the parabolic rendition of matters.

As before, I underscore the parabolic material, the simile itself, which affords perspective on the classification of the parable: particular to the exegetical task — or adapted thereto, as the case may be. It remains to note that there is, in addition, one parable that falls into neither classification, treated in rubric C at the end.

We find nine parables not generated by the particular exegetical task at hand, not systematically replicating the situation or transaction predicated upon the base-verse and demanded by the exegesis thereof. And there are thirty-six instances (counting three ambiguous items) in which the parable is particular to its exegetical task, tracking the case that is generalized by the simile, commonly but not invariably narrative in execution. If we collect the nine parables that appear to enjoy an autonomous existence and to be adapted to the exegetical task, not invented for it, what we have is miscellaneous:

1. a king who, with his troops, went out into the field. His troops said to him, "Give us hot white bread."
2. A king had great wealth. He had a young son and had to go overseas. He said, "If I leave my wealth in the hands of my son, he will go and squander it. Lo, I shall appoint a guardian for him until he comes of age."
3. Someone who said to his fellow, "Sell me your ass." The other said, "All right." "Will you let me try it out?"
4. Someone sitting at a crossroads. Before him were two paths. One of them began in clear ground but ended in thorns. The other began in thorns but ended in clear ground
5. A king had a field, which he handed over to tenant-farmers. The tenant-farmers began to steal the produce of the field that was owing to the king, so he took it from them and handed it over to their children
6. one said to his fellow, 'I am going to sell you as a slave, to be delivered at some time in the future.'
7. A man handed his son over to a teacher, who would take him about and show things to him and say to him, "All these trees are yours, all these vines are yours, all these olive trees are yours."

8. a reliable person was in a town, with whom everyone deposited their bailments for safe-keeping. When one of them would come to retrieve his property, the reliable man would produce and hand over the object, since he knew precisely where it was.
9. the king's butcher knows precisely how much the king is spending on his table

I see no traits that characterize the autonomous parables but not the tailor-made exegetical ones, nor even conventions to which they adhere. If there was a corpus of parables that circulated beyond documentary limits, I cannot point to the qualities that distinguish items in that corpus from the parables that are particular to documents.

To the compilers of Sifré to Deuteronomy, the exegetical parable presented a fine medium to advance the work of clarifying theological, but not Halakhic, messages of the book of Deuteronomy, and three-fourths of all the parables identified as such ("to what is the matter likened?") are devoted to that one task. That is so whether or not the *Nimshal* is articulated and matched to the *Mashal* in so many words. The parabolic conventions that transcend the particular exegetical cases before us generally involve the king/prince/ally/queen, in various commonplace relationships, but rarely can we reconstruct a considerable narrative account of those relationships. Once we have our king/prince/ally or king/queen, what happens to them or what they say or do generally proves fragmentary and not very illuminating. The lesson they embody turns out, even in the parables not particular to the exegetical setting, to emerge primarily within the exegetical setting for the purposes of which they have been adapted.

## XII. The *Mashal* in Song of Songs Rabbah

The whole of Song of Songs serves as a *Mashal* for God's and Israel's love for one another, which is why the Rabbinic sages adopted the Song in the canon. Given the task of the document — to articulate the parabolic character of the Torah's song, we cannot find surprising the compilers' systematic resort — fifty-six entries — to the exegetical parable as principal medium of their exposition. The question that once more engages us in the present context is, does the *Mashal* stand on its own, or does it require the exegetical context to bear specific meaning? At stake is the autonomy of the parable: does it represent writing distinct from documentary tasks but then adapted to the realization of those tasks? Or is the parable integral to the documentary writing of Song of Songs Rabbah in particular?[3]

As in the Tannaite Midrash-compilations, so here too, the parable in Song of Songs Rabbah is more often an invention of the exegete of a particular passage than an adaptation by him of a ready-made narrative of exemplary quality. In three-fourths of the exegetical parables, the parabolic representations of relationships and transactions and even static similes respond to the exegetical tasks of a highly particular sort. Lest we doubt it, the *Nimshal* explicitly shows that they are linked to the accomplishment of those tasks. It follows from that persistent pattern that those items were written in the context of compiling this particular document. In one fourth of the whole, the matter is ambiguous, for reasons to be specified. These entries may or may not have responded to the tasks of compiling an exegetical exposition of Song of Songs Rabbah in particular.

In sum: 48 out of 59 parables, or 80%, assuredly originate within the framework of the documentary writing, and the other 20% may or may not undertake a comparable documentary task. Parabolic writing, like narrative writing, defined one of the media for the accomplishment of the tasks facing compilers of documents. If they drew upon a corpus of extra-documentary writing, e.g., broadly circulating parables, fully formed and available through a labor of adaptation, there is slight evidence in Song of Songs Rabbah to suggest so. Do the parables circulate independent of their documentary context? In approximately four-fifths of the instances, the parable is constructed in response to the case it is meant to clarify through a process of imaginative generalization. It is comprised therefore by the counterpart-players or counterpart-transactions set forth by the components of the verse subject to clarification and application. The parable then is integral to the exegetical process, applying the principle of the verse under discussion to exemplary cases. That is made explicit in the vast majority of instances.

## XIII. The *Mashal* in Lamentations Rabbah

In Lamentations Rabbah the parable provides a subordinated medium of exegesis and exposition, eighteen in all against the document's forty-nine authentic stories, many of them elaborate and protracted. We find fourteen exegetical parables, a pair in the Halakhic realm occurs, and an unfamiliar utilization of the parable makes its appearance as well. When we recall that Song of Songs Rabbah required no fewer than fifty-six exegetical parables, but yielded only seven authentic narratives, none of them comparable to the massive constructions of Lamentations Rabbah, the picture is clear. The compilers of each document knew precisely what types of narratives they required to accomplish their purpose and deliver their message, and they accordingly subordinated the narrative to their documentary purposes.

## XIV. A Diachronic View of the Parable: Three Propositions

The following generalizations emerge from the eight documents surveyed in this account of the parable.

### 1. The Parable Serves the Document and Responds to its Program

If we know the purpose of the document, we also can come to a fairly reliable prospect of how an authorship will find the parable useful and if so, how — in what form, for what purpose — it will serve. Halakhic documents choose the Halakhic parable, exegetical documents, the exegetical kind.

The Mishnah is principally a Halakhic statement, and the Mishnah's parables are similes that re-present Halakhic situations; they are not exegetical and they are not narrative. The Tosefta is a complex of types of writing and takes over but augments the Mishnah's repertoire. Tractate Abot uses parabolic materials to embody lessons of wisdom, and these ignore the marker, *Mashal,* but employ their own signal, "to what is he to be likened" without "A parable." The comparison then is to contrasting situations, If A, then X, if B, then Y. The Mishnah's similes meet their match in tractate Abot. Sifra finds use for both the Halakhic and the exegetical parable; Sifré to Numbers and its companion for Deuteronomy practically ignore the former and concentrate on the latter. Sifré to Deuteronomy in particular asks the exegetical parable to address broad, theological questions, with special reference to the Song of Moses at the end. Song of Songs Rabbah builds its many parables on Scripture's own generative parable, and Lamentations Rabbah assigns to parables a modest part of its burden, preferring another kind of narrative altogether.

The documents then present no uniformity in the type or use of parables. In each case we may correlate the type and use of parables with the documentary program in general. What about form-history, the diachronic perspective promised in the title of this book? So far as a form-history of the parable can be constructed, it forms a detail of the encompassing documentary history of forms; the parable has little autonomous standing beyond the boundaries of the documents that utilize the form for their distinctive purposes, signified, commonly, not only by topic but also by a particular choice of rhetoric, e.g., the Halakhic in one context, the exegetical in another.

**2. The Rabbinic Parable Ordinarily, though not Always, Articulates the Details of the *Mashal* in Response the Requirements of the *Nimshal***

That result is reinforced when we ask whence the parable to begin with: does it begin in the *Mashal* — the parable viewed autonomous of all particularity — or in the *Nimshal* — the point of contact between the parabolic narrative and its documentary occasion. Has the exegetical task provoked the formation of the simile and thus the parable, or did the parable take shape independent of the exegetical or Halakhic or theological or even biographical circumstance?

The governing criterion is the question: is the parable in every last detail particular to the exegetical context, or is it necessary to adjust the parable to that context? We know that such a necessity comes into play when a detail of a parable proves superfluous, playing no role in the exposition of the base-verse or context. Overall, then, the answer to the question for our documents is, the expository task, defined by the *Nimshal*, whether Halakhic or exegetical, most of the time — 75-80% of the sample — defines the program and traits of the parable. In constructing parables the exegetical task is primary, the construction of a pertinent, illuminating simile only secondary and derivative. We find little evidence that permits us to describe an autonomous corpus of narratives awaiting the parabolic vocation: stories of general motif awaiting case-by-case particularization.

### 3. Not "*The Parable*," an Autonomous Literary Genre, but *Parabolic Writing*, Part of, and Just Another Option in, the Composition of a Rabbinic Canonical Document

On its own, then, the *Mashal* has no form-history autonomous of the canonical documents. The diachronic approach yields evidence for testing a null hypothesis. What should we have anticipated were the *Mashal* to form an independent genre of writing? It is writing that we do not find in abundance in any of our documents: writing adapted for the particular setting but not a comfortable fit in that setting. For the opposite, the governing hypothesis, what we should have expected if the *Mashal* is defined by its documentary context is what has turned up, both in general and in detail: ample evidence that most of the time, if not always, the *Mashal* forms the outcome of the *Nimshal.*

There is no evidence of a vast, free-floating corpus of similes and exemplary narratives, snatched from on high and adapted to local purposes. Rather, we find the evidence of a mode of thought and expression, involving similes and metaphors of transactions. In the formation of most, though not all, exegetical parables in our documents, the generative force derives not from the fixed conventions of the abstract players, the king, the prince but from the transactions they embody, and these transactions are particular to the verse under study as set forth by the Rabbinic exegetes. Like chess pieces, the nameless kings and princes and queens are moved hither and yon, to reconstitute a relationship or a transaction in terms analogous to mathematical symbols: purely abstract, very precise.

The marker, *Mashal* on its own, outside of particular documentary settings, bears no fixed, universal traits of substance, only of form: the signal stands for itself, the context — the task defined by the composition of which the *Mashal* forms a principal part — defines all else, and the documents determine the context for most of their various compositions. Then is there no fixed corpus of stories, traveling here and there and serving diverse tasks? What collections of parables prove is that in detail, where it matters, there is none. What we see here is that, transcending documentary lines, more often than not, is simply the pattern, "There was a king who...." The rest of the differentiated *Mashal*, e.g., "...had such and so," "who said such and such," "who did so and so" — with the result that such and such happened — all that realizes the *Mashal* in its specificity and context in most though not all instances proves particular to the specific context, not characteristic of the *Mashal* wherever it surfaces. The conception that a corpus of stories (parables) or fixed, conventional comparisons (similes, metaphors) surfaced promiscuously to be adapted for the use of a particular piece of writing finds little support but much contrary evidence in the repertoire of cases we have examined in documentary sequence.

So we cannot speak of *the* Parable, a fixed corpus of narratives that make their way hither and yon through the far reaches of a single, unitary "Rabbinic tradition," ignoring the lines of documentary boundaries. We can only differentiate by documents and consequently speak of how diverse documentary authorships in realizing their program and its tasks resorted, where they did, to the signal, *Mashal.* What then does the marker, *Mashal,* signal? The advent of some sort of static simile or dynamic metaphorical narrative, which will be brief, anecdotal, and abstract.

That signal never alludes to particular transactions or events, that is, invoking a specific moment in Israel's history to clarify another such moment. It homogenizes, humanizes, through concretization and particularization. When a king or other principal player is named, the signal, *Ma'aseh,* is invoked, and *Mashal* is not, even though the narrative that follows is indistinguishable in its indicative qualities from a *Mashal.* Common to all *Meshalim* in the Rabbinic corpus then are only some few rules of writing. These include one that is fixed: the signal, *Mashal,* never deals with determinate actors, e.g., named kings, queens, and princes and princesses, only with shadowy "there was a king" and his wife, the queen, his son or daughter..

## XIV. The Precedent (*Ma'aseh*) and the Parable (*Mashal*) in Diachronic View and the Documentary Hypothesis

The fulcrum of interpretation and analysis, for narrative as much as for all other kinds of canonical writing in formative Judaism, is the document. Narratives no less than expository, exegetical, and analytical writing, form part of the documentary self-definition of the Rabbinic canonical writings. The fulcrum of interpretation and analysis, for narrative as much as for all other kinds of canonical writing in formative Judaism, therefore is the document. It is analytically meaningless to talk about "the Rabbinic story" or "the Rabbinic narrative" or "the Rabbinic parable" or "the Aggadah" or "the Rabbinic folk-tale" or any comparable, generic category that ignores documentary boundaries. The principal, and primary, analytical initiative commences with the document — the traits of *its* corpus of narratives.[4]

So the *Ma'aseh* and the *Mashal,* the precedent and the parable, change places in the unfolding in ordinal sequence of the eight documents probed here. The precedent begins subject to precise definition of form and function but loses particularity later on, and the proverb starts off serving a variety of purposes but later on comes to focus on some few, well-differentiated ones, which it serves with great effect. But that shift corresponds not only, or not mainly, to the ordinal sequence of the documents — first the Mishnah, then the Tosefta, then Sifra and the two Sifrés, finally the Rabbah-Midrash-compilations. Rather, it corresponds to the character of the documentary assignments, the Mishnah and the Tosefta requiring a Halakhic form, the precedent, with its clearly defined, *Sitz-im-Leben,* for a Halakhic function, and the Midrash-exegetical compilations seeking an Aggadic form, the parable, with its power of universalization and concretization at the same time, for a Midrash-exegetical function. The curious insistence of the framers of Sifré to

Deuteronomy that the parable serve *only* Aggadic-exegetical purposes and *never* intervene in the Halakhic expositions covering Deuteronomy 12-26, makes sense in this context.

The diachronic view of the precedent and the parable is readily stated. The precedent, well-defined and used with precision in the earlier, Halakhic documents of our probe, loses its particular functional definition in the later, Aggadic ones, and ultimately, the marker, *Ma'aseh*, comes to signal everything and its opposite. It also loses importance and becomes random and haphazard. The parable, rare and not fully articulated in the earlier, Halakhic documents, gains particularity and precise definition in the later, Aggadic-exegetical ones, and ultimately is differentiated and richly instantiated in precisely the document where parabolic thinking permeates. The two forms change places, the one deemed most useful in Halakhic discourse losing currency in the Aggadic compilations, and the one natural to Aggadic-exegetical purposes — how better explain a theological or ethical proposition than by appeal to a concrete, exemplary case conveyed as an abstract narrative to a universal audience? — gaining in prominence and utility, hence in precision and consistent differentiation.

Rabbinic narratives, represented by the precedent and the parable, respond to the documentary program and policy of the authorships that employ them. The result is easily summed up: the *Ma'aseh*, a Halakhic form, is the form of choice of Halakhic documents, and the *Mashal,* an Aggadic-exegetical form, is the narrative form of choice of Midrash-exegetical ones. Within the documentary hypothesis for the analysis of the canonical documents of formative Rabbinic Judaism, that result stands to reason. But it contradicts the hypothesis that documentary lines do not make a difference, and documentary boundaries bear no significance.[5]

### XVI. Concluding Observation on the Parable in Matthew 13

Clearly in the Rabbinic canon the union of the *Nimshal* and the *Mashal* — the situation or transaction to be clarified (Nimshal) and the abstract rendition of that situation or transaction in narrative form (*Mashal*) — defines the purpose of the parable. It is to render accessible, clarify the situation or transaction at issue. The parable forms a means to an end. In context of every Rabbinic document, the parable does not require interpretation but is immediately matched to the situation subject to its illumination. And in no Rabbinic document does the parable routinely require exegesis. It forms a medium of and not a challenge to exegesis.

But in Matthew's Gospel *the parable itself* is what requires interpretation and explanation. It does not decipher the mystery, it *is* the mystery. Only the disciples know the meaning of the *Mashal*, and there is no articulated *Nimshal* at all. Take for example Mt. 13:3-9, the parable of the sower, ending, "He who has ears, let him hear." The disciples then make explicit the puzzle of the parable: "Why do you speak too them in parables? They are told, "To you have been given to know the secrets of the kingdom of heaven, but to them it has not been given...This is why I speak to them in parables, because, seeing, they do not see, and hearing, they do not hear, nor do they understand" (Mt. 13:10, 13). As if to underscore the obscurity of parables, Matthew proceeds to collect a set of parables of the kingdom of heaven (Mt. 13:24-34), which he then unpacks for the disciples alone (Mt. 36-7): "Then he left the crowds and went into the house. And the disciples came to him, saying, 'Explain to us the parable of the weeds of the field,' which Jesus proceeds to do.

The upshot is clear. Given a parable stripped down to its essential elements and out of all documentary context, we should readily identify a Matthean parable by the (articulated) absence of a *Nimshal* joined to the *Mashal*. So too, a blind test of whether or not we may locate the documentary origin of any parable will yield a similar result, because parables are subordinate in form and other indicative traits of narrative to the documentary program of the compilations that preserve and use them. We cannot speak of "The Parable," but only parables in canonical context.

In the matter of the parable, another approach, rejecting the documentary theory, has been explored. Here is my reading of the alternative.

## XVII. An Afterword: David Stern, *Parables in Midrash. Narrative and Exegesis in Rabbinic Literature.* Cambridge, 1991: Harvard University Press

The intimidating title, promising to cover four enormous subjects, "parables," "Midrash," "narrative," and "exegesis," the work in fact is a revised dissertation, with the strengths and weaknesses of the genre. It is compendious and very well researched; it contains a large number of interesting observations of detail. But it is more of a collection of information and opinions on a number of topics than a well-argued, thoughtfully-crafted statement of a particular proposition on the general theme at hand. The bridge from the detail to the main point proves shaky. The result is an occasionally-interesting but rather prolix and unfocussed work, a bit pretentiously claiming to accomplish more than is actually achieved, but, still, valuable for what in fact is given.

Dealing with the *mashal* as it occurs in two dozen passages in Lamentations Rabbah, which are given in an appendix in the Hebrew texts in two recensions and in translation as well, the monograph, on the strength of which its author gained a tenured professorship at the University of Pennsylvania, deals with these topics: composition and exegesis, rhetoric, poetics, thematics, the mashal in context, and the mashal in Hebrew literature. The mashal, though represented by a remarkably tiny sample, is treated as uniform, the representations of the form in various, diverse documents not being differentiated; so too "Midrash" is treated as everywhere the same thing, being defined as "the study and interpretation of Scripture by the Rabbis in Late Antiquity." Consequently, the contemporary tools of form-analysis and criticism, on the one side, and of the systematic differentiation of documents by their indicative traits of rhetoric, topic, and logic of coherence, on the other, are denied the author. The result is a rather general and unanalytical treatment of the subject. But that does not deny the book a hearing, since the author provides a full, though somewhat repetitious, account of the scholarly literature and problems, and his treatment of the texts he discusses, if a bit prolix, contains interesting ad hoc observations. A brief survey of the main points yields sound reason to value the book.

COMPOSITION AND EXEGESIS: the mashal or parable is to be distinguished from a table: "a fable utilizes anthropomorphic animals or plants to portray the particularly theriomorphic or phytomorphic features of human behavior. A parable suggests a sort of parallels between an imagined fictional event and an immediate, 'real' situation confronting the parable's author and his audience." Parables in Rabbinic literature are "preserved not in narrative contexts but in exegetical ones, as part of Midrash...There is no important formal or functional difference between meshalim recorded as parts of narratives and those presented as exegeses of Midrashim of verses." Parables are to be distinguished from allegories, on the one side, and the ma'aseh, or precedent ("example or exemplum, an anecdote told to exemplify or illustrate a lesson"). While Stern concedes that the explanation that accompanies the narrative of the mashal., called the nimshal, first occurs only in Medieval documents, he includes in his discussion a full account of that quite distinct development. Indeed, much of the chapter on poetics invokes the nimshal, so we are asked to understand Rabbinic literature of late antiquity only by appeal to literary forms not found in the writings of late antiquity, a rather confusing mode of analysis.

RHETORIC: the occasions of the mashal are spelled out. The mashal serves for three purposes: illustration, "secret speech," and "rhetorical narrative." Stern sees the mashal as "a story that turns allusiveness to effect in order to persuade its audience of the value of a certain idea or approach or feeling." The key word here is "allusiveness," which Stern does not define with clarity.

POETICS: the center of the book is the interest in "the relationship between exegesis and narrative. "The Rabbinic mashal can be defined as a parabolic narrative that claims to be exegesis and serves the purposes of ideology." That definition would prove more compelling if it did not serve equally well a variety of other forms in the Rabbinic literature. Much of the rest of the discussion concerns the nimshal, as I said, leaving open a variety of questions concerning the mashal in late antiquity. But the results are not wholly without interest. Stern's most interesting point is this: "among the most distinctive characteristics of the mashal's poetics is the strategically placed point of discontinuity, technically called a gap." Much of the exposition, alas, proceeds to "disparities between narrative and nimshal," leaving us once more somewhat puzzled as to Stern's program. Lamentations Rabbah is not a medieval document, but much of the exposition of the data spills over into the consideration of kinds of mashal-writing that came to the surface much later than that document; that presents a considerable puzzle, if we want to grasp precisely what Stern wishes to say, indeed, even to define that about which he is writing; sometimes late antique writing, sometimes medieval; sometimes, indeed, the mashal in particular, other times Midrash in general.

Indeed, the confusion is intensified by recurring efforts to define the mashal, each fabricated for its context, thus, later in the same chapter, "the mashal is essentially mimetic narrative. It is about events and characters, and particularly one character — the king, or God. Beyond all else, the mashal represents the greatest effort to imagine God in all Rabbinic literature." That definition bears more enthusiasm than enlightenment, since the conception that the "king" in the Mashal means "God" in particular relies upon the particular cases at hand; the point is not so much demonstrated as alleged with gusto.

THEMATICS: "the Midrashic mashal is a type of ideological narrative, which seeks to impress the truth and validity of a world-view...upon its audience. In any particular mashal, that world-view is refracted within the mashal's specific message, its theme or thesis." This new definition would prove more useful if it did not define equally well every other type of writing in Rabbinic literature. Thus the chapter treats, further, "apologetics, polemics, eulogy and consolation, complaint, regret and warning," and on and on; that is, various mashals are classified in various ways. None of the classifications encompasses only the mashal, so the results are indeterminate and again somewhat puzzling.

THE MASHAL IN CONTEXT: in their seemingly haphazard positions in these collections [Talmud, Midrash], the meshalim are no different from the rest of the contents. The structure and composition of these documents are famously difficult to identify. Despite a few recent attempts to demonstrate the 'integrity' — the formal and thematic coherence — of the various Midrashic collections, they remain to all appearances more like anthologies of traditional Rabbinic interpretations that an anonymous editor has selected and recorded than like self-contained, logically structured books in their own right." Stern does not then see any differences of a general character between, e.g., Sifra and Leviticus Rabbah, both on Leviticus; or the Tosefta and the Talmud of the Land of Israel, both on the Mishnah. This awry view makes difficult for him the determination of the context in which the mashal does, or does not, occur, why here, not there, being questions that, by definition, he finds he cannot answer. That further accounts for his difficulty in seeing formal differences in the mashal as it occurs in the several distinct documents. So he concedes at the outset, "the 'contextual' interpretation of Midrash — reading a Midrashic passage in its literary, documentary context — is a very problematic venture. The larger literary units that we most comfortably use in reading and interpreting the meaning of literary works — the document as a whole, chapters, even subsections in chapters or discrete narrative or legal sections in a work like the Bible — do not constitute significant units of meaning for Midrash."

That explains why Stern sees the units as "fragmentary, miscellaneous, and atomistic." Other views of the documentary character of the Rabbinic corpus are not examined, and the remainder of the chapter replicates in detail the deeply confused character of Stern's reading of the whole. That makes all the more regrettable Stern's failure to understand his own results. After a systematic study, he concludes, "The passages just discussed all show how Midrashic discourse is organized: in recognizable units of discourse, in literary forms like the petihta, the mashal, the enumeration, the series. These forms comprise the genres or subgenres of Midrash. They constitute its language, and they maintain themselves in Midrashic literature formally and rhetorically, even when they combine with one another. The combinatory pattern of these units is essentially additive. The petihta-form provides a frame for the mashal, which in turn is made to serve the special rhetoric of the petihta; but neither form is required to surrender its distinctive structure or formal identity when it joins with the other. Similarly, a mashal can be constructed in the image of an aggadic narrative or ma'aseh, with its own lesson or homily, but it can simultaneously be employed so as to exploit its own parabolic strengths as a paradigmatic, representational narrative." Quite what Stern means to say is not entirely clear, but the main point is precisely that of form-analysis: there are fixed forms, they do govern, and they characterize one kind of writing, rather than some other. Having produced exactly the results that form-analysis of documents has yielded, Stern is left unable to explain his own data. That is because he has not come to grips with the position he rejects without discussion, quite out of hand, that documents make a difference. Once he has declared the literature chaotic, he cannot recognize the points of order he himself identifies. The concluding chapter, the Mashal in Hebrew literature," need not detain us, since it is tacked on, dissertation-style, to cover whatever might have been left out in the substantive chapters.

The strengths of Stern's dissertation are his own. They lie in his ad hoc observations about this and that. In his rambling, sometimes unfocussed discussions of the specific passages in Lamentations Rabbah he has chosen to discuss in detail, he makes numerous interesting observations. Though this is not a work of mature scholarship, it is more than a mere collection and arrangement of information, and we may hope for better things to come from its author.

The weaknesses of the dissertation are those of the genre; the prose I have cited suffices to show that he writes abominably. Stern proves a good graduate student, thorough in compiling opinions on various topics, but embarrassingly selective in dealing with published results that the author does not wish to address at all. He covers a broad range of subjects, but has not got a well crafted thesis to present to make the topical program cohere and form an important proposition and thesis upon a well-crafted problem. So the work is at the same time too general and rambling and altogether too specific, not bridging the gap between the detail and the main point. As a dissertation it certainly is above average; as an account of the parable, this overweight book is more encyclopedic than interesting.

## ENDNOTES

[1] See Clemens Thoma and Simon Lauer, *Die Gleichnisse der Rabbinen.* I. *Pesiqta deRav Kahana. Einleitung, Übersetzung, Parallelen, Kommentar, Texte* (Bern, Frankfurt am Main, New York, 1986: Peter Lang); Clemens Thoma and Simon Lauer, *Die Gleichnisse der Rabbinen.* II. *Von der Erschaffung der Welt bis zum Tod Abrahams: Bereschit Rabba 1-63.* (Bern, Frankfurt am Main, New York, 1991: Peter Lang); Clemens Thoma and Hanspeter Ernst, *Die Gleichnisse der Rabbinen.* III. *Von Isaak bis Zum Schilfmeer. Ber R 63-100, ShemR 1-22.* (Bern, Frankfurt am Main, New York, 1996: Peter Lang). Clemens Thoma and Hanspeter Ernst, *Die Gleichnisse der Rabbinen.* IV. *Vom Lied des Mose bis zum Bundesbuch: ShemR 23-30* . (Bern, Frankfurt am Main, New York, 2000: Peter Lang). While he collects the parables of a specified document, he does not then characterize the lot of them or differentiate one document's parables from those of another. So he prepared the way for work he did not then do.

[2] That is, the *Mashal* is assumed to conform to a uniform program throughout the Rabbinic canon, or even throughout all Judaic ("Jewish") writings. And Gospels-scholarship has tended to take the *Mashal* as a fixed genre of writing even for Christian documents.

[3] And along these same lines of Comparative Midrash, why does Lamentations Rabbah opt, among Rabbinic narrative types, for the authentic story rather than the parable. Its selection of parables is hardly comparable to that of Song of Songs Rabbah in volume or in documentary importance.

[4] We may therefore speak of the narrative such as a parable (*Mashal)* or a case/precedent *(Ma'aseh)* in the Mishnah or the Tosefta or Sifra or one or another of the Midrash-compilations or of the Talmuds, and only then ask how the *Mashal* or *Ma'aseh* as represented by the one document compares or contrasts with that set forth in another. And that is the fact, even though a given narrative may serve the purposes of more than a single document. I discuss the fact that some few compositions move from document to document in *Extra- and Non-Documentary Writing in the Canon of Formative Judaism.* I. *The Pointless Parallel: Hans-Jürgen Becker and the Myth of the Autonomous Tradition in Rabbinic Documents.* Binghamton 2001: Global Publications. ACADEMIC STUDIES IN THE HISTORY OF JUDAISM SERIES; *Extra- and Non-Documentary Writing in the Canon of Formative Judaism.* II. *Paltry Parallels. The Negligible Proportion and Peripheral Role of Free-Standing Compositions in Rabbinic Documents.* Binghamton 2001: Global Publications ACADEMIC STUDIES IN THE HISTORY OF JUDAISM SERIES; *Extra- and Non-Documentary Writing in the Canon of Formative Judaism.* III. *Peripatetic Parallels.* Binghamton, 2001: Global Publications. ACADEMIC STUDIES IN THE HISTORY OF JUDAISM SERIES. Second edition, revised, of *The Peripatetic Saying: The Problem of the Thrice-Told Tale in Talmudic Literature.* Chico, 1985: Scholars Press for Brown Judaic Studies.

[5] In the following I respond to critics in a systematic fashion: *The Documentary Foundation of Rabbinic Culture. Mopping Up after Debates with Gerald L. Bruns, S. J. D. Cohen, Arnold Maria Goldberg, Susan Handelman, Christine Hayes, James Kugel, Peter Schaefer, Eliezer Segal, E. P. Sanders, and Lawrence H. Schiffman.* Atlanta, 1995: Scholars Press for South Florida Studies in the History of Judaism; *Are the Talmuds Interchangeable? Christine Hayes's Blunder.* Atlanta, 1996: Scholars Press for South Florida Studies on the History of Judaism; *Judaic Law from Jesus to the Mishnah. A Systematic Reply to Professor E. P. Sanders.* Atlanta, 1993: Scholars Press for South Florida Studies in the History of Judaism; *Are There Really Tannaitic Parallels to the Gospels? A Refutation of Morton Smith.* Atlanta,

1993: Scholars Press for South Florida Studies in the History of Judaism; *Why There Never Was a "Talmud of Caesarea." Saul Lieberman's Mistakes.* Atlanta, 1994: Scholars Press for South Florida Studies in the History of Judaism; to James Kugel in *Canon and Connection: Intertextuality in Judaism.* Lanham, 1986: University Press of America. *Studies in Judaism* Series; *Midrash as Literature: The Primacy of Documentary Discourse.* Lanham, 1987: University Press of America *Studies in Judaism* series.

# Appendix

**Bibliography of Jacob Neusner**
**as of November 1, 2006**

### 1. *The pre-critical stage.*

*A Life of Yohanan ben Zakkai.* Leiden, 1962: Brill. Awarded the Abraham Berliner Prize in Jewish History, Jewish Theological Seminary of America, 1962. Second edition, completely revised, 1970.

French: *Vie de Yohanan ben Zakkai.* Paris, 2000: Clio.
Italian: Ferrara, 2007: Gallio Editori.
Japanese: Tokyo, 2007: Lithon Publishing House

*A History of the Jews in Babylonia.* Leiden: Brill, 1965-1970. I-V. Reprinted: Atlanta, 1999: Scholars Press for South Florida Studies in the History of Judaism. Now: Lanham, MD: University Press of America.

I. *A History of the Jews in Babylonia. The Parthian Period.* 1965. Second printing, revised, 1969. Third printing: Chico, 1984: Scholars Press for Brown Judaic Studies.
II. *A History of the Jews in Babylonia. The Early Sasanian Period.* 1966.
III. *A History of the Jews in Babylonia. From Shapur I to Shapur II.* 1968.
IV. *A History of the Jews in Babylonia. The Age of Shapur II.* 1969.
V. *A History of the Jews in Babylonia. Later Sasanian Times.* 1970.

French: *Histoire des Juifs de Babylonie.* Tome I. *L'epoque parthe.* Paris, 1997: Clio
French: *Histoire des Juifs de Babylonie.* II-V. Planned by Centre Clio/ Centre d'Études Juives/École des Hautes Études, Paris. Paris, 2007: Editions d Cerf.

*Aphrahat and Judaism. The Christian Jewish Argument in Fourth Century Iran.* Leiden, 1971: Brill. Reprint: Atlanta, 1999: Scholars Press for South Florida Studies in the History of Judaism.

### 2. *The beginning of the critical enterprise.*

*Development of a Legend. Studies on the Traditions Concerning Yohanan ben Zakkai.* Leiden, 1970: Brill. Reprinted: Binghamton, 2002: Global Publications. CLASSICS OF JUDAIC SERIES.

*The Rabbinic Traditions about the Pharisees before 70.* Leiden, 1971: Brill. I-III. Second printing: Atlanta, 1999: Scholars Press for South Florida Studies in the History of Judaism. Third printing: Eugene, OR 2005: Wipf and Stock. DOVE STUDIES IN BIBLE, LANGUAGE, HISTORY SERIES.

I. *The Rabbinic Traditions about the Pharisees before 70. The Masters.*
II. *The Rabbinic Traditions about the Pharisees before 70. The Houses.*
III. *The Rabbinic Traditions about the Pharisees before 70. Conclusions.*

*Eliezer ben Hyrcanus. The Tradition and the Man.* Leiden, 1973: Brill. Reprint: Eugene OR 2003: Wipf and Stock Publishers

I. *Eliezer ben Hyrcanus. The Tradition and the Man. The Tradition.*
II. *Eliezer ben Hyrcanus. The Tradition and the Man. The Man.*

### 3. *Literature*

### Describing the Canon, Document by Document.
### The Stage of Translation, Form-Analysis, and Exegesis

*A History of the Mishnaic Law of Purities.* Leiden, 1974-1977: Brill. I-XXII. Reprinted: Eugene OR 2007: Wipf & Stock

I. *Kelim. Chapters One through Eleven.* 1974.
II. *Kelim. Chapters Twelve through Thirty.* 1974.
III. *Kelim. Literary and Historical Problems.* 1974.
IV. *Ohalot. Commentary.* 1975.
V. *Ohalot. Literary and Historical Problems.* 1975.
VI. *Negaim. Mishnah-Tosefta.* 1975.
VII. *Negaim. Sifra.* 1975.
VIII. *Negaim. Literary and Historical Problems.* 1975.
IX. *Parah. Commentary.* 1976.
X. *Parah. Literary and Historical Problems.* 1976.

XI. *Tohorot. Commentary,* 1976.
XII. *Tohorot. Literary and Historical Problems.* 1976.
XIII. *Miqvaot. Commentary.* 1976.
XIV. *Miqvaot. Literary and Historical Problems.* 1976.
XV. *Niddah. Commentary.* 1976.
XVI. *Niddah. Literary and Historical Problems.* 1976.
XVII. *Makhshirin.* 1977.
XVIII. *Zabim.* 1977.
XIX. *Tebul Yom. Yadayim.* 1977.
XX. *Uqsin. Cumulative Index, Parts I-XX.* 1977.
XXI. *The Redaction and Formulation of the Order of Purities in the Mishnah and Tosefta.*
XXII. *The Mishnaic System of Uncleanness. Its Context and History.*

*The Judaic Law of Baptism. Tractate Miqvaot in the Mishnah and the Tosefta. A Form-Analytical Translation and Commentary, and a Legal and Religious History.* Atlanta, 1995: Scholars Press for South Florida Studies in the History of Judaism. Second Printing of *A History of the Mishnaic Law of Purities.* Volumes XIII and XIV.

*The Tosefta: Its Structure and its Sources*. Atlanta, 1986: Scholars Press for Brown Judaic Studies. Reprise of pertinent results in *Purities* I-XXI.

*A History of the Mishnaic Law of Holy Things*. Leiden, Brill: 1979. I-VI. Reprinted: Eugene OR 2007: Wipf & Stock

I. *Zebahim. Translation and Explanation.*
II. *Menahot. Translation and Explanation.*
III. *Hullin, Bekhorot. Translation and Explanation.*
IV. *Arakhin, Temurah. Translation and Explanation.*
V. *Keritot, Meilah, Tamid, Middot, Qinnim. Translation and Explanation.*
VI. *The Mishnaic System of Sacrifice and Sanctuary.*

*Form Analysis and Exegesis: A Fresh Approach to the Interpretation of Mishnah.* Minneapolis, 1980: University of Minnesota Press.

*A History of the Mishnaic Law of Women.* Leiden, Brill: 1979-1980. I-V. Reprinted: Eugene OR 2007: Wipf & Stock

I. *Yebamot. Translation and Explanation.*
II. *Ketubot. Translation and Explanation.*

III. *Nedarim, Nazir. Translation and Explanation.*
IV. *Sotah, Gittin, Qiddushin. Translation and Explanation.*
V. *The Mishnaic System of Women.*

*A History of the Mishnaic Law of Appointed Times.* Leiden, Brill: 1981-1983. I-V. Reprinted: Eugene OR 2007: Wipf & Stock

I. *Shabbat. Translation and Explanation.*
II. *Erubin, Pesahim. Translation and Explanation.*
III. *Sheqalim, Yoma, Sukkah. Translation and Explanation.*
IV. *Besah, Rosh Hashanah, Taanit, Megillah, Moed Qatan, Hagigah. Translation and Explanation.*
V. *The Mishnaic System of Appointed Times.*

*A History of the Mishnaic Law of Damages.* Leiden, Brill: 1983-1985. I-V. Reprinted: Eugene OR 2007: Wipf & Stock

I. *Baba Qamma. Translation and Explanation.*
II. *Baba Mesia. Translation and Explanation.*
III. *Baba Batra, Sanhedrin, Makkot. Translation and Explanation.*
IV. *Shebuot, Eduyyot, Abodah Zarah, Abot, Horayyot. Translation and Explanation.*
V. *The Mishnaic System of Damages.*

*The Mishnah. A New Translation.* New Haven and London, 1987: Yale University Press. *Choice* Outstanding Academic Book List, 1989. Second printing: 1990. Paperbound edition: 1991. CD Rom edition: Logos, 1996. CD Rom/ Web edition: OakTree Software, Inc. Altamonte Springs, FL.

Editor: *The Law of Agriculture in the Mishnah and the Tosefta.* Leiden, 2005: E. J. Brill.

I. *A History of the Mishnaic Law of Agriculture. Berakhot, Peah.*
II. *Demai, Kilayim., Shebiit*
III. *Terumot, Maaserot, Maaser Sheni, Hallah, Orlah, Bikkurim*

*The Tosefta. Translated from the Hebrew.* N.Y., 1977-1980: Ktav. II-VI.

I. Editor: *The Tosefta. Translated from the Hebrew. I. The First Division Zeraim.* N.Y., 1985: Ktav.

II. *The Tosefta. Translated from the Hebrew. The Second Division. Moed.* Second printing: Atlanta, 1999: Scholars Press for USF Academic Commentary Series.

III. *The Tosefta. Translated from the Hebrew. The Third Division. Nashim.* Second printing: Atlanta, 1999: Scholars Press for USF Academic Commentary Series.

IV. *The Tosefta. Translated from the Hebrew. The Fourth Division. Neziqin.* Second printing: Atlanta, 1999: Scholars Press for USF Academic Commentary Series.

V. *The Tosefta. Translated from the Hebrew. The Fifth Division. Qodoshim.* Second printing: Atlanta, 1997: Scholars Press for USF Academic Commentary Series.

VI. *The Tosefta. Translated from the Hebrew. The Sixth Division. Tohorot.* Second printing: Atlanta, 1990: Scholars Press for *South Florida Studies in the History of Judaism.* With a new preface.

Reprint: *The Tosefta in English.* I. *Zeraim, Moed, and Nashim.* Peabody, 2003: Hendrickson Publications. With a new introduction.
Reprint: *The Tosefta in English.* II. *Neziqin, Qodoshim, and Toharot.* Peabody, 2003: Hendrickson Publications.

*The Talmud of the Land of Israel. A Preliminary Translation and Explanation.* Chicago: The University of Chicago Press: 1982-1993. IX-XII, XIV-XV, XVII-XXXV.

IX. *Hallah.* 1991
X. *Orlah. Bikkurim.* 1991.
XI. *Shabbat.* 1991.
XII. *Erubin.* 1990.
XIV. *Yoma.* 1990.
XV. *Sheqalim.* 1990.
XVII. *Sukkah.* 1988.
XVIII. *Besah. Taanit.* 1987.
XIX. *Megillah.* 1987.
XX. *Hagigah. Moed Qatan.* 1986.
XXI. *Yebamot.* 1986.
XXII. *Ketubot.* 1985.
XXIII. *Nedarim* 1985.
XXIV. *Nazir.* 1985.
XXV. *Gittin.* 1985
XXVI. *Qiddushin.* 1984.
XXVII. *Sotah.* 1984.

XXVIII *Baba Qamma*. 1984.
XXIX. *Baba Mesia*. 1984.
XXX. *Baba Batra*. 1984.
XXXI. *Sanhedrin. Makkot*. 1984.
XXXII. *Shebuot*. 1983.
XXXIII. *Abodah Zarah*. 1982.
XXXIV. *Horayot. Niddah*. 1982
XXXV. *Introduction. Taxonomy*.

Edited: *In the Margins of the Yerushalmi. Notes on the English Translation*. Chico, 1983: Scholars Press for Brown Judaic Studies. Now: Lanham, MD: University Press of America.

*Torah from Our Sages: Pirke Avot. A New American Translation and Explanation*. Chappaqua, 1983: Rossel. Paperback edition: 1987. In print: S. Orange, 2005: Behrman House.

*Law as Literature*. Chico, 1983: Scholars Press. = *Semeia. An Experimental Journal for Biblical Criticism* Volume 27. Co-edited with William Scott Green. Second printing: Eugene OR, 2006: Wipf & Stock

*The Talmud of Babylonia. An American Translation*. Chico, then Atlanta: 1984-1995: Scholars Press for Brown Judaic Studies.

I. *Tractate Berakhot*
II.A. *Tractate Shabbat. Chapters One and Two.*
II.B. *Tractate Shabbat Chapters Three through Six*
II.C. *Tractate Shabbat Chapters Seven through Ten*
II.D. *Tractate Shabbat Chapters Eleven through Seventeen*
II.E. *Tractate Shabbat Chapters Eighteen through Twenty-Four*
III.A. *Tractate Erubin. Chapters One and Two*
III.B. *Tractate Erubin, Chapters Three and Four*
III.C. *Tractate Erubin, Chapters Five and Six*
III.D. *Tractate Erubin, Chapters Seven through Ten*
IV.A. *Tractate Pesahim. Chapter One*
IV.B. *Tractate Pesahim. Chapters Two and Three*
IV.C. *Tractate Pesahim. Chapters Four through Six*
IV.D. *Tractate Pesahim. Chapters Seven and Eight*
IV.E. *Tractate Pesahim. Chapters Nine and Ten*
V.A. *Tractate Yoma. Chapters One and Two*
V.B. *Tractate Yoma. Chapters Three through Five*
V.C. *Tractate Yoma. Chapters Six through Eight*

VI. *Tractate Sukkah*
XI. *Tractate Moed Qatan*
XII. *Tractate Hagigah*
XIII.A. *Tractate Yebamot. Chapters One through Three*
XIII.B. *Tractate Yebamot. Chapters Four through Six*
XIII.C. *Tractate Yebamot. Chapters Seven through Nine*
XIII.D. *Tractate Yebamot. Chapters Ten through Sixteen*
XIV.A. *Tractate Ketubot. Chapters One through Three*
XIV.B. *Tractate Ketubot. Chapters Four through Seven*
XIV.C. *Tractate Ketubot. Chapters Eight through Thirteen*
XV.A. *Tractate Nedarim. Chapters One through Four*
XV.B. *Tractate Nedarim. Chapters Five through Eleven*
XVII. *Tractate Sotah*
XVIII.A. *Tractate Gittin. Chapters One through Three*
XVIII.B. *Tractate Gittin. Chapters Four and Five*
XVIII.C. *Tractate Gittin. Chapters Six through Nine*
XIX.A. *Tractate Qiddushin. Chapter One*
XIX.B. *Tractate Qiddushin. Chapters Two through Four*
XX.A. *Tractate Baba Qamma. Chapters One through Three*
XX.B. *Tractate Baba Qamma. Chapters Four through Seven*
XX.C. *Tractate Baba Qamma. Chapters Eight through Ten*
XXI.A. *Tractate Baba Mesia. Introduction. Chapters One and Two*
XXI.B. *Tractate Baba Mesia. Chapters Three and Four*
XXI.C. *Tractate Baba Mesia. Chapters Five and Six*
XXI.D. *Tractate Baba Mesia. Chapters Seven through Ten*
XXII.A. *Tractate Baba Batra. Chapters One and Two*
XXII.B. *Tractate Baba Batra. Chapter Three*
XXII.C. *Tractate Baba Batra. Chapters Four through Six*
XXII.D *Tractate Baba Batra. Chapters Seven and Eight*
XXII. *Tractate Baba Batra. Chapters Nine and Ten*
XXII.A. *Tractate Sanhedrin. Chapters One through Three*
XXII.B. *Tractate Sanhedrin Chapters Four through Eight*
XXII.C. *Tractate Sanhedrin Chapters Nine through Eleven*
XXIV. *Tractate Makkot*
XXV.A. *Tractate Abodah Zarah. Chapters One and Two*
XXV.B. *Tractate Abodah Zarah. Chapters Three, Four, and Five*
XXVII.A. *Tractate Shebuot. Chapters One through Three*
XXVII.B. *Tractate Shebuot. Chapters Four through Eight*
XXVIII.A. *Tractate Zebahim. Chapters One through Three*
XXVIII.B. *Tractate Zebahim. Chapters Four through Eight*
XXVIII.C. *Tractate Zebahim. Chapters Nine through Fourteen*
XXIX.A. *Tractate Menahot. Chapters One through Three*

XXIX.B. *Tractate Menahot. Chapters Four through Seven*
XXIX.C. *Tractate Menahot. Chapters Eight through Thirteen*
XXXI.A. *Tractate Bekhorot. Chapters One through Four*
XXXI.B. *Tractate Bekhorot. Chapters Five through Nine*
XXXII. *Tractate Arakhin*
XXXIII. *Tractate Temurah*
XXXIV. *Tractate Keritot*
XXXVI.A. *Tractate Niddah. Chapters One through Three*
XXXVI.B. *Tractate Niddah. Chapters Four through Ten*

For Leviticus Rabbah, see below, *Judaism and Scripture: The Evidence of Leviticus Rabbah*

*Genesis Rabbah. The Judaic Commentary on Genesis. A New American Translation.* Atlanta, 1985: Scholars Press for Brown Judaic Studies. Now: Lanham: University Press of America. I. *Genesis Rabbah. The Judaic Commentary on Genesis. A New American Translation. Parashiyyot One through Thirty-Three. Genesis 1:1-8:14.*

*Genesis Rabbah. The Judaic Commentary on Genesis. A New American Translation.* Atlanta, 1985: Scholars Press for Brown Judaic Studies. II. *Genesis Rabbah. The Judaic Commentary on Genesis. A New American Translation. Parashiyyot Thirty-Four through Sixty-Seven. Genesis 8:15-28:9.*

*Genesis Rabbah. The Judaic Commentary on Genesis. A New American Translation.* Atlanta, 1985: Scholars Press for Brown Judaic Studies. III. *Genesis Rabbah. The Judaic Commentary on Genesis. A New American Translation. Parashiyyot Sixty-Eight through One Hundred. Genesis 28:10-50:26.*

*Sifra. The Judaic Commentary on Leviticus. A New Translation. The Leper. Leviticus 13:1-14:57.* Chico, 1985: Scholars Press for Brown Judaic Studies. Now: Lanham: University Press of America. [With a section by Roger Brooks.] Based on *A History of the Mishnaic Law of Purities. VI. Negaim. Sifra.*

*Sifré to Numbers. An American Translation.* I. *1-58.* Atlanta, 1986: Scholars Press for Brown Judaic Studies. Now: Lanham: University Press of America.

*Sifré to Numbers. An American Translation.* II. *59-115.* Atlanta, 1986: Scholars Press for Brown Judaic Studies. Now: Lanham: University Press of

America. The translation of Parashiyyot 116-161 is given in *The Components of the Rabbinic Documents: From the Whole to the Parts.* XII. *Sifré to Numbers.*

*The Fathers According to Rabbi Nathan. An Analytical Translation and Explanation.* Atlanta, 1986: Scholars Press for Brown Judaic Studies. Now: Lanham: University Press of America.

*Pesiqta deRab Kahana. An Analytical Translation and Explanation.* I. *1-14.* Atlanta, 1987: Scholars Press for Brown Judaic Studies. Now: Lanham: University Press of America.

*Pesiqta deRab Kahana. An Analytical Translation and Explanation.* II. *15-28. With an Introduction to Pesiqta deRab Kahana.* Atlanta, 1987: Scholars Press for Brown Judaic Studies. Now: Lanham: University Press of America.

For Pesiqta Rabbati, see below, *From Tradition to Imitation. The Plan and Program of Pesiqta deRab Kahana and Pesiqta Rabbati.*

*Sifré to Deuteronomy. An Analytical Translation.* Atlanta, 1987: Scholars Press for Brown Judaic Studies. Now: Lanham: University Press of America. I. *Pisqaot One through One Hundred Forty-Three. Debarim, Waethanan, Eqeb, Re'eh.*

*Sifré to Deuteronomy. An Analytical Translation.* Atlanta, 1987: Scholars Press for Brown Judaic Studies. Now: Lanham: University Press of America. II. *Pisqaot One Hundred Forty-Four through Three Hundred Fifty-Seven. Shofetim, Ki Tese, Ki Tabo, Nesabim, Ha'azinu, Zot Habberakhah.*

*Sifra. An Analytical Translation.* Atlanta, 1988: Scholars Press for Brown Judaic Studies. Now: Lanham: University Press of America. I. *Introduction* and *Vayyiqra Dibura Denedabah* and *Vayiqqra Dibura Dehobah.*

*Sifra. An Analytical Translation.* Atlanta, 1988: Scholars Press for Brown Judaic Studies. Now: Lanham: University Press of America. II. *Sav, Shemini, Tazria, Negaim, Mesora,* and *Zabim*

*Sifra. An Analytical Translation.* Atlanta, 1988: Scholars Press for Brown Judaic Studies. Now: Lanham: University Press of America. III. *Aharé Mot, Qedoshim, Emor, Behar,* and *Behuqotai.*

*Mekhilta Attributed to R. Ishmael. An Analytical Translation.* Atlanta, 1988: Scholars Press for Brown Judaic Studies. Now: Lanham: University Press of America. I. *Pisha, Beshallah, Shirata, and Vayassa.*

*Mekhilta Attributed to R. Ishmael. An Analytical Translation.* Atlanta, 1988: Scholars Press for Brown Judaic Studies. Now: Lanham: University Press of America. II. *Amalek, Bahodesh, Neziqin, Kaspa and Shabbata*

*Translating the Classics of Judaism. In Theory and in Practice*. Atlanta, 1989: Scholars Press for Brown Judaic Studies.

*Lamentations Rabbah. An Analytical Translation.* Atlanta, 1989: Scholars Press for Brown Judaic Studies. Now: Lanham: University Press of America.

*Esther Rabbah I. An Analytical Translation.* Atlanta, 1989: Scholars Press for Brown Judaic Studies. Now: Lanham: University Press of America.

*Ruth Rabbah. An Analytical Translation.* Atlanta, 1989: Scholars Press for Brown Judaic Studies. Now: Lanham: University Press of America.

*Song of Songs Rabbah. An Analytical Translation.* Volume One. *Song of Songs Rabbah to Song Chapters One through Three.* Atlanta, 1990: Scholars Press for Brown Judaic Studies. Now: Lanham: University Press of America.

*Song of Songs Rabbah. An Analytical Translation.* Volume Two. *Song of Songs Rabbah to Song Chapters Four through Eight.* Atlanta, 1990: Scholars Press for Brown Judaic Studies. Now: Lanham: University Press of America.

*Texts without Boundaries. Protocols of Non-Documentary Writing in the Rabbinic Canon,* Lanham MD, 2002: University Press of America. STUDIES IN JUDAISM SERIES. Volume One. *The Mishnah, Tractate Abot, and the Tosefta*

*Texts without Boundaries. Protocols of Non-Documentary Writing in the Rabbinic Canon,* Lanham MD, 2002: University Press of America. STUDIES IN JUDAISM SERIES. Volume Two. *Sifra and Sifré to Numbers.*

*Texts without Boundaries. Protocols of Non-Documentary Writing in the Rabbinic Canon,* Lanham MD, 2002: University Press of America. STUDIES IN JUDAISM SERIES. Volume Three. *Sifré to Deuteronomy and Mekhilta Attributed to R. Ishmael*

*Texts without Boundaries. Protocols of Non-Documentary Writing in the Rabbinic Canon,* Lanham MD, 2002: University Press of America. STUDIES IN JUDAISM SERIES. Volume Four. *Leviticus Rabbah*

*Rabbinic Narrative: A Documentary Perspective.* Volume One. *Forms, Types, and Distribution of Narratives in the Mishnah, Tractate Abot, and the Tosefta.* Leiden, 2003: E. J. Brill. THE BRILL REFERENCE LIBRARY OF JUDAISM

*Rabbinic Narrative: A Documentary Perspective.* Volume Two. *Forms, Types, and Distribution of Narratives in Sifra, Sifré to Numbers, and Sifré to Deuteronomy.* Leiden, 2003: E. J. Brill. THE BRILL REFERENCE LIBRARY OF JUDAISM

*Rabbinic Narrative: A Documentary Perspective.* Volume Three. *Forms, Types, and Distribution of Narratives in Song of Songs Rabbah and Lamentations Rabbah. And a Reprise of Fathers According to Rabbi Nathan Text A.* Leiden, 2003: E. J. Brill. THE BRILL REFERENCE LIBRARY OF JUDAISM

*Rabbinic Narrative. A Documentary Perspective.* Volume Four. *The Precedent and the Parable in Diachronic View.* Leiden, 2003: E. J. Brill. THE BRILL REFERENCE LIBRARY OF JUDAISM

## 4. *History of Ideas, Law, and Literature*

### Introducing the Documents, Comparing and Contrasting the Documentary Components of the Canon of Formative Judaism

*Invitation to the Talmud. A Teaching Book.* N.Y., 1973: Harper & Row. Second printing, 1974. Paperback edition, 1975. Reprinted: 1982. Second edition, completely revised, San Francisco, 1984: Harper & Row. Paperback edition: 1988. Second printing, in paperback, of the second edition: Atlanta, 1998: Scholars Press for South Florida Studies in the History of Judaism. Third printing of the second edition: Binghamton, 2001: Global Publications. Fourth printing of the second edition: Eugene, OR: Wipf & Stock, Publishers.

*The Mishnah before 70.* Atlanta, 1987: Scholars Press for Brown Judaic Studies. [Reprise of pertinent results of *A History of the Mishnah Law of Purities* Volumes. III, V, VIII, X, XII, XIV, XVI, XVII, and XVIII.]

*The Integrity of Leviticus Rabbah. The Problem of the Autonomy of a Rabbinic Document*. Chico, 1985: Scholars Press for Brown Judaic Studies.

*Comparative Midrash: The Plan and Program of Genesis Rabbah and Leviticus Rabbah.* Atlanta, 1986: Scholars Press for Brown Judaic Studies. Now: Lanham: University Press of America.

*From Tradition to Imitation. The Plan and Program of Pesiqta deRab Kahana and Pesiqta Rabbati.* Atlanta, 1987: Scholars Press for Brown Judaic Studies. [With a fresh translation of Pesiqta Rabbati *Pisqaot* 1-5, 15.]

*Canon and Connection: Intertextuality in Judaism.* Lanham, 1986: University Press of America. *Studies in Judaism* Series.

*Midrash as Literature: The Primacy of Documentary Discourse.* Lanham, 1987: University Press of America *Studies in Judaism* series. Reprint: Eugene OR 2003: Wipf and Stock Publishers

*The Bavli and its Sources: The Question of Tradition in the Case of Tractate Sukkah.* Atlanta, 1987: Scholars Press for Brown Judaic Studies.

*Invitation to Midrash: The Working of Rabbinic Bible Interpretation. A Teaching Book.* San Francisco, 1988: Harper & Row. Second printing, in paperback: Atlanta, 1998: Scholars Press for South Florida Studies in the History of Judaism.

*What Is Midrash?* Philadelphia,1987: Fortress Press. Second printing: Atlanta, 1994: Scholars Press.

*Sifré to Deuteronomy. An Introduction to the Rhetorical, Logical, and Topical Program.* Atlanta, 1987: Scholars Press for Brown Judaic Studies.

*Uniting the Dual Torah: Sifra and the Problem of the Mishnah.* Cambridge and New York, 1989: Cambridge University Press.

*Sifra in Perspective: The Documentary Comparison of the Midrashim of Ancient Judaism* Atlanta, 1988: Scholars Press for Brown Judaic Studies.

*Mekhilta Attributed to R. Ishmael. An Introduction to Judaism's First Scriptural Encyclopaedia.* Atlanta, 1988: Scholars Press for Brown Judaic Studies.

*The Midrash Compilations of the Sixth and Seventh Centuries. An Introduction to the Rhetorical Logical, and Topical Program.* I. *Lamentations Rabbah.* Atlanta, 1990: Scholars Press for Brown Judaic Studies

*The Midrash Compilations of the Sixth and Seventh Centuries: An Introduction to the Rhetorical Logical, and Topical Program.* II. *Esther Rabbah I.* Atlanta, 1990: Scholars Press for Brown Judaic Studies

*The Midrash Compilations of the Sixth and Seventh Centuries: An Introduction to the Rhetorical Logical, and Topical Program.* III. *Ruth Rabbah.* Atlanta, 1990: Scholars Press for Brown Judaic Studies

*The Midrash Compilations of the Sixth and Seventh Centuries: An Introduction to the Rhetorical Logical, and Topical Program.* IV. *Song of Songs Rabbah.* Atlanta, 1990: Scholars Press for Brown Judaic Studies

*A Midrash Reader.* Minneapolis, 1990: Augsburg-Fortress. Second printing: Atlanta, 1994: Scholars Press.

*Making the Classics in Judaism: The Three Stages of Literary Formation.* Atlanta, 1990: Scholars Press for Brown Judaic Studies.

*The Mishnah. An Introduction.* Northvale, N.J., 1989: Jason Aronson, Inc. Paperback edition: 1994. Reprinted 2004: Rowman and Littlefield.

*The Midrash. An Introduction.* Northvale, 1990: Jason Aronson, Inc. Paperback edition: 1994. . Reprinted 2005: Rowman and Littlefield

*The Yerushalmi. The Talmud of the Land of Israel. An Introduction.* Northvale, 1992: Jason Aronson, Inc. . Reprinted 2004: Rowman and Littlefield

*The Tosefta. An Introduction.* Atlanta, 1992: Scholars Press for South Florida Studies in the History of Judaism. Now: Lanham, UNIVERSITY PRESS OF AMERICA STUDIES IN JUDAISM SERIES.

*The Bavli. The Talmud of Babylonia. An Introduction.* Atlanta, 1992: Scholars Press for South Florida Studies in the History of Judaism.

*The Canonical History of Ideas. The Place of the So-called Tannaite Midrashim, Mekhilta Attributed to R. Ishmael, Sifra, Sifré to Numbers, and Sifré to Deuteronomy.* Atlanta, 1990: Scholars Press for South Florida Studies in the History of Judaism.

*The Talmud: Close Encounters.* Minneapolis, 1991: Fortress Press. Second printing, 1996. Reprint: Eugene OR 2004: Wipf and Stock.

*Tradition as Selectivity: Scripture, Mishnah, Tosefta, and Midrash in the Talmud of Babylonia. The Case of Tractate Arakhin.* Atlanta, 1990: Scholars Press for South Florida Studies in the History of Judaism.

*Language as Taxonomy. The Rules for Using Hebrew and Aramaic in the Babylonian Talmud.* Atlanta, 1990: Scholars Press for South Florida Studies in the History of Judaism.

*The Bavli That Might Have Been: The Tosefta's Theory of Mishnah-Commentary Compared with That of the Babylonian Talmud.* Atlanta, 1990: Scholars Press for South Florida Studies in the History of Judaism.

*The Rules of Composition of the Talmud of Babylonia. The Cogency of the Bavli's Composite.* Atlanta, 1991: Scholars Press for South Florida Studies in the History of Judaism.

*The Bavli's One Voice: Types and Forms of Analytical Discourse and their Fixed Order of Appearance.* Atlanta, 1991: Scholars Press for South Florida Studies in the History of Judaism. Now: Lanham, MD: University Press of America.

*The Bavli's One Statement. The Metapropositional Program of Babylonian Talmud Tractate Zebahim Chapters One and Five.* Atlanta, 1991: Scholars Press for South Florida Studies in the History of Judaism.

*How the Bavli Shaped Rabbinic Discourse.* Atlanta, 1991: Scholars Press for South Florida Studies in the History of Judaism.

*The Bavli's Massive Miscellanies. The Problem of Agglutinative Discourse in the Talmud of Babylonia.* Atlanta, 1992: Scholars Press for South Florida Studies in the History of Judaism.

*Sources and Traditions. Types of Composition in the Talmud of Babylonia.* Atlanta, 1992: Scholars Press for South Florida Studies in the History of Judaism.

*The Law Behind the Laws. The Bavli's Essential Discourse.* Atlanta, 1992: Scholars Press for South Florida Studies in the History of Judaism.

*The Bavli's Primary Discourse. Mishnah Commentary, its Rhetorical Paradigms and their Theological Implications in the Talmud of Babylonia Tractate Moed Qatan.* Atlanta, 1992: Scholars Press for South Florida Studies in the History of Judaism.

*The Discourse of the Bavli: Language, Literature, and Symbolism. Five Recent Findings.* Atlanta, 1991: Scholars Press for South Florida Studies in the History of Judaism.

*How to Study the Bavli: The Languages, Literatures, and Lessons of the Talmud of Babylonia.* Atlanta, 1992: Scholars Press for South Florida Studies in the History of Judaism.

*Form-Analytical Comparison in Rabbinic Judaism. Structure and Form in* The Fathers *and* The Fathers According to Rabbi Nathan. Atlanta, 1992: Scholars Press for South Florida Studies in the History of Judaism.

*The Bavli's Intellectual Character. The Generative Problematic in Bavli Baba Qamma Chapter One and Bavli Shabbat Chapter One.* Atlanta, 1992: Scholars Press for South Florida Studies in the History of Judaism.

*Decoding the Talmud's Exegetical Program: From Detail to Principle in the Bavli's Quest for Generalization. Tractate Shabbat.* Atlanta, 1992: Scholars Press for South Florida Studies in the History of Judaism.

*The Principal Parts of the Bavli's Discourse: A Final Taxonomy. Mishnah-Commentary, Sources, Traditions, and Agglutinative Miscellanies.* Atlanta, 1992: Scholars Press for South Florida Studies in the History of Judaism.

*The Torah in the Talmud. A Taxonomy of the Uses of Scripture in the Talmuds. Tractate Qiddushin in the Talmud of Babylonia and the Talmud of the Land of Israel.* I. *Bavli Qiddushin Chapter One.* Atlanta, 1993: Scholars Press for South Florida Studies in the History of Judaism.

*The Torah in the Talmud. A Taxonomy of the Uses of Scripture in the Talmuds. Tractate Qiddushin in the Talmud of Babylonia and the Talmud of the Land of Israel.* II. *Yerushalmi Qiddushin Chapter One. And a Comparison of the Uses of Scripture by the Two Talmuds.* Atlanta, 1993: Scholars Press for South Florida Studies in the History of Judaism.

*The Bavli's Unique Voice. A Systematic Comparison of the Talmud of Babylonia and the Talmud of the Land of Israel.* Volume One. *Bavli and Yerushalmi Qiddushin Chapter One Compared and Contrasted.* Atlanta, 1993: Scholars Press for South Florida Studies in the History of Judaism.

*The Bavli's Unique Voice. A Systematic Comparison of the Talmud of Babylonia and the Talmud of the Land of Israel.* Volume Two. *Yerushalmi's, Bavli's, and Other Canonical Documents' Treatment of the Program of Mishnah-Tractate Sukkah Chapters One, Two, and Four Compared and Contrasted. A Reprise and Revision of* The Bavli and its Sources. Atlanta, 1993: Scholars Press for South Florida Studies in the History of Judaism.

*The Bavli's Unique Voice. A Systematic Comparison of the Talmud of Babylonia and the Talmud of the Land of Israel.* Volume Three. *Bavli and Yerushalmi to Selected Mishnah-Chapters in the Division of Moed. Erubin Chapter One, and Moed Qatan Chapter Three.* Atlanta, 1993: Scholars Press for South Florida Studies in the History of Judaism.

*The Bavli's Unique Voice. A Systematic Comparison of the Talmud of Babylonia and the Talmud of the Land of Israel.* Volume Four. *Bavli and Yerushalmi to Selected Mishnah-Chapters in the Division of Nashim. Gittin Chapter Five and Nedarim Chapter One. And Niddah Chapter One.* Atlanta, 1993: Scholars Press for South Florida Studies in the History of Judaism.

*The Bavli's Unique Voice. A Systematic Comparison of the Talmud of Babylonia and the Talmud of the Land of Israel.* Volume Five. *Bavli and Yerushalmi to Selected Mishnah-Chapters in the Division of Neziqin. Baba Mesia Chapter One and Makkot Chapters One and Two.* Atlanta, 1993: Scholars Press for South Florida Studies in the History of Judaism.

*The Bavli's Unique Voice. A Systematic Comparison of the Talmud of Babylonia and the Talmud of the Land of Israel.* Volume Six. *Bavli and Yerushalmi to a Miscellany of Mishnah-Chapters. Gittin Chapter One, Qiddushin Chapter Two, and Hagigah Chapter Three.* Atlanta, 1993: Scholars Press for South Florida Studies in the History of Judaism.

*The Bavli's Unique Voice.* Volume Seven. *What Is Unique about the Bavli in Context? An Answer Based on Inductive Description, Analysis, and Comparison.* Atlanta, 1993: Scholars Press for South Florida Studies in the History of Judaism.

*From Text to Historical Context in Rabbinic Judaism: Historical Facts in Systemic Documents.* I. *The Mishnah, Tosefta, Abot, Sifra, Sifré to Numbers, and Sifré to Deuteronomy.* Atlanta, 1993: Scholars Press for South Florida Studies in the History of Judaism.

*From Text to Historical Context in Rabbinic Judaism: Historical Facts in Systemic Documents.* II. *The Later Midrash-Compilations: Genesis Rabbah, Leviticus Rabbah, Pesiqta deRab Kahana.* Atlanta, 1994: Scholars Press for South Florida Studies in the History of Judaism.

*From Text to Historical Context in Rabbinic Judaism: Historical Facts in Systemic Documents.* III. *The Latest Midrash-Compilations: Song of Songs Rabbah, Ruth Rabbah, Esther Rabbah I, and Lamentations Rabbah.* Atlanta, 1994: Scholars Press for South Florida Studies in the History of Judaism.

*Introduction to Rabbinic Literature.* N.Y., 1994: Doubleday. The Doubleday Anchor Reference Library. Religious Book Club Selection, 1994. Paperback edition: 1999.

Italian: Bologna, 2007: Edizioni Piemme

*Where the Talmud Comes From: A Talmudic Phenomenology. Identifying the Free-Standing Building Blocks of Talmudic Discourse.* Atlanta, 1995: Scholars Press for South Florida Studies in the History of Judaism.

*The Initial Phases of the Talmud's Judaism.* Atlanta, 1995: Scholars Press for South Florida Studies in the History of Judaism. I. *Exegesis of Scripture.*

*The Initial Phases of the Talmud's Judaism.* Atlanta, 1995: Scholars Press for South Florida Studies in the History of Judaism. II. *Exemplary Virtue.*

*The Initial Phases of the Talmud's Judaism.* Atlanta, 1995: Scholars Press for South Florida Studies in the History of Judaism. III. *Social Ethics.*

*The Initial Phases of the Talmud's Judaism.* Atlanta, 1995: Scholars Press for South Florida Studies in the History of Judaism. IV. *Theology.*

*Talmudic Dialectics: Types and Forms.* Atlanta, 1995: Scholars Press for South Florida Studies in the History of Judaism. I. *Introduction. Tractate Berakhot and the Divisions of Appointed Times and Women.*

*Talmudic Dialectics: Types and Forms.* Atlanta, 1995: Scholars Press for South Florida Studies in the History of Judaism. II. *The Divisions of Damages and Holy Things and Tractate Niddah.*

*Rationality and Structure: The Bavli's Anomalous Juxtapositions.* Atlanta, 1997: Scholars Press for South Florida Studies in the History of Judaism. Now: Lanham,, MD.: University Press of America.

*The Modes of Thought of Rabbinic Judaism.* I. *Types of Analysis.* Binghamton 2000: Global Publications. ACADEMIC STUDIES IN THE HISTORY OF JUDAISM SERIES.

*The Modes of Thought of Rabbinic Judaism.* II. *Types of Argumentation.* Binghamton 2000: Global Publications. ACADEMIC STUDIES IN THE HISTORY OF JUDAISM SERIES.

Second printing, condensed and revised; under the title, *Analysis and Argumentation in Rabbinic Judaism.* Lanham, 2003: University Press of America.

*Extra- and Non-Documentary Writing in the Canon of Formative Judaism.* I. *The Pointless Parallel: Hans-Jürgen Becker and the Myth of the Autonomous Tradition in Rabbinic Documents.* Binghamton 2001: Global Publications. ACADEMIC STUDIES IN THE HISTORY OF JUDAISM SERIES.

*Extra- and Non-Documentary Writing in the Canon of Formative Judaism.* II. *Paltry Parallels. The Negligible Proportion and Peripheral Role of Free-Standing Compositions in Rabbinic Documents.* Binghamton 2001: Global PublicationsACADEMIC STUDIES IN THE HISTORY OF JUDAISM SERIES

*Extra- and Non-Documentary Writing in the Canon of Formative Judaism.* III. *Peripatetic Parallels.* Binghamton, 2001: Global Publications. ACADEMIC STUDIES IN THE HISTORY OF JUDAISM SERIES. Second edition, revised, of *The Peripatetic Saying: The Problem of the Thrice-Told Tale in Talmudic Literature.* Chico, 1985: Scholars Press for Brown Judaic Studies.

*How the Halakhah Unfolds*: I. *Moed Qatan in the Mishnah, Tosefta, Yerushalmi, and Bavli.* Lanham 2006: University Press of America.

*How the Halakhah Unfolds*: II. *Nazir in the Mishnah, Tosefta, Yerushalmi, and Bavli.* Lanham 2006: University Press of America. Part A. *Mishnah Tractate Nazir. Tosefta Tractate Nazir. Yerushalmi Tractate Nazir.*

*How the Halakhah Unfolds*: II. *Nazir in the Mishnah, Tosefta, Yerushalmi, and Bavli.* Lanham 2006: University Press of America. Part B. *Bavli Tractate Nazir. Yerushalmi-Bavli Nazir Systematically Compared. Nazir Viewed Whole.*

*How the Halakhah Unfolds.* III. Abodah Zarah *in the Mishnah, Tosefta, Yerushalmi, and Bavli.* Lanham 2006: University Press of America. Part A. Mishnah Tractate Abodah Zarah. Tosefta Tractate Abodah Zarah. Yerushalmi Tractate Abodah Zarah.

*How the Halakhah Unfolds.* III. Abodah Zarah *in the Mishnah, Tosefta, Yerushalmi, and Bavli.* Lanham 2006: University Press of America. Part B. *Bavli Tractate Abodah Zarah. Yerushalmi-Bavli Abodah Zarah Systematically Compared. Abodah Zarah Viewed Whole.*

## 5. *Religion*

### Reconstructing and Interpreting the History of the Formation of Judaism

*From Politics to Piety. The Emergence of Pharisaic Judaism.* Englewood Cliffs, 1973: Prentice-Hall. Second printing, N.Y., 1978: Ktav. Reprint: Eugene OR 2003: Wipf and Stock Publishers

Japanese translation: *Parisai Ha towa Nanika. Seifi Kara Keiken e.* Tokyo, 1988: Kyo Bun Kwan.

*The Idea of Purity in Ancient Judaism. The Haskell Lectures, 1972-1973.* Leiden, 1973: E. J. Brill. Second printing: Eugene OR, 2006: Wipf & Stock.

*Judaism. The Evidence of the Mishnah.* Chicago, 1981: University of Chicago Press. *Choice*, "Outstanding academic book list" 1982-3. Paperback edition: 1984. Second printing, 1985. Third printing, 1986. Second edition, augmented: Atlanta, 1987: Scholars Press for Brown Judaic Studies. Reprint, Eugene, OR, 2003: Wipf and Stock.

*Hayyahadut le'edut hammishnah.* Hebrew translation of *Judaism. The Evidence of the Mishnah.* Tel Aviv, 1987: Sifriat Poalim.
*Il Giudaismo nella testimonianza della Mishnah.* Italian translation by Giorgio Volpe. Bologna, 1995: Centro editoriale Dehoniane.

*Judaism without Christianity. An Introduction to the Religious System of the Mishnah in Historical Context.* Hoboken, 1991: Ktav Publishing House. Abbreviated version of *Judaism* : *The Evidence of the Mishnah.*

*Judaism in Society: The Evidence of the Yerushalmi. Toward the Natural History of a Religion.* Chicago, 1983: The University of Chicago Press. *Choice,* "Outstanding Academic Book List, 1984-1985." Second printing, with a new preface: Atlanta, 1991: Scholars Press for South Florida Studies in the History of Judaism. Reprint, Eugene, OR, 2003: Wipf and Stock.

*Judaism and Scripture: The Evidence of Leviticus Rabbah.* Chicago, 1986: The University of Chicago Press. [Fresh translation of Margulies' text and systematic analysis of problems of composition and redaction.] Jewish Book Club Selection, 1986. Reprint, Eugene, OR, 2003: Wipf and Stock.

*Judaism: The Classical Statement. The Evidence of the Bavli.* Chicago, 1986: University of Chicago Press. *Choice,* "Outstanding Academic Book List, 1987." Reprint, Eugene, OR, 2003: Wipf and Stock.

*Judaism and Story: The Evidence of The Fathers According to Rabbi Nathan.* Chicago, 1992: University of Chicago Press. Reprint, Eugene, OR, 2003: Wipf and Stock.

*Ancient Israel after Catastrophe. The Religious World-View of the Mishnah. The Richard Lectures for 1982.* Charlottesville, 1983: The University Press of Virginia.

*The Foundations of Judaism. Method, Teleology, Doctrine.* Philadelphia, 1983-5: Fortress Press. I-III. I. *Midrash in Context. Exegesis in Formative Judaism.* Second printing: Atlanta, 1988: Scholars Press for Brown Judaic Studies.

*The Foundations of Judaism. Method, Teleology, Doctrine.* Philadelphia, 1983-5: Fortress Press. I-III. II. *Messiah in Context. Israel's History and Destiny in Formative Judaism.* Second printing: Lanham, 1988: University Press of America. Studies in Judaism series.

*The Foundations of Judaism. Method, Teleology, Doctrine.* Philadelphia, 1983-5: Fortress Press. I-III. III. *Torah: From Scroll to Symbol in Formative Judaism.* Second printing: Atlanta, 1988: Scholars Press for Brown Judaic Studies.

*The Foundations of Judaism.* Philadelphia, 1988: Fortress. Abridged edition of the foregoing trilogy. Second printing: Atlanta, 1994: Scholars Press for South Florida Studies in the History of Judaism.

*Grondslagen van het Jodendom: Tora, Misjna, Messias.* Translated by Liesbeth Mok and Klaas A. D. Smelik. Boxtel and Leuven, 1991: Katholieke Bijbelstichting and Vlaamse Bijbelstichting.

Italian translation: *I fondamenti del giudaismo.* Translated by Piero Stefani. Firenze, 1992: Editrice la Giuntina.

*From Description to Conviction. Essays on the History and Theology of Judaism.* Atlanta, 1987: Scholars Press for Brown Judaic Studies.

*The Oral Torah. The Sacred Books of Judaism. An Introduction.* San Francisco, 1985: Harper & Row. Paperback: 1987. Bnai Brith Jewish Book Club Selection, 1986. Second printing: Atlanta, 1991: Scholars Press for South Florida Studies in the History of Judaism.

Editor: *Scriptures of the Oral Torah. Sanctification and Salvation in the Sacred Books of Judaism.* San Francisco, 1987: Harper & Row. Jewish Book Club Selection, 1988. Second printing: Atlanta, 1990: Scholars Press for Brown Judaic Studies.

*Vanquished Nation, Broken Spirit. The Virtues of the Heart in Formative Judaism.* New York, 1987: Cambridge University Press. Jewish Book Club selection, 1987.

Editor: *"To See Ourselves as Others See Us." Jews, Christians, ""Others" in Late Antiquity.* Chico, 1985: Scholars Press. *Studies in the Humanities.*

Editor: *Judaic Perspectives on Ancient Israel.* Philadelphia, 1987: Fortress Press. Reprint: Eugene, OR, 2004: Wipf and Stock.

Editor: *Judaisms and their Messiahs in the Beginning of Christianity.* New York, 1987: Cambridge University Press. [Edited with William Scott Green]

Editor: *Goodenough's Jewish Symbols. An Abridged Edition.* Princeton, 1988: Princeton University Press. Paperback edition: 1992.

*Judaism in the Beginning of Christianity.* Philadelphia, 1983: Fortress. British edition, London, 1984: SPCK. Second US printing, 1988. Third printing, 1990. Fifth US printing,1994.

French translation: *Le judaisme a l'aube du christianisme.* Paris, 1986: Editions du Cerf.

German translation: *Judentum in frühchristlicher Zeit.* Stuttgart, 1988: Calwerverlag.

Dutch translation: *De Joodse wieg van het Christendom*. Kampen, 1987: J. H. Kok.

Norwegian translation: *Jødedommen i den første kristne tid.* Trondheim, 1987: Tapir Publishers, University of Trondheim. Translated by Johan B. Hygen.

Italian translation: *Il Giudaismo nei primi secoli del Christianismo.* Brescia, 1989: Morcelliano.

Japanese translation: *Iesu Jidai No Yudayakyo*. Tokyo, 1992: Kyo Bun Kwan.

*Judaism in the Matrix of Christianity.* Philadelphia, 1986: Fortress Press. British edition, Edinburgh, 1988, T. & T. Collins. Second printing, with a new introduction: Atlanta, 1990: Scholars Press for South Florida Studies in the History of Judaism.

*Judaism and Christianity in the Age of Constantine. Issues of the Initial Confrontation.* Chicago, 1987: University of Chicago Press.

*Death and Birth of Judaism. The Impact of Christianity, Secularism, and the Holocaust on Jewish Faith,* New York, 1987: Basic Books. Second printing: Atlanta, 1993: Scholars Press for South Florida Studies in the History of Judaism. Now: Lanham MD, 2000: University Press of America.

*Self-Fulfilling Prophecy: Exile and Return in the History of Judaism.* Boston, 1987: Beacon Press. Second printing: Atlanta, 1990: Scholars Press for South Florida Studies in the History of Judaism. With a new introduction. Now: Lanham, Md.: University Press of America.

Editor: *Goodenough on History of Religion and on Judaism.* Atlanta, 1986: Scholars Press for Brown Judaic Studies.

Editor: *Science, Magic, and Religion in Concert and in Conflict. Judaic, Christian, Philosophical, and Social Scientific Perspectives.* New York, 1988: Oxford University Press. Paperback edition: 1993.

*The Enchantments of Judaism. Rites of Transformation from Birth through Death.* New York, 1987: Basic Books. Judaic Book Club selection, September, 1987. Jewish Book Club selection, October, 1987. Second printing: Atlanta, 1991: Scholars Press for University of South Florida Studies in the History of Judaism. Now: Lanham: University Press of America. Edition on tape: Princeton, 1992: Recording for the Blind. Third printing: Lanham, 2005: University Press of America.

*Judaism and its Social Metaphors. Israel in the History of Jewish Thought.* N.Y., 1988: Cambridge University Press.

*The Incarnation of God: The Character of Divinity in Formative Judaism.* Philadelphia, 1988: Fortress Press. Reprinted: Atlanta, 1992: Scholars Press for South Florida Studies in the History of Judaism. Reprinted: Binghamton, 2000: Global Publications. CLASSICS OF JUDAIC SERIES.

*Writing with Scripture: The Authority and Uses of the Hebrew Bible in the Torah of Formative Judaism.* Philadelphia, 1989: Fortress Press. Second printing: Atlanta, 1994: Scholars Press for South Florida Studies in the History of Judaism. Reprint, Eugene, OR, 2003: Wipf and Stock.

*The Making of the Mind of Judaism.* Atlanta, 1987: Scholars Press for Brown Judaic Studies.

Reprint, revised: *Rabbinic Judaism's Generative Logic.* I. *The Making of the Mind of Judaism.* Binghamton, 2002: Global Publications. ACADEMIC STUDIES IN THE HISTORY OF JUDAISM SERIES.

*The Formation of the Jewish Intellect. Making Connections and Drawing Conclusions in the Traditional System of Judaism.* Atlanta, 1988: Scholars Press for Brown Judaic Studies.

Reprint, revised: *Rabbinic Judaism's Generative Logic.* II. *The Formation of the Jewish Intellect.* Binghamton, 2002: Global Publications. ACADEMIC STUDIES IN THE HISTORY OF JUDAISM SERIES.

*The Economics of the Mishnah.* Chicago, 1989: The University of Chicago Press. Reprint: Atlanta, 1998: Scholars Press for South Florida Studies in the History of Judaism.

*Rabbinic Political Theory: Religion and Politics in the Mishnah.* Chicago, 1991: The University of Chicago Press.

*The Philosophical Mishnah.* Volume I. *The Initial Probe.* Atlanta, 1989: Scholars Press for Brown Judaic Studies. Now: Lanham MD: University Press of America.

*The Philosophical Mishnah.* Volume II. *The Tractates' Agenda. From Abodah Zarah to Moed Qatan.* Atlanta, 1989: Scholars Press for Brown Judaic Studies. . Now: Lanham MD: University Press of America.

*The Philosophical Mishnah.* Volume III. *The Tractates' Agenda. From Nazir to Zebahim.* Atlanta, 1989: Scholars Press for Brown Judaic Studies. . Now: Lanham MD: University Press of America.

*The Philosophical Mishnah.* Volume IV. *The Repertoire.* Atlanta, 1989: Scholars Press for Brown Judaic Studies. Now: Lanham MD: University Press of America.

*Judaism as Philosophy. The Method and Message of the Mishnah.* Columbia, 1991: University of South Carolina Press.

Paperback edition: Baltimore, 1999: The Johns Hopkins University Press. Reprinted: Eugene, OR, 2004: Wipf & Stock.

*Torah through the Ages. A Short History of Judaism.* New York and London, 1990: Trinity Press International and SCM. Reprinted, Eugene OR, 2004: Wipf & Stock

*From Literature to Theology in Formative Judaism. Three Preliminary Studies.* Atlanta, 1989: Scholars Press for Brown Judaic Studies.

Edited: *The Christian and Judaic Invention of History.* Atlanta, 1990: Scholars Press for American Academy of Religion. Studies in Religion series.

Edited: *Essays in Jewish Historiography* [=*History and Theory* Beiheft 27, edited by Ada Rapoport-Albert]. With a new Introduction and an Appendix. Atlanta, 1991: Scholars Press for South Florida Studies in the History of Judaism.

*Symbol and Theology in Early Judaism.* Minneapolis, 1991: Fortress Press.

Reprint: Atlanta, 1999: Scholars Press for South Florida Studies in the History of Judaism.

*The Transformation of Judaism. From Philosophy to Religion.* Champaign, 1992: University of Illinois Press.

Paperback edition: Baltimore, 1999: The Johns Hopkins University Press. Reprinted: Eugene, 2004: Wipf and Stock.

*Talmudic Thinking: Language, Logic, and Law.* Columbia, 1992: University of South Carolina Press.

*The Emergence of Judaism. Jewish Religion in Response to the Critical issues of the First Six Centuries.* Lanham, 2000: University Press of America. STUDIES IN JUDAISM SERIES.

German translation: *Die Gestaltwerdung des Judentums. Die jüdische Religion als Antwort auf die kritischen Herausforderungen der ersten sechs Jahrhunderte der christlichen Ära.* Frankfurt-am-Main, Bern and N.Y., 1994: Verlag Peter Lang. *Judentum und Umwelt.* Translated and edited by Johann Maier.

*Judaism and Zoroastrianism at the Dusk of Late Antiquity. How Two Ancient Faiths Wrote Down Their Great Traditions.* Atlanta, 1993: Scholars Press for South Florida Studies in the History of Judaism. Now: Lanham, University Press of America.

*Purity in Rabbinic Judaism. A Systematic Account of the Sources, Media, Effects, and Removal of Uncleanness.* Atlanta, 1993: Scholars Press for South Florida Studies in the History of Judaism.

*Rabbinic Literature and the New Testament. What We Cannot Show, We Do Not Know.* Philadelphia, 1993: Trinity Press International. Reprint, Eugene, OR 2004: Wipf & Stock.

*Judaismo Rabinico.* [Five lectures in Spanish, given in Madrid in 1991.], Madrid, 1991: *El Olivo. Documentacion y estudios para el dialogo entre Judios y Cristianos.*

*Androgynous Judaism. Masculine and Feminine in the Dual Torah.* Macon, 1993: Mercer University Press. Jewish Book Club Selection. Reprint, Eugene, OR, 2003: Wipf and Stock.

*Judaism States its Theology: The Talmudic Re-Presentation.* Atlanta, 1993: Scholars Press for South Florida Studies in the History of Judaism.

*The Judaism Behind the Texts. The Generative Premises of Rabbinic Literature.* I. *The Mishnah.* A. *The Division of Agriculture.* Atlanta, 1993: Scholars Press for South Florida Studies in the History of Judaism.

*The Judaism Behind the Texts. The Generative Premises of Rabbinic Literature.* I. *The Mishnah.* B. *The Divisions of Appointed Times, Women, and Damages (through Sanhedrin).* Atlanta, 1993: Scholars Press for South Florida Studies in the History of Judaism.

*The Judaism Behind the Texts. The Generative Premises of Rabbinic Literature.* I. *The Mishnah.* C. *The Divisions of Damages (from Makkot), Holy Things and Purities.* Atlanta, 1993: Scholars Press for South Florida Studies in the History of Judaism.

*The Judaism Behind the Texts. The Generative Premises of Rabbinic Literature.* II. *The Tosefta, Tractate Abot, and the Earlier Midrash-Compilations: Sifra, Sifré to Numbers, and Sifré to Deuteronomy.* Atlanta, 1993.: Scholars Press for South Florida Studies in the History of Judaism.

*The Judaism Behind the Texts. The Generative Premises of Rabbinic Literature.* III. *The Later Midrash-Compilations: Genesis Rabbah, Leviticus Rabbah and Pesiqta deRab Kahana.* Atlanta, 1994: Scholars Press for South Florida Studies in the History of Judaism.

*The Judaism Behind the Texts. The Generative Premises of Rabbinic Literature.* IV. *The Latest Midrash-Compilations: Song of Songs Rabbah, Ruth Rabbah, Esther Rabbah I, and Lamentations Rabbati. And The Fathers According to Rabbi Nathan.* Atlanta, 1994: Scholars Press for South Florida Studies in the History of Judaism.

*The Judaism Behind the Texts. The Generative Premises of Rabbinic Literature.* V. *The Talmuds of the Land of Israel and Babylonia.* Atlanta, 1994: Scholars Press for South Florida Studies in the History of Judaism.

*The Judaism the Rabbis Take for Granted.* Atlanta, 1995: Scholars Press for South Florida Studies in the History of Judaism.

*Rabbinic Judaism. The Documentary History of the Formative Age.* Bethesda, 1994: CDL Press.

*Judaism's Theological Voice: The Melody of the Talmud.* Chicago, 1995: The University of Chicago Press.

*Rabbinic Judaism. Structure and System.* Minneapolis, 1996: Fortress Press.

Reprint: Atlanta, 1999: Scholars Press for South Florida Studies in the History of Judaism.

*The Presence of the Past, the Pastness of the Present. History, Time, and Paradigm in Rabbinic Judaism.* Bethesda, 1996: CDL Press.

Second edition, revised and augmented by six new chapters: *The Idea of History in Rabbinic Judaism*. Leiden, 2004: E. J. Brill.

*Jerusalem and Athens: The Congruity of Talmudic and Classical Philosophy.* Leiden, 1997: E. J. Brill. *Supplements to the Journal for the Study of Judaism.*

Italian: Ferrara, 2005: Gallio Editori.

*The Theology of Rabbinic Judaism. A Prolegomenon.* Atlanta, 1997: Scholars Press for South Florida Studies on the History of Judaism.

*The Halakhah of the Oral Torah. A Religious Commentary. Introduction.* And Volume One. Part One. *Between Israel and God. Faith, Thanksgiving: Tractate Berakhot. Enlandisement. Tractates Kilayim, Shebi'it, and 'Orlah.* Atlanta, 1997. Scholars Press for South Florida Studies in the History of Judaism. [The remainder of this project, originally planned for twenty-four volumes, was recast as *The Halakhah: An Encyclopaedia of the Law of Judaism*.]

*The Theological Grammar of the Oral Torah.* Binghamton, 1999: Dowling College Press/Global Publications of Binghamton University [SUNY]. I. *Vocabulary: Native Categories.* Epitomized in *Handbook of Rabbinic Theology,* below.

*The Theological Grammar of the Oral Torah.* Binghamton, 1999: Dowling College Press/Global Publications of Binghamton University [SUNY]. II. *Syntax: Connections and Constructions.* Epitomized in *Handbook of Rabbinic Theology,* below.

*The Theological Grammar of the Oral Torah.* Binghamton, 1999: Dowling College Press/Global Publications of Binghamton University [SUNY]. III. *Semantics: Models of Analysis, Explanation and Anticipation.* Epitomized in *Handbook of Rabbinic Theology,* below.

*Theological Dictionary of Rabbinic Judaism.* Lanham, MD 2005: University Press of America. Second edition, revised, of *The Theological Grammar of the Oral Torah.* I. *Principal Theological Categories.*

*Theological Dictionary of Rabbinic Judaism.* Lanham, MD 2005: University Press of America. Second edition, revised, of *The Theological Grammar of the Oral Torah.* II. *Making Connections and Building Constructions.*

*Theological Dictionary of Rabbinic Judaism.* Lanham, MD 2005: University Press of America. Second edition, revised, of *The Theological Grammar of the Oral Torah.* III. *Models of Analysis, Explanation, and Anticipation.*

*The Theology of the Oral Torah. Revealing the Justice of God.* Kingston and Montreal, 1999: McGill-Queen's University Press and Ithaca, 1999: Cornell University Press. Epitomized in *Handbook of Rabbinic Theology,* below.

*Rabbinic Judaism: Theological System.* Boston and Leiden, 2003: E. J. Brill. Condensation of *The Theology of the Oral Torah.*

*The Halakhah: An Encyclopaedia of the Law of Judaism.* Volume I. *Between Israel and God.* Part A. *Faith, Thanksgiving, Enlandisement: Possession and Partnership.* Leiden, 1999: E. J. Brill. THE BRILL REFERENCE LIBRARY OF JUDAISM.

*The Halakhah: An Encyclopaedia of the Law of Judaism.* Volume II. *Between Israel and God.* Part B. *Transcendent Transactions: Where Heaven and Earth Intersect.* Leiden, 1999: E. J. Brill. THE BRILL REFERENCE LIBRARY OF JUDAISM.

*The Halakhah: An Encyclopaedia of the Law of Judaism.* Volume III. *Within Israel's Social Order.* Leiden, 1999: E. J. Brill. THE BRILL REFERENCE LIBRARY OF JUDAISM

*The Halakhah: An Encyclopaedia of the Law of Judaism.* Volume IV. *Inside the Walls of the Israelite Household.* Part A. *At the Meeting of Time and Space. Sanctification in the Here and Now: The Table and the Bed. Sanctification and the Marital Bond. The Desacralization of the Household: The Bed.* Leiden, 1999: E. J. Brill. THE BRILL REFERENCE LIBRARY OF JUDAISM.

*The Halakhah: An Encyclopaedia of the Law of Judaism.* Volume V. *Inside the Walls of the Israelite Household.* Part B. *The Desacralization of the Household: The Table. Foci, Sources, and Dissemination of Uncleanness. Purification from the Pollution of Death.* Leiden, 1999: E. J. Brill. THE BRILL REFERENCE LIBRARY OF JUDAISM.

*The Theology of the Halakhah.* Leiden, 2001: E. J. Brill. BRILL REFERENCE LIBRARY OF ANCIENT JUDAISM. EPITOMIZED in *Handbook of Rabbinic Theology,* below.

*Scripture and the Generative Premises of the Halakhah. A Systematic Inquiry.* I. *Halakhah Based Principally on Scripture and Halakhic Categories Autonomous of Scripture.* Binghamton, 2000: Global Publications. ACADEMIC STUDIES IN ANCIENT JUDAISM series.

*Scripture and the Generative Premises of the Halakhah. A Systematic Inquiry.* II. *Scripture's Topics Derivatively Amplified in the Halakhah.* Binghamton, 2000: Global Publications. ACADEMIC STUDIES IN ANCIENT JUDAISM series.

*Scripture and the Generative Premises of the Halakhah. A Systematic Inquiry.* III. *Scripture's Topics Independently Developed in the Halakhah. From the Babas through Miqvaot.* Binghamton, 2000: Global Publications. ACADEMIC STUDIES IN ANCIENT JUDAISM series.

*Scripture and the Generative Premises of the Halakhah. A Systematic Inquiry.* IV. *Scripture's Topics Independently Developed in the Halakhah. From Moed Qatan through Zebahim.* Binghamton, 2000: Global Publications. ACADEMIC STUDIES IN ANCIENT JUDAISM series.

Second printing, revised and condensed: under the title, *The Torah and the Halakhah: The Four Relationships.* Lanham, 2003: University Press of America.

*The Four Stages of Rabbinic Judaism.* London, 2000: Routledge. E-book edition, London, 2001: Taylor and Francis.

*How the Rabbis Liberated Women.* Atlanta, 1999: Scholars Press for South Florida Studies in the History of Judaism. Now: Lanham, MD: University Press of America.

*From Scripture to 70. The Pre-Rabbinic Beginnings of the Halakhah.* Atlanta, 1999: Scholars Press for South Florida Studies in the History of Judaism.

*What, Exactly, Did the Rabbinic Sages Mean by "the Oral Torah"? An Inductive Answer to the Question of Rabbinic Judaism.* Atlanta, 1999: Scholars Press for South Florida Studies in the History of Judaism. Now: Lanham, MD: University Press of America.

*The Halakhah and the Aggadah: Theological Perspectives.* Atlanta, 2000: Scholars Press for South Florida Studies in the History of Judaism.

*The Mishnah: Social Perspectives.* Leiden, 1999: E. J. Brill. Paperback reprint: 2002.

*The Mishnah: Religious Perspectives.* Leiden, 1999: E. J. Brill Paperback reprint: 2002.

*The Messiah in Ancient Judaism* [With William Scott Green.] Leiden, 2005: E. J. Brill. THE BRILL REFERENCE LIBRARY OF JUDAISM.

*Recovering Judaism: The Universal Dimension of Jewish Religion.* Minneapolis, 2000: Fortress Press

*How Judaism Reads the Bible.* Baltimore, 1999: Chizuk Amuno Congregation. Published lecture.

*The Unity of Rabbinic Discourse.* Volume One. *Aggadah in the Halakhah.* Lanham, 2000: University Press of America. STUDIES IN JUDAISM SERIES.

*The Unity of Rabbinic Discourse.* Volume Two. *Halakhah in the Aggadah.* Lanham, 2000: University Press of America. STUDIES IN JUDAISM SERIES.

*The Unity of Rabbinic Discourse.* Volume Three. *Halakhah and Aggadah in Concert.* Lanham, 2000: University Press of America. STUDIES IN JUDAISM SERIES.

*Dual Discourse, Single Judaism. The Category-Formations of the Halakhah and of the Aggadah Defined, Compared, and Contrasted.* Lanham, 2000: University Press of America. STUDIES IN JUDAISM SERIES.

*Judaism's Story of Creation: Scripture, Halakhah, Aggadah.* Leiden, 2000: E. J. Brill. THE BRILL REFERENCE LIBRARY OF JUDAISM.

*The Aggadic Role in Halakhic Discourse.* Volume One. *An Initial Probe: Three Tractates: Moed Qatan, Nazir, and Horayot. The Mishnah and the Tosefta: The Division of Purities. The Mishnah, the Tosefta, and the Yerushalmi:. The Division of Agriculture. The Mishnah-Tosefta-Bavli: The Division of Holy Things.* Lanham, 2000: University Press of America. Studies in Judaism Series.

*The Aggadic Role in Halakhic Discourse.* Volume Two. *The Mishnah, Tosefta, Yerushalmi, and Bavli to Tractate Berakhot, the Division of Appointed Times and the Division of Women.* Lanham, 2000: University Press of America. Studies in Judaism SERIES.

*The Aggadic Role in Halakhic Discourse.* Volume Three. *The. Mishnah, Tosefta, Yerushalmi, and Bavli to the Division of Damages and Tractate Niddah. Sifra and the two Sifrés.* Lanham, 2000: University Press of America. Studies in Judaism SERIES.

*The Social Teaching of Rabbinic Judaism.* I. *Corporate Israel and the Individual Israelite.* Leiden, 2001: E. J. Brill. THE BRILL REFERENCE LIBRARY OF JUDAISM.

*The Social Teaching of Rabbinic Judaism.* II. *Between Israelites.* Leiden, 2001: E. J. Brill. THE BRILL REFERENCE LIBRARY OF JUDAISM.

*The Social Teaching of Rabbinic Judaism.* III. *God's Presence in Israel.* Leiden, 2001: E. J. Brill. THE BRILL REFERENCE LIBRARY OF JUDAISM.

*A Theological Commentary to the Midrash*: I. *Pesiqta deRab Kahana.* Lanham, 2001: University Press of America. Studies in Judaism SERIES.

*A Theological Commentary to the Midrash*: II. *Genesis Rabbah.* Lanham, 2001: University Press of America. Studies in Judaism SERIES.

*A Theological Commentary to the Midrash*: III. *Song of Songs Rabbah.* Lanham, 2001: University Press of America. Studies in Judaism SERIES.

*A Theological Commentary to the Midrash.* IV. *Leviticus Rabbah.* Lanham, 2001: University Press of America. Studies in Judaism SERIES.

*A Theological Commentary to the Midrash*: V. *Lamentations Rabbati.* Lanham, 2001: University Press of America. Studies in Judaism SERIES

*A Theological Commentary to the Midrash.* VI. *Ruth Rabbah and Esther Rabbah I.* Lanham, 2001: University Press of America. Studies in Judaism Series

*A Theological Commentary to the Midrash.* VII. *Sifra.* Lanham, 2001: University Press of America. Studies in Judaism Series

*A Theological Commentary to the Midrash,* VIII. *Sifré to Numbers and Sifré to Deuteronomy.* Lanham, 2001: University Press of America. Studies in Judaism Series

*A Theological Commentary to the Midrash.* IX. *Mekhilta Attributed to R. Ishmael.* Lanham, 2001: University Press of America. Studies in Judaism Series

*The Theological Foundations of Rabbinic Midrash.* Lanham, 2006: University Press of America Studies in Judaism series.

Editor: *The Mishnah in Contemporary Study.* Volume One. Leiden, 2002: E. J. Brill. [Edited with Alan J. Avery-Peck.]

*Handbook of Rabbinic Theology: Language, System, Structure.* Leiden, 2003: E. J. Brill. Epitomization of *Theological Grammar of the Oral Torah, Theology of the Oral Torah: Revealing the Justice of God,* and *Theology of the Halakhah.*

*The Perfect Torah.* Leiden, 2003: E. J. Brill, Leiden.

*Making God's Word Work: Guide to the Mishnah.* N.Y., 2004: Continuum.

*Rabbinic Categories: Construction and Comparison.* Leiden, 2005: E. J. Brill

Editor: *The Encyclopaedia of Midrash: Bible-Interpretation in Formative Judaism.* Leiden, 2004: E. J. Brill. The Brill Reference Library of Judaism. [Edited with Alan J. Avery-Peck.] In three volumes. Volume One.

Editor: *The Encyclopaedia of Midrash: Bible-Interpretation in Formative Judaism.* Leiden, 2004: E. J. Brill. The Brill Reference Library of Judaism. [Edited with Alan J. Avery-Peck.] In three volumes. Volume Two.

Editor: *The Mishnah in Contemporary Study.* Volume Two. Leiden, 2006: E. J. Brill. [Edited with Alan J. Avery-Peck.]

*The Religious Meaning of History,* Cincinnati, 2004: Central Conference of American Rabbis-Hebrew Union College-Jewish Institute of Religion. Joint Commission for Sustaining Rabbinic Education. Series: SCHOLARS OF THE 21ST CENTURY.

*Performing Israel's Faith: Narrative and Law in Rabbinic Theology.* Waco, 2005: Baylor University Press. H"

*Contours of Coherence in Rabbinic Judaism.* Leiden, 2005: E. J. Brill.

*Is Scripture the Origin of the Halakhah?* Lanham, 2005: University Press of America.

*The Vitality of Rabbinic Imagination: The Mishnah against the Bible and Qumran.* Lanham, 2005: University Press of America

*How Important Was the Destruction of the Second Temple in the Formation of Rabbinic Judaism?* Lanham, 2005: University Press of America.

*Praxis and Parable: The Divergent Discourses of Rabbinic Judaism. How Halakhic and Aggadic Documents Treat the Bestiary Common to Them Both.* Lanham, 2005: University Press of America

*The Implicit Norms of Rabbinic Judaism. The Bedrock of a Classical Religion.* Lanham, 2005: University Press of America

*Chapters in the Formative History of Judaism Current Questions and Enduring Answers* Lanham, 2006: University Press of America.

*Halakhic Theology: A Sourcebook.* Lanham 2005: University Press of America.

*Jeremiah in Talmud and Midrash. A Source Book.* Lanham, 2006: University Press of America STUDIES IN JUDAISM SERIES

*Rabbi Jeremiah.* Lanham, 2006: University Press of America STUDIES IN JUDAISM SERIES

*Amos in Talmud and Midrash. A Source Book.* Lanham, 2007: University Press of America STUDIES IN JUDAISM SERIES

*Hosea in Talmud and Midrash. A Source Book.* Lanham, 2007: University Press of America STUDIES IN JUDAISM SERIES

*Micah and Joel in Talmud and Midrash. A Source Book.* Lanham: University Press of America STUDIES IN JUDAISM SERIES

*Habakkuk, Jonah, Nahum, and Obadiah in Talmud and Midrash. A Source Book.* Lanham, 2007: University Press of America STUDIES IN JUDAISM SERIES

*Zephaniah, Haggai, Zechariah, and Malachi in Talmud and Midrash. A Source Book.* Lanham, 2007: University Press of America STUDIES IN JUDAISM SERIES

*Ezekiel in Talmud and Midrash. A Source Book.* Lanham, 2007: University Press of America STUDIES IN JUDAISM SERIES

*Isaiah in Talmud and Midrash. A Source Book.* A. *Mishnah, Tosefta, Tannaite Midrash-Compilations, Yerushalmi and Associated Midrash-Compilations.* Lanham, 2007: University Press of America STUDIES IN JUDAISM SERIES.

*Isaiah in Talmud and Midrash. A Source Book.* B. *The Later Midrash-Compilations and the Bavli.* Lanham, 2007: University Press of America STUDIES IN JUDAISM SERIES.

*The Rabbis, the Law, and the Prophets*, Offered to Brill.

**Now underway**

*Torah Revealed, Torah Fulfilled: Scriptural Laws in Formative Judaism and Earliest Christianity*. Grand Rapids, 2006: Baker Academic. With Baruch A. Levine and Bruce D. Chilton

*The Rabbinic Utopia. The Normative Vision of the Social Order in Classical Judaism*

*The Rabbinic Dystopia. The Rabbinic Anti-system*

**6. *Talmudic Hermeneutics***

*The Talmud of Babylonia. An Academic Commentary.* Atlanta, 1994-1996, 1999: Scholars Press for *USF Academic Commentary Series*. Now: Lanham, MD. University Press of America

I. *Bavli Tractate Berakhot*
II.A. *Bavli Tractate Shabbat. Chapters One through Twelve*

II.B. *Bavli Tractate Shabbat. Chapters Thirteen through Twenty-Four*
III.A. *Bavli Tractate Erubin. Chapters One through Five*
III.B. *Bavli Tractate Erubin. Chapters Six through Eleven*
IV.A. *Bavli Tractate Pesahim. Chapters One through Seven.*
IV.B. *Bavli Tractate Pesahim. Chapters Eight through Eleven.*
V. *Bavli Tractate Yoma*
VI. *Bavli Tractate Sukkah*
VII. *Bavli Tractate Besah*
VIII. *Bavli Tractate Rosh Hashanah*
IX. *Bavli Tractate Taanit* [1999]
X. *Bavli Tractate Megillah*
XI. *Bavli Tractate Moed Qatan*
XII. *Bavli Tractate Hagigah*
XIII.A. *Bavli Tractate Yebamot. Chapters One through Eight*
XIII.B. *Bavli Tractate Yebamot. Chapters Nine through Seventeen*
XIV.A. *Bavli Tractate Ketubot. Chapters One through Six*
XIV.B. *Bavli Tractate Ketubot. Chapters Seven through Fourteen*
XV. *Bavli Tractate Nedarim*
XVI. *Bavli Tractate Nazir* [1999]
XVII. *Bavli Tractate Sotah*
XVIII. *Bavli Tractate Gittin*
XIX. *Bavli Tractate Qiddushin*
XX. *Bavli Tractate Baba Qamma*
XXI.A. *Bavli Tractate Baba Mesia. Chapters One through Six*
XXI.B. *Bavli Tractate Baba Mesia. Chapters Seven through Eleven*
XXII.A *Bavli Tractate Baba Batra. Chapters One through Six*
XXII.B *Bavli Tractate Baba Batra. Chapters Seven through Eleven*
XXIII.A . *Bavli Tractate Sanhedrin. Chapters One through Seven*
XXIII.B. *Bavli Tractate Sanhedrin. Chapters Eight through Twelve*
XXIV. *Bavli Tractate Makkot*
XXV. *Bavli Tractate Abodah Zarah*
XXVI. *Bavli Tractate Horayot*
XXVII. *Bavli Tractate Shebuot*
XXVIII.A. *Bavli Tractate Zebahim. Chapters One through Seven*
XXVIII.B. *Bavli Tractate Zebahim. Chapters Eight through Fifteen*
XXIX.A . *Bavli Tractate Menahot. Chapters One through Six*
XXIX.B . *Bavli Tractate Menahot. Chapters Seven through Fourteen*
XXX. *Bavli Tractate Hullin*
XXXI. *Bavli Tractate Bekhorot*
XXXII. *Bavli Tractate Arakhin*
XXXIII *Bavli Tractate Temurah*
XXXIV. *Bavli Tractate Keritot*

XXXV. *Bavli Tractate Meilah and Tamid*
XXXVI. *Bavli Tractate Niddah*

*The Babylonian Talmud. Translation and Commentary.* Peabody, 2005: Hendrickson Publishing Co. Second printing of *The Talmud of Babylonia. An Academic Commentary.* Also published as a CD.

i. *Berakhot*
ii. *Shabbat*
iii. *Erubin*
iv. *Pesahim*
v. *Yoma-Sukkah*
vi. *Taanit-Megillah-Moed Qatan-Hagigah*
vii. *Besah-Rosh Hashanah*
viii. *Yebamot*
ix. *Ketubot*
x. *Nedarim-Nazir*
xi. *Sotah-Gittin*
xii. *Qiddushin*
xiii. *Baba Qamma*
xiv. *Baba Mesia*
xv. *Baba Batra*
xvi. *Sanhedrin*
xvii. *Makkot-Abodah Zarah-Horayot*
xviii. *Shebuot-Zebahim*
xix. *Menahot*
xx. *Hullin*
xxi. *Bekhorot-Arakhin-Temurah*
xxii. *Keritot-Meilah-Tamid-Niddah*

*The Talmud of Babylonia. A Complete Outline.* Atlanta, 1995-6: Scholars Press for *USF Academic Commentary Series.* Now: Lanham, MD. University Press of America

I.A. *Tractate Berakhot and the Division of Appointed Times. Berakhot, Shabbat, and Erubin.*
I.B. *Tractate Berakhot and the Division of Appointed Times. Pesahim through Hagigah.*
II.A. *The Division of Women. Yebamot through Ketubot*
II.B. *The Division of Women. Nedarim through Qiddushin*
III.A. *The Division of Damages. Baba Qamma through Baba Batra*
III.B. *The Division of Damages. Sanhedrin through Horayot*

IV.A. *The Division of Holy Things and Tractate Niddah. Zebahim through Hullin*
IV.B. *The Division of Holy Things and Tractate Niddah. Bekhorot through Niddah*

*The Talmud of the Land of Israel. An Academic Commentary to the Second, Third, and Fourth Divisions.* Atlanta, 1998-1999: Scholars Press for *USF Academic Commentary Series.* Now: Lanham, MD. University Press of America.

I. *Yerushalmi Tractate Berakhot*
II.A *Yerushalmi Tractate Shabbat. Chapters One through Ten*
II.B *Yerushalmi Tractate Shabbat. Chapters Eleven through Twenty-Four. And the Structure of Yerushalmi Shabbat*
III. *Yerushalmi Tractate Erubin*
IV. *Yerushalmi Tractate Yoma*
V.A *Yerushalmi Tractate Pesahim. Chapters One through Six.*
V.B *Yerushalmi Tractate Pesahim. Chapters Seven through Ten. And the Structure of Yerushalmi Pesahim*
VI. *Yerushalmi Tractate Sukkah*
VII. *Yerushalmi Tractate Besah*
VIII. *Yerushalmi Tractate Taanit*
IX. *Yerushalmi Tractate Megillah*
X. *Yerushalmi Tractate Rosh Hashanah*
XI. *Yerushalmi Tractate Hagigah*
XII. *Yerushalmi Tractate Moed Qatan*
XIII.A. *Yerushalmi Tractate Yebamot. Chapters One through Ten*
XIII.B. *Yerushalmi Tractate Yebamot. Chapters Eleven through Seventeen. And the Structure of Yerushalmi Yebamot*
XIV. *Yerushalmi Tractate Ketubot*
XV. *Yerushalmi Tractate Nedarim*
XVI. *Yerushalmi Tractate Nazir*
XVII. *Yerushalmi Tractate Gittin*
XVIII. *Yerushalmi Tractate Qiddushin*
XIX. *Yerushalmi Tractate Sotah*
XX. *Yerushalmi Tractate Baba Qamma*
XXI. *Yerushalmi Tractate Baba Mesia*
XXII. *Yerushalmi Tractate Baba Batra*
XXIII. *Yerushalmi Tractate Sanhedrin*
XXIV. *Yerushalmi Tractate Makkot*
XXV. *Yerushalmi Tractate Shebuot*
XXVI. *Yerushalmi Tractate Abodah Zarah*

XXVII. *Yerushalmi Tractate Horayot*
XXVIII. *Yerushalmi Tractate Niddah*

*The Talmud of the Land of Israel. Translation and Commentary. The Second, Third, and Fourth Divisions.* Peabody, 2007: Hendrickson Publishing Co. Second printing of *The Talmud of the Land of Israel. An Academic Commentary.* Also published as a CD.

i. *Berakhot and Shabbat*
ii. *Erubin and Yoma*
iii. *Pesahim and Sukkah*
iv. *Besah, Taanit, Megillah, Rosh Hashanah*
v. *Hagigah, Moed Qatan, Yebamot*
vi. *Ketubot, Nedarim*
vii. *Nazir, Gittin, Qiddushin*
viii. *Sotah, Baba Qamma, Baba Mesia*
ix. *Baba Batra, Sanhedrin, Makkot*
x. *Shebuot , Abodah Zarah, Horayot, Niddah*

*The Talmud of The Land of Israel. An Outline of the Second, Third, and Fourth Divisions.* Atlanta, 1995-6: Scholars Press for USF Academic Commentary Series. Now: Lanham, MD. University Press of America

I.A. *Tractate Berakhot and the Division of Appointed Times. Berakhot and Shabbat*
I.B. *Tractate Berakhot and the Division of Appointed Times. Erubin, Yoma, and Besah*
I.C. *Tractate Berakhot and the Division of Appointed Times. Pesahim and Sukkah*
I.D. *Tractate Berakhot and the Division of Appointed Times. Taanit, Megillah, Rosh Hashanah, Hagigah, and Moed Qatan*
II.A. *The Division of Women. Yebamot to Nedarim*
II.B. *The Division of Women. Nazir to Sotah*
III.A. *The Division of Damages and Tractate Niddah. Baba Qamma, Baba Mesia, Baba Batra, Horayot, and Niddah*
III.B. *The Division of Damages and Tractate Niddah. Sanhedrin, Makkot, Shebuot, and Abodah Zarah*

*The Two Talmuds Compared.* Atlanta, 1995-6: Scholars Press for USF Academic Commentary Series. *The Talmud of the Land of Israel. An Academic Commentary to the Second, Third, and Fourth Divisions.* Atlanta, 1998-1999: Scholars Press for *USF Academic Commentary Series.* Now: Lanham, MD. University Press of America.

I.A. *Tractate Berakhot and the Division of Appointed Times in the Talmud of the Land of Israel and the Talmud of Babylonia. Yerushalmi Tractate Berakhot*

I.B. *Tractate Berakhot and the Division of Appointed Times in the Talmud of the Land of Israel and the Talmud of Babylonia. Tractate Shabbat.*

I.C. *Tractate Berakhot and the Division of Appointed Times in the Talmud of the Land of Israel and the Talmud of Babylonia. Tractate Erubin*

I.D. *Tractate Berakhot and the Division of Appointed Times in the Talmud of the Land of Israel and the Talmud of Babylonia. Tractates Yoma and Sukkah*

I.E. *Tractate Berakhot and the Division of Appointed Times in the Talmud of the Land of Israel and the Talmud of Babylonia. Tractate Pesahim*

I.F. *Tractate Berakhot and the Division of Appointed Times in the Talmud of the Land of Israel and the Talmud of Babylonia. Tractates Besah, Taanit, and Megillah*

I.G. *Tractate Berakhot and the Division of Appointed Times in the Talmud of the Land of Israel and the Talmud of Babylonia. Tractates Rosh Hashanah, Hagigah, and Moed Qatan*

II.A. *The Division of Women in the Talmud of the Land of Israel and the Talmud of Babylonia. Tractates Yebamot and Ketubot.*

II.B. *The Division of Women in the Talmud of the Land of Israel and the Talmud of Babylonia. Tractates Nedarim, Nazir, and Sotah.*

II.C. *The Division of Women in the Talmud of the Land of Israel and the Talmud of Babylonia. Tractates Qiddushin and Gittin.*

III.A. *The Division of Damages and Tractate Niddah in the Talmud of the Land of Israel and the Talmud of Babylonia. Tractates Baba Qamma and Baba Mesia*

III.B. *The Division of Damages and Tractate Niddah in the Talmud of the Land of Israel and the Talmud of Babylonia. Baba Batra and Niddah.*

III.C. *The Division of Damages and Tractate Niddah. Sanhedrin and Makkot.*

III.D. *The Division of Damages and Tractate Niddah. Shebuot, Abodah Zarah, and Horayot.*

*The Components of the Rabbinic Documents: From the Whole to the Parts.* I. *Sifra.* Atlanta, 1997: Scholars Press for USF Academic Commentary Series.

Part i. *Introduction. And Parts One through Three, Chapters One through Ninety-Eight*
Part ii. *Parts Four through Nine. Chapters Ninety-Nine through One Hundred Ninety-Four*
Part iii. *Parts Ten through Thirteen. Chapters One Hundred Ninety-Five through Two Hundred Seventy-Seven*
Part iv. *A Topical and Methodical Outline of Sifra*

*The Components of the Rabbinic Documents: From the Whole to the Parts.* II. *Esther Rabbah I.* Atlanta, 1997: Scholars Press for USF Academic Commentary Series.

*The Components of the Rabbinic Documents: From the Whole to the Parts.* III. *Ruth Rabbah.* Atlanta, 1997: Scholars Press for USF Academic Commentary Series.

*The Components of the Rabbinic Documents: From the Whole to the Parts.* IV. *Lamentations Rabbati.* Atlanta, 1997: Scholars Press for USF Academic Commentary Series.

*The Components of the Rabbinic Documents: From the Whole to the Parts.* V. *Song of Songs Rabbah.* Atlanta, 1997: Scholars Press for USF Academic Commentary Series.

Part i. *Introduction. And Parashiyyot One through Four*
Part ii. *Parashiyyot Five through Eight. And a Topical and Methodical Outline of Song of Songs Rabbah*

*The Components of the Rabbinic Documents: From the Whole to the Parts.* VI. *The Fathers Attributed to Rabbi Nathan.* Atlanta, 1997: Scholars Press for USF Academic Commentary Series.

*The Components of the Rabbinic Documents: From the Whole to the Parts.* VII. *Sifré to Deuteronomy.* Atlanta, 1997: Scholars Press for USF Academic Commentary Series.

Part i. *Introduction. And Parts One through Four*
Part ii. *Parts Five through Ten*
Part iii. *A Topical and Methodical Outline of Sifré to Deuteronomy*

*The Components of the Rabbinic Documents: From the Whole to the Parts.* VIII. *Mekhilta Attributed to R. Ishmael.* Atlanta, 1997: Scholars Press for USF Academic Commentary Series

Part i. *Introduction. Pisha, Beshallah and Shirata*
Part ii *Vayassa, Amalek, Bahodesh, Neziqin, Kaspa and Shabbata*
Part iii. *A Topical and Methodical Outline of Mekhilta Attributed to R. Ishmael.*

*The Components of the Rabbinic Documents: From the Whole to the Parts.* IX. Atlanta, 1998: Scholars Press for USF Academic Commentary Series. Now: Lanham, University Press of America.

Part i. *Introduction. Genesis Rabbah Chapters One through Twenty-One*
Part ii. *Genesis Rabbah Chapters Twenty-Two through Forty-Eight*
Part iii. *Genesis Rabbah Chapters Forty-Nine through Seventy-Three*
Part iv. *Genesis Rabbah Chapters Seventy-Four through One Hundred*
Part v. *A Topical and Methodical Outline of Genesis Rabbah. Bereshit through Vaere, Chapters One through Fifty-Seven*
Part vi. *A Topical and Methodical Outline of Genesis Rabbah. Hayye Sarah through Miqqes. Chapters Fifty-Eight through One Hundred*

*The Components of the Rabbinic Documents: From the Whole to the Parts.* X. *Leviticus Rabbah.* Atlanta, 1998: Scholars Press for USF Academic Commentary Series.

Part i. *Introduction. Leviticus Rabbah Parashiyyot One through Seventeen*
Part ii. *Leviticus Rabbah Parashiyyot Eighteen through Thirty-Seven*
Part iii. *Leviticus Rabbah. A Topical and Methodical Outline*

*The Components of the Rabbinic Documents: From the Whole to the Parts.* XI. *Pesiqta deRab Kahana.* Atlanta, 1998: Scholars Press for USF Academic Commentary Series.

Part i. *Introduction. Pesiqta deRab Kahana Pisqaot One through Eleven*
Part ii. *Pesiqta deRab Kahana Pisqaot Twelve through Twenty-Eight*
Part iii. *Pesiqta deRab Kahana. A Topical and Methodical Outline*

*The Components of the Rabbinic Documents: From the Whole to the Parts.* XII. *Sifré to Numbers.* Atlanta, 1998: Scholars Press for USF Academic Commentary Series.

Part i. *Introduction. Pisqaot One through Eighty-Four*
Part ii *Pisqaot Eighty-Five through One Hundred Twenty-Two*
Part iii *Pisqaot One Hundred Twenty-Three through One Hundred Sixty-One*
Part iv *Sifré to Numbers. A Topical and Methodical Outline*

*The Rabbinic Midrash.* Peabody, 2003: Hendrickson Publishing Co. Second printing, in twelve volumes, of *The Components of the Rabbinic Documents: From the Whole to the Parts.*

*Judaism and the Interpretation of Scripture: Introduction to* The Rabbinic Midrash. Peabody, 2005: Hendrickson.

*The Documentary Form-History of Rabbinic Literature.* I. *The Documentary Forms of the Mishnah.* Atlanta, 1998: Scholars Press for USF Academic Commentary Series.

*The Documentary Form-History of Rabbinic Literature* II. *The Aggadic Sector: Tractate Abot, Abot deRabbi Natan, Sifra, Sifré to Numbers, and Sifré to Deuteronomy.* Atlanta, 1998: Scholars Press for USF Academic Commentary Series.

*The Documentary Form-History of Rabbinic Literature* III. *The Aggadic Sector: Mekhilta Attributed to R. Ishmael and Genesis Rabbah.* Atlanta, 1998: Scholars Press for USF Academic Commentary Series.

*The Documentary Form-History of Rabbinic Literature* IV. *The Aggadic Sector: Leviticus Rabbah, and Pesiqta deRab Kahana.* Atlanta, 1998: Scholars Press for USF Academic Commentary Series.

*The Documentary Form-History of Rabbinic Literature* V. *The Aggadic Sector: Song of Songs Rabbah, Ruth Rabbah, Lamentations Rabbati, and Esther Rabbah I.* Atlanta, 1998: Scholars Press for USF Academic Commentary Series.

*The Documentary Form-History of Rabbinic Literature.* VI. *The Halakhic Sector. The Talmud of the Land of Israel.* A. *Berakhot and Shabbat through Taanit.* Atlanta, 1998: Scholars Press for USF Academic Commentary Series.

*The Documentary Form-History of Rabbinic Literature.* VI. *The Halakhic Sector. The Talmud of the Land of Israel.* B. *Megillah through Qiddushin.* Atlanta, 1998: Scholars Press for USF Academic Commentary Series.

*The Documentary Form-History of Rabbinic Literature.* VI. *The Halakhic Sector. The Talmud of the Land of Israel.* C. *Sotah through Horayot and Niddah.* Atlanta, 1998: Scholars Press for USF Academic Commentary Series.

*The Documentary Form-History of Rabbinic Literature.* VII. *The Halakhic Sector. The Talmud of Babylonia.* A. *Tractates Berakhot and Shabbat through Pesahim.* Atlanta, 1998: Scholars Press for USF Academic Commentary Series.

*The Documentary Form-History of Rabbinic Literature.* VII. *The Halakhic Sector. The Talmud of Babylonia.* B. *Tractates Yoma through Ketubot.* Atlanta, 1998: Scholars Press for USF Academic Commentary Series.

*The Documentary Form-History of Rabbinic Literature.* VII. *The Halakhic Sector. The Talmud of Babylonia.* C. *Tractates Nedarim through Baba Mesia.* Atlanta, 1998: Scholars Press for USF Academic Commentary Series.

*The Documentary Form-History of Rabbinic Literature.* VII. *The Halakhic Sector. The Talmud of Babylonia.* D. *Tractates Baba Batra through Horayot.* Atlanta, 1998: Scholars Press for USF Academic Commentary Series.

*The Documentary Form-History of Rabbinic Literature.* VII. *The Halakhic Sector. The Talmud of Babylonia.* E. *Tractates Zebahim through Bekhorot.* Atlanta, 1998: Scholars Press for USF Academic Commentary Series.

*The Documentary Form-History of Rabbinic Literature.* VII. *The Halakhic Sector. The Talmud of Babylonia.* F. *Tractates Arakhin through Niddah. And Conclusions.* Atlanta, 1998: Scholars Press for USF Academic Commentary Series.

*The Native Category-Formations of the Aggadah.* I. *The Later Midrash-Compilations.* Lanham, 2000: University Press of America. Studies in Judaism Series.

*The Native Category-Formations of the Aggadah.* II. *The Earlier Midrash-Compilations.* Lanham, 2000: University Press of America. Studies in Judaism Series.

*The Hermeneutics of the Rabbinic Category-Formations: An Introduction.* Lanham, 2000: University Press of America. Studies in Judaism SERIES.

*The Comparative Hermeneutics of Rabbinic Judaism.* Volume One. *Introduction. Berakhot and Seder Mo'ed.* Binghamton, 2000: Global Publications. ACADEMIC STUDIES IN ANCIENT JUDAISM series

*The Comparative Hermeneutics of Rabbinic Judaism.* Volume Two. *Seder Nashim.* Binghamton, 2000: Global Publications. ACADEMIC STUDIES IN ANCIENT JUDAISM series.

*The Comparative Hermeneutics of Rabbinic Judaism.* Volume Three. *Seder Neziqin.* Binghamton, 2000: Global Publications. ACADEMIC STUDIES IN ANCIENT JUDAISM series.

*The Comparative Hermeneutics of Rabbinic Judaism.* Volume Four. *Seder Qodoshim.* Binghamton, 2000: Global Publications. ACADEMIC STUDIES IN ANCIENT JUDAISM series.

*The Comparative Hermeneutics of Rabbinic Judaism.* Volume Five. *Seder Tohorot.* Part *Kelim through Parah.* Binghamton, 2000: Global Publications. ACADEMIC STUDIES IN ANCIENT JUDAISM series.

*The Comparative Hermeneutics of Rabbinic Judaism.* Volume Six. *Seder Tohorot. Tohorot through Uqsin.* Binghamton, 2000: Global Publications. ACADEMIC STUDIES IN ANCIENT JUDAISM series.

*The Comparative Hermeneutics of Rabbinic Judaism.* Volume Seven *The Generic Hermeneutics of the Halakhah. A Handbook.* Binghamton, 2000: Global Publications. ACADEMIC STUDIES IN ANCIENT JUDAISM series.

Volumes One through Seven: Second printing, condensed, under the title, *Halakhic Hermeneutics,* Lanham, 2003: University Press of America.

*The Comparative Hermeneutics of Rabbinic Judaism.* Volume Eight. *Why This, Not That? Ways Not Taken in the Halakhic Category-Formations of the Mishnah-Tosefta-Yerushalmi-Bavli.* Binghamton, 2000: Global Publications. ACADEMIC STUDIES IN ANCIENT JUDAISM series.

Second printing, revised; under the title, *Why This, Not That? Ways Not Taken in the Halakhic Category-Formations of the Mishnah-Tosefta-Yerushalmi-Bavli.* Lanham, 2003: University Press of America.

*Intellectual Templates of the Law of Judaism.* Lanham, 2006: University Press of America.

*Analytical Templates of the Bavli.* Lanham, 2006: University Press of America.

## 7. *Constructive and Comparative Theology* From Description to Conviction

*Fellowship in Judaism. The First Century and Today.* London, 1963: Valentine, Mitchell. Reprint, Eugene,, OR, 2005: Wipf and Stock. NYC 2006: On line edition: Center for Online Judaic Studies: www.cojs.org

*History and Torah. Essays on Jewish Learning.* London, 1965: Valentine, Mitchell. N.Y., 1964: Schocken Books. Paperback, N.Y., 1967: Schocken.

*Judaism in the Secular Age. Essays on Fellowship, Community, and Freedom.* London, 1970: Valentine Mitchell. N.Y., 1970: Ktav.

Editor: *Contemporary Judaic Fellowship. In Theory and in Practice.* N.Y., 1972: Ktav.

Editor: *Understanding Jewish Theology. Classical Themes and Modern Perspectives.* N.Y., 1973: Ktav. Fifth printing: 1992. Sixth printing: Binghamton 2001: Global Publications/SUNY. In CLASSICS IN JUDAIC STUDIES.

*The Glory of God Is Intelligence. Four Lectures on the Role of Intellect in Judaism.* Provo, 1978: Religious Studies Center, Brigham Young University. *Religious Studies Monograph Series* Volume III. Introduction by S. Kent Brown.

*The Jewish War against the Jews. Reflections on Golah, Shoah, and Torah.* N.Y., 1984: Ktav.

*Stranger at Home. Zionism, "The Holocaust," and American Judaism.* Chicago, 1980: University of Chicago Press. Paperback edition, 1985. Second printing, 1985. Third printing, 1988. Paperback reprint: Atlanta, 1997: Scholars Press for South Florida-Rochester-St. Louis Studies on Religion and the Social Order. Reprint, Eugene, OR, 2003: Wipf and Stock.

*Tzedakah. Can Jewish Philanthropy Buy Jewish Survival?* Chappaqua, 1982: Rossel. Second printing, 1983. Fourth printing, 1988. Fifth printing:

Atlanta, 1990: Scholars Press for Brown Judaic Studies. Sixth printing, 1997: Union of American Hebrew Congregations.

*Israel in America. A Too-Comfortable Exile?* Boston, 1985: Beacon. Paperback edition, 1986. Second printing: Lanham, 1990: University Press of America Studies in Judaism series. Third printing: 1994.

Edited: *To Grow in Wisdom. An Anthology of Abraham Joshua Heschel.* New York, 1989: Madison Books. [With Noam M. M. Neusner]

*Who, Where, and What Is "Israel"? Zionist Perspectives on Israeli and American Judaism.* Lanham, 1989: University Press of America Studies in Judaism.

*The Religious World of Contemporary Judaism: Observations and Convictions.* Atlanta, 1989: Scholars Press for Brown Judaic Studies.

*The Bible and Us. A Priest and a Rabbi Read the Scriptures Together.* With Andrew M. Greeley. N.Y., 1990: Warner Books. Trade paperback edition: 1991. Jewish Book Club alternative selection.

Portuguese translation: *A Bíblia e Nós. Um padre e um rabino interpretam as Sagradas Escrituras.* São Paulo, 1994: Editora Siciliano.

Spanish translation: *La Biblia y Nosotros*. Madrid, 1995: Editora Planeta

*Common Ground. A Priest and a Rabbi Read the Scriptures Together.* Second edition, revised of the foregoing title. Cleveland, 1996: Pilgrim Press. Reprint: Eugene, OR 2005: Wipf and Stock.

*Jews and Christians: The Myth of a Common Tradition.* New York and London, 1990: Trinity Press International and SCM Press. Reprint: Binghamton, 2001: Global Publications. Reprint: Eugene, OR, 2003: Wipf and Stock, Publishers.

*The Foundations of the Theology of Judaism. An Anthology.* I. *God.* Northvale, 1990: Jason Aronson, Inc. A main selection of the Jewish Book Club. . Reprinted 2004: Rowman and Littlefield

*The Foundations of the Theology of Judaism. An Anthology.* II. *Torah* Atlanta, 1992: Scholars Press for South Florida Studies in the History of Judaism.

*The Foundations of the Theology of Judaism. An Anthology.* III. *Israel.* Atlanta, 1992: Scholars Press for South Florida Studies in the History of Judaism.

*Telling Tales: Making Sense of Christian and Judaic Nonsense. The Urgency and Basis for Judaeo-Christian Dialogue.* Louisville, 1993: Westminster-John Knox Press.

*A Rabbi Talks with Jesus. An Intermillennial, Interfaith Exchange.* N.Y., 1993: Doubleday. Jewish Book Club Main Selection, February, 1993. Paperback edition: N.Y., 1994: Image Books.

*A Rabbi Talks with Jesus.* Second edition Montreal and Kingston, 2000: McGill-Queen's University Press. And Ithaca, 2000: Cornell University Press. Second printing, 2001. Book of the Month Club selection, 2002.

Italian translation: *Disputa immaginaria tra un rabbino e Gesus: Quale maestro seguire?* Casale Monferrato, 1996: Redizioni Piemme.

Swedish translation: *En rabbin medtalar med Jesus.* Stockholm, 1996: Verbum

German translation: *Ein Rabbi Spricht mit Jesus. Ein jüdisch-christlicher Dialogue.* Munich, 1997: Claudius Verlag.

Polish translation under contract.

Russian translation under contract. By Boris Dynin. Moscow, 2006: Gesher Publishing Co.

Editor *Judaism Transcends Catastrophe: God, Torah, and Israel beyond the Holocaust.* Macon, GA, 1994: Mercer University Press. I. *Faith Renewed: The Judaic Affirmation beyond the Holocaust*

Editor *Judaism Transcends Catastrophe: God, Torah, and Israel beyond the Holocaust.* Macon, GA, 1995: Mercer University Press. II. *God Commands.*

Editor *Judaism Transcends Catastrophe: God, Torah, and Israel beyond the Holocaust.* Macon, GA, 1996: Mercer University Press. III. *The Torah Teaches.*

Editor *Judaism Transcends Catastrophe: God, Torah, and Israel beyond the Holocaust.* Macon, GA, 1997: Mercer University Press. IV. *Eternal Israel Endures.*

Editor *Judaism Transcends Catastrophe: God, Torah, and Israel beyond the Holocaust.* Macon, GA, 1997: Mercer University Press. V. *Faith Seeking Understanding: The Tasks of Theology in Twenty-First Century Judaism*

*Jewish and Christian Doctrines: The Classics Compared.* With Bruce D. Chilton. London, 1999: Routledge. E-book edition, London, 2001: Taylor and Francis.

*Judaism in the New Testament. Practices and Beliefs.* London, 1995: Routledge [With Bruce D. Chilton]. E-book edition, London, 2001: Taylor and Francis.

*Types of Authority in Formative Christianity and Judaism. Institutional, Charismatic, and Intellectual.* With Bruce D. Chilton. London, 1999: Routledge. E-book edition, London, 2001: Taylor and Francis.

*The Intellectual Foundations of Christian and Jewish Discourse: The Philosophy of Religious Argument.* London, 1997: Routledge. [With Bruce D. Chilton.] .E-book edition, London, 2001: Taylor and Francis.

*Christianity and Judaism: The Formative Categories.* With Bruce D. Chilton. I. *Revelation. The Torah and the Bible.* Philadelphia, 1995: Trinity Press International. Reprint: Eugene, 2004: Wipf and Stock.

*Christianity and Judaism: The Formative Categories.* With Bruce D. Chilton. II. *The Body of Faith: Israel and Church.* Philadelphia, 1997: Trinity Press International. Reprint: Eugene, 2004: Wipf and Stock.

*Christianity and Judaism: The Formative Categories.* With Bruce D. Chilton. III. *God in the World.* Philadelphia, 1997: Trinity Press International. Reprint, Eugene, OR, 2004:Wipf and Stock.

*Judaeo-Christian Debates. God, Kingdom, Messiah.* With Bruce D. Chilton. Minneapolis, 1998: Fortress Press. *Choice* List of Fifty Best Academic Books of 1998.

*Children of the Flesh, Children of the Promise. An Argument with Paul about Judaism as an Ethnic Religion.* Cleveland, 1995: Pilgrim Press. Second printing: Eugene OR, 2005: Wipfs and Stock.

Editor: *Forging a Common Future: Catholic, Judaic, and Protestant Relations for a New Millennium.* Cleveland, 1997: Pilgrim Press.

*Virtues and Vices: Stories of the Moral Life.* With Andrew M. Greeley and Mary G. Durkin. Louisville, 1999: Westminster/John Knox Press. Catholic Book Club Selection, 1999.

*Comparing Spiritualities: Formative Christianity and Judaism on Finding Life and Meeting Death.* [With Bruce D. Chilton] Harrisburg, 2000: Trinity Press International

Editor: *The Missing Jesus: Rabbinic Judaism and the New Testament.* Leiden & Boston, 2003: E. J. Brill. Edited with Craig Evans and Bruce D. Chilton

Editor: *The Brother of Jesus. James the Just and his Mission.* Louisville, 2001: Westminster/John Knox Press. [With Bruce D. Chilton.]

*Talmud Torah: Ways to God's Presence through Learning.* Lanham, MD 2002: University Press of America STUDIES IN JUDAISM SERIES.

*Classical Christianity and Rabbinic Judaism: Comparing Theologies.* With Bruce D. Chilton. Grand Rapids, 2004: Baker Academic.

*Theology of Normative Judaism: A Source Book.* Lanham, 2005: University Press of America.

*Judaism in Monologue and Dialogue.*. Lanham, 2005: University Press of America.

### UNDERWAY

*Law and Gospel.* I. *Mark.* Leiden, 2006: E. J. Brill. Edited with Bruce D. Chilton.

## 8. Exposition of Problems of Method and *Auseinandersetzungen* with Other Viewpoints

Editor: *The Formation of the Babylonian Talmud. Studies on the Achievements of Late Nineteenth and Twentieth Century Historical and Literary-Critical Research.* Leiden, 1970: Brill. Reprint: Eugene OR 2003: Wipf and Stock Publishers

Editor: *The Modern Study of the Mishnah.* Leiden, 1973: Brill. Reprint: Eugene OR 2003: Wipf and Stock Publishers

Editor: *Soviet Views of Talmudic Judaism. Five Papers by Yu. A. Solodukho.* Leiden, 1973: Brill. Reprint: Eugene OR 2003: Wipf and Stock Publishers

*From Mishnah to Scripture. The Problem of the Unattributed Saying.* Chico, 1984: Scholars Press for Brown Judaic Studies. Reprise and reworking of materials in *A History of the Mishnaic Law of Purities.*

*In Search of Talmudic Biography. The Problem of the Attributed Saying.* Chico, 1984: Scholars Press for Brown Judaic Studies. Reprise and reworking of materials in *Eliezer ben Hyrcanus. The Tradition and the Man.*

*The Peripatetic Saying: The Problem of the Thrice-Told Tale in Talmudic Literature.* Chico, 1985: Scholars Press for Brown Judaic Studies. Reprise and reworking of materials in *Development of a Legend; Rabbinic Traditions about the Pharisees before 70* I-III. For the second edition, see above, *Peripatetic Parallels.*

*The Memorized Torah. The Mnemonic System of the Mishnah.* Chico, 1985: Scholars Press for Brown Judaic Studies. Reprise and reworking of materials in *Rabbinic Traditions about the Pharisees before 70* I and III, and *A History of the Mishnaic Law of Purities* XXI.

*Oral Tradition in Judaism: The Case of the Mishnah.* N.Y., 1987: Garland Publishing Co. *Albert Bates Lord Monograph Series* of the journal, *Oral Tradition.* Restatement of results in various works on the Mishnah together with a fresh account of the problem.

Editor: *The Study of Ancient Judaism.* N.Y., 1981: Ktav. Second printing: Atlanta, 1992: Scholars Press for South Florida Studies in the History of Judaism.

I. *The Study of Ancient Judaism: Mishnah, Midrash, Siddur.*

II. *The Study of Ancient Judaism: The Palestinian and Babylonian Talmuds.*

Editor: *Take Judaism, for Example. Studies toward the Comparison of Religions.* Chicago, 1983: University of Chicago Press. Second printing: Atlanta, 1992: Scholars Press for South Florida Studies in the History of Judaism.

Reprint: Binghamton, 2001: Global Publications, CLASSICS IN JUDAIC STUDIES SERIES. Reprint, Eugene, OR, 2003: Wipf and Stock.

*Method and Meaning in Ancient Judaism*. Missoula, 1979: Scholars Press for Brown Judaic Studies. Second printing, 1983.

*Method and Meaning in Ancient Judaism. Second Series*. Chico, 1980: Scholars Press for Brown Judaic Studies.

*Method and Meaning in Ancient Judaism. Third Series*. Chico, 1980: Scholars Press for Brown Judaic Studies.

*Method and Meaning in Ancient Judaism. Fourth Series*. Atlanta, 1989: Scholars Press for Brown Judaic Studies.

*Ancient Judaism. Debates and Disputes*. Chico, 1984: Scholars Press for Brown Judaic Studies.

*Ancient Judaism. Debates and Disputes. Second Series*. Atlanta, 1990: Scholars Press for South Florida Studies in the History of Judaism.

*Ancient Judaism. Debates and Disputes. Third Series. Essays on the Formation of Judaism, Dating Sayings, Method in the History of Judaism, the Historical Jesus, Publishing Too Much, and Other Current Issues*. Atlanta, 1993: Scholars Press for South Florida Studies in the History of Judaism.

*Ancient Judaism. Debates and Disputes. Fourth Series. Historical, Literary, Theological, and Religious Issues*. Atlanta, 1996: Scholars Press for South Florida Studies in the History of Judaism.

*The Public Side of Learning. The Political Consequences of Scholarship in the Context of Judaism*. Chico, 1985: Scholars Press for the American Academy of Religion *Studies in Religion* Series.

*Reading and Believing: Ancient Judaism and Contemporary Gullibility*. Atlanta, 1986: Scholars Press for Brown Judaic Studies. Now: Lanham, University Press of America.

*Ancient Judaism and Modern Category-Formation. "Judaism," "Midrash," "Messianism," and Canon in the Past Quarter-Century*. Lanham, 1986: University Press of America *Studies in Judaism* Series.

*Struggle for the Jewish Mind. Debates and Disputes on Judaism Then and Now.* Lanham, 1987: University Press of America. *Studies in Judaism* series.

*First Principles of Systemic Analysis. The Case of Judaism in the History of Religion.* Lanham, 1988: University Press of America. *Studies in Judaism* series.

*The Systemic Analysis of Judaism.* Atlanta, 1988: Scholars Press for Brown Judaic Studies.

*Why No Gospels in Talmudic Judaism?* Atlanta, 1988: Scholars Press for Brown Judaic Studies. Now: Lanham MD, 2001: University Press of America STUDIES IN JUDAISM series.

*Paradigms in Passage: Patterns of Change in the Contemporary Study of Judaism.* Lanham, 1988: University Press of America. STUDIES IN JUDAISM SERIES.

*Wrong Ways and Right Ways in the Study of Formative Judaism. Critical Method and Literature, History, and the History of Religion.* Atlanta, 1988: Scholars Press for Brown Judaic Studies.

*The Ecology of Religion: From Writing to Religion in the Study of Judaism.* Nashville, 1989: Abingdon. Paperback edition: Atlanta, 1997: Scholars Press for South Florida Studies in the History of Judaism.

*The Social Study of Judaism. Essays and Reflections.* Volume I. Atlanta, 1989: Scholars Press for Brown Judaic Studies.

*The Social Study of Judaism. Essays and Reflections.* Volume II. Atlanta, 1989: Scholars Press for Brown Judaic Studies.

Edited: *The Social Foundations of Judaism.* Edited with Calvin Goldscheider. Englewood Cliffs, 1989: Prentice Hall. Reprint: Eugene, OR, 2004: Wipf & Stock.

Edited: *Religious Writings and Religious Systems. Systemic Analysis of Holy Books in Christianity, Islam, Buddhism, Greco-Roman Religions, Ancient Israel, and Judaism* (Atlanta, 1989: Scholars Press for Brown Studies in Religion). Volume I. *Islam, Buddhism, Greco-Roman Religions, Ancient Israel, and Judaism.*

Edited: *Religious Writings and Religious Systems. Systemic Analysis of Holy Books in Christianity, Islam, Buddhism, Greco-Roman Religions, Ancient Israel, and Judaism* (Atlanta, 1989: Scholars Press for Brown Studies in Religion). Volume II. *Christianity.*

*Studying Classical Judaism: A Primer.* Louisville, 1991: Westminster/John Knox Press.

*Judaic Law from Jesus to the Mishnah. A Systematic Reply to Professor E. P. Sanders.* Atlanta, 1993: Scholars Press for South Florida Studies in the History of Judaism.

*Are There Really Tannaitic Parallels to the Gospels? A Refutation of Morton Smith.* Atlanta, 1993: Scholars Press for South Florida Studies in the History of Judaism.

*Why There Never Was a "Talmud of Caesarea." Saul Lieberman's Mistakes.* Atlanta, 1994: Scholars Press for South Florida Studies in the History of Judaism.

*The Documentary Foundation of Rabbinic Culture. Mopping Up after Debates with Gerald L. Bruns, S. J. D. Cohen, Arnold Maria Goldberg, Susan Handelman, Christine Hayes, James Kugel, Peter Schaefer, Eliezer Segal, E. P. Sanders, and Lawrence H. Schiffman.* Atlanta, 1995: Scholars Press for South Florida Studies in the History of Judaism.

Editor: *Religion and the Social Order. What Kinds of Lessons Does History Teach? Papers at the Conference on the Historical Study of Religion and Society.* Atlanta, 1995: Scholars Press for South Florida-St. Louis-Rochester Studies in Religion and the Social Order.

Editor: *Religion and the Political Order: The Ideal Politics of Christianity, Islam, and Judaism.* Atlanta, 1996: Scholars Press for South Florida-St. Louis-Rochester Studies in Religion and the Social Order.

*Are the Talmuds Interchangeable? Christine Hayes's Blunder.* Atlanta, 1996: Scholars Press for South Florida Studies on the History of Judaism.

*The Place of the Tosefta in the Halakhah of Formative Judaism. What Alberdina Houtman Didn't Notice.* Atlanta, 1998: Scholars Press for South Florida Studies in the History of Judaism.

Editor: *Judaism in Late Antiquity.* Volume One. *Literary and Archaeological Sources.* In the series *Handbuch der Orientalistik. Judaistik.* Leiden, 1995: E. J. Brill. Volume XVI.

Editor: *Judaism in Late Antiquity.* Volume Two. *Historical Syntheses.* In the series *Handbuch der Orientalistik. Judaistik.* Leiden, 1995: E. J. Brill. Volume XVII.

Volumes One and Two: Single-volume Paperback edition: Boston, 2002: E. J. Brill.

Editor: *Judaism in Late Antiquity.* Volume Three. *Where We Stand: Issues and Debates.* Part One. In the series, *Handbuch der Orientalistik. Judaistik.* Leiden, 1999: E. J. Brill. Edited with Alan J. Avery-Peck. Paperback edition: Boston, 2002: E. J. Brill.

Editor: *Judaism in Late Antiquity.* Volume Three. *Where We Stand: Issues and Debates.* Part Two. In the series, *Handbuch der Orientalistik. Judaistik.* Leiden, 1999: E. J. Brill. Edited with Alan J. Avery-Peck. Paperback edition: Boston, 2002: E. J. Brill.

Editor: *Judaism in Late Antiquity.* Volume Three. *Where We Stand: Issues and Debates.* Part Three. In the series, *Handbuch der Orientalistik. Judaistik.* Leiden, 2000: E. J. Brill. Edited with Alan J. Avery-Peck. Paperback edition: Boston, 2002: E. J. Brill.

Editor: *Judaism in Late Antiquity.* Volume Three. *Where We Stand: Issues and Debates.* Part Four. *The Problem of the Synagogue.* In the series, *Handbuch der Orientalistik. Judaistik.* Leiden, 2000: E. J. Brill. Edited with Alan J. Avery-Peck. Paperback edition: Boston, 2002: E. J. Brill.

*Volume three parts one through four: Single-volume Paperback edition: Boston 2002, E. K. Brill.*

Editor: *Judaism in Late Antiquity.* Volume Four. *Death, Life-after-Death, Resurrection, and the World to Come in the Judaisms of Antiquity.* In the series, *Handbuch der Orientalistik. Judaistik.* Leiden, 1999: E. J. Brill. Edited with Alan J. Avery-Peck. Paperback edition: Boston, 2002: E. J. Brill.

Editor: *Judaism in Late Antiquity.* Volume Five. *Judaism at Qumran.* Part One. *Theory of Israel, Way of Life.* In the series, *Handbuch der Orientalistik.*

*Judaistik.* Leiden, 1999: E. J. Brill. Edited with Alan J. Avery-Peck. Paperback edition: Boston, 2002: E. J. Brill.

Editor: *Judaism in Late Antiquity.* Volume Five. *Judaism at Qumran.* Part Two *World View.* In the series, *Handbuch der Orientalistik. Judaistik.* Leiden, 1999: E. J. Brill. Edited with Alan J. Avery-Peck. Paperback edition: Boston, 2002: E. J. Brill.

Volumes Four and Five: Single-volume Paperback edition: Boston 2002, E. J. Brill.

*How Adin Steinsaltz Misrepresents the Talmud. Four False Propositions from his "Reference Guide."* Atlanta, 1998: Scholars Press for South Florida Studies in the History of Judaism.

Editor: *Religious Belief and Economic Behavior. Judaism, Christianity, Islam.* Atlanta, 1999: Scholars Press for South Florida Studies in the History of Judaism.

Editor: *Religion and Economics: New Perspectives.* Binghamton, 2000: Global Publications. ACADEMIC STUDIES OF RELIGION AND THE SOCIAL ORDER. With Bruce D. Chilton.

*Editor:* Judaism in Late Antiquity. *Part Five.* The Judaism of Qumran:. A Systemic Reading of the Dead Sea Scrolls. *Volume One.* Way of Life. *LEIDEN, 2000: E. J. Brill. Handbuch der Orientalistik.*

*Editor:* Judaism in Late Antiquity. *Part Five.* The Judaism of Qumran. A Systemic Reading of the Dead Sea Scrolls. *Volume Two.* World View and Theory of Israel. *LEIDEN, 2000: E. J. Brill. Handbuch der Orientalistik. Edited with Alan J. Avery-Peck and Bruce D. Chilton*

Contemporary Views of Ancient Judaism: Disputes and Debates. *Binghamton, 2001: Global Publications. ACADEMIC STUDIES IN THE HISTORY OF JUDAISM SERIES.*

*Editor:* Religious Texts and Material Contexts. *Lanham, 2001: University Press of America. STUDIES IN FORMATIVE JUDAISM SERIES. Edited with James F. Strange.*

*The Three Questions of Formative Judaism: History, Literature, and Religion.* Leiden, 2003: E. J. Brill. THE BRILL REFERENCE LIBRARY OF JUDAISM.

*UNDERWAY*

Building Blocks of Rabbinic Tradition The Documentary Approach to the Study of Formative Judaism. *Lanham, 2007: University Press of America. STUDIES IN JUDAISM SERIES.*

### 9. *Restatement of Results*

**Systematic *Haute Vulgarisation* for the wider scholarly world**

*Early Rabbinic Judaism. Historical Studies in Religion, Literature, and Art.* Leiden, 1975: Brill.

*The Academic Study of Judaism. Essays and Reflections*. N.Y., 1975: Ktav Publishing House. Second printing, Chico, 1982: Scholars Press for Brown Judaic Studies.

*The Academic Study of Judaism. Second Series*. N.Y., 1977: Ktav Publishing House.

*The Academic Study of Judaism. Third Series. Three Contexts of Jewish Learning.* N.Y., 1980: Ktav Publishing House.

*Talmudic Judaism in Sasanian Babylonia. Essays and Studies*. Leiden, 1976: Brill.

*Judaism in the American Humanities*. Chico, 1981: Scholars Press for Brown Judaic Studies.

*Judaism in the American Humanities.* Second Series. *Jewish Learning and the New Humanities.* Chico, 1983: Scholars Press for Brown Judaic Studies.

*Das pharisäische und talmudische Judentum.* Tuebingen, 1984: J.C.B.Mohr (Paul Siebeck). Edited by Hermann Lichtenberger. Foreword by Martin Hengel.

*Formative Judaism. Religious, Historical, and Literary Studies. First Series.* Chico, 1982: Scholars Press for Brown Judaic Studies.

*Formative Judaism. Religious, Historical, and Literary Studies. Second Series.* Chico, 1983: Scholars Press for Brown Judaic Studies.

*Formative Judaism. Religious, Historical, and Literary Studies. Third Series. Torah, Pharisees, and Rabbis.* Chico, 1983: Scholars Press for Brown Judaic Studies.

*Formative Judaism. Religious, Historical, and Literary Studies. Fourth Series. Problems of Classification and Composition.* Chico, 1984: Scholars Press for Brown Judaic Studies.

*Formative Judaism. Religious, Historical, and Literary Studies. Fifth Series. Revisioning the Written Records of a Nascent Religion.* Chico, 1985: Scholars Press for Brown Judaic Studies.

*Formative Judaism. Religious, Historical, and Literary Studies. Sixth Series.* Atlanta, 1989: Scholars Press for Brown Judaic Studies.

*Formative Judaism. Religious, Historical, and Literary Studies. Seventh Series. The Formation of Judaism, Intentionality, Feminization of Judaism, and Other Current Results.* Atlanta, 1993: Scholars Press for South Florida Studies in the History of Judaism.

*Major Trends in Formative Judaism. First Series. Society and Symbol in Political Crisis.* Chico, 1983: Scholars Press for Brown Judaic Studies. Now: Lanham, University Press of America.

*Major Trends in Formative Judaism. Second Series. Texts, Contents, and Contexts.* Chico, 1984: Scholars Press for Brown Judaic Studies. Now: Lanham, University Press of America.

*Major Trends in Formative Judaism. Third Series. The Three Stages in the Formation of Judaism.* Chico, 1985: Scholars Press for Brown Judaic Studies. Now: Lanham, University Press of America.

*Major Trends in Formative Judaism.* Fourth Series *Category-Formation, Literature, and Philosophy. Lanham, 2002: University Press of America* STUDIES IN JUDAISM SERIES.

*Major Trends in Formative Judaism. Fifth Series. Comparisons, History, Religion. Reviews* Lanham, 2002: University Press of America STUDIES IN JUDAISM SERIES.

*The Religious Study of Judaism. Description, Analysis, Interpretation.* Volume One. Lanham, 1986: University Press of America *Studies in Judaism* Series.

*The Religious Study of Judaism. Description, Analysis, Interpretation.* Volume Two. *The Centrality of Context.* Lanham, 1986: University Press of America *Studies in Judaism* Series.

*The Religious Study of Judaism. Description, Analysis, Interpretation.* Volume Three. *Context, Text, and Circumstance.* Lanham, 1987: University Press of America *Studies in Judaism* Series.

*The Religious Study of Judaism. Description, Analysis, Interpretation.* Volume Four. *Ideas of History, Ethics, Ontology, and Religion in Formative Judaism.* Lanham, 1988: University Press of America *Studies in Judaism* Series.

*Understanding Seeking Faith. Essays on the Case of Judaism.* Volume One. *Debates on Method, Reports of Results.* Atlanta, 1986: Scholars Press for Brown Judaic Studies.

*Understanding Seeking Faith. Essays on the Case of Judaism.* Volume Two. *Literature, Religion, and the Social Study of Judaism.* Atlanta, 1987: Scholars Press for Brown Judaic Studies.

*Understanding Seeking Faith. Essays on the Case of Judaism.* Volume Three. *Society, History, and the Political and Philosophical Uses of Judaism.* Atlanta, 1989: Scholars Press for Brown Judaic Studies.

*The Pharisees. Rabbinic Perspectives.* N.Y., 1985: Ktav Publishing House. Reprise of *Rabbinic Traditions about the Pharisees before 70.* I-III.

*Israel and Iran in Talmudic Times. A Political History.* Lanham, 1986: University Press of America *Studies in Judaism* Series. Reprise of materials in *A History of the Jews in Babylonia* II-V, parts of chapter one of each volume. Jewish Book Club selection, 1988.

*Judaism, Christianity, and Zoroastrianism in Talmudic Babylonia.* Lanham, 1986: University Press of America *Studies in Judaism* Series. Reprise of materials in *A History of the Jews in Babylonia* II-V, parts of chapter one of each volume and of *Aphrahat and Judaism.* Reprinted: Atlanta, 1990: Scholars Press for Brown Judaic Studies.

*Israel's Politics in Sasanian Iran. Jewish Self-Government in Talmudic Times.* Lanham, 1986: University Press of America Studies in Judaism Series. Reprise of materials in *A History of the Jews in Babylonia* II-V, parts of chapter two of each volume.

*The Wonder-Working Lawyers of Talmudic Babylonia. The Theory and Practice of Judaism in its Formative Age.* Lanham, 1987: University Press of America Studies in Judaism. Reprise of materials in *A History of the Jews in Babylonia* II-V.

*School, Court, Public Administration: Judaism and its Institutions in Talmudic Babylonia.* Atlanta, 1987: Scholars Press for Brown Judaic Studies. Reprise of materials in *A History of the Jews in Babylonia* III-V.

*A Religion of Pots and Pans? Modes of Philosophical and Theological Discourse in Ancient Judaism. Essays and a Program.* Atlanta, 1988: Scholars Press for Brown Judaic Studies.

*Medium and Message in Judaism. First Series.* Atlanta, 1989: Scholars Press for Brown Judaic Studies.

*Lectures on Judaism in the Academy and in the Humanities.* Atlanta, 1990: Scholars Press for South Florida Studies in the History of Judaism.

*Lectures on Judaism in the History of Religion.* Atlanta, 1990: Scholars Press for South Florida Studies in the History of Judaism.

*The Formation of Judaism in Retrospect and Prospect.* Atlanta, 1991: Scholars Press for South Florida Studies in the History of Judaism.

*The Twentieth Century Construction of "Judaism." Essays on the Religion of Torah in the History of Religion.* Atlanta, 1991: Scholars Press for South Florida Studies in the History of Judaism.

*The City of God in Judaism. And Other Methodological and Comparative Studies.* Atlanta, 1991: Scholars Press for South Florida Studies in the History of Judaism.

*Åbo Addresses. And Other Recent Essays on Judaism in Time and Eternity.* Atlanta, 1994: Scholars Press for South Florida Studies in the History of Judaism.

*Rabbinic Judaism in the Formative Age: Disputes and Debates.* Atlanta, 1994: Scholars Press for South Florida Studies in the History of Judaism.

*Judaism after the Death of "the Death of God." The Canterbury Addresses and Other Essays on the Renaissance of Judaism in Contemporary Jewry.* Atlanta, 1994: Scholars Press for South Florida Studies in the History of Judaism.

*Understanding Seeking Faith. Essays on the Case of Judaism.* Volume Four. *Judaism Then and Now.* Atlanta, 1995: Scholars Press for South Florida Studies in the History of Judaism.

*Formative Judaism. New Series. Current Issues and Arguments.* Volume One. Atlanta, 1996: Scholars Press for South Florida Studies in the History of Judaism.

*Religion and Law: How through Halakhah Judaism Sets Forth its Theology and Philosophy.* Atlanta, 1996: Scholars Press for South Florida Studies in the History of Judaism.

*Uppsala Addresses. And Other Recent Essays and Reviews on Judaism Then and Now.* Atlanta, 1996: Scholars Press for South Florida Studies in the History of Judaism.

*Formative Judaism. New Series. Current Issues and Arguments.* Volume Two. *Chapters on Form-History, Documentary Description, and the Social, Religious, and Theological Study of Judaism.* Atlanta, 1997: Scholars Press for South Florida Studies in the History of Judaism.

*The Mind of Classical Judaism.* I. *The Philosophy and Political Economy of Formative Judaism. The Mishnah's System of the Social Order.* Atlanta, 1997: Scholars Press for South Florida Studies in the History of Judaism.

*The Mind of Classical Judaism.* II. *Modes of Thought: Making Connections and Drawing Conclusions.* Atlanta, 1997: Scholars Press for South Florida Studies in the History of Judaism.

*The Mind of Classical Judaism.* III. *From Philosophy to Religion.* Atlanta, 1997: Scholars Press for South Florida Studies in the History of Judaism.

*The Mind of Classical Judaism.* IV. *What is "Israel"? Social Thought in the Formative Age.* Atlanta, 1997: Scholars Press for South Florida Studies in the History of Judaism.

*Messages to Moscow. And Other Current Lectures on Learning and Community in Judaism.* Atlanta, 1998: Scholars Press for South Florida Studies in the History of Judaism

*Jewish Law from Moses to the Mishnah. The Hiram College Lectures on Religion for 1999 and Other Papers.* Atlanta, 1998: Scholars Press for South Florida Studies in the History of Judaism.

*A Reader's Guide to the Talmud.* Leiden, 2001: E. J. Brill.

*How the Talmud Works.* Leiden, 2002: E. J. Brill.

*The Halakhah. Religious and Historical Perspectives.* Leiden, 2002: E. J. Brill.

*Formative Judaism: History, Hermeneutics, Law and Religion. Ten Recent Essays.* Binghamton, 2000: Global Publications. ACADEMIC STUDIES IN THE HISTORY OF JUDAISM SERIES.

### 10. *Toward the Creation of a New Academy:*

#### i. Scholarly Books Organized and Edited

Editor: *Report of the 1965-1966 Seminar on Religions in Antiquity.* Hanover, 1966: Dartmouth College Comparative Studies Center. Reprinted, 1984.

Editor: *Religions in Antiquity. Essays in Memory of Erwin Ramsdell Goodenough.* Leiden, 1968: Brill. Supplements to *Numen.* Vol. XIV. Second printing, 1970; third printing, 1972. Reprint: Eugene OR, 2004: Wipf and Stock

Editor: *Christianity, Judaism, and Other Greco-Roman Cults. Studies for Morton Smith at Sixty.* Leiden, 1975: Brill. Reprint: Eugene OR 2004: Wipf and Stock.

I. *New Testament*
II. *Early Christianity.*
III. *Judaism before 70.*
IV. *Judaism after 70. Other Greco-Roman Cults.*

Editor: *Essays in Honor of Yigael Yadin.* [Edited with Geza Vermes]. Special issue of *Journal of Jewish Studies,* 1982.

Editor: *The New Humanities and Academic Disciplines. The Case of Jewish Studies.* Madison, 1984: University of Wisconsin Press. On graduate education in Judaic studies. Second printing: Eugene, OR: 2004: Wipf and Stock.

Editor: *New Perspectives on Ancient Judaism.* I. *Contents and Contexts in Judaic and Christian Interpretation. Formative Judaism.* Lanham, 1987: University Press *Studies in Judaism* series. [Essays in honor of Howard Clark Kee.] Second printing: Atlanta, 1990: Scholars Press for Brown Judaic Studies.

Editor: *New Perspectives on Ancient Judaism.* II. *Contents and Contexts in Judaic and Christian Interpretation. Ancient Israel. Formative Christianity.* Lanham, 1987: University Press *Studies in Judaism* series. [Essays in honor of Howard Clark Kee.]

Editor: *New Perspectives on Ancient Judaism.* III. *Judaic and Christian Interpretation of Texts: Contents and Contexts.* Lanham, 1987: University Press *Studies in Judaism* series.

Editor: *The Social World of Formative Christianity and Judaism. Essays in Honor of Howard Clark Kee.* Philadelphia, 1988: Fortress Press. [Edited with Peder Borgen, Ernest S. Frerichs, and Richard Horsley].

*Editor: From Ancient Israel to Modern Judaism. Intellect in Quest of Understanding. Essays in Honor of Marvin Fox.* Atlanta, 1989: Scholars Press for Brown Judaic Studies. I-IV.

I. *What Is at Stake in the Judaic Quest for Understanding? Judaic Learning and the Locus of Education. Ancient Israel. Formative Christianity. Judaism in the Formative Age: Religion.*

II. *Judaism in the Formative Age: Theology and Literature. Judaism in the Middle Ages: The Encounter with Christianity. The Encounter with Scripture. Philosophy and Theology.*

III. *Judaism in the Middle Ages: Philosophers. Hasidism. Messianism in Modern Times. The Modern Age: Philosophy.*

IV. *The Modern Age: Theology, Literature, History.*

*Editor: Approaches to Ancient Judaism.* Volume Six. *Studies in the Ethnography and Literature of Judaism.* Atlanta, 1989: Scholars Press for Brown Judaic Studies.

*Editor: Approaches to Ancient Judaism.* New Series. Volume One. Atlanta, 1991: Scholars Press for South Florida Studies in the History of Judaism.

*Editor: Approaches to Ancient Judaism.* New Series. Volume Two. Atlanta, 1991: Scholars Press for South Florida Studies in the History of Judaism.

Editor: *Approaches to Ancient Judaism.* New Series. Volume Three. *Historical and Literary Studies.* Atlanta, 1993: Scholars Press for South Florida Studies in the History of Judaism.

Editor: *Approaches to Ancient Judaism.* New Series. Volume Four. *Religious and Theological Studies.* Atlanta, 1993: Scholars Press for South Florida Studies in the History of Judaism.

Editor: *The Origins of Judaism. Religion, History, and Literature in Late Antiquity.* With William Scott Green. New York, 1991: Garland Press. Twenty volumes of reprinted scholarly essays, with introductions.

i. *Normative Judaism*
ii. *Normative Judaism*
iii. *Normative Judaism*
iv. *The Pharisees and Other Sects*
v. *The Pharisees and Other Sects*
vi. *Judaism and Christianity in the First Century*
vii. *Judaism and Christianity in the First Century*
viii. *Controversies in the Study of Judaic Religion and Theology*
ix. *History of the Jews in the Second and First Centuries B.C.*
x. *History of the Jews in the Second and First Centuries B.C.*
xi. *History of the Jews in the First Century of the Common Era*
xii. *History of the Jews in the Second Century of the Common Era*
xiii *History of the Jews in the Second through Seventh Centuries of the Common Era*
xiv. *History of the Jews in the Second through Seventh Centuries of the Common Era*
xv. *The Literature of Formative Judaism: The Mishnah and the Tosefta*
xvi. *The Literature of Formative Judaism: The Talmuds*
xvii *The Literature of Formative Judaism: The Midrash-Compilations*
xviii *The Literature of Formative Judaism: The Midrash-Compilations*
xix. *The Literature of Formative Judaism: The Targumim and Other Jewish Writings in Late Antiquity*
xx. *The Literature of Formative Judaism: Controversies on the Literature of Formative Judaism*

Editor: *Judaism in Cold War America: 1945-1990.* New York, 1993: Garland Press. Ten volumes of reprinted scholarly essays, with introductions.

i. *The Challenge of America: Can Judaism Survive in Freedom?*
ii. *In the Aftermath of the Holocaust*
iii. *Israel and Zion in American Judaism: The Zionist Fulfillment*
iv. *Judaism and Christianity: The New Relationship*
v. *The Religious Renewal of Jewry*
vi. *The Reformation of Reform Judaism*
vii. *Conserving Conservative Judaism*
viii. *The Alteration of Orthodoxy*
ix. *The Academy and Traditions of Jewish Learning*
x. *The Rabbinate in America: Reshaping an Ancient Calling*

Editor: *Approaches to Ancient Judaism.* New Series. Volume Seven. Atlanta, 1995: Scholars Press for South Florida Studies in the History of Judaism.

Editor: *Approaches to Ancient Judaism.* New Series. Volume Eight. Atlanta, 1995: Scholars Press for South Florida Studies in the History of Judaism.

Editor: *Approaches to Ancient Judaism.* New Series. Volume Nine. Atlanta, 1996: Scholars Press for South Florida Studies in the History of Judaism.

*Ancient Judaism: Religious and Theological Perspectives.* First Series. Atlanta, 1996: Scholars Press for South Florida Studies in the History of Judaism.

Editor: *Approaches to Ancient Judaism.* New Series. Volume Ten. Atlanta, 1997: Scholars Press for South Florida Studies in the History of Judaism.

Editor: *Approaches to Ancient Judaism.* New Series. Volume Eleven. Atlanta, 1997: Scholars Press for South Florida Studies in the History of Judaism.

Editor: *Approaches to Ancient Judaism.* New Series. Volume Twelve. Atlanta, 1997: Scholars Press for South Florida Studies in the History of Judaism.

Editor: *Approaches to Ancient Judaism.* New Series. Volume Thirteen. Atlanta, 1998: Scholars Press for South Florida Studies in the History of Judaism.

Chairman of the Editorial Board: *The Annual of Rabbinic Judaism: Ancient, Medieval and Modern.* Leiden, 1998: E. J. Brill. Volume I.

Editor: *Approaches to Ancient Judaism.* New Series. Volume Fourteen. Atlanta, 1998: Scholars Press for South Florida Studies in the History of Judaism.

Editor: *Approaches to Ancient Judaism.* New Series. Volume Fifteen. Atlanta, 1999: Scholars Press for South Florida Studies in the History of Judaism.

Chairman of the Editorial Board: *The Annual of Rabbinic Judaism: Ancient, Medieval and Modern.* Leiden, 1999: E. J. Brill. Volume II.

Editor: *Approaches to Ancient Judaism.* New Series. Volume Sixteen. Atlanta, 1999: Scholars Press for South Florida Studies in the History of Judaism.

Chairman of the Editorial Board: *The Annual of Rabbinic Judaism: Ancient, Medieval and Modern.* Leiden, 2000: E. J. Brill. Volume III.

Editor: *Marvin Fox: Collected Essays on Philosophy and on Judaism.* Binghamton 2001: Global Publications. ACADEMIC STUDIES IN THE HISTORY OF JUDAISM SERIES.

I. *Greek Philosophy, Maimonides*
II. *Some Philosophers*
III. *Ethics, Reflections*

Chairman of the Editorial Board: *The Review of Rabbinic Judaism: Ancient, Medieval and Modern.* Leiden, 2001: E. J. Brill. Volume IV, Nos. 1-2.

Chairman of the Editorial Board: *The Review of Rabbinic Judaism: Ancient, Medieval and Modern.* Leiden, 2002: E. J. Brill. Volume V, Nos. 1-3.

Chairman of the Editorial Board: *The Review of Rabbinic Judaism: Ancient, Medieval and Modern.* Leiden, 2003: E. J. Brill. Volume VI, Nos. 1-3.

Chairman of the Editorial Board: *The Review of Rabbinic Judaism: Ancient, Medieval and Modern.* Leiden, 2004: E. J. Brill. Volume VII

Chairman of the Editorial Board: *The Review of Rabbinic Judaism: Ancient, Medieval and Modern.* Leiden, 2005: E. J. Brill. Volume VIII

Editor: *George W. E. Nickelsburg in Perspective: An On-Going Dialogue of Learning.* [With Alan J. Avery-Peck] Leiden, 2003: E. J. Brill. JOURNAL FOR THE STUDY OF JUDAISM SUPPLEMENTS. VOLUME ONE

Editor: *George W. E. Nickelsburg in Perspective: An On-Going Dialogue of Learning.* [With Alan J. Avery-Peck. Leiden, 2003: E. J. Brill. JOURNAL FOR THE STUDY OF JUDAISM SUPPLEMENTS. VOLUME TWO

Editor: *When Judaism and Christianity Began: Essays in Memory of Anthony J. Saldarini*. [With Daniel Harrington, Alan J. Avery-Peck]. Leiden & Boston, 2003: E. J. Brill SUPPLEMENTS TO JOURNAL FOR THE STUDY OF JUDAISM. VOLUME ONE.

Editor: *When Judaism and Christianity Began: Essays in Memory of Anthony J. Saldarini*. [With Daniel Harrington, Alan J. Avery-Peck]. Leiden & Boston, 2003: E. J. Brill SUPPLEMENTS TO JOURNAL FOR THE STUDY OF JUDAISM. VOLUME TWO.

*How Not to Study Judaism: Examples and Counter-examples.* Lanham, 2004: University Press of America. I. *Parables, Rabbinic Narratives, Rabbis' Biographies, Rabbis' Disputes*

*How Not to Study Judaism: Examples and Counter-examples.* Lanham, 2004: University Press of America. II. *Ethnicity and Identity versus Culture and Religion, How Not to Write A Book on Judaism. Point and Counterpoint*

*Parsing the Torah. Surveying the History, Literature, Religion, and Theology of Formative Judaism.* Lanham, 2005: University Press of America.

Italian translation: *Analizzando la Torah. Capitoli di autobiografia intellettuale* Brescia, 2006: Editrice Morcelliana.

Editor: *Ancient Israel, Judaism, and Christianity in Contemporary Perspective. Essays in memory of Karl-Johan Illman.* Lanham, 2005: University Press of America. Edited with Alan J. Avery-Peck, Antti Laato, Risto Nurmela, and Karl-Gustav Sandelin.

### 11. *Toward the Creation of the New Academy:* (ii). Providing Textbooks for Undergraduate Instruction and Trade Books for the Public at Large.

*The Way of Torah. An Introduction to Judaism.* Encino, 1970: Dickenson Publishing Co. In *Living Religion of Man* Series, edited by Frederick Streng. Second printing, 1971. Third printing, 1971. Second edition, revised, 1973. Third printing, 1976. Third edition, thoroughly revised, Belmont: 1979: Wadsworth Publishing Co. Third printing, l980. Fourth printing, 1982. Fifth printing, 1983. Sixth printing, 1985. Seventh printing, 1986. Fourth edition, completely revised and rewritten: 1988. Second printing: 1988. Third printing, 1990. Fourth printing: 1991. Fifth edition, revised and augmented: 1992. Sixth edition: in *Living Religion of Man* Series, edited by Charles Hallisey. Belmont, 1997:Wadsworth/Thompson International. Seventh Edition: Belmont, 2003: Wadsworth/Thompson International.

Editor: *Life of Torah. Readings in the Jewish Religious Experience.* Encino, 1974: Dickenson Publishing Co. Third printing, Belmont, 1980: Wadsworth. Sixth printing, 1984. Seventh printing, 1987.

Editor: *Signposts on the Way of Torah. A Reader for* The Way of Torah. In *Living Religion of Man* Series, edited by Charles Hallisey. Belmont, 1998: Wadsworth/Thompson International.

*There We Sat Down. Talmudic Judaism in the Making.* Nashville, 1972: Abingdon. Second printing, N.Y., 1978: Ktav. . Reprint: Eugene OR 2006: Wipf and Stock Publishers

*American Judaism. Adventure in Modernity.* Englewood Cliffs, 1972: Prentice-Hall. Second printing, 1973. Third printing, 1976. Fourth printing, N.Y., 1978: Ktav.

Editor: *Understanding Rabbinic Judaism. From Talmudic to Modern Times.* N.Y., 1974: Ktav. Second printing, 1977. Fourth printing, 1985. Reprint: Binghamton 2001: Global Publications/SUNY. In ACADEMIC CLASSICS OF JUDAISM SERIES. Reprint: Eugene OR 2003: Wipf and Stock Publishers

*First Century Judaism in Crisis. Yohanan ben Zakkai and the Renaissance of Torah.* Nashville, 1975: Abingdon. Second printing, N.Y., 1981: Ktav. Third printing: Eugene OR, 2006: Wipf & Stock

*Between Time and Eternity. The Essentials of Judaism.* Encino, 1976: Dickenson Publishing Co. Fifth printing, Belmont, 1983: Wadsworth. Sixth printing, 1987. Reprint: Eugene OR, 2005: Wipf and Stock.

Editor: *Understanding American Judaism. Toward the Description of a Modern Religion.* N.Y., 1975: Ktav. I-II. Reprint: Eugene OR 2003: Wipf and Stock Publishers

I. *Understanding American Judaism. Toward the Description of a Modern Religion. The Synagogue and the Rabbi.*

II. *Understanding American Judaism. Toward the Description of a Modern Religion. The Sectors of American Judaism: Reform, Orthodoxy, Conservatism, and Reconstructionism.*

*Our Sages, God, and Israel. An Anthology of the Yerushalmi*. Chappaqua, 1984: Rossel. 1985 selection, Jewish Book Club.

*How To Grade Your Professors and Other Unexpected Advice*. Boston, 1984: Beacon. Second printing: 1984. Third printing: Eugene OR 2006: Wipf & Stock.

*Genesis and Judaism: The Perspective of Genesis Rabbah. An Analytical Anthology*. Atlanta, 1986: Scholars Press for Brown Judaic Studies.

*Christian Faith and the Bible of Judaism*. Grand Rapids, 1987: Wm. B. Eerdmans Publishing Co. Second printing: Atlanta, 1990: Scholars Press for Brown Judaic Studies.

*Confronting Creation: How Judaism Reads Genesis. An Anthology of Genesis Rabbah*. Columbia, 1991: University of South Carolina Press. Reprint: Eugene, OR, 2005: Wipf & Stock.

*From Testament to Torah: An Introduction to Judaism in its Formative Age*. Englewood Cliffs, 1987: Prentice Hall.

*An Introduction to Judaism. Textbook and Anthology*. Louisville, 1992: Westminster/John Knox Press. Second printing: 1999.

*A Short History of Judaism. Three Meals, Three Epochs*. Minneapolis, 1992: Fortress Press.

Editor: *World Religions in America. An Introduction*. Louisville, 1994: Westminster/John Knox Press. Library Guild Selection, Methodist Church Libraries, 1994. Jewish Book Club Selection for July 1995. Third printing: 1996. Fourth printing, 1998. Second edition: 1999. Reprinted annually. Third edition: 2003. Fourth printing of the third edition: 2004. Fifth printing of the third edition: 2005.

*Sources of the Transformation of Judaism: From Philosophy to Religion in the Classics of Judaism. A Reader*. Atlanta, 1992: Scholars Press for South Florida Studies in the History of Judaism.

*Fortress Introduction to American Judaism: What the Books Say, What the People Do* Minneapolis, 1993: Fortress Press. Reprinted: Eugene, OR 2004: Wipf and Stock.

*Israel's Love Affair with God: Song of Songs.* Philadelphia, 1993: Trinity Press International. The Bible of Judaism Library.

*"Your People Will be My People:" The Mother of the Messiah in Judaism. How the Rabbis Read the Book of Ruth. An Anthology of Ruth Rabbah.* Philadelphia, 1994: Trinity Press International. The Bible of Judaism Library.

*The Woman Who Saved Israel: How the Rabbis Read the Book of Esther. An Anthology of Esther Rabbah.* Philadelphia, 1994: Trinity Press International. The Bible of Judaism Library.

*The Classics of Judaism. An Introduction to Mishnah, Talmud, and Midrash.* Louisville, 1995: Westminster/John Knox Press.

*Classical Judaism: Torah, Learning, Virtue. An Anthology of the Mishnah, Talmud, and Midrash.* I. *Torah.* Essen and New York, 1993: Peter Lang.

*Classical Judaism: Torah, Learning, Virtue. An Anthology of the Mishnah, Talmud, and Midrash.* II. *Learning.* Essen and New York, 1993: Peter Lang.

*Classical Judaism: Torah, Learning, Virtue. An Anthology of the Mishnah, Talmud, and Midrash.* III. *Virtue.* Essen and New York, 1993: Peter Lang.

*How Judaism Reads the Torah.* I. *How Judaism Reads the Ten Commandments. An Anthology of the Mekhilta Attributed to R. Ishmael.* Essen and New York, 1994: Peter Lang.

*How Judaism Reads the Torah.* II. *"You Shall Love Your Neighbor as Yourself:" How Judaism Defines the Covenant to Be a Holy People. An Anthology of Sifra to Leviticus.* Essen and New York, 1994: Peter Lang.

*How Judaism Reads the Torah.* III. *Wayward Women in the Wilderness. An Anthology of Sifré to Numbers.* Essen and New York, 1994: Peter Lang.

*How Judaism Reads the Torah.* IV. *"I Deal Death and I Give Life." How Classical Judaism Confronts Holocaust. An Anthology of Sifré to Deuteronomy.* Essen and New York, 1994: Peter Lang.

*Conservative, American, and Jewish — I Wouldn't Want It Any Other Way* Lafayette, 1993: Huntington House. Selection, Jewish Book Club, March, 1994.

*Scripture and Midrash in Judaism.* [1] *Exegesis An Anthology of Sifra and the two Sifrés.* Frankfurt and New York, 1994: Peter Lang.

*Scripture and Midrash in Judaism.* [2] *Proposition. An Anthology of Genesis Rabbah, Leviticus Rabbah, Pesiqta deRab Kahana.* Frankfurt and New York, 1995: Peter Lang.

*Scripture and Midrash in Judaism.* [3] *Theology. An Anthology of Lamentations Rabbati, Song of Songs Rabbah, Esther Rabbah, Ruth Rabbah.* Frankfurt and New York, 1995: Peter Lang

*The Talmudic Anthology:* I. *Torah: Issues of Ethics.* Frankfurt and New York, 1995: Verlag Peter Lang.

*The Talmudic Anthology:* II. *God: Issues of Theology.* Frankfurt and New York, 1995: Verlag Peter Lang.

*The Talmud Anthology:* III. *Israel: Issues of Public Policy.* Frankfurt and New York, 1995: Verlag Peter Lang.

Editor *The Religion Factor: An Introduction to How Religion Matters.* Louisville, 1996: Westminster/John Knox. [Edited with William Scott Green.]

*Judaism in Modern Times. An Introduction and Reader.* Oxford 1995: Blackwell.

*Iudaismul in Timpurile moderne.* *Colectia Judaica*. Translation into Romanian. Bucharest, 2004: Editura Hasefer

*Beyond Catastrophe: The Rabbis' Reading of Isaiah's Vision. Israelite Messiah-Prophecies in Formative Judaism. An Anthology of Pesiqta deRab Kahana for the Seven Sabbaths after the Ninth of Ab.* Atlanta, 1996: Scholars Press for South Florida Studies in the History of Judaism.

*The Price of Excellence. Universities in Conflict during the Cold War Era.* New York, 1995: Continuum. [With Noam M. M. Neusner]. Second printing: Lanham 2004: University Press of America.

*Trading Places: The Intersecting Histories of Christianity and Rabbinic Judaism.* Cleveland, 1997: Pilgrim Press. [With Bruce D. Chilton]. Reprint: Eugene, OR, 2004: Wipf and Stock.

*Trading Places. A Reader and Sourcebook on the Intersecting Histories of Christianity and Rabbinic Judaism.* Cleveland, 1997: Pilgrim Press. [With Bruce D. Chilton] Reprint: Eugene, OR, 2004: Wipf and Stock.

*The Mishnah. Introduction and Reader. An Anthology.* Philadelphia, 1992: Trinity Press International. Library of Rabbinic Literature. Reprinted Eugene, OR, 2004: Wipf and Stock.

*The Talmud. Introduction and Reader.* Atlanta, 1995: Scholars Press for South Florida Studies in the History of Judaism

*Understanding the Talmud: A Dialogic Approach.* Hoboken, 2004: Ktav Publishing House. [Reissue of the foregoing, revised.]

Editor: *Dictionary of Judaism in the Biblical Period, from 450 B.C. to 600 A.D.* N.Y., 1995: MacMillan Publishing Co. Two volumes.

One volume reprint: N.Y., 1999: Hendrickson Publishing Co.

*The Book of Jewish Wisdom. The Talmud of the Well-Considered Life.* N.Y., 1996: Continuum. [With Noam M. M. Neusner]. Reprint: Binghamton, 2001: Global Publications, CLASSICS IN JUDAIC STUDIES SERIES.

*Reaffirming Higher Education.* New Brunswick, 2000: Transaction Publishers. [With Noam M. M. Neusner]

Editor: *The Pilgrim Library of World Religions.* I. *Christianity, Judaism, Islam, Buddhism, and Hinduism on God.* Cleveland, 1997: Pilgrim Press.

Editor: *The Pilgrim Library of World Religions.* II. *Judaism, Islam, Buddhism, Hinduism and Christianity on Sacred Texts and Authority.* Cleveland, 1998: Pilgrim Press. Second printing: Eugene Or, 2006: Wipf & Stock.

Editor: *The Pilgrim Library of World Religions.* III. *Buddhism, Hinduism Christianity, Judaism, and Islam, on Evil and Suffering.* Cleveland, 1999: Pilgrim Press. Second printing: Eugene Or, 2006: Wipf & Stock.

Editor *The Pilgrim Library of World Religions.* IV. *Islam, Buddhism, Hinduism, Christianity, and Judaism on Woman and the Family.* Cleveland, 1999: Pilgrim Press. Second printing: Eugene Or, 2006: Wipf & Stock.

*Editor* *The Pilgim Library of World Religions.* V. *Hinduism, Christianity, Judaism, Islam, and Buddhism on the Afterlife.* Cleveland, 2000: Pilgrim Press.

*Comparing Religions Through Law: Judaism and Islam.* [With Tamara Sonn] London, 1999: Routledge. E-book edition, London, 2001: Taylor and Francis.

*Judaism and Islam in Practice. A Source Book of the Classical Age.* [With Tamara Sonn & Jonathan Brockopp] London, 2000: Routledge. E-book edition, London, 2001: Taylor and Francis.

Editor: *Comparing Religious Traditions.* I. *Judaism, Christianity, Islam, Hinduism, and Buddhism on the Ethics of Family Life: What Do We Owe One Another?* Belmont, 2000: Wadsworth Publishing Co.

Editor: *Comparing Religious Traditions.* II. *Judaism, Christianity, Islam, Hinduism, and Buddhism on Making an Honest Living: What Do We Owe the Community?* Belmont, 2000: Wadsworth Publishing Co.

Editor: *Comparing Religious Traditions.* III. *Judaism, Christianity, Islam, Hinduism, and Buddhism on Virtue: What Do We Owe Ourselves?* Belmont, 2000: Wadsworth Publishing Co.

Editor-in-Chief: *The Encyclopaedia of Judaism.* [With William Scott Green and Alan J. Avery-Peck] In three volumes. Leiden, 1999: E. J. Brill & NYC, 1999: Continuum. Under the Auspices of the Museum of Jewish Heritage. Volume I. CD Edition: Leiden, 2003: E. J. Brill, covering Volumes I-III and Supplements I-II.

Editor-in-Chief: *The Encyclopaedia of Judaism.* [With William Scott Green and Alan J. Avery-Peck] In three volumes. Leiden, 1999: E. J. Brill & NYC, 1999: Continuum. Under the Auspices of the Museum of Jewish Heritage. Volume II. CD Edition: Leiden, 2003: E. J. Brill, covering Volumes I-III and Supplements I-II.

Editor-in-Chief: *The Encyclopaedia of Judaism.* [With William Scott Green and Alan J. Avery-Peck] ] In three volumes. Leiden, 1999: E. J. Brill & NYC, 1999: Continuum. Under the Auspices of the Museum of Jewish Heritage. Volume III. CD Edition: Leiden, 2003: E. J. Brill, covering Volumes I-III and Supplements I-II.

Award: "Book of the Year" Citation, Choice, 2000.
Award: American Libraries (American Library Association): Outstanding Reference Sources 2001, selected by Reference Users' Service Association of ALA.

Editor-in-Chief: *The Encyclopaedia of Judaism. Supplement One.* [With Alan J. Avery-Peck and William Scott Green] Leiden, 2002: E. J. Brill & NYC, 2002: Continuum. CD Edition: Leiden, 2003: E. J. Brill, covering Volumes I-III and Supplements I-II.

Editor-in-Chief: *Encyclopaedia of Judaism. Supplement Two.* [With Alan J. Avery-Peck and William Scott Green] Leiden, 2003: E. J. Brill & NYC, 2003: Continuum.

CD Edition: Leiden, 2003: E. J. Brill, covering Volumes I-III and Supplements I-II.

Editor-in-chief: *Encyclopaedia of Judaism. Second Edition.* [With Alan J. Avery-Peck and William Scott Green.] Leiden and Boston, 2005: Brill, Volume One. A-E

Editor-in-chief: *Encyclopaedia of Judaism. Second Edition.* [With Alan J. Avery-Peck and William Scott Green.] Leiden and Boston, 2005: Brill, Volume Two. F-K

Editor-in-chief: *Encyclopaedia of Judaism. Second Edition* [With Alan J. Avery-Peck and William Scott Green.] Leiden and Boston, 2005: Brill, Volume III. L-Ra

Editor-in-chief: *Encyclopaedia of Judaism. Second Edition..* [With Alan J. Avery-Peck and William Scott Green.] Leiden and Boston, 2005: Brill, Volume IV. Re-Z.

Editor: *The Companion to Judaism.* [With Alan J. Avery-Peck] Oxford, 2000: Blackwells. Paperback edition: 2003.

Editor: *The Blackwell Reader in Judaism.* [With Alan J. Avery-Peck] Oxford, 2000: Blackwells. Paperback edition: 2003. Second printing: 2005.

*Judaism When Christianity Began: A Survey of Belief and Practice.* Louisville 2003: Westminster/John Knox Press.

*Transformations in Ancient Judaism: Textual Evidence for Creative Responses to Crisis.* Peabody, 2004: Hendrickson.

*Judaism. An Introduction.* London and New York, 2002: Penguin. In the RELIGION SERIES edited by John Hinells. Second printing: 2003.

Portuguese translation: *Introdução ao Judaismo.* Rio de Janeiro, 2004: Imago.
Japanese translation: Tokyo, 2005: Khobunkwan.

Edited: *The 2002 Mathers Lecture, the 2001 Rosen Lecture, and Other Queen's University Essays in the Study of Judaism.* Binghamton, 2002: Global Publications. ACADEMIC STUDIES IN THE HISTORY OF JUDAISM SERIES.

Editor: *Judaism from to Muhammad. An Interpretation. Turning Points and Focal Points.* Leiden, 2005: E. J. Brill [Edited with William Scott Green.]

Editor: *Faith, Truth, and Freedom: The Expulsion of Professor Gerd Luedemann from the Theology Faculty of Goettingen University. Symposium and Documents.* Binghamton, 2002: Global Publications. ACADEMIC STUDIES ON RELIGION AND THE SOCIAL ORDER SERIES.

*Three Faiths, One God. The Formative Faith and Practice of Judaism, Christianity, and Islam* [With Bruce D. Chilton & William A. Graham.] Leiden and Boston, 2002: E. J. Brill.

Edited: *Judaism: Major Traits. Theology, Philosophy, Practice. Articles selected from The Encyclopaedia of Judaism.* Boston and Leiden, 2006: E. J. Brill. [With Alan J. Avery-Peck and William Scott Green]

Editor: *God's Rule: The Politics of World Religions.* Washington DC, 2003: Georgetown University Press. Nominated for 2003 Christopher Award.

*Questions and Answers: Intellectual Foundations of Judaism for the Non-Jew.* Peabody, 2005: Hendrickson.

*Neusner on Judaism.* Aldershott, 2004: Ashgate Publishers. ASHGATE CONTEMPORARY THINKERS ON RELIGION. COLLECTED WORKS, General Editor: John Hinnells. Volume One. *History.*

*Neusner on Judaism.* Aldershott, 2005: Ashgate Publishers. ASHGATE CONTEMPORARY THINKERS ON RELIGION. COLLECTED WORKS, General Editor: John Hinnells. Volume Two: *Literature.*

*Neusner on Judaism.* Aldershott, 2006: Ashgate Publishers. ASHGATE CONTEMPORARY THINKERS ON RELIGION. COLLECTED WORKS, General Editor: John Hinnells. Volume Three, *Religion and Theology*

*The Dictionary of Judaism.* London and New York, 2003: Routledge. With Alan J. Avery-Peck.

Editor: *Dictionary of Ancient Rabbis. Selections from the Jewish Encyclopaedia.* Peabody, 2003: Hendrickson.

*Emergence of Judaism.* Louisville, 2004: Westminster/John Knox Press.

*Rabbinic Literature. An Essential Guide.* Nashville, 2005: Abingdon.

*Theology in Action. How the Rabbis of Formative Judaism Present Theology (Aggadah) in the Medium of Law (Halakhah). An Anthology.* Lanham, 2006: University Press of America.

*The Talmud: Law, Theology, Narrative. A Reader.* Lanham, 2005: University Press of America

*Religious Foundations of Western Civilization. Judaism, Christianity, Islam.* Nashville, 2005: Abingdon.

*Judaism in Contemporary Context.* London, 2006: Valentine, Mitchell.

Editor: *Altruism in World Religions.* Washington, 2005: Georgetown University Press.

*Reading Scripture with the Rabbis. The Five Books of Moses. An Anthology.* Lanham, 2007: University Press of America

*The Talmud. What It Is and What It Says.* Lanham, 2006: Rowman and Littlefield.

*Judaism. The Basics.* London and New York, 2006: Routledge

Editor: *In Quest of the Historical Pharisees.* Edited with Bruce D. Chilton. Waco, 2006: Baylor University Press.

Editor: *Historical Knowledge in Biblical Antiquity.* Blandford Forum, 2006: Deo Publishing. Edited with Bruce D. Chilton and William Scott Green.

**Also Underway**

Editor-in-chief: *Dictionary of Religious Writings in Antiquity. 300 B.C.E. to 600 C.E.* Leiden and Boston, 2007: E. J. Brill. Volumes I-II.

Editor: *Religious Resources of Tolerance*

Editor: *The Golden Rule in world religions.* Washington, 2009: Georgetown University Press.

*A Heart of Wisdom: The Year in Service to God. Essential Texts of Rabbinic Judaism relating to the calendar and holy days.* With Seymour Rossel. Edited by David A. Altshuler.

### 12. *Toward the Creation of the New Academy*

### (iii) Facing the Future. Children's Textbooks

*Learn Mishnah.* S. Orange NJ, 1978: Behrman. Reprinted many times since.

Italian translation: *Come si studia la Mishna.* Rome, 1983: Unione delle Communità Israelitiche Italiane.

*Learn Talmud.* S. Orange NJ, 1979: Behrman. Reprinted many times since.

*Meet Our Sages.* S. Orange NJ, 1980: Behrman. Reprinted many times since.

*Mitzvah.* Chappaqua, 1981: Rossel. Subsequently: S. Orange NJ, 1980: Behrman. Reprinted: 1983. Third printing: 1985. Reprinted many times since.

### 13. *Bound Articles, Archival Collection*

Neusner Papers. Collected articles. Harvard College Library VJUD 750.284 Volumes 1-208 to date.

Neusner File. Collected papers. American Jewish Archives, 3101 Clifton Avenue, Cincinnati OH 45220.

STUDIES IN JUDAISM
TITLES IN THE SERIES
PUBLISHED BY UNIVERSITY PRESS OF AMERICA

Judith Z. Abrams
*The Babylonian Talmud: A Topical Guide*, 2002.

Roger David Aus
*Matthew 1-2 and the Virginal Conception: In Light of Palestinian and Hellenistic Judaic Traditions on the Birth of Israel's First Redeemer, Moses*, 2004.

*My Name Is "Legion": Palestinian Judaic Traditions in Mark 5:1-20 and Other Gospel Texts*, 2003.

Alan L. Berger, Harry James Cargas, and Susan E. Nowak
*The Continuing Agony: From the Carmelite Convent to the Crosses at Auschwitz*, 2004.

S. Daniel Breslauer
*Creating a Judaism without Religion: A Postmodern Jewish Possibility*, 2001.

Bruce Chilton
*Targumic Approaches to the Gospels: Essays in the Mutual Definition of Judaism and Christianity*, 1986.

David Ellenson
*Tradition in Transition: Orthodoxy, Halakhah, and the Boundaries of Modern Jewish Identity*, 1989.

Roberta Rosenberg Farber and Simcha Fishbane
*Jewish Studies in Violence: A Collection of Essays*, 2007.

Paul V. M. Flesher
*New Perspectives on Ancient Judaism, Volume 5: Society and Literature in Analysis*, 1990.

Marvin Fox
*Collected Essays on Philosophy and on Judaism, Volume One: Greek Philosophy, Maimonides*, 2003.

*Collected Essays on Philosophy and on Judaism, Volume Two: Some Philosophers*, 2003.

*Collected Essays on Philosophy and on Judaism, Volume Three: Ethics, Reflections*, 2003.

Zev Garber

*Methodology in the Academic Teaching of Judaism*, 1986.

Zev Garber, Alan L. Berger, and Richard Libowitz

*Methodology in the Academic Teaching of the Holocaust* ,1988.

Abraham Gross

*Spirituality and Law: Courting Martyrdom in Christianity and Judaism*, 2005.

Harold S. Himmelfarb and Sergio DellaPergola

*Jewish Education Worldwide: Cross-Cultural Perspectives*, 1989.

William Kluback

*The Idea of Humanity: Hermann Cohen's Legacy to Philosophy and Theology*, 1987.

Samuel Morell

*Studies in the Judicial Methodology of Rabbi David ibn Abi Zimra*, 2004.

Jacob Neusner

*Amos in Talmud and Midrash*, 2006.

*Ancient Israel, Judaism, and Christianity in Contemporary Perspective*, 2006.

*The Aggadic Role in Halakhic Discourses: Volume I*, 2001.

*The Aggadic Role in Halakhic Discourses: Volume II*, 2001.

*The Aggadic Role in Halakhic Discourses: Volume III*, 2001.

*Analysis and Argumentation in Rabbinic Judaism*, 2003.

*Analytical Templates of the Bavli*, 2006.

*Ancient Judaism and Modern Category-Formation: "Judaism," "Midrash," "Messianism," and Canon in the Past Quarter Century*, 1986.

*Bologna Addresses and Other Recent Papers*, 2007.

*Building Blocks of Rabbinic Tradition: The Documentary Approach to the Study of Formative Judaism*, 2007.

*Canon and Connection: Intertextuality in Judaism*, 1987.

*Chapters in the Formative History of Judaism*, 2006.

*Dual Discourse, Single Judaism*, 2001.

*The Emergence of Judaism: Jewish Religion in Response to the Critical Issues of the First Six Centuries*, 2000.
*Ezekiel in Talmud and Midrash*, 2007.

*First Principles of Systemic Analysis: The Case of Judaism within the History of Religion*, 1988.

*Habakkuk, Jonah, Nahum, and Obadiah in Talmud and Midrash: A Source Book*, 2007.

*The Halakhah and the Aggadah*, 2001.

*Halakhic Hermeneutics*, 2003.

*Halakhic Theology: A Sourcebook*, 2006.

*The Hermeneutics of Rabbinic Category Formations*, 2001.

*Hosea in Talmud and Midrash*, 2006.

*How Important Was the Destruction of the Second Temple in the Formation of Rabbinic Judaism?* 2006.

*How Not to Study Judaism, Examples and Counter-Examples, Volume One: Parables, Rabbinic Narratives, Rabbis' Biographies, Rabbis' Disputes*, 2004.

*How Not to Study Judaism, Examples and Counter-Examples, Volume Two: Ethnicity and Identity Versus Culture and Religion, How Not to Write a Book on Judaism, Point and Counterpoint, 2004.*

*How the Halakhah Unfolds: Moed Qatan in the Mishnah, Tosefta, Yerushalmi, and Bavli*, 2006.

*How the Halakhah Unfolds, Volume II, Part A: Nazir in the Mishnah, Tosefta, Yerushalmi, and Bavli*, 2007.

*How the Halakhah Unfolds, Volume II, Part B: Nazir in the Mishnah, Tosefta, Yerushalmi, and Bavli*, 2007.

*How the Halakhah Unfolds, Volume III, Part A: Abodah Zarah in the Mishnah, Tosefta, Yerushalmi, and Bavli*, 2007.

*How the Halakhah Unfolds, Volume III, Part B: Abodah Zarah in the Mishnah, Tosefta, Yerushalmi, and Bavli*, 2007.

*The Implicit Norms of Rabbinic Judaism*, 2006.

*Intellectual Templates of the Law of Judaism*, 2006.

*Isaiah in Talmud and Midrash: A Source Book, Part A*, 2007.

*Isaiah in Talmud and Midrash: A Source Book, Part B*, 2007.

*Is Scripture the Origin of the Halakhah?* 2005

*Israel and Iran in Talmudic Times: A Political History*, 1986.

*Israel's Politics in Sasanian Iran: Self-Government in Talmudic Times*, 1986.

*Jeremiah in Talmud and Midrash: A Source Book*, 2006.

*Judaism in Monologue and Dialogue*, 2005.

*Major Trends in Formative Judaism, Fourth Series*, 2002.

*Major Trends in Formative Judaism, Fifth Series*, 2002.

*Messiah in Context: Israel's History and Destiny in Formative Judaism*, 1988.

*Micah and Joel in Talmud and Midrash*, 2006.

*The Native Category – Formations of the Aggadah: The Later Midrash-Compilations – Volume I*, 2000.

*The Native Category – Formations of the Aggadah: The Earlier Midrash-Compilations – Volume II*, 2000.

*Paradigms in Passage: Patterns of Change in the Contemporary Study of Judaism*, 1988.

*Parsing the Torah*, 2005.

*Praxis and Parable: The Divergent Discourses of Rabbinic Judaism*, 2006.

*Rabbi Jeremiah*, 2006.

*Rabbinic Theology and Israelite Prophecy: Primacy of the Torah, Narrative of the World to Come, Doctrine of Repentance and Atonement, and the Systematization of Theology in the Rabbis' Reading of the Prophets,* 2007.

*The Rabbinic Utopia*, 2007.

*Reading Scripture with the Rabbis: The Five Books of Moses*, 2006.

*The Religious Study of Judaism: Description, Analysis, Interpretation, Volume 1*, 1986.

*The Religious Study of Judaism: Description, Analysis, Interpretation, Volume 2*, 1986.

*The Religious Study of Judaism: Context, Text, Circumstance, Volume 3,* 1987.

*The Religious Study of Judaism: Description, Analysis, Interpretation, Volume 4*, 1988.

*Struggle for the Jewish Mind: Debates and Disputes on Judaism Then and Now,* 1988.

*The Talmud Law, Theology, Narrative: A Sourcebook*, 2005.

*Talmud Torah: Ways to God's Presence through Learning: An Exercise in Practical Theology,* 2002.

*Texts Without Boundaries: Protocols of Non-Documentary Writing in the Rabbinic Canon: Volume I: The Mishnah, Tractate Abot, and the Tosefta,* 2002.

*Texts Without Boundaries: Protocols of Non-Documentary Writing in the Rabbinic Canon: Volume II: Sifra and Sifre to Numbers*, 2002.

*Texts Without Boundaries: Protocols of Non-Documentary Writing in the Rabbinic Canon: Volume III: Sifre to Deuteronomy and Mekhilta Attributed to Rabbi Ishmael,* 2002.

*Texts Without Boundaries: Protocols of Non-Documentary Writing in the Rabbinic Canon: Volume IV: Leviticus Rabbah*, 2002.

*A Theological Commentary to the Midrash – Volume I: Pesiqta deRab Kahana,* 2001.

*A Theological Commentary to the Midrash – Volume II: Genesis Raba,* 2001.

*A Theological Commentary to the Midrash – Volume III: Song of Songs Rabbah,* 2001.

*A Theological Commentary to the Midrash – Volume IV: Leviticus Rabbah,* 2001.

*A Theological Commentary to the Midrash – Volume V: Lamentations Rabbati,* 2001.

*A Theological Commentary to the Midrash – Volume VI: Ruth Rabbah and Esther Rabbah,* 2001.

*A Theological Commentary to the Midrash – Volume VII: Sifra,* 2001.

*A Theological Commentary to the Midrash – Volume VIII: Sifre to Numbers and Sifre to Deuteronomy,* 2001.

*A Theological Commentary to the Midrash – Volume IX: Mekhilta Attributed to Rabbi Ishmael,* 2001.

*Theological Dictionary of Rabbinic Judaism: Part One: Principal Theological Categories*, 2005.

*Theological Dictionary of Rabbinic Judaism: Part Two: Making Connections and Building Constructions*, 2005.

*Theological Dictionary of Rabbinic Judaism: Part Three: Models of Analysis, Explanation, and Anticipation,* 2005.

*The Theological Foundations of Rabbinic Midrash*, 2006.

*Theology of Normative Judaism: A Source Book*, 2005.

*Theology in Action: How the Rabbis of the Talmud Present Theology (Aggadah) in the Medium of the Law (Halakhah). An Anthology*, 2006.

*The Torah and the Halakhah: The Four Relationships*, 2003.

*The Unity of Rabbinic Discourse: Volume I: Aggadah in the Halakhah*, 2001.

*The Unity of Rabbinic Discourse: Volume II: Halakhah in the Aggadah*, 2001.

*The Unity of Rabbinic Discourse: Volume III: Halakhah and Aggadah in Concert,* 2001.

*The Vitality of Rabbinic Imagination: The Mishnah Against the Bible and Qumran*, 2005.

*Who, Where and What is "Israel?": Zionist Perspectives on Israeli and American Judaism*, 1989.

*The Wonder-Working Lawyers of Talmudic Babylonia: The Theory and Practice of Judaism in its Formative Age*, 1987.

*Zephaniah, Haggai, Zechariah, and Malachi in Talmud and Midrash: A Source Book*, 2007.

Jacob Neusner and Renest S. Frerichs

*New Perspectives on Ancient Judaism, Volume 2: Judaic and Christian Interpretation of Texts: Contents and Contexts,* 1987.

*New Perspectives on Ancient Judaism, Volume 3: Judaic and Christian Interpretation of Texts: Contents and Contexts,* 1987

Jacob Neusner and James F. Strange

*Religious Texts and Material Contexts*, 2001.

David Novak and Norbert M. Samuelson

*Creation and the End of Days: Judaism and Scientific Cosmology*, 1986.

*Proceedings of the Academy for Jewish Philosophy*, 1990.

Risto Nurmela

*The Mouth of the Lord Has Spoken: Inner-Biblical Allusions in Second and Third Isaiah,* 2006.

Aaron D. Panken

*The Rhetoric of Innovation: Self-Conscious Legal Change in Rabbinic Literature*, 2005.

Norbert M. Samuelson

*Studies in Jewish Philosophy: Collected Essays of the Academy for Jewish Philosophy, 1980-1985*, 1987.

Benjamin Edidin Scolnic

*Alcimus, Enemy of the Maccabees*, 2004.

*If the Egyptians Drowned in the Red Sea, Where Are the Pharoah's Chariots?: Exploring the Historical Dimension of the Bible*, 2005.

Rivka Ulmer

*Pesiqta Rabbati: A Synoptic Edition of Pesiqta Rabbati Based Upon All Extant Manuscripts and the Editio Preceps, Volume III*, 2002.

Manfred Vogel

*A Quest for a Theology of Judaism: The Divine, the Human and the Ethical Dimensions in the Structure-of-Faith of Judaism Essays in Constructive Theology*, 1987.

Anita Weiner

*Renewal: Reconnecting Soviet Jewry to the Soviet People: A Decade of American Jewish Joint Distribution Committee (AJJDC) Activities in the Former Soviet Union 1988-1998*, 2003.

Eugene Weiner and Anita Weiner

*Israel-A Precarious Sanctuary: War, Death and the Jewish People*, 1989.

*The Martyr's Conviction: A Sociological Analysis*, 2002.

Leslie S. Wilson

*The Serpent Symbol in the Ancient Near East: Nahash and Asherah: Death, Life, and Healing*, 2001.